ESKIMOS OF
NORTHWESTERN ALASKA

US/IBP SYNTHESIS SERIES

This volume is a contribution to the International Biological Program. The United States effort was sponsored by the National Academy of Sciences through the National Committee for the IBP. The lead federal agency in providing support for IBP has been the National Science Foundation.

Views expressed in this volume do not necessarily represent those of the National Academy of Sciences or the National Science Foundation.

Vol. 1   MAN IN THE ANDES: A Multidisciplinary Study of High-Altitude Quechua/edited by Paul T. Baker and Michael A. Little

Vol. 2   CHILE-CALIFORNIA MEDITERRANEAN SCRUB ATLAS: A Comparative Analysis/edited by Norman J. W. Thrower and David E. Bradbury

Vol. 3   CONVERGENT EVOLUTION IN WARM DESERTS: An Examination of Strategies and Patterns in Deserts of Argentina and the United States/edited by Gordon H. Orians and Otto T. Solbrig

Vol. 4   MESQUITE: Its Biology in Two Desert Ecosystems/edited by B. B. Simpson

Vol. 5   CONVERGENT EVOLUTION IN CHILE AND CALIFORNIA: Mediterranean Climate Ecosystems/edited by Harold A. Mooney

Vol. 6   CREOSOTE BUSH: Biology and Chemistry of *Larrea* in New World Deserts/edited by T. J. Mabry, J. H. Hunziker, and D. R. DiFeo, Jr.

Vol. 7   BIG BIOLOGY: The US/IBP/W. Frank Blair

Vol. 8   ESKIMOS OF NORTHWESTERN ALASKA: A Biological Perspective/edited by Paul L. Jamison, Stephen L. Zegura, and Frederick A. Milan

Additional volumes in preparation.

US/IBP SYNTHESIS SERIES | 8

ESKIMOS OF NORTHWESTERN ALASKA

A Biological Perspective

Edited by

Paul L. Jamison
Indiana University

Stephen L. Zegura
University of Arizona

Frederick A. Milan
University of Alaska

Dowden, Hutchinson & Ross, Inc.
Stroudsburg   Pennsylvania

Library of Congress Cataloging in Publication Data

Main entry under title:
Eskimos of northwestern Alaska.
  (U.S./IBP synthesis series; 8)
  Includes bibliographical references and index.
  1. Eskimos—Alaska—Anthropometry. 2. Eskimos—Alaska—Population.
3. Eskimos—Alaska—Health and hygiene. I. Jamison, Paul L. II. Zegura, Stephen
L. III. Milan, Frederick A. IV. Series.
E99.E7E75   572.8'97   77-18941
ISBN 0-87933-319-7

Distributed world wide by Academic Press,
a subsidiary of Harcourt Brace Jovanovich,
Publishers.

FOREWORD

This book is one of a series of volumes reporting results of research by U.S. scientists participating in the International Biological Program (IBP). As one of the fifty-eight nations taking part in the IBP during the period of July 1967 to June 1974, the United States organized a number of large, multidisciplinary studies pertinent to the central IBP theme of "the biological basis of productivity and human welfare."

These multidisciplinary studies (Integrated Research Programs) directed toward an understanding of the structure and function of major ecological or human systems have been a distinctive feature of the U.S. participation in the IBP. Many of the detailed investigations that represent individual contributions to the overall objectives of each Integrated Research Program have been published in the journal literature. The main purpose of this series of books is to accomplish a synthesis of the many contributions for each principal program and thus answer the larger questions pertinent to the structure and function of the major systems that have been studied.

Publications Committee: US/IBP
Gabriel Lasker
Robert B. Platt
Frederick E. Smith
W. Frank Blair, Chairman

FOREWORD

Prior to initiation of the International Biological Program (IBP) in 1964, biomedical studies of so-called primitive populations were limited investigations for the greater part. They represented the interests and expertise of one or, at most, of a very small number of scientists in any given instance. However, as a result of numerous such investigations over the course of years, extensive collections had been made all over the world of blood group antigens, innumerable studies carried out of physiological adaptations to harsh environments, and questionably comparable anthropometric measurements taken *ad infinitum.* Ethnographic, demographic, sociological, health, and disease data had been compiled, independently, and without reference to the other variables collected by different scientists working on different populations or even the same population at different times. The frustrations that resulted from attempts to interpret, integrate, and compare these isolated mountains of information grew, and by 1960 resulted in recognition of the need for comprehensive and coordinated investigations, particularly of some populations facing early disruption or extinction.

The first formal and effective meeting to resolve this problem convened in Geneva, November 27, to December 3, 1962. Eleven members and their consultants representing six nations comprised the World Health Organization's Scientific Committee on Research in Population Genetics of Primitive Groups. J. V. Neel was elected chairman; J. Guiant, vice chairman; and N. A. Barnicot and R. L. Kirk, rapporteurs. The twenty-six-page report of the meeting (WHO Technical Report, 1964, #279) outlined a plan for the comprehensive study of genetic structure and ecological factors, both physical and social, on primitive populations. This plan became the basic study design for all of the IBP Human Adaptability Studies that were to follow.

Informal discussions of comprehensive studies in the western Arctic began immediately. It was at one of these meetings in February 1965 in Fairbanks that I first met Frederick Milan. He was to become program director of the study of the Eskimo of northwestern Alaska and he was responsible for the success of four years of field research. Several informal discussions were followed by formal joint Canadian-U.S. meetings that culminated in the working party conference at Point Barrow, November 17-22, 1967. This working party detailed the data to be collected and the methods to be employed to insure, insofar as possible, comparability of the data to be obtained for all studies of circumpolar populations. The highlight of the workshop was the meeting of nine representatives of the scientific group with the Wainwright Village Council.

Separate and uncoordinated studies had been conducted in Wainwright at an accelerating rate since 1955 in which varying numbers of villagers had been examined, photographed, poked, bled, and pestered as though they were human novelties. The village council was understandably reluctant to commit its fellow villagers to further annoyance. This reluctance was an unequivocal demonstration of the major pitfall in conducting uncoordinated studies of such population groups. Resistance immediately diminished with the assurance that a villagewide study was planned in which the whole community would participate and services such as dental examinations would be rendered. The pledge of cooperation, from which the villagers never waivered during the four years of intensive study, came when the point was made that the results of the study would constitute a description and record of the Eskimo people as they were now that could be read by generations to come. Therefore, it is with the publication of this volume that our pledge to the community of Wainwright is made good.

The concentration at the University of Wisconsin of scientists interested in the Eskimo, together with the tireless and ingenious efforts of Fred Milan, put the first research party into the field by July 1968, even before actual funding was available under the auspices of the IBP. Eight of the contributors to this volume were then located at the University of Wisconsin. By 1972 none of those participants in the field work, and only I among those at the Point Barrow Conference and meeting with the Wainwright Village Council, remained at Wisconsin. Herein rests the hazard of comprehensive, and thus long-term investigations such as this and others promoted by the IBP.

The time lapse and dispersion of organizers and participants preclude the fulfillment of the studies' objectives, unless there is one essential ingredient: retention of interest and responsibility of some individual or individuals from the earliest part of the investigation to achieve integration and publication of the research results. Paul Jamison and Stephen Zegura were members of the first field party in 1968. Without them this report would never have been compiled and published and the study of the Eskimo of northwestern Alaska never completed.

Richard H. Osborne
University of Wisconsin
Madison

PREFACE

The North Slope of Alaska has long been an area of interest for researchers representing a variety of academic disciplines, including the social, biological, and physical sciences. It is the aim of this volume to present basic biological information about the Eskimo populations living in this portion of Alaska. The various contributions reflect a particular perspective—that of human biology. The scope of human biology has been defined as "the study of the nature, development, causes and origins of variations in human populations at the molecular, cellular, tissue and whole body levels. In particular, emphasis is given to the relationship between genetic and environmental factors in producing this variation, as it occurs both within and between populations" (IAHB, 1967: 319). Thus, the studies reported here focus primarily on the biological variation of northwest Alaskan Eskimos.

Elucidating this variation required considerable interdisciplinary cooperation. Topics investigated included demography, morphology, biochemistry, biomedical parameters, nutrition, physiology, genetics, and behavior. The individual reports are primarily descriptive in nature and frequently comparative in approach; they concentrate on presenting data and results. The extensive summary chapter at the end of the volume attempts to coordinate and integrate these contributions. Should this synthesis prove synergistic, it will furnish a base for disseminating information across disciplinary boundaries more effectively than in the past.

These investigations took place as part of an International Study of Circumpolar Peoples under the auspices of the Human Adaptability component of the International Biological Program (IBP). Financial support for the Eskimo research project came from the National Institutes of Health (specifically the National Institute of Dental Research and the National Institute of General Medical Sciences), the National Science Foundation, the Smithsonian Institution, the Wenner-Gren Foundation, the Air Force Office of Scientific Research, and the Office of Naval Research. Many people in addition to the authors of individual chapters participated in the preparation of this volume. They include: Sharon Devlin, Harriet Greenland, Fruma Klass, Kay McKinley, Karon Jamison, and Ronald Royce. The Human Adaptability Coordinating Office, University Park, Pennsylvania, provided for most of the costs of preparing this book while the Authropology Departments of Indiana University and the University of Arizona both provided support at crucial times. Paul

Baker, director of the Human Adaptability Coordinating Office deserves special thanks for his unstinting guidance and encouragement of the IBP synthesis volume concept and this volume.

Recently, in addition to academic interests, commercial interests have entered northern Alaska with a promise of vast economic returns for concomitantly high risks. The development of what may be enormous oil reserves on the North Slope has caused both natives and immigrants to anticipate another in a long series of "booms" for Alaska. Not since the heyday of the whaling industry in the middle of the nineteenth century has there been the prospect of events so quickly changing the status and life of these Eskimos.

Whether or not they ultimately benefit from the process of extracting oil from their land, the Eskimos will not escape the encounter unscathed. The timing of this research, therefore, may be fortuitous. If economic and social factors impose radical changes on these people, research such as has been conducted over the past years may prove impossible in the future. But a baseline will have been established from which change can be measured in subsequent work.

Finally, this research obviously could not have been conducted without the cooperation of the inhabitants of the villages of Wainwright, Barrow, Point Hope, Kaktovik, and Anaktuvuk Pass, Alaska. Therefore, it is to these people that we dedicate this volume, with sincere appreciation for their patience and understanding during the hectic visitations of the investigating teams.

Paul L. Jamison
Stephen L. Zegura

CONTENTS

Foreword *by US/IBP Publications Committee*   v
Foreword *by Richard H. Osborne*   vii
Preface   ix
List of Contributors   xvii

1: **Multidisciplinary Research on Northwest Alaskan Eskimos**   1
   Frederick A. Milan

   Chronology of Fieldwork, 3   Summary, 7

2: **The Eskimo Population System: Linguistic Framework**
   and Skeletal Remains   8
   Stephen L. Zegura

   The Eskimo Population System, 8   Linguistic Framework,
   8   Archaeological Perspective, 10   Skeletal Remains, 11
   Relationship of Linguistic Classification to Eskimo Biological Differentiation, 21

3: **Ethnohistory of the Research Populations**   31
   Paul L. Jamison

   Research Area, 31   History of the Villages, 32   Population
   Size, 34   Cultural Groupings, 36

4: **Anthropometric Variation**   40
   Paul L. Jamison

   Adult Measurements, 40   Growth Measurements, 65   Age
   and Secular Trends, 77

5: **Dermatoglyphic Variation**   79
   Robert J. Meier

   Correlation of Digital Ridge Counts and Pattern Intensity,
   79   Basic Terminology, 80   Results, 81   Summary of

                                                                   xi

Digital Dermatoglyphic Research, 87   Summary of Palmar
Dermatoglyphic Research, 91   Planned Research for the
Eskimo Dermatoglyphic Data, 93

6: **Eskimo Craniofacial Studies**   94
   A. A. Dahlberg, R. Cederquist, J. Mayhall, and D. Owen

   Craniofacial Growth and Morphology, 94   Measurements,
   105   Intermaxillary Relationships, 106   Morphology of
   the Dentition, 107   Oral Epidemiology, 108   Saliva Analysis for Secretion of Blood Group Substances, 112
   Summary, 112

7: **Biochemical Variation: The Development of Biochemical**
   Normal Ranges for Eskimo Populations   114
   Ronald H. Laessig, Frank P. Pauls, Toni A. Paskey, and
   Thomas H. Schwartz

   Materials and Methods, 114   Results, 116   Conclusions,
   124

8: **Biochemical Variation: Carbonic Anhydrase**   125
   Mary Jane Moore

   Study Population, 125   Qualitative Study, 126   Quantitative Study, 127   Population Comparisons, 130   Discussion,
   132   Summary and Conclusions, 133

9: **Biochemical Variation: Bone Mineral Content**   134
   Richard B. Mazess and Warren Mather

   Methods, 134   Discussion, 137

10: **Nutrition Studies: The Aboriginal Eskimo Diet—A**
    Modern Perspective   139
    H. H. Draper

    Vitamin Content, 140   Minerals, 140   Energy, 141
    Impact of Modern Diet, 144

11: Nutrition Studies: An Appraisal of the Modern North
      Alaskan Eskimo Diet   145
      R. Raines Bell and Christine A. Heller

      Evaluations of Nutrients, 147   Southwestern Tundra
      Villages, 154

12: Nutrition Studies: Biochemical Assessment of Nutritional
      Status   157
      J. G. Bergan and R. Raines Bell

13: Nutrition Studies: Clinical Observations on Nutritional
      Health   162
      M. J. Colbert, G. V. Mann, and L. M. Hursh

      Characteristics of the Villages and Villagers, 162   Provi-
      sion for Medical Care, 163   Examinations, 163   Clinical
      Conditions,   164

14: Metabolic Parameters: Aspects of Cholesterol, Lipid, and
      Carbohydrate Metabolism   174
      Sheldon A. Feldman, Arthur Rubenstein, C. Bruce Taylor,
      Kang-Jey Ho, and Lena Lewis

      Cholesterol Metabolism, 174   Lipid and Carbohydrate
      Metabolism, 178

15: Metabolic Parameters: Lactose and Sucrose Tolerance   184
      R. Raines Bell, H. H. Draper, and J. G. Bergan

      Lactose Intolerance, 184   Sucrose Intolerance, 186

16: Metabolic Parameters: Plasma Vitamin E and Cholesterol
      Levels in Alaskan Eskimos   189
      H. H. Draper and Catherine C. K. Wei Wo

      Methods, 189   Results, 190   Discussion, 195

17: **Exercise Physiology**   198
Donald W. Rennie

Methods, 199   Results, 203   Discussion, 211   Summary,
215

18: **General Health**   217
Anthony B. Way

Review of Literature, 217   International Biological Program Study, 219   Conclusions, 220

19: **Demography and Population Parameters of the Present**
Inhabitants of Northwest Alaska   222
Frederick A. Milan

Historical Background of the Population, 222   Point
Hope, 228   Barrow, 229   Discussion and Summary, 230

20: **Behavioral Studies: Cognitive Development**   233
Carol Fleisher Feldman, Benjamin Lee, J. Dickson McLean,
David B. Pillemer, and James R. Murray

21: **Behavioral Studies: A Psychometric Study at Barrow Day**
School   237
R. Darrell Bock

Working Hypotheses, 238   Results, 247   Discussion, 259
Summary, 260

22: **Multidisciplinary Research: A Case Study in Eskimo**
Human Biology   262
Stephen L. Zegura and Paul L. Jamison

Results from the IBP Eskimo Study, 262   Biological
Change: Evolution, Growth, and Aging, 265   Biological
Variability Within Northwestern Alaska, 273   Synergistic
Relationships: Diet Interactions, 279   Overview, 286

Appendix A: Funding Sources for the IBP Project   288
Appendix B: Tapescript of English-Inupiat Concept Knowledge
             Test   290
             Carol Fleischer Feldman

References   293

Index   315

LIST OF CONTRIBUTORS

R. Raines Bell
Assistant Professor of Nutrition, Department of Human Resources and Family Studies, University of Illinois, Urbana, Illinois

J. G. Bergan
Assistant Professor of Nutrition, Department of Food and Nutritional Science, University of Rhode Island, Kingston, Rhode Island

R. Darrell Bock
Professor, Department of Education, University of Chicago, Chicago, Illinois

K. R. Cederquist
5715 South Drexel Avenue, Apartment 214, Chicago, Illinois

M. J. Colbert
University of Illinois Medical Center, P.O. Box 6998, Chicago, Illinois

Albert A. Dahlberg
Professor, Zoller Memorial Dental Clinic and Department of Anthropology, University of Chicago, Chicago, Illinois

Harold H. Draper
Professor and Chairman, Department of Nutrition, University of Guelph, Guelph, Ontario, Canada

Carol F. Feldman
Assistant Professor, Department of Psychology, University of Houston, Houston, Texas

Sheldon A. Feldman
Deceased

Christine A. Heller
    Nutritionist, US Public Health Service (Ret.), Anchorage, Alaska

Kang-Jey Ho
    Associate Professor of Pathology, Birmingham Medical Center, University of Alabama, Birmingham, Alabama

L. M. Hursh
    Director of Health Services, University of Illinois, Urbana, Illinois

Paul L. Jamison
    Assistant Professor of Anthropology, Department of Anthropology, Indiana University, Bloomington, Indiana

Ronald H. Laessig
    Associate Professor of Preventive Medicine, Chief of Clinical Chemistry, and Assistant Director, State Laboratories of Hygiene, University of Wisconsin Medical Center, Madison, Wisconsin

Benjamin Lee
    Graduate Student, Department of Anthropology, University of Chicago, Chicago, Illinois.

Lena Lewis
    Staff Researcher, Cleveland Clinic, Cleveland, Ohio

J. Dickson McLean
    Assistant Professor, Department of Psychology, University of Kentucky, Lexington, Kentucky

G. V. Mann
    Division of Nutrition, School of Medicine, Vanderbilt University, Nashville, Tennessee

Warren Mather
    Department of Radiology (Medical Physics), University of Wisconsin Hospital, Madison, Wisconsin

John Mayhall
    Department of Anthropology, University of Toronto, Toronto, Ontario, Canada

Richard B. Mazess

Department of Radiology (Medical Physics), University of Wisconsin Hospital, Madison, Wisconsin

Robert J. Meier

Associate Professor and Chairman, Department of Anthropology, Indiana University, Bloomington, Indiana

Frederick A. Milan

Adjunct Professor and Senior Researcher, Department of Anthropology and Institute of Arctic Biology, University of Alaska, College, Alaska

Mary Jane Moore

Assistant Professor, Department of Anthropology, San Diego State University, San Diego, California

James R. Murray

National Opinion Research Center, Chicago, Illinois

Richard H. Osborne

Professor, Department of Anthropology, University of Wisconsin, Madison, Wisconsin

David Owen

Department of Pediatric Dentistry, University of Maryland Dental School, Baltimore, Maryland

Toni A. Paskey

Laboratory Technician, State Laboratories of Hygiene, University of Wisconsin, Madison, Wisconsin

Frank P. Pauls

Chief, Section of Laboratories, Department of Health and Social Services, State of Alaska, Juneau, Alaska

David P. Pillemer

Graduate Student, School of Education, Program in Human Development, Harvard University, Cambridge, Massachusetts

Donald W. Rennie

Professor of Physiology, Department of Physiology, School of Medicine, State University of New York at Buffalo, Buffalo, New York

Arthur Rubenstein
Professor of Medicine, University of Chicago Hospitals and Clinics, Chicago, Illinois

Thomas A. Schwartz
Chief Chemist, Multiphasic Screening Program, State Division of Health, Madison, Wisconsin

C. Bruce Taylor
Associate Chief of Staff for Research, Veterans Administration Hospital, Albany, New York

Anthony B. Way
Department of Preventive Medicine and Community Health, Texas Tech University School of Medicine and Department of Anthropology, Texas Tech University, Lubbock, Texas

Catherine C. K. Wei Wo
Research Assistant, Department of Food Science, University of Illinois, Urbana, Illinois

Stephen L. Zegura
Assistant Professor of Anthropology, Department of Anthropology, University of Arizona, Tucson, Arizona

ESKIMOS OF
NORTHWESTERN ALASKA

1

Multidisciplinary Research on Northwest Alaskan Eskimos

Frederick A. Milan

This study of the Eskimo of northwestern Alaska was carried out within the context of the Human Adaptability (HA) component of the International Biological Program (IBP). The IBP was a ten-year, sixty-nation research endeavor that sought to examine the biological basis of human welfare and productivity using multidisciplinary research teams. The objective of the Eskimo study was to examine the biological and behavioral factors responsible for long-term survival of a human population in an arctic environment (Milan, 1968). Low temperatures, seasonal extremes in light and darkness, snow cover for two-thirds of the year, and relatively meager ecological resources characterize this environment. Despite these environmental "constraints," the Eskimos have occupied such areas of northern Alaska for generations.

It was our contention in initiating this research that human cultural and biological adaptation could not be fully understood outside the context of the evolutionary process. In agreement with Mazess (1975) we considered "adaptation" a generic as much as a genetic term. Population stability may indicate adjustment or adaptation, but the stress and strain of life in particular environments must be considered as well as other evidence for cultural and biological adaptation. The latter could include psychological accommodation, physiological acclimatization, developmental adaptation, or genetic adaptation. According to Baker (1965a) phenotypic plasticity, which applies to both behavior and form, has been an important evolutionary development. With such complexity of human adaptation emphasized early in the planning of the IBP, multidisciplinary studies were recognized as necessary (Baker, 1965b). Specific traits do not exist in isolation but in complexes possessed by individuals as members of populations. Accordingly, like the other IBP/HA studies, the Eskimo study was multidisciplinary in nature and focused on an analysis of populations.

This study of Eskimos in the United States was also part of a larger study of circumpolar poeple. From 1967 through 1976, IBP scientists from the USSR, Japan, Canada, Norway, Finland, West Germany, France, and the United States conducted HA research projects on the indigenous human populations living in the circumpolar zone. This volume presents results of

1

the U.S. study. Results from the international study will be presented elsewhere (Milan, in press).

For many scientists the IBP provided an opportunity to continue research already started. However, for these and other workers initiating new projects, an international symposium held at Burg Wartenstein, Austria, in 1964 provided the impetus for most of the HA studies (Weiner, 1976). This symposium was summarized by the World Health Organization (WHO) in a brief report, *Research in Population Genetics of Primitive Groups* (1964). A more extensive treatment of the results of the symposium appeared in a volume edited by Baker and Weiner (1966), *The Biology of Human Adaptability*. W. S. Laughlin and W. J. A. Hildes summarized the current knowledge about arctic populations in a chapter on genetics and anthropology (Laughlin), and health and physiological adaptations (Hildes).

Laughlin, a productive researcher on the prehistory and human biology of Eskimos and Aleuts for some thirty-five years, saw the advantages of working within the IBP, and he must be accorded full credit for the initiation and early planning of the Eskimo study on both national and international levels.

The U.S. National Committee for the IBP held its first meeting in Washington in March 1965. Present at this meeting were members of the HA subcommittee (F. Sargent, chairman; S. Robinson; D. B. Shimkin; J. V. Neel; and W. S. Laughlin). The late J. S. Hart, a member of the National Research Council and chairman of Human Adaptability for Canada, suggested to his counterpart in the United States, F. Sargent, that researchers from their respective countries should pursue joint cooperative studies on arctic populations. As a result I was invited by Sargent to assume responsibility for U.S. participation in the project planning meetings on circumpolar peoples.

The first of these meetings was organized in Ottawa on November 25, 1966; here, Laughlin outlined a research proposal to study the community of Wainwright, Alaska. A second meeting was held in late March and early April 1967 in Winnipeg. Conferees at this meeting decided that a working party conference should be scheduled for Thanksgiving week at the Naval Arctic Research Laboratory (NARL), Point Barrow, Alaska. Those invited to this conference were scientists interested in or actually working in the Arctic.

The next step in my participation in the planning occurred on August 21, 1967 when the assistant executive secretary of the U.S. National Committee for the IBP asked me to be program director for the Eskimo study. The IBP/HA sponsored Point Barrow Working Party Conference was held in November 1967 with Hildes of Canada as the convener and myself as the chairman. In attendance were some forty-one scientists representing the United States, Canada, Denmark, Sweden, Norway, France, and Japan. The week-long conference resulted in a general agreement about the methods for study of northern peoples under IBP auspices. This agreement was necessary, since it was prior to publication of the IBP instructional manuals, and an important aim of the IBP was cross-national comparison of data collected by similar methods. The proceedings of this conference were published in mimeo-graphed form (Milan, 1967).

One important event during the Point Barrow conference was a meeting between the scientists and residents of the village of Wainwright. Nine investi-gators, flown from Barrow in Cessna 180 aircraft, met with seven members of the Wainwright village council to explain the research program and to obtain their informed consent for the proposed study.

In the keynote address at the conference, Laughlin (1970) described the purpose of studying Eskimos and their population systems. Wainwright was selected as the main U.S. study site for the following reasons:

1. It was accessible, through the logistic capabilities of the Naval Arctic Research Laboratory at Point Barrow, Alaska.
2. Previous studies carried out since 1955 had familiarized the vil-lagers with researchers and vice versa (Milan, 1964a, 1964b; Milan and Evonuk, 1967) and had provided a wealth of informa-tion about the Wainwright hunter and his environment (Nelson, 1969).
3. It had a demonstrable long-term viability as a community, and adequate population size for analysis.
4. Residents were friendly and cooperative in their attitudes towards researchers.

CHRONOLOGY OF FIELDWORK

All of the investigators assembled at the Naval Arctic Research Laboratory in July of 1968 for the first field season. Personnel and equipment were trans-ported the ninety miles to Wainwright by light aircraft belonging to the NARL. Earlier, NARL had delivered two research buildings to Wainwright by tractor-train. While in the village the scientific personnel occupied three NARL research buildings, and they also used the Bureau of Indian Affairs (BIA) schoolhouse and the National Guard armory. Permission for the use of these facilities had been obtained from the responsible governmental agencies. Weekly flights from NARL at Point Barrow brought in food and equipment. Details of the funding sources for the project are listed in Appendix A.

Wainwright—1968

During July and August of 1968, 269 (91%) of the available Eskimo in-habitants of Wainwright were examined and information was obtained on the following: (1) genealogy and family history (F. A. Milan); (2) photography and anthroposcopy (W. S. Laughlin); (3) anthropometry (P. L. Jamison and

S. L. Zegura); (4) medical examinations including ECG (R. B. Rice and D. Robinhold); (5) X-rays of chest, head, wrist, and ankles (J. Pegg, R. T. Bates, and T. Bates); (6) complete dental examinations including X-rays, dental casts, and saliva collections (A. A. Dahlberg, T. Dahlberg, D. Owen, and T. Mayhall); (7) serological and epidemiological collections including 30-ml blood samples from 196 subjects and 100 throat cultures (F. Pauls); (8) bone mineral scannings of the radius and ulna of 100 individuals (R. Mazess); (9) physiological tests of maximal O_2 consumption, maximum anaerobic power, lung volumes, and other standard respiratory parameters on forty male and eleven female subjects, as well as a three-mile endurance run in which over half the villagers participated (D. Rennie, R. Fitts, and P. Di Prampero—a visiting scientist from Milan, Italy); and (10) biological rhythms investigations on ten subjects (J. Bohlen).

In addition to these investigations within the confines of Wainwright, a survey by boat and on foot was made of the location of old village settlements forty miles up the coast (Milan and Jamison). Also, aerial photos of old village sites were taken using equipment of the U.S. Army's Cold Land Research Establishment at Dartmouth College (Milan).

It should be emphasized that most investigators used equipment and supplies from their own research laboratories and that most data analysis costs were borne by their home institutions. The Alaska State Department of Health provided a nurse and portable X-ray machine in return for copies of the information on the exposed plates. These X-rays were read by C. Dotter and his resident, D. Wishart, at the University of Oregon Medical School.

The physicians, one of whom (Robinhold) was in the Public Health Service (PHS), provided medical care for the villagers and referral service for the Barrow PHS Hospital. The dental team led by Dahlberg, who went on active duty as a commander in the Dental Corps of the PHS for the summer, likewise provided dental care for the local populace.

Governmental agency support of this research included the Neighborhood Youth Corps of the Office of Economic Opportunity, which paid the wages of six Wainwright teenagers who helped the dental and radiological teams and the epidemiologist. As mentioned above, the BIA allowed us to use the school building in Wainwright as a medical and examination clinic, kitchen, and as sleeping quarters; and the Alaska National Guard armory served as a dental clinic.

The study of circadian and circannual biorhythms continued through the year after the initial research visit to Wainwright. Additional trips were scheduled to last twenty days each to bracket the two solstices and the two equinoxes. J. Bohlen was assisted in this research by S. Bohlen and B. Bohlen and by two nurses (twins) who were also scientific subjects in a longitudinal time-displacement study. This phase of the study was mainly supported by NASA funds of F. Halberg, director of Laboratories of Periodicity Analysis in the Medical School at the University of Minnesota.

Wainwright—1969

Four researchers spent three weeks in Wainwright during January and February 1969, with the primary goal of undertaking a nutritional survey (Milan and Jamison assisted H. Sauberlich and W. Goad from the U.S. Army's Medical and Nutritional Research Laboratory at Fitzsimmons Hospital). This nutrition study included estimates of the type and amounts of foods eaten, measurements of hemoglobin and hematocrit levels, and collections of urine from all members of the National Guard. The children were also remeasured as part of a longitudinal growth study (Jamison).

The main field party returned to Wainwright in June. This group consisted of twenty persons and included the principal investigator and demographer (Milan); the dental team (same personnel as 1968 with an undergraduate assistant replacing Owen); the chronobiologist, J. Bohlen, and his assistants; two psychologists (D. Bock and C. Feldman); and anthropometrist (Jamison); a dermatoglyphic specialist (R. Meier); a physician (A. B. Way); a Finnish opthalmologist (H. Forsius); and epidemiologist (W. Thompson), who worked with F. Pauls; two exercise physiologists (Fitts and L. Sinclair); the bone mineral physicist (R. Mazess); and a cook (L. Fisher, a former Wainwright school teacher). Local hired personnel consisted of a handyman (H. Bodfish), a cook's helper (L. Kagak), and two village health aides (E. Ungadruk and L. Shoudla).

From our point of view the village population cooperated as well as they had the previous year. The medical personnel again provided free dental and medical care. Dr. Forsius, working under temporary licensure obtained from the director of the State Department of Health, treated one case of glaucoma, measured the degree of refraction of eyes, and fitted new glasses for fifty persons on the basis of his prescriptions, in addition to his own research activities. Dr. Dippe, chief of opthalmology at the Alaskan Native Health Center in Anchorage, provided equipment in exchange for these services.

The summer field party left by mid-August, although some research still continued. Jamison and Meier visited Anaktuvuk Pass in the Brooks Range and collected anthropometric and dermatoglyphic data on all available adult residents of this community. This collection increased their samples, since Wainwrighters have relatives in that village. In September a psychiatrist (E. F. Foulks) commenced the first of a series of regular visits to Wainwright. The chronobiology team also continued their work in September.

Expanded Field Research—1970

During discussions among the researchers in the field and after returning it was apparent that many wanted to expand the research focus beyond Wainwright. Accordingly, Point Hope was selected as the site of a second major effort, with the hope that Barrow could be visited the following year. Rather than being restricted to the Eskimo population of Wainwright, the focus was now on the entire population of north Alaska. The mayor of Point Hope and its village council were contacted for permission to conduct the research.

The field party was scheduled to arrive in Point Hope in early July. Several investigators arrived in Alaska in June to continue or initiate work in other villages. The anthropometric and dermatoglyphic team visited Anaktuvuk Pass to continue data collection begun the year before. J. Brøsted, a student at the University of Copenhagen, accompanied them. W. Mather measured bone mineral content of eighty older Eskimo men and women at the Barrow hospital during the same time period.

The main field party in Point Hope included the same demographic, anthropometric, dermatoglyphic, bone mineral, and dental specialists as before. Additions included P. Walker and M. Kulesz on the dental team; M. J. Moore assisting in serology; D. McLean aiding the psychologist, C. Feldman; a new exercise physiology team (P. Hogan, D. Wilson, and M. Wilson); two physicians (S. Feldman and T. Lewin, a member of the Anatomy Department of the University of Gothenburg, Sweden); and H. Draper, a nutritional biochemist who would initiate a major nutritional study. Local hired personnel in Point Hope included two cooks (R. Oviuk and L. Nashookpuk), two clinic helpers (J. Lane and J. Howarth), and two messengers paid by the Neighborhood Youth Corps. The village census listed 353 resident of Point Hope and we saw 230 in our examinations.

After their research in Point Hope, the anthropometrist and dermatoglyphic specialist visited Kaktovik on Barter Island. Thus the regional coverage of the research continued to expand.

Barrow—1971

A sample of residents of the large village of Barrow (population 1,856, according to the BIA) was studied during the summer of 1971. About 300 individuals came through the examination clinic held in the BIA schoolhouse.

The following personnel made up the Barrow research team:

Anthropometry	P. L. Jamison
Demography	F. A. Milan
Dentistry	A. A. Dahlberg, T. Dahlberg, and T. Forti
Dermatoglyphics	R. Meier
Epidemiology	D. Bosman
Exercise Physiology	D. Wilson, M. Wilson, and R. Washburn
Hemispheric Dominance	D. Kolakowski and R. Sternback
Photography	H. Hudson

Psychology	D. Bock, C. Feldman, W. Fitzgerald, and D. Likens
Medicine	S. Feldman and S. Haroldson (from the School of Public Health, Gothenburg, Sweden)
Serology	F. Pauls and R. Palczer

In addition, local hired personnel in Barrow consisted of E. MacLean assisting the demographer, and three clinic helpers: E. Ahkvgak, H. Panigeo, and N. Taalak.

Wainwright—1972

The final research activity in the field occurred in the summer of 1972 when a small field party visited Wainwright to continue a longitudinal cranio-facial growth study (the Dahlbergs and C. Merbs) and to make skin color measurements and examine cerumen (G. Pawson and S. Petrakis). After leaving Wainwright the dental/craniofacial team including Leda Milan continued on to Old Harbor, Kodiak Island, to reexamine a population they had studied a decade earlier.

SUMMARY

The specific aims of this research were to study the biological and behavioral processes responsible for the adaptation, population maintenance, and recent population increase of Eskimos living in villages in the arctic environment of north Alaska. To this end, multidisciplinary studies were conducted over the period 1968 through 1972. The following chapters will present results of these studies.

2

The Eskimo Population System: Linguistic Framework and Skeletal Remains

Stephen L. Zegura

For the study of north Alaskan Eskimo diversity, an anthropological framework is needed. Data for the framework come from both linguistics and the archaeological remains of earlier Eskimo populations.

THE ESKIMO POPULATION SYSTEM

The Eskimo population is difficult to divide into unambiguous subgroups because of contradictory linguistic, cultural, and biological evidence. Linguists see a major twofold division of the Eskimo based entirely on language: western (Yupik) versus eastern (Inuit or Inupik), with the dividing line occurring at Norton Sound (Dumond, 1965). Cultural anthropologists see ecological adaptations as the essence of the primary division between western (from the mouth of the Mackenzie River through coastal Alaska to the eastern edge of Siberia) and central-eastern (from Mackenzie Bay to Greenland). The latter group can be further subdivided, based on the importance of caribou hunting as a means of subsistence for the central Eskimo (Powers, 1967). In general, physical anthropologists stress a twofold division between western and eastern Eskimos; some place the boundary at Norton Sound, as do the linguists, while others place the division east of Point Barrow (Hrdlička, 1930; Levin, 1963; Zegura, in press).

At present the Eskimo population system is probably larger than ever before. According to Krauss (1973), a good estimate for 1972 would be 95,000 (± 5%), distributed as follows: Greenland, 43,000; Canada, 17,000; Alaska, 34,000; Siberia, 1,000.

LINGUISTIC FRAMEWORK

The most complete summarizations of internal Eskaleutian (Eskimo-Aleut) linguistic relationships are those of Dumond (1965) and Krauss (1973).

Dumond (1965) presents an Eskaleutian genetic language classification portraying linguistic similarities as derived from both structural and lexicostatistical examination. His classification is based principally on the work of Hammerich (1958), Hirsch (1954), and a series of papers by Swadesh (1951, 1952b, 1954, 1958). Swadesh and Hirsch both used a glottochronological approach, while Hammerich relied on comprehension of stories as an indicator of linguistic relationship. Glottochronology is a particular kind of lexicostatistical technique defined by Hymes (1960) as "the study of rate of change in language, and the use of the rate for historical inference, especially for the estimation of time depths to provide a pattern of internal relationships within a language family." The technique was originally formulated by Swadesh (1950), and many of its early applications involved American Indian and Eskaleutian languages (Swadesh, 1951, 1952a, 1952b, 1954, 1958). In view of the many criticisms of glottochronology as a means for accurately estimating the dates of language group divergences, the safest strategy would be to treat the results of glottochronological studies not as indicators of absolute time, but rather as a relative grouping device (Bergsland, 1958; Bergsland and Vogt, 1962; Chretien, 1962; Fodor, 1961, 1965; Zegura, 1971).

The review of the Eskimo-Aleut language family by Krauss (1973) presents a linguistic taxonomic subdivision of Eskaleutian based on all available linguistic information, and drawing on a bibliography of over 800 items. The classifications of Dumond and Krauss are very similar, although Krauss pays more attention to dialect differentiation than does Dumond. The linguistic classification presented in Fig. 2-1 is a combination of their classifications.

Table 2-1 gives an estimate of the number of speakers of the major linguistic subdivisions portrayed in Fig. 2-1. Thus, of the nearly 95,000 Eskimos living today, approximately 83,000 are considered speakers of their

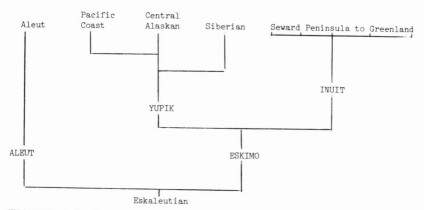

FIGURE 2-1. *Genetic classification of some internal Eskaleutian linguistic relationships (after Dumond, 1965, and Krauss, 1973).*

native language. Most native speakers are in the Inuit category and are termed "eastern" Eskimos by linguists. All Alaskan Inuit dialects are mutually intelligible, and their speakers can be considered to form a single linguistic community. The five study populations dealt with in this volume (Anaktuvuk Pass, Barrow, Kaktovik, Point Hope, and Wainwright) are all Inuit-speaking groups. Two distinct subdialects of Inuit are represented in these five populations: one in Point Hope and the other in Anaktuvuk Pass, Barrow, Kaktovik, and Wainwright. This second subdialect, incidentally, is nearly identical with Mackenzie Delta Inuit, so that the Alaska-Canada border is linguistically artificial (Krauss, 1973).

ARCHAEOLOGICAL PERSPECTIVE

According to Bandi (1969), Eskimo prehistory began when the Epi-Gravettian people arrived in Arctic North America between 8,000 and 15,000 years ago. These migrants most probably came from Siberia across the Bering land bridge. Bandi believes that these Eskimo ancestors possessed a culture that differed from the familiar maritime culture of historic Arctic North America and Greenland. In fact, he hypothesizes that the early American Epi-Gravettian people were oriented primarily toward the interior regions of the land bridge and later toward the rivers of Alaska, and that adaptations to life on the coast set in only gradually. ("American Epi-Gravettian" is a collective term that includes both the Northwest Microblade tradition and the more recent Arctic Small-Tool tradition.)

The maritime adaptations of the modern Eskimo probably began somewhere in southwestern Alaska, around 2000 B.C. From this focus maritime

TABLE 2-1   *Estimated Numbers of Native Eskimo Speakers*

Subdivision	Speakers
Yupik	
Siberian	1,500
Central Alaskan	14,500
Pacific Coast	2,000
Inuit	65,000[*]
Total	83,000

Adapted from Krauss (1973).

[*]From Alaska, 6,000; from Canada, 16,000; from Greenland, 43,000.

cultures then disseminated to the Asiatic side of the Bering Strait and to northern Alaska. The direct ancestors of modern Eskimos are represented by the Thule culture, which first appeared in northern Alaska between 900 and 1100 A.D. This culture subsequently spread eastward across Canada to Greenland. Thus, the Eskimo maritime adaptation can tentatively be traced back about 4,000 years. This time depth agrees well with linguistic evidence suggesting that the Eskimo and Aleut languages separated at least 4,500 years ago (Bandi, 1969; Dumond, 1965).

Recent work by Laughlin (1975) provides a slightly different answer to the question of Eskimo origins. He presents striking evidence for human occupation spanning the last 8,700 years inside Nikolski Bay near Umnak Island in the Aleutians. Both the absolute dating of the events inside Nikolski Bay and the identification of Asiatic elements in the artifact assemblages have led Laughlin to hypothesize that the earliest Aleuts and Eskimos were part of a single population system that expanded along the Siberian coasts and across the southern coasts of Beringia. According to Laughlin, those who reached Nikolski Bay became Aleuts while those who migrated closer to the old mouth of the Kuskokwim River and farther north became Eskimos. These postulated migrations would have occurred much earlier than 4,000 years ago, the time depth commonly assumed for Eskimo maritime adaptations.

SKELETAL REMAINS

Literature: A Historical Perspective

The Eskimo skeleton has been the subject of an extensive body of work in both physical anthropology and biometry. The major emphasis of this work has been the description of the Eskimo skull, usually in outmoded typological terms. According to Jørgensen (1953), the Danish anatomist Jacob Winslow published the first description of an Eskimo cranium in the year 1722. This cranium was found by V. Riecke near Disko just off the west coast of Greenland. However, it was not until 1817 that an Eskimo skull was collected for scientific purposes. This skull was taken from the rocks of St. Lawrence Island by the Kotzebue Party and was the subject of a phrenological report by Gall in 1822 (Hrdlička, 1930; Zegura, in press).

The first detailed study of Eskimo craniology was Fürst and Hansen's *Crania Grøenlandica* (1915), a catalog of measurements and observations of 380 Greenlandic Eskimos. In their well-illustrated catalog Fürst and Hansen reviewed previous research on Eskimo skeletal remains in Greenland and presented a comprehensive list of metric and morphological characters of the Greenland Eskimo.

Hrdlička (1930) then gave a historical résumé of all publications dealing with western Eskimo skull measurements from 1839 to 1923. (In this context the term "western" is geographically defined and includes Eskimos of Alaska, Siberia, St. Lawrence Island, Kodiak Island, and St. Michael Island.) Hrdlička's 1930 report also presented data on 1,283 skulls, mostly from the western Eskimo area. This was the most ambitious study of Eskimo craniology until Hrdlička's 1942 Eskimo cranial catalog, which contains measurements on over 2,200 Eskimo skulls. Hrdlička's 1930 study had also included measurements on long bones, but these measurements formed only a minor portion of the treatise. In 1937 Morant, a biometrician, combined the data from Hrdlička (1930) and Fürst and Hansen (1915), and presented the first major analysis of Eskimo *inter*population affinities. This analysis was based on Pearson's Coefficient of Racial Likeness (Zegura, in press).

Hrdlička's 1942 catalog of Eskimo crania represents the largest repository of information on Eskimo crania that has been published to date. He listed nineteen cranial measurements and calculated eight indices for the crania of over 2,200 Eskimos, 2,100 of whom were adults. The only postcranial measurements given relate to stature estimations based on femur length. The 1942 catalog covers material from Alaska, Canada, Greenland, and associated islands, including a small series from Siberia. In 1944 Hrdlička also published a cranial catalog of supposedly non-Eskimo people of the Northwest Coast, Alaska, and Siberia; however, he erroneously included the Eskimos from Kodiak Island.

Hundreds of reports and studies in some way involve the Eskimo skeleton. Those mentioned above are major studies of historical import; much of the extant data on skeletons dealing with the presumed ancestors of the five north Alaskan study populations in this volume appear in Hrdlička's 1942 catalog. Other important data sources for the history of these five populations are the works of Stewart (1959), Debetz (1959), and Lester and Shapiro (1968).

Stewart (1959) reviews the skeletal material from the vicinity of Point Barrow. The report deals primarily with cranial measurements and attempts to clarify the provenience of the many skeletal series from this area. Debetz's (1959) paper remains the only published report on the cranial remains of the important Ipiutak material from Point Hope. The Ipiutak series represents the oldest skeletal series of Alaskan Eskimos of sufficient size for statistical treatment. The dating is uncertain but many archaeologists consider the Ipiutak culture to be between 1,500 and 2,000 years old (Debetz, 1959; Rainey, 1971). The major significance of the Ipiutak series lies in the prospect of unraveling the origin of these people whose culture is unlike any other known in the Arctic (Rainey, 1971). Lester and Shapiro (1968) also include 47 Ipiutak skeletons in their study of the Eskimo vertebral column, the only other publication dealing with Ipiutak skeletal remains. The remainder of the 295 skeletons used by Lester and Shapiro come from the Tigara, a group which lived at Point Hope from approximately 1300 to 1700 A.D.

Craniofacial Morphology

Collins (1951:441) summarizes what he considers to be the total morphological pattern of the Eskimo skull as follows:

> In its most characteristic form the Eskimo skull exhibits a combination of features that makes it one of the most distinctive and easily recognized of all human types. The vault is extremely long, narrow, and high with a ridge-like elevation . . . extending along the top from front to back. The face is high and broad, and, what is most unusual, broader than the skull itself. The cheek bones are very prominent and the orbits are high. In contrast to the massiveness of the face as a whole, the nose is extremely narrow and the brow ridges only slightly developed. The nasal depression is shallow and the nasal bones are very narrow, usually having a "pinched-up" appearance. The Eskimo jaw is large and heavy, the upper part or ascending ramus, being very wide and having an outward flare at the back which gives the face its characteristic squarish shape. Another distinguishing feature of the Eskimo skull is the unusual thickness of the tympanic plate, the bony edge bordering the ear opening. Bony swellings or overgrowths on the lower and upper jaws and palate, known respectively as mandibular, maxillary and palatine tori, also occur . . . frequently among the Eskimo . . . . It is suggested here that these features which are especially characteristic of the Eskimo —the "pinched-up" nasal bones, thickened tympanic plate and mandibular and palatine tori—may be of equal if not greater significance genetically than purely metrical features such as head length, head breadth, *etc.*

> The specialized type of skull just described—long, narrow, high—is not universal among the Eskimos, though it predominates in parts of West and East Greenland, the Mackenzie Delta, and in parts of northern Alaska.

Collins's description is couched in outmoded typological terms; however, it does give a good indication of what a "typical" Eskimo skull looks like. But little attention it paid to *intra-* and *inter*population variation. For instance, sexual dimorphism is not considered, and the differences in cranial morphology throughout the geographic distribution of the Eskimo are not adequately discussed. Subsequent univariate and multivariate analyses of 609 Eskimoid crania which come from twelve populations that cover the entire geographic distribution of the Eskimo-Aleut language family have shown both sexual dimorphism and *inter*population differences (Zegura, 1971, 1975, in press). Male Eskimo crania are differentiated from female Eskimo crania primarily on the basis of the following traits: males have larger mastoids, a more protruding glabellar region, a broader face across the zygomatic arches, a longer basion-nasion chord, and a longer nasal region. Thus, size-oriented measurements seem to reflect sexual dimorphism more readily than shape-dependent variables. Substantial morphological differentiation was seen across the geographic distribution of the Eskimo. Univariate results supported the value of the cranial vault as an importnat *inter*population indicator. This finding is concordant with the general consensus of arctic specialists that facial dimensions remain relatively constant across the geographic distribution of the Eskimo while head form changes from dolichocranic in the east to brachycranic in the west.

Some general tendencies shown by the Eskimo in nonmetric craniofacial traits include: more mandibular than palatine tori, auditory exostoses less frequent than in American Indians, pronounced thickening of the tympanic plate, tympanic dehiscences prevalent, concave or straight nasal profile, round auditory meatuses, chin less pronounced than in American Indians, frequent absence of third molars, supernumerary molar cusps rare, frequent three-rooted lower first molars, marked shoveling of incisors, absence of Carabelli's cusp, and frequent enamel pearls (Collins, 1951; Greene, 1967; Laughlin, 1963, Zegura, in press).

Postcranial Remains

Far more is known about the cranial morphology of the Eskimos than about their postcranial remains. The principal reason for this discrepancy is the bias of the skeleton collectors in the early twentieth century. Crania were easier to collect and often thought to be more important for answering questions of Eskimo origins, for tracing population movements, and for assessing population affinities. As a result there are many fewer entire skeletons preserved than crania. Also, there have been fewer studies of Eskimo postcranial materials. In fact, there have been no extensive publications specifically relating to the Eskimo postcranial skeleton comparable to the work of Hrdlička (1942) on cranial material. Often, postcranial material is discussed almost parenthetically after an extensive discussion of cranial remains, usually with the intention of estimating stature from long bones. Typical of these latter reports are the works of Jørgensen (1953) and Hrdlička (1930, 1942).

Mean values for stature in males vary from 159 cm for a combined sample of eighty-six Greenlandic Eskimos to 166.5 cm for thirteen Point Hope Eskimos (Hrdlicka, 1942). For females, means range from 147.5 cm for four Naujan Eskimos to 154.6 for a heterogeneous sample from north and northeast Alaska (Hrdlicka, 1942; Jørgensen, 1953). These estimates of stature were based on bicondylar length of the femur, and it should be noted that Stewart (1939) cautions that the widely used stature reconstruction formulae of Pearson underestimated Eskimo stature by at least 3 cm. In summary, the Eskimo are short people, with stature decreasing eastward across their geographic distribution. Their relatively short stature is a function of short limbs rather than short torsos (Hrdlička, 1930; Zegura, in press).

The Eskimo vertebral column has been the subject of numerous studies (Lester and Shapiro, 1968; Merbs, 1969; Merbs and Wilson, 1962; Stewart, 1931, 1953, 1956). These investigations have uncovered an unusually high frequency of anomalies and pathological changes. Indeed, on the basis of an examination of 295 skeletons from Point Hope (47 Ipiutak and 248 Tigara) Lester and Shapiro (1968) conclude that these Eskimos have a much higher incidence of lumbar vertebral arch defects (spondylolysis) than do other ethnic groups. This condition, separate neural arches, increases with age in both incidence and extent, is probably not congenital, and indicates a possible hereditary disposition to weakness of the lumbar area.

Skeletal Remains from Anaktuvuk Pass, Barrow, Kaktovik, Point Hope, and Wainwright

Of the five villages, only Barrow and Point Hope have enough time depths for investigation of prehistoric populations. Also, these two villages are the only sources of skeletal collections large enough for statistical analyses. There are no skeletal collections from Wainwright. Anaktuvuk Pass is represented by a single skeleton at the Smithsonian Institution. Kaktovik is situated on Barter Island, and Hrdlička's 1942 catalog lists only eight skulls (two males and six females) from Barter Island; they are at the National Museum of Canada. Thus, the discussion of the skeletal remains of the five study populations will focus on Barrow and Point Hope.

Table 2-2 lists the extant skeletal collections from the vicinity of Point Barrow, Alaska (Stewart, 1959). The skeletal material represents 332 individuals; however, in most cases only the skull was collected. Fewer than fifty skeletons in various states of completeness are present in the collections. Stewart (1959) lists sixteen craniometric measurements and seven indices for most of the material and calculates t-tests for the differences between the means of the combined recent material versus the combined old (Birnirk) material. Very few of the t-tests showed statistically significant differences between the means. The major differences were mainly in the vault dimensions and associated indices. In general, the combined Birnirk sample tended to indicate longer, narrower, and higher-headed skulls than the combined sample of recent material. Thus, while the face remained largely the same through a period of roughly 1000 years the vault shifted from long, narrow, and high to short, broad, and less high. Stewart (1959) interprets these morphological changes as due to population replacement, perhaps from the interior, rather than representing an ancestral-descendant sequence from Birnirk to the recent inhabitants of Point Barrow.

Possible stature changes during this time interval cannot be adequately

TABLE 2-2 *Distribution of Skeletal Materials (Mostly Skulls) from the*
Vicinity of Point Barrow, Alaska

Sites in geographical order from Northeast to Southwest	Collector	Present Location	No. of Males	No. of Females
Recent (found on surface, without cultural association; 18th to early 20th century, A.D.)				
Point Barrow	Stefánsson	Amer. Museum Nat. History	44	49
Point Barrow	Ray	Smithsonian	5	3
Nixeruk	Ford	Smithsonian	27	28
Barrow	Van Valin	Wistar Inst.	21	14
Barrow	Hrdlička	Smithsonian	16	22
Utkiavik	Ford	Smithsonian	13	18
Total			126	134
Old (burials associated with Birnirk culture; A.D. 500–900)[*]				
Birnirk (Piginik)	Ford	Smithsonian	1	4
Kugok	Ford	Smithsonian	3	3
Nunavak	Hopson	Univ. Penn	3	6
Kugusugaruk	Van Valin	Smithsonian, Wistar Inst.	28	24
Total			35	37

Adapted from Stewart (1959).

[*]The Birnirk culture directly precedes the appearance of the Thule culture at Barrow.

investigated because Ford brought back only nine skeletons (seven Birnirk and two recent), and the only published long-bone measurements come from a portion of the Van Valin Birnirk collection. Hrdlička (1930) reported these long-bone measurements in summary form, and Stewart (1959) concludes that these members of the Birnirk culture did not differ appreciably in stature from a miscellaneous group of recent Steward Peninsula Eskimos. Table 2-3 presents the means and standard deviations for an extensive craniometric measurement battery for the Nixeruk series, dated provisionally as being from the eighteenth to the nineteenth century A.D.

TABLE 2-3 *Means and Standard Deviations of 74 Craniometric Measurements for the Nixeruk (Point Barrow) Series and a Recent Point Hope Series*

Measurement	Nixeruk				Point Hope			
	Males (15)		Females (12)		Males (61)		Females (36)	
	Mean	S.D.	Mean	S.D.	Mean	S.D.	Mean	S.D.
1. Glabello-occipital length	186.6	3.5	178.1	5.1	183.6	4.8	174.6	5.3
2. Nasio-occipital length	183.5	3.0	175.9	5.1	180.0	4.9	172.6	4.7
3. Nasion-basion length	105.3	2.9	100.2	3.5	104.7	4.1	99.5	4.3
4. Basion-bregma height	136.6	4.3	131.3	3.3	139.7	4.4	133.9	4.6
5. Maximum cranial breadth	138.6	2.8	134.2	3.5	138.8	4.3	134.9	2.8
6. Maximum frontal breadth	114.7	4.5	110.2	4.1	115.5	4.3	111.4	3.1
7. Bistephanic breadth	108.6	4.7	105.3	4.1	110.6	5.4	107.1	4.2
8. Bimalar breadth	117.9	3.6	108.9	4.5	117.3	4.6	109.8	3.7
9. Bizygomatic breadth	140.5	3.7	130.8	3.3	143.0	4.6	133.1	3.7
10. Biauricular breadth	128.9	3.0	122.0	2.6	129.4	4.1	123.7	3.0
11. Minimum cranial breadth	76.2	3.6	68.2	1.8	73.8	3.2	70.2	3.7
12. Biasterionic breadth	109.3	4.4	105.5	3.0	109.3	4.0	106.0	3.6
13. Basion-prosthion length	101.0	3.7	95.4	4.6	101.2	3.8	95.5	3.9
14. Nasion-prosthion height	70.4	2.5	66.0	3.2	69.4	4.0	65.7	4.0
15. Bijugal breadth	123.2	4.2	115.2	4.1	125.6	4.2	117.4	3.4
16. Nasal breadth	24.3	1.4	22.9	1.4	23.6	1.6	22.8	1.5
17. Palate breadth, external	62.9	4.1	56.8	3.7	64.4	2.9	61.4	2.6
18. Palate length, internal	46.8	1.5	44.8	2.8	47.0	3.1	44.1	2.7
19. Mastoid length	26.5	2.6	22.8	2.2	26.0	3.4	21.3	3.1
20. Mastoid width	11.7	2.8	8.5	2.1	12.8	2.0	9.1	1.9
21. Malar length, inferior	40.9	2.9	36.8	3.5	39.8	2.7	37.4	2.6
22. Malar length, maximum	58.9	3.4	54.1	3.7	57.4	3.6	53.7	2.6
23. Cheek height	43.7	3.0	41.9	3.5	43.5	3.7	41.4	2.5
24. Frontomalare anterior – zygomaxillary anterior length	47.5	2.9	44.6	2.0	47.5	2.4	44.5	2.5

TABLE 2-3 *Continued*

	Nixeruk				Point Hope			
	Males (15)		Females (12)		Males (61)		Females (36)	
Measurement	Mean	S.D.	Mean	S.D.	Mean	S.D.	Mean	S.D.
25. Nasal height	55.8	2.1	51.8	1.9	54.0	2.5	50.8	2.1
26. Orbit height	37.0	1.9	35.4	1.4	36.5	1.7	35.8	1.8
27. Orbit breadth	42.5	1.1	40.0	1.4	42.0	1.4	40.1	1.4
28. Minimum zygomatic arch height	7.9	1.2	6.9	1.7	8.5	1.3	6.6	1.1
29. Foramen magnum length	37.9	2.0	37.1	2.6	39.6	2.2	37.7	1.6
30. Bimaxillary chord	100.2	4.0	94.8	5.7	102.8	5.0	96.3	4.7
31. Zygomaxillary subtense	22.2	2.9	19.8	2.0	22.1	2.4	20.9	2.0
32. Bifrontal chord	103.3	2.6	97.9	3.1	102.9	3.3	98.3	3.3
33. Nasio-frontal subtense	16.1	2.1	14.8	1.8	15.1	2.2	14.4	1.5
34. Bi-orbital breadth	103.0	3.0	97.6	3.0	102.2	3.0	98.3	3.7
35. Dacryon subtense	11.0	2.3	8.9	1.4	10.0	2.2	8.9	2.4
36. Interorbital breadth	22.1	2.0	20.8	1.6	22.3	1.8	21.0	1.3
37. Nasio-dacryal subtense	11.6	1.8	10.5	1.4	11.8	1.8	10.2	1.4
38. Simotic chord	6.1	1.8	5.5	1.8	5.2	1.6	5.3	1.7
39. Simotic subtense	2.6	.6	2.2	.9	2.6	.9	2.0	.7
40. Glabella projection	3.7	1.4	2.2	.9	3.9	1.1	2.0	.9
41. Nasion-bregma chord	112.1	3.1	108.8	3.3	112.7	4.4	109.5	3.6
42. Nasion-bregma subtense	25.2	1.9	24.7	1.5	25.7	2.4	25.7	1.9
43. Nasion-subtense fraction	51.7	2.1	48.7	1.9	52.4	3.0	50.0	2.6
44. Bregma-lambda chord	108.5	7.6	104.5	5.3	110.1	4.7	104.9	5.5
45. Bregma-lambda subtense	20.2	2.8	20.8	2.6	23.5	2.3	22.3	2.6
46. Bregma-subtense fraction	51.3	5.3	51.6	2.7	53.5	4.4	49.8	4.4
47. Lambda-opisthion chord	99.6	3.5	95.8	4.4	97.6	5.1	94.8	5.2
48. Lambda-opisthion subtense	30.0	2.5	27.2	3.4	27.7	2.8	26.6	3.0
49. Lambda-subtense fraction	50.1	5.5	42.8	4.9	51.1	7.1	45.8	5.4
50. Rhinial chord	55.7	4.1	53.0	4.6	56.6	4.6	54.3	5.2
51. Rhinial subtense	18.9	2.3	15.5	2.0	17.8	2.6	15.9	2.1

52. Bregma radius	116.1	3.4	111.5	2.7	118.2	3.8	113.4	3.4
53. Lambda radius	103.2	3.9	100.0	4.2	101.9	4.4	97.8	4.1
54. Opisthion radius	35.3	3.0	36.1	3.8	38.0	3.1	35.8	2.9
55. Basion radius	10.8	2.9	10.5	2.8	11.8	3.0	11.0	2.4
56. Nasion radius	94.5	2.2	89.4	2.9	93.7	4.1	88.6	3.0
57. Prosthion radius	102.1	3.5	95.1	3.1	101.8	4.3	96.2	4.1
58. Subspinale radius	97.1	3.3	89.8	2.6	96.7	4.2	91.0	3.7
59. Rhinion radius	98.7	3.4	91.0	4.1	97.3	4.7	91.4	3.4
60. Nasion angle (basion-prosthion)*	66.8	3.0	66.4	2.2	67.6	2.6	67.0	2.7
61. Prosthion angle (basion-nasion)*	73.4	2.6	74.5	2.6	73.1	2.6	73.7	3.1
62. Basion angle (nasion-prosthion)*	39.7	1.7	39.3	1.9	39.3	2.1	39.3	2.5
63. Nasion angle (basion-bregma)*	77.7	2.9	77.6	2.5	79.9	2.6	79.5	2.2
64. Basion angle (bregma-nasion)*	53.5	2.9	54.1	2.2	52.6	2.4	53.5	2.1
65. Bregma angle (basion-nasion)*	48.7	1.3	48.2	1.6	47.5	2.1	47.0	2.1
66. Zygomaxillary angle	132.3	4.9	134.8	3.4	133.4	4.5	133.1	4.4
67. Nasio-frontal angle	145.3	4.5	146.5	4.0	147.3	4.3	147.4	3.3
68. Dacryal angle	149.9	6.3	154.2	3.9	152.3	5.9	154.3	7.3
69. Nasio-dacryal angle	87.5	9.2	89.9	7.2	87.3	8.7	92.3	8.1
70. Simotic angle	97.9	14.0	104.2	19.9	91.8	20.0	105.2	16.9
71. Frontal angle	131.4	3.0	130.8	2.1	130.7	3.4	129.4	2.9
72. Parietal angle	139.1	3.8	136.8	3.9	133.8	3.3	133.8	3.5
73. Occipital angle	117.5	3.6	120.5	5.3	120.1	4.8	121.1	5.0
74. Rhinial angle	111.9	5.6	119.4	7.5	115.6	9.1	119.4	6.9

For complete definitions of the craniometric measurements, see Zegura (1971). Linear measurements were taken to the nearest millimeter, angular measurements were calculated to the nearest degree; bilateral measurements were taken on the left side.

*The chord subtended by the angle is indicated inside the parentheses.

19

Skeletal remains from Point Hope are much more plentiful than from the vicinity of Barrow; however, most of the material remains unanalyzed. Hrdlička's 1942 catalog reports cranial measurements and indices on 281 individuals (163 males and 118 females), divided into two groups: "older" burials and "later" burials. Unfortunately, adequate archaeological provenience data are lacking and much of the material actually represents surface collections. Dating for the "later" burials is probably late nineteenth to early twentieth century. The older burials may be slightly earlier but probably postdate the Tigara culture (1300-1700 A.D.). In addition to these materials some 500 usable skeletons with good provenience data were collected by Larsen and Rainey between 1939 and 1941 (Rainey, 1971). In 1941 Harry Shapiro of the American Museum of Natural History undertook the analysis of these materials and has not yet completed the project. The importance of this skeletal collection cannot be overemphasized. The collection spans at least five distinct cultural periods (Near Ipiutak, ca. 500-100 B.C.; Ipiutak, ca. 100 B.C.-ca. 500 A.D.; Birnirk, ca. 500-900 A.D.; Western Thule, ca. 900-1300 A.D.; and Tigara, ca. 1300-1700 A.D.) extending over 2,000 years (Rainey, 1971). When these materials are completely analyzed much will be learned about the former inhabitants of Point Hope.

The only publications dealing with these 500 skeletons are those of Debetz (1959) and Lester and Shapiro (1968). Debetz's short paper lists means for nineteen craniometric variables, two facial angles, and seven long-bone measurements. His sample included seventy-one Ipiutak skeletons (thirty-six males; thirty-five females) and 238 Tigara skeletons (113 males; 125 females). Incomplete preservation caused the sample sizes to differ widely for different measurements. Also, it should be noted that only forty-seven of the seventy-one "Ipiutak" skeletons had good provenience data and are recognized as belonging to the main Ipiutak burial by Shapiro. The rest are near Ipiutak and/or undated burials found on the grounds of the Ipiutak cemetery (Debetz, 1959). Debetz (1959) concluded that there were no substantial differences between the Tigara and the Ipiutak proper (the forty-seven skeletons with secure provenience). There were, however, some statistically significant differences between them although he did not report the pertinent statistical tests. Debetz noted that the Ipiutak had a lower cranial vault than the Tigara. Also, the characteristic Eskimo dominance of bizygomatic breadth over cranial breadth was present in the Tigara, but the relationship was reversed in the Ipiutak. Finally, the Tigara's long bones were larger than the Ipiutak's. Debetz felt that on typological grounds the enigmatic inland-oriented Ipiutak were not the direct ancestors of the maritime-oriented Tigara. Instead, he pointed to typological similarities between the Ipiutak and the Yukaghir from Siberia.

Lester and Shapiro (1968) compared the incidence of spondylolysis among the Tigara and Ipiutak skeletons. The vertebral arch defect investigated is a separation, or lysis, through the *pars interarticularis*, which divides the vertebra into two parts: one, the body and superior articular process; the other, the neural arch and inferior articular processes (Lester and Shapiro, 1968). The Tigara were found to have a much higher incidence of the lesion (Tigara: 111 lesions in 248 skeletons, or 45%; Ipiutak: ten lesions in forty-seven skeletons, or 21%). The combined incidence (121 lesions in 295 skeletons, or 41%) was higher than that found in other ethnic groups (Lester and Shapiro, 1968).

Definitive *inter*population comparisons of the skeletal remains at Point Hope must await the published analysis of the huge series of skeletons collected by Larsen and Rainey. Point Hope represents the longest continuously inhabited site in Alaska. It presents a unique opportunity to unravel the evolutionary history of the Eskimo during the last 2,500 years. As Table 2-3 shows, craniometric measurements for a series of recent Point Hope crania are very similar to those for the Nixeruk (Point Barrow) series. This similarity points to a close phenotypic relationship, which can be demonstrated by biological-distance studies and cluster analyses.

RELATIONSHIP OF LINGUISTIC CLASSIFICATION TO ESKIMO BIOLOGICAL DIFFERENTIATION

For placement of the north Alaskan Eskimo within the context of overall Eskimo diversity a biological distance study was undertaken (Zegura, 1975). The results of the biological distance analyses can be compared with the linguistic framework presented in Fig. 2-1. Data consist of seventy-four craniometric measurements taken on a total of 609 Eskaleutian crania. Of the seventy-four craniometric variables fifty-nine are linear dimensions of the head and face and the remaining fifteen are computed angles. These variables are listed in Table 2-3. The sample comprised the crania of 353 males and 256 females distributed in twelve populations raning in size from twenty-one to 109 and in chronological age from approximately the middle of the seventeenth century to around 1900 (see Table 2-4 for details of sample composition). The sample was chosen to cover the entire geographical distribution (see Fig. 2-2) of the Eskimo-Aleut stock as well as the major linguistic subdivisions in Fig. 2-1. The major caveat in the application of a linguistic model to a skeletal series is ascertaining what language these people spoke. I have tried to deal with this problem by choosing as recent a sample as possible. Still, in many cases there is no direct proof that the skeletal series chosen actually belonged to the language group that I assigned them to in terms of the linguistic classification in Fig. 2-1 (Zegura, 1975).

One of the most direct ways to demonstrate the concordance of language and biology would be to correlate the biological distances with the quantity, one minus shared cognate percentage (Friedlaender, 1969; Spielman et al., 1974). Unfortunately, the necessary cognate percentages are not available.

TABLE 2-4 *Sample Composition of Craniometric Study Populations*

Population	Male	Female	Total	Linguistic Group[*]	Date (Century)
(1) Nunivak Island	39	32	71	Central Alaskan Yupik	Late 19th– early 20th
(2) Nelson Island	11	10	21	Central Alaskan Yupik	Late 19th– early 20th
(3) Kuskokwim River (below Old Bethel)	18	12	30	Central Alaskan Yupik	Late 19th– early 20th
(4) Wales	19	11	30	Inuit	Late 19th– early 20th
(5) Sadlermiut (Southampton Is.)	23	26	49	Inuit	19th
(6) Kagamil Island	28	32	60	Aleut	18th–19th
(7) Point Hope	61	36	97	Inuit	Late 19th– early 20th
(8) St. Lawrence Is.	71	38	109	Siberian Yupik	Late 18th– 19th
(9) Point Barrow (Nixeruk)	15	12	27	Inuit	18th–19th
(10) Kodiak Island	24	14	38	Pacific Coast Yupik	17th–18th
(11) Chirikof Island	17	13	30	Pacific Coast Yupik	19th(probably)
(12) Umanak, Greenland	27	20	47	Inuit	19th–early 20th
Totals	353	256	609		

[*]As shown in Fig. 2.1.

The relevant linguistic comparisons that appear in the literature include the following cognate percentages: Aleut vs Proto-Eskimo (36.5%); Aleut vs Inuit (25%); Inuit vs Central Alaskan Yupik (56–65%); Siberian Yupik vs Central Alaskan Yupik (65%); and Inuit vs Inuit (88.5%) (Dumond, 1965; Krauss, 1973; Swadesh, 1958). The lack of quantitative linguistic data thus necessitates a qualitative comparison between biology and language.

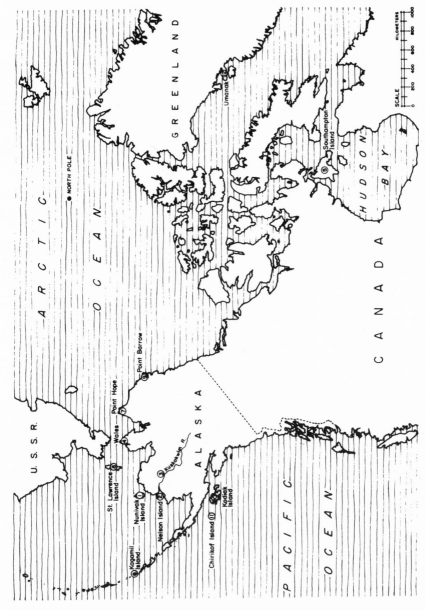

FIGURE 2-2. *Geographic distribution of 12 skeletal populations used in biological-distance and cluster analyses (from Zegura, 1975).*

23

Multiple discriminate function and canonical variate analyses (multivariate statistical procedures) of the craniometric data were undertaken for each sex as a first step in the assessment of biological and linguistic congruence. By "congruence" I mean the degree of correspondence between arrangements of objects in a classification. The twelve study populations were assigned to groups according to their putative linguistic affiliation and the subsequent multivariate analyses were based on the terminal groups given in the linguistic classification (Fig. 2-1).

The basic logic of discriminant function analysis involves the following four-step procedure (Zegura, 1971):

1. Find the linear functions(s) which maximally separate the known groups.
2. Calculate the importance of each function.
3. Calculate a discriminant score for each individual on each function.
4. Convert this score to a probability of being a member of each group.

Discriminant function analysis can be included within the more general structure of the branch of multivariate statistics called canonical analysis (McKeon, 1966). Here the discriminant functions are replaced by canonical variates and the discriminant score of an individual on a particular function is replaced by the analogous quantity, the value of a particular canonical variate for an individual. The mathematics of the two techniques are essentially the same, and the computer program used for the analyses (BMD07M) combines elements from both techniques (Dixon, 1970).

Two portions of computer output from the multivariate analyses are of interest: the "hits" and "misses" tables and the Mahalanobis' distances which can be calculated from the canonical variable means (McKeon, 1966). The probability of group membership of each specimen is computed employing Bayes' theorem, and individuals are assigned to that group for which their probability of group membership is highest. The assignments based on group membership probabilities can then be combined into a "hits" and "misses" table wherein a "hit" denotes the assignment of a subject to the population that he actually does come from and a "miss" denotes an incorrect linguistic group assignment. This is one of the best ways to assess the separateness of the different linguistic groupings in terms of biological parameters (Zegura, 1971). For the analysis of male subjects, 311 of 353 specimens were correctly assigned to their putative linguistic group—a "hit" rate of 88%. For the female subjects, 242 of 256 specimens were correctly assigned—a "hit" rate of 95%. The overall "hit" rate for the two analyses was 553 of 609, or 91%. These results imply that biological differentiation parallels linguistic differentiation.

The final attempt to assess taxonomic congruence of biological and linguistic information involves a cluster analysis of Mahalanobis' D^2 values for male and female subjects in the twelve original populations. According to Rao (1952), the first step in studying biological differences between populations is the construction of an index by which one can measure the resemblance between groups. The majority opinion is that Mahalanobis' D^2 represents the best available distance statistic for use on craniometric data. Mahalanobis formulated this statistic in a series of papers (Mahalanobis, 1925, 1930, 1936) and the pertinent concepts, as well as computational details, are clearly explained in Rao (1952), Rightmire (1969), and Mahalanobis et al. (1949) among others.

Mahalanobis' D^2 assumes multivariate normal distributions for the variates as well as homogeneous dispersion matrices and correlations for the different populations. Most craniometric materials probably approximate these assumptions to some extent (Rao, 1952). The D^2 statistic satisfies the two following fundamental postulates of distance in topological spaces:

The distance between groups is not less than zero.

The sum of distances of a group from two other groups is not less than the distance between the two other groups (triangle law of distance). (Rao, 1952:352.)

In addition, D^2 seems to adhere to the two following empirical requirements stipulated by Rao (1952:353):

The distance must not decrease when additional characters are considered.

The increase in distance by the addition of some characters to a suitably chosen set must be relatively small so that the group constellations arrived at on the basis of the chosen set are not distorted when additional characters are considered.

The equation for D^2 is of the form:

$$D_p^2 = \sum_{i=1}^{p} \sum_{j=1}^{p} w^{ij}(\bar{x}_{i1} - \bar{x}_{i2})(\bar{x}_{j1} - \bar{x}_{j2}) \qquad (2.1)$$

where p = number of variables and
    $\bar{x}_{i1}$ = mean value of character i in population 1.
    $\bar{x}_{i2}$ = mean value of character i in population 2.
    $\bar{x}_{j1}$ = mean value of character j in population 1.
    $\bar{x}_{j2}$ = mean value of character j in population 2.
    w^{ij} = an element in the inverse of the pooled within dispersion matrix.

The distance between all $g(g - 1)/2$ pairs of populations is then calculated in this manner.

The value of D^2 for any pair of populations can be tested for statistical significance by the Hotelling T^2 statistic. This tests the null hypothesis that the two population mean vectors are identical (H_2) against the alternative that they are not. The test statistic is

$$T^2 = \frac{N_1 N_2}{N_1 + N_2} \; D^2 \tag{2.2}$$

where (N_1) and (N_2) represent the sample sizes. The quantity

$$F = \frac{(N - g - r + 1)}{r(N - g)} \; T^2 \tag{2.3}$$

has the variance ratio (F) distribution with degrees of freedom (r) and $(N - g - r + 1)$ where (N) = total sample size, (g) = number of groups, and (r) = number of variables (Dixon, 1970; Morrison, 1967).

The mathematical similarity between Mahalanobis' distance statistic and discriminant function analysis becomes apparent when one considers that the sum of the squared discriminant coefficients is equal to Mahalanobis' D^2 in the two-group case using the transformed variate procedure of Rao (1952). In this alternative procedure for calculating a discriminate function the correlations among the various measurements are first corrected for by finding equations which transform the measurements into new uncorrelated variables all with the same (unit) variance. Then, the discriminant function coefficients are found as the differences between the means of the two populations in these uncorrelated variables. Rao (1952) states that in this case $D^2 p$ is the variance of the discriminant function. Thus, both $D^2 p$ and the discriminant function can be calculated with the same procedure (Zegura, 1971).

The values for the Mahalanobis statistic are listed in Table 2-5, based on data in Zegura (1971). The cluster analysis dendrographs shown in Figs. 2-3 and 2-4 contain information about both within-group and between-group distances. The numbers on the ordinate represent the distance values at which clusters are formed. This axis gives within-cluster distance information by giving the distance from the origin at which two adjacent groups are connected. The other axis gives between-group distances—i.e., it gives the distance between two adjacent objects (McCammon and Wenninger, 1970).

Fig. 2-3 (D^2 analysis for male subjects) shows rather good concordance with linguistic affiliation. The tightest cluster involves Point Hope and Point Barrow (the two Inuit populations in the north Alaskan Eskimo study). Nelson Island and Kuskokwim River represent the next tightest cluster: two of the three Central Alaskan Yupik groups in the analysis. The third close grouping involves Wales and Sadlermiut (again, two Inuit groups). The top

TABLE 2-5 *Mahalanobis' Distances: Males (Below Diagonal) and Females (Above Diagonal)*

Group*	1	2	3	4	5	6	7	8	9	10	11	12
1		22.4	20.5	22.0	23.1	72.1	26.4	36.0	24.9	57.8	77.5	38.1
2	24.5		12.5+	23.4+	31.4	63.0	34.2	42.3	38.8	53.8	68.4	40.3
3	24.8	17.6+		26.0	30.4	53.2	32.4	30.9	38.9	40.7	75.6	39.9
4	17.7	23.7	28.1		17.6+	81.9	24.7	41.3	35.3	68.4	81.3	26.9
5	26.0	21.6	25.2	16.8		78.7	20.0	31.8	30.4	59.2	87.2	22.8
6	54.7	45.1	39.3	58.6	66.4		63.7	50.9	83.1	30.9	121.1	108.4
7	26.8	32.2	27.5	18.9	25.2	54.1		19.5	16.0+	40.5	72.9	35.4
8	39.0	35.7	22.7	36.2	36.5	36.9	19.0		32.5	34.5	100.6	48.3
9	34.2	32.6	36.8	27.1	31.2	53.9	13.6	22.4		61.8	88.7	41.5
10	54.7	43.1	37.4	53.5	58.4	32.7	36.3	28.2	40.7		81.8	85.4
11	67.0	51.1	57.4	73.6	74.6	62.0	58.4	63.0	52.5	41.1		98.8
12	31.3	42.4	43.6	21.6	22.1	83.7	22.0	42.9	28.3	60.3	75.2	

The Spearman Rank-Order Correlation coefficient between the corresponding distances for males and for females is +.92.

*Key for group numbering is given in Table 2.4.

+These values are <u>not</u> statistically significant at the 5% level for 66 simultaneous tests.

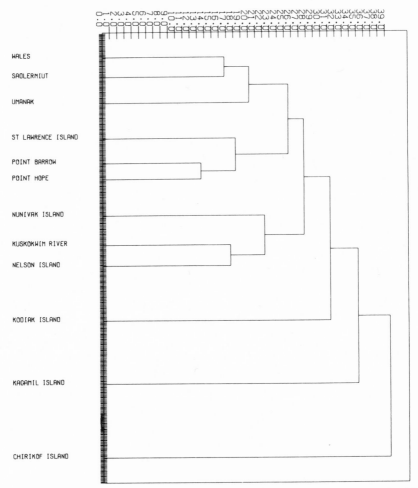

FIGURE 2-3. *Male Eskaleutians: unweighted pair-group (Average-Link) clustering of Mahalanobis's* D^2 *distances (from Zegura, 1975).*

six populations in Fig. 2-3 form a higher-order cluster that represents the five Inuit groups plus St. Lawrence Island. The next three populations are the three Central Alaskan Yupik groups. The preferential joining of the Inuit groups with the Central Alaskan Yupik groups rather than with the Pacific Coast Yupik populations is predictable from ethnohistoric information (Hrdlička, 1930). The aberrant position of Chirikof Island is also to be expected because of small sample size, uncertain provenience, slight cranial deformation, and the possibility of Russian admixture (Zegura, 1971). Overall, therefore, the concordance between biology and linguistics is quite remarkable for the D^2 analysis on male subjects.

The D^2 analysis on female subjects also shows good concordance between biology and linguistics (Fig. 2-4). The same three pairs of populations that

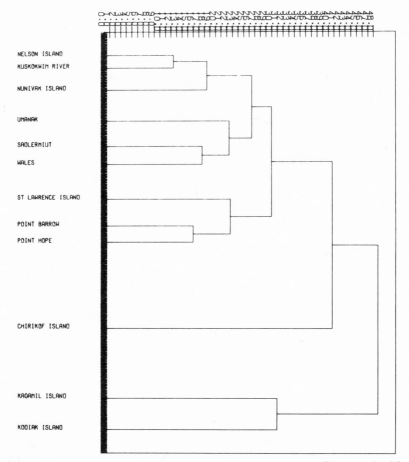

FIGURE 2-4. *Female Eskaleutians: unweighted pair-group (Average-Link) clustering of Mahalanobis's* D^2 *distances (from Zegura, 1975).*

joined first in the analysis of male subjects also joined first here, though the order differs. The Central Alaskan Yupik cluster appears at the top of Fig. 2-4, followed by the Inuit cluster and St. Lawrence Island. Here, however, Kagamil Island, an Aleut group, joins Kodiak Island, a Pacific Coast Yupik group, with Chirikof Island, the other Pacific Coast Yupik group, left to join the other populations rather than Kodiak Island. The close phenotypic resemblance of Kodiak Islanders and the Aleuts was not unexpected. In fact, this striking similarity had been noted many time by Hrdlička, who actually included Kodiak Islanders with the Aleuts as non-Eskimoid peoples rather than with the Eskimo when publishing his cranial catalogs in the 1940s (Hrdlička, 1942, 1944). Thus, although there are deviations from a 1:1 correspondence for females between the D^2 analysis clusters and linguistic affiliation, the overall degree of concordance is rather high.

The results of the cluster analyses demonstrate a close phenotypic similarity between the Point Barrow and Point Hope cranial remains during the last two centuries. These two populations form tight first-order clusters in both analyses for male and female subjects, thereby suggesting a phenotypic unity for a portion of the North Alaskan Eskimo population system. The Aleut population (Kagamil Island) is well differentiated from the Eskimo groups, except for Kodiak Island. In turn, the Eskimo groups form distinct biological clusters which have demonstrable linguistic correlates. The outliers are confined to the two Pacific Coast Yupik groups, Chirikof Island and Kodiak Island. The slight cranial deformation noted in these two groups (although absent in the rest) may have been the reason for their peripheral placement.

3

Ethnohistory of the Research Populations

Paul L. Jamison

In Chapter 2, Zegura presented an archaeological, linguistic, and biological perspective of the Eskimo that encompassed, geographically, parts of four nations in two hemispheres. In this chapter the geographical focus will be much narrower, to concentrate on the ethnohistorical background of the study populations.*

RESEARCH AREA

Four of the villages visited by members of the IBP team are located on what is commonly called the North Slope of Alaska or, more appropriately, the Arctic Coastal Plain (Milan, 1964a). This is a vast expanse of tundra entirely within the Arctic Circle; it is flat, treeless, and relatively featureless. During the summer months countless lakes and meandering streams dot the landscape. Snow covers the ground from September to May and permafrost underlies it year-round.

A number of rivers drain the area, and most of them flow north out of the Brooks Range, the northwesternmost extension of the major continental mountain system of North America. This mountain range roughly bounds the study area. The coastal plain slopes from the broken foothills of the Brooks Range in the south to the Arctic Ocean in the north. To the east and west, respectively, the Alaska-Canada border at Demarcation Point and the DeLong Mountains near Capes Seppings and Thompson provide convenient boundaries (Fig. 3-1).

At present there are six predominantly Eskimo villages within the approximately 100,000-square-mile area of the Arctic Coastal Plain, all on the coast. From west to east they are: Point Hope, Point Lay, Wainwright, Barrow, Nuiksut, and Kaktovik (on Barter Island). Two of the villages, Point Lay and Nuiksut, are old village sites that have been recently reoccupied by people

*Additional information on historical aspects of these populations will be found in the discussion of demographic parameters in Chapter 19.

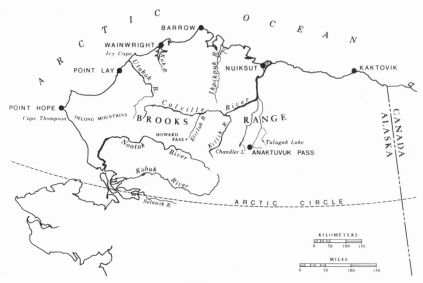

FIGURE 3-1. *Map of northern Alaska.*

from Wainwright and Barrow, respectively. This reoccupation occurred after the completion of the research phase of the IBP so these villages will not be considered in this report. An entire research team spent one or more summers in Wainwright, Point Hope, and Barrow. Kaktovik and a fifth village, Anaktuvuk Pass, were visted at least once by a smaller research team.

Anaktuvuk Pass is situated in the interior of Alaska, and its name is descriptive. The village is located in a broad pass that transects the Brooks Range. Although Anaktuvuk Pass is not on the coastal plain, the cultural and ecological focus of its inhabitants has always been directed northwards. On any basis except their present location the residents of this village should be included in a discussion of the inhabitants of the Arctic Coastal Plain rather than grouped with other Eskimo aggregations to the southwest and east or with Indian tribes to the south.

HISTORY OF THE VILLAGES

The archaeological record indicates that Point Hope and Barrow have the longest history at, or very near, their present location (Larsen and Rainey, 1948; Ford, 1959; and Bandi, 1969). The spectacular Ipiutak site identified and excavated by Larsen and Rainey at Point Hope dates from the time of Christ. "Near Ipiutak" materials at this same site may date from 500 years earlier. Birnirk, an archaeological site located near Point Barrow, dates from 500 to 900 A.D., according to Bandi. Because of favorable conditions for sea mammal hunting at both of these locations, they probably have been occupied for as long as the Eskimo have been sea mammal hunters.

Wainwright does not have as extensive a past. As an established village it dates from 1904, when the schoolhouse was constructed (Milan, 1964a). Before this date Eskimos lived along the Kuk River and at its mouth, Wainwright Inlet, for an indeterminate amount of time (Fig. 3-1). The establishment of educational and then medical and economic institutions just north of Wainwright Inlet attracted natives from a wide area. Unfortunately, there has been little archaeological work in the vicinity.

Kaktovik has had a similar but even more recent history (Chance, 1966). It became a permanent village at its present location in the late 1940s and early 1950s. The impetus for this development initially came from the United States Coast and Geodetic Survey and the military. The permanence of the location was assured in 1953-54 when construction began on the Barter Island radar station, part of the Distant Early Warning (DEW-line) system. Prior to this time the current residents of Kaktovik lived in Barrow and in small family groups scattered along the northeastern coast of Alaska.

Occupation of the interior of Alaska is not as easy to define because one must rely almost entirely on the archaeological record. The Eskimos living there were, to a large extent, seminomadic wanderers within a particular territory (Ingstad, 1954; Gubser, 1965; Campbell, 1968). Most of the archaeological work in the interior has been undertaken in two areas: the Anaktuvuk Pass region (Solecki, 1950; Campbell, 1962) and the area between Anaktuvuk Pass and the headwaters of either the Noatak River (Irving, 1953) or the Colville River (Hall, 1968, 1970). The former region has been populated for around 200-300 years in its most recent occupation. Before this time there were sporadic occupations of the Central Brooks Range by different, discontinuous societies (Campbell, 1962).

Since 1900 there has been a trend for the coastal and inland Eskimo of northern Alaska to congregate in fewer and fewer locations (Jamison, 1968). The inland people gradually left the Brooks Range to seek residence on the coast where better opportunities existed. A decline in the size of the caribou herds in the interior contributed to this migration since caribou were a primary basis of inland subsistence. By 1920 the Brooks Range was nearly uninhabited. Then in 1938 three families returned inland and were soon followed by several others (Gubser, 1965).

In 1947, according to Gubser, there were two groups of Eskimo living in the vicinity of Anaktuvuk Pass. Five families lived at Chandler Lake and eight families on the Killik River. In 1947 those at Chandler Lake moved to Tulugak Lake and shortly thereafter the Killik River families joined them. Again, however, outside influences were important in localizing the people. A monthly postal service was established at the summit of Anaktuvuk Pass in 1951 and most of the families moved there that year. In 1960 a schoolteacher began conducting school in the village and this induced the remaining two families to join the rest at the present location (Gubser, 1965).

POPULATION SIZE

Table 3-1 gives population figures for these five villages as of the 1970 census. The total population of 3,027 Eskimos *may* be the largest number the area has supported since the mid-nineteenth century. According to Milan (1970 and this volume), the population of these villages is increasing rapidly.

There is considerable uncertainty about the size of the aboriginal population of northern Alaska. Earliest estimates must be based on the impressionistic statements of early explorers such as Cook (1818), who sailed as far north as Icy Cape in the late 1770s, Kotzebue (1821), and Beechey (1831). Members of Beechey's crew reached Point Barrow during the voyage of H.M.S. *Blossom* to the Arctic Coast in 1826-27.

Census data exist for northern Alaska for the years 1880 and 1890. Petroff (1884) indicates that a Captain E. E. Smith, ice-pilot on the U.S. steamer *Thomas Corwin,* counted 1,102 natives living at thirteen coastal locations between Point Hope and the mouth of the Colville River in 1880. In the next census Porter (1893) reports, 1,019 natives living at seven coastal sites between Points Hope and Barrow. Petroff listed the Colville, Kuk, Noatak, Kobuk, Selawik, and Buckland as the known rivers of that day. He states, "The natives on the coast and whalers report the existence of settlements farther up on all these rivers, with the exception of the Colville River, whose headwaters no white man has ever visited" (p. 2).

TABLE 3-1 *Population Estimates for the Research Villages*

Village	Size
Point Hope	386
Wainwright	315
Barrow	2104
Kaktovik	123
Anaktuvuk Pass	99
Total	3027

From census data for 1970.

This deficiency was remedied only a few years later when Lieutenant George M. Stoney and his men explored the Kobuk River and much of the western Brooks Range (Stoney, 1899). In 1886 Stoney sent Ensign Howard to meet a party of Eskimo who were going to travel down the Colville River to trade with the Point Barrow Eskimos. Howard's route took him up the Noatak River, through Howard Pass and up the Etivluk River, then down the Colville on the north side of the Brooks Range, and finally down the Ikpikpuk River to the coast (see Fig. 3-1). He encountered several hundred natives on this journey.

Another basis for population estimates comes from accounts of the number of people attending traditional trading fairs during the summer. Larsen and Rainey (1948) quote an informant who recalled seeing 160 tents pitched at Tulareaq, a trading center at the mouth of the Utokok River, with "maybe" ten persons a tent. Larsen and Rainey felt that this number should be halved, and that perhaps 800 people were assembled. Another trading center was Negalik at the mouth of the Colville River. Spencer (1959) cites a Barrow native who counted 400 tents at Negalik one year in the early 1900s. Since this trading center drew people from as far away as the Noatak River in the west and the Mackenzie delta in the east, Spencer feels that there could well have been 1,500 natives present.

Larsen and Rainey (1948) estimate a population of 3,000 for all of Arctic Alaska between 1895 and 1905. This figure included those people living on the southwest side of the Brooks Range and along the Noatak, Kobuk, and Selawik rivers all the way to Hotham Inlet, an area much broader than the one under study here. Gubser (1965), on the basis of archaeological and ethnohistorical data, estimates that about 1,000 Eskimos lived in the Brooks Range in the 1880s. By combining the counts of Petroff (1884) or Porter (1893) with Gubser's estimate, one obtains a figure of approximately 2,000 for the population of the North Slope in the late 1800s.

Almost universally, however, writers concerned with the Eskimo of that time maintain that they suffered a marked decline in population in the 1800s. The coastal and inland groups that came into contact with whalers often encountered strange diseases to which they had no natural immunity. In addition, periodic food shortages often led to starvation or movements from one area to another. John Simpson, for example, counted 309 people at Nuwuk (a village north of the present town of Barrow, now abandoned) and 250 people at Utkeagvik (the Inuit name for Barrow) in 1852–53 (Spencer, 1959). By 1882–83 the populations at these two locations were 150 and 130, respectively, according to Ray (1885). Simpson indicates that forty natives died of influenza in Nuwuk in 1851, and there were twenty-seven deaths in Nuwuk and forty in Utkeagvik from a famine in 1853–54. Brower (1942) recalls two incidents around 1900 when 126 Eskimos died in a measles epidemic at Barrow and perhaps as many as 200 inland people died on their way back home after contracting influenza while they were visiting Barrow. Certainly, events in the early contact period had a detrimental effect on the size of the Eskimo population in northern Alaska, but the precise magnitude of this effect will probably never be known.

CULTURAL GROUPINGS

The most comprehensive attempt to deal with the cultural groupings of these Eskimos was Spencer's, in *The North Alaskan Eskimo* (1959). He emphasized an ecological basis for dividing the people into two general groups: The Nunamiut, people of the land, and the Tareumiut, people of the sea. These terms are derivative of native designations for the two groups and they recognize a basic difference in subsistence patterns. The Nunamiut specialized in hunting caribou and lived inland, while the Tareumiut built their life around sea mammal hunting and resided on the coast. Although Spencer indicates that these terms were indicative of a way of life rather than tribal designations (p. 14), he later goes on to give them considerable biological significance when he states, "Nunamiut is distinguished from Tareumiut not only on the basis of way of life but also because of the absence of kinship ties between them. Kinship extends within an ecological area, never across its boundaries" (pp. 22-23). It is important of course to recognize that Spencer is speaking of the "ethnographic present" in this regard, which for our purposes can be reckoned as a time before European contact.

In addition to the general headings of "land" and "sea" people, there was also a proliferation of names for smaller groups. All of these names had the suffix "miut," meaning "dwellers at" (Milan, 1964a) or "inhabitants of" (Gubser, 1965). These terms frequently were names for topographic or geographic features of the landscape. They were not universal, however, since one group might call another by a different name than that group used for itself. A few examples of these names will illustrate the situation. Wainwright is located near the Kuk River (*kuuk* itself means river) and its people were called Kuungmiut by Barrow residents. Wainwrighters call their village Ulurunik and therefore they consider themselves Ulurunikamiut.

Point Hope is situated on a spit of land that vaguely resembles a finger pointing. For this reason the village was called Tikerak, which means "index finger" (Van Stone, 1962). The people here were called Tikeraamiut by their own designation and that of their neighbors.

The inhabitants of Anaktuvuk Pass are the only remnants of what Hall (1970) calls the eastern Nunamiut, who still live in the interior of North Alaska. Specifically, the Nunamiut included in this study represent two small groups—the Killikmiut, named for the Killik River, and the Tulugak Lake people or Tulugakmiut. Other researchers use the term Nunatagmiut for the inland Eskimo.

Barrow residents would have been referred to by their residence in one of the two older villages in the region of the present location: either Nuwukmiut for the village of Nuwuk, located north of Barrow, or Utkeavigmiut for Utkeavik, the native designation for the present site of Barrow. Since most of the residents of Kaktovik originated from Barrow they also would have been called Nuwukmiut or Utkeavigmiut.

Today these designations do not convey a great deal of meaning when applied to people living in the present villages of Wainwright, Point Hope, Anaktuvuk Pass, Barrow, and Kaktovik. While Burch and Correll (1972) are able to list "at least" thirty-seven regional groups for the mid-nineteenth century population of north Alaska, in the recent past there has been considerable movement of people and a concentration of what were formerly seminomadic groups in fewer and fewer locations. The result of this movement has been that people now living at Wainwright, for instance, may cite a variety of "miut" suffix groups when asked where they come from.

Did these regional or territorial groupings have any biological significance? Spencer (1959), who felt the only meaningful terms were Nunamiut and Tareumiut, saw this division as ecological, cultural, and biological—there were two breeding populations on the North Coastal Plain. About the other regional designations he states, "One can only refer to the various subgroupings by name with the understanding that these are meaningful only in the sense of geographical divisions within each cultural and ecological area" (p. 22).

Oswalt (1967), when speaking of the Tareumiut and the Nunamiut, used the term "tribe" for each. He acknowledged that they did not fit the term precisely, but he states,

> Certain social and cultural ties, such as those pertaining to marriage and ceremonial gatherings, were stronger within a tribe. A tribe is designated as the people within certain villages, hamlets or camps who were considered by outsiders, and by themselves, as being set off from other such units and having a sense of in-group identity. (pp. 2-3)

Few ethnographers follow Oswalt in referring to these Eskimo groupings as "tribes;" most concentrate on the smaller groupings and refer to them as "bands" (Gubser, 1965; Damas, 1969; Hall, 1970).

Both Hall (1970) and Burch (1970) appear to discount the significance of the cultural differences between Tareumiut and Nunamiut. Hall refers to "the high degree of cultural uniformity" between them, particularly in nonmaterial aspects of their culture. Burch emphasizes, "the Eskimos operated in terms of the same general social system, in both inland and coastal areas" (p. 52). Burch identifies three major patterns of yearly cycle in northern Alaska:

. . . the people who spent virtually the entire year at or near the coast, living in permanent villages which sometimes had several hundred inhabitants.

. . . those individuals, relatively few in number, who lived in small camps far inland. . . . These "true inlanders," if they got to the coast at all, did so only for a few weeks in summer when they attended the summer "trade fairs."

. . . those who spend half the year inland and the other half on the coast. . . .

Spencer (1959) also discounted the significance of the smaller regional groupings, but Gubser (1965) indicated that the Nunamiut of the Anaktuvuk Pass region felt a definite territorial affinity and considered themselves distinct from the coastal people *and* the Eskimos who lived inland along the Kobuk River. Campbell (1968) was more specific:

. . . if a Nunamiut married outside his band, he (or she) was more likely to marry an Eskimo from another Nunamiut band than an Eskimo from, for instance, the Kobuk or Point Barrow. A very large majority of a Nunamiut's relatives who lived outside his own band consequently belonged to other Nunamiut bands. (p. 3)

Among the Tareumiut, Rainey (1947) identified the Tikeraamiut as a distinct group of coastal Eskimos. He said they considered themselves to be one people affiliated with a single village. Van Stone (1962) added support to this contention by indicating that there was considerable village endogamy among the residents of Point Hope in the past.

Burch and Correll (1972) are the most explicit on the biological significance of these groups. They state,

. . . marriage tended to be within rather than between regional groups. . . . endogamy resulted from the simple fact that contact and familiarity between males and females were greater within than between regional groups. Each group thus constituted a "deme" in that it was a partially isolated population of individuals having an intimate temporal and spatial relation to one another. (p. 24)

On this ethnographic basis, it seems apparent that numerous populations were present in northern Alaska prior to European contact. However, the ethnographers have also described various cultural practices of the Alaskan Eskimo that would have produced gene flow between these populations. The coastal people lived in permanent villages for the greater part of the year, and the inland natives lived in seminomadic bands. The size of either grouping could expand or contract, depending upon local circumstances. Membership was an individual choice: ". . . each individual was free, either with or without his immediate relatives, to settle where he chose, provided he could establish some claim of kinship. . . ." (Spencer, 1959:22). The matter of kinship was very important; a "stranger" who was not recognized as a kinsman of one's own group, ran the risk of being killed.

Kinship claims might be extended between villages, bands, or even regional groups through actual genetic ties or partnerships between nonkin. The partnerships formalized relationships for reciprocal trading and mutual protection when traveling in the partner's territory (Burch, 1970; Burch and Correll, 1972). To demonstrate good faith, they might also include spouse exchange (Rubel, 1961; Spencer, 1958, 1968; Hennigh, 1970). Hennigh (1970) specified three general situations in which the north Alaskan Eskimo felt it was legitimate to exchange wives: (1) to settle marital disputes, (2) to reinforce the status of important people, and (3) to produce kinsmen for one's children.

In Hennigh's model, the first two situations were more likely to occur within a village or band. Thus they would not enhance gene flow across regional boundaries. The third situation could and did produce gene flow (Milan, personal communication based on genealogical information), as its avowed purpose was to broaden kinship relationships. Children of couples who engaged in spouse exchange, whether or not they were actually biologically related, had certain mutual rights and obligations toward each other. The kinship terminology reflected this situation with an elaborate set of terms to cover all conceivable relationships (Heinrich, 1955, 1960; Posposil and Laughlin, 1963). Of primary interest, however, is the amount of gene flow that such a situation would have produced.

Spencer (1958) felt that spouse exchange unions were rarely more than a few days in duration. If that is true, then on the basis of probability it would be more likely for a woman to become pregnant by her mate than by her mate's exchange partner. Therefore, the effect of spouse exchange on gene flow between regional groups would depend on its frequency, its duration, and its timing in reference to the woman's reproductive cycle.

Adoption, a fairly widespread phenomenon among Eskimos, would also distribute genes between groups if children were adopted out of their own village or group. Such does not seem to have been the general situation (Milan, 1964a). Children would be adopted within the group by childless couples or relatives, or to replace a child who had recently died. Both adoption and spouse exchange must be kept in mind when interpreting the biological similarities and differences of the regional groups, but their genetic effect need not have been a major influence. Migration, on the other hand, must have considerably altered the composition of present-day villages.

4

Anthropometric Variation

Paul L. Jamison

This chapter will deal with two general categories of data: (1) adult anthropometric measurements and (2) growth measurements on children and subadults. For the purposes of this analysis I have chosen age twenty as the point of separation of adults and subadults. The subjects came from Wainwright (1968-1971), Point Hope (1970), Barrow (1971), Anaktuvuk Pass (1969 and 1970) and Kaktovik (1970), in north Alaska.

During the first research season in Wainwright in 1968, two anthropometrists took measurements on the population. S. L. Zegura and I each measured half of the variables in the measurement battery. During subsequent visits to Wainwright I remeasured a number of the individuals for those variables originally determined by Zegura. A comparison of our results (Jamison and Zegura, 1974) led to "correction" factors that could be applied to Zegura's data where there were systematic differences in our results. Therefore, with the exception of approximately half of the measurement battery on thirty male and twenty-one female Wainwright subjects, I took all of the anthropometric measurements reported in this chapter. Measurement techniques were basically those of Hertzeberg et al. (1963), with exceptions as noted in Jamison and Zegura (1970) and Jamison (1972).

ADULT MEASUREMENTS

A general anthropometric description of north Alaskan Eskimos does not quite correspond to the traditional description of Eskimo morphology. Further, morphological differences can be examined between the sexes, between hybridized and nonhybridized subjects, and among different village populations.

Anthropometric Description

One of the classic descriptions of Alaskan Eskimo morphology is that of A. Hrdlička in his *Anthropological Survey in Alaska* (1930). He enumerates the following characteristics of the western Eskimo based on those he and his coworkers measured in the Yukon River area and on Nunivak and St. Lawrence Islands:

> Submedium to medium stature
> High relative sitting height due to a relatively long trunk and somewhat short limbs, especially their distal segments
> Large chests; broad in females and deep in males
> Hands and feet small but relatively broad in comparison to their length
> High mesocephaly to moderate brachycephaly in head form while the head itself is large
> Face large in all dimensions, particularly its breadth
> Broad, high nose
> Large ears, particularly their length or height (pp. 239-249)

Laughlin (1963), in an otherwise very similar description, adds an additional dimension, "A common misconception about Eskimos is that they are fat or chubby. . . . Though muscular, with heavy bones, they have little fat even at advanced ages" (p. 7).

One difficulty for the reader of such descriptions is knowing what was the point of reference of their authors. Does the Eskimo have short limbs compared to all other populations or relative to some standard population? In Hrdlička's case, the reference population was his Old American series of U.S. whites (1925). In this report I will use the same basis of comparison along with additional white samples to determine how well the north Alaskan Eskimos of today fit this traditional description. (This use of the Old American series is intended strictly as a reference point rather than as any suggestion of "normal" or "modal" for the human species as a whole.)

Tables 4-1 and 4-2 give sample sizes, means, standard deviations, and coefficients of variation for thirty-nine measurements taken on male and female nonhybrid adult subjects. Except for head circumference and the skinfold measurements, these tables demonstrate the unsurprising fact that anthropometric means, except for skinfold thicknesses, are larger for men than for women. These tables will be discussed further under sexual dimorphism.

Tables 4-3 through 4-5 are designed to answer the question of how well north Alaskan Eskimos fit the classic description of Eskimo morphology. The basis of comparison is initially Hrdlička's Old American series but additional white samples are also used because all of the relevant measurements were not taken on the Old Americans. If attention is focused only on the means in these tables, Hrdlička's 1930 description of Eskimos holds up quite well. However, the terms "large" and "small" could more properly be viewed as relative to body size in the populations concerned, rather than as absolute statements. Accordingly, the ratios listed in Tables 4-3 to 4-5 are of particular interest. These ratios, it must be noted, were derived from means of variables rather than individual data because only means were cited in the literature.

TABLE 4-1 *Body Measurements of Adult Nonhybrid Eskimos (cm)*

Variable		Males				Females		
	n	Mean	S.D.	C.V.	N	Mean	S.D.	C.V.
Weight (kg)	109	71.2	12.0	15.6	117	64.5	15.7	22.3
Sitting ht.	132	87.7	3.2	3.6	140	82.7	3.5	4.2
Stature	132	166.1	5.4	3.2	140	154.2	5.8	3.8
Biacromial br.	132	39.0	2.0	5.1	140	35.8	1.8	5.0
Arm lg.	132	71.5	3.0	4.3	140	65.9	3.0	4.5
Bicondylar br.	132	7.3	0.4	5.5	140	6.6	0.5	7.8
Humerus lg.	104	31.3	1.7	5.3	112	29.1	1.5	5.0
Radius lg.	104	24.2	1.2	4.9	112	22.3	1.1	4.9
Chest br.	132	30.2	2.1	7.0	140	27.7	2.2	7.8
Chest dp.	132	23.1	2.4	10.2	140	21.6	3.0	14.1
Biiliac br.	132	30.1	2.0	6.6	140	29.3	2.2	7.6
Tibiale ht.	104	42.6	2.0	4.8	113	39.8	2.5	6.4
Spherion ht.	104	8.8	0.9	9.9	113	8.3	0.9	10.4
Foot br.	132	10.0	0.5	5.3	140	9.1	0.6	7.0
Foot lg.	132	25.3	1.0	4.0	140	23.1	1.1	4.6
Ankle br.	132	7.4	0.4	4.9	140	6.7	0.4	6.0
Calf circ.	132	34.4	2.5	7.1	140	33.6	3.2	9.7
Mid-up. arm circ.	132	30.3	2.7	9.0	140	29.3	4.1	14.0
Forearm circ.	132	27.7	2.0	7.2	140	25.4	2.8	10.9
Wrist br.	132	6.1	0.3	4.4	140	5.5	0.3	5.2
Hand br.	132	8.5	0.4	4.1	140	7.7	0.4	4.5
Hand lg.-bone	132	19.2	0.8	4.3	140	17.8	0.9	4.9
Hand lg.-crease	132	18.4	0.7	3.9	140	17.1	0.8	4.4
Flank skfld.	132	1.0	0.7	64.7	131	1.7	1.0	62.3
Subsc. skfld.	132	1.2	0.8	65.6	138	1.9	1.2	60.8
Triceps Skfld.	132	0.9	0.6	59.8	138	2.0	1.0	49.7

TABLE 4-2 *Head Measurements of Adult Nonhybrid Eskimos (cm)*

Variable		Males				Females		
	N	Mean	S.D.	C.V.	N	Mean	S.D.	C.V.
Head circ.	132	56.9	1.7	2.9	98	63.9	17.2	27.0
Head lg.	132	19.4	0.7	3.4	140	18.7	0.7	3.6
Head br.	132	15.6	0.6	3.6	140	15.0	0.5	3.2
Min. frontal br.	132	10.5	0.5	4.9	140	10.2	0.4	4.4
Bizygomatic br.	132	15.2	0.6	3.6	140	14.2	0.5	3.8
Bigonial br.	132	11.8	0.7	5.7	140	11.0	0.6	5.1
Tot. facial ht.	132	12.4	0.7	5.7	140	11.3	0.6	5.6
Up. facial ht.	132	7.4	0.6	7.6	140	6.7	0.5	7.5
Nose ht.	132	5.4	0.5	9.3	140	4.8	0.4	9.4
Nose br.	132	4.0	0.3	6.9	140	3.6	0.3	7.6
Symphyseal ht.	132	4.5	0.4	9.4	140	4.0	0.4	11.3
Ear ht.	132	7.3	0.6	8.3	140	6.8	0.5	7.4
Ear br.	132	3.8	0.3	8.1	140	3.5	0.2	7.1

Submedium to medium stature. Hrdlička (1930) cites 165 cm as "medium" stature for males across all populations. By this criterion, the north Alaskan Eskimo males can certainly be described as medium in stature or even submedium, given secular changes that have been occurring. In Tables 4-3 and 4-4, Eskimo males average 4.5-9.5 cm shorter than whites, and Eskimo females are 7.6-8.6 cm shorter. This size difference will be important to the rest of the comparisons.

High relative sitting height. The data in Tables 4-3 and 4-4 do not support this conclusion for the north Alaskans. Their relative sitting heights are very similar to those of the whites, for both sexes.

Short limbs, especially their distal segments. Tibiale height/stature and radius length/stature ratios demonstrate a close similarity between the Eskimo and the white series. Therefore, the forearms and lower legs of these Eskimos are not shorter than those of whites when expressed relative to height. The brachial indices suggest the same thing: the forearm lengths of Eskimos are quite similar to those of whites when expressed as a proportion of upper arm length.

Large chests. Chest dimension means shown in Tables 4-3 and 4-4 are somewhat larger among Eskimos than among whites, and when the depth of the chest is expressed as a percentage of its breadth, the Eskimos again have larger index values. However, chest dimensions are not among the most accurate anthropometric measurements (Jamison and Zegura, 1974; Jamison, 1972; Osborne and Goldstein, 1972), so these results should not be heavily stressed.

Hands and feet small but broad. When foot and hand size are considered in relation to stature, the data do not indicate that north Alaskan Eskimos have extremities that are smaller than those of whites. However, the foot indices are considerably higher for the Eskimos, indicating feet that are broad relative to their length. The same cannot be said for Eskimo hands.

High mesocephaly to moderate brachycephaly, and large heads. If a cephalic index of eighty is the borderline between mesocephaly and brachycephaly (Hooton, 1946), then these Eskimos have low brachycephalic head forms. On the other hand, the overall size of the Eskimo head is comparable to that seen in whites. With the Eskimos' shorter stature, relatively large heads may be inferred.

Face large, particularly its breadth. For total facial height, bizygomatic breadth, and bigonial breadth, the means for Eskimos exceed those for the white series. In addition, the facial indices of the Eskimo males and females are in the broad-faced range (less than 84, according to Hooton).

Broad, high nose. Nose heights among the north Alaskans are similar to those of whites but nose breadths are greater, as can also be seen in the nasal indices in Tables 4-3 and 4-4.

Large ears, particularly their height. This is quite true of the north Alaskan Eskimos. Their ears are decidedly longer than those of whites, and the ear

TABLE 4-3 *Measurements of North Alaskan Eskimo Males and of Whites (cm)*

Variable	Eskimos	Old Americans[*]	Air Force[+]	Cleveland[‡]
Weight (kg)	71.2	68.3	73.4	--
Sitting ht.	87.7	92.3	91.4	88.6
Stature	166.1	174.4	175.6	170.6
Chest breadth	30.2	29.8	30.5	27.3
Chest depth	23.1	21.7	22.9	20.8
Tibiale ht.	42.6	--	--	44.3
Spherion ht.	8.8	--	8.8	7.3
Humerus length	31.3	--	33.2	33.3
Radius length	24.2	--	25.3	24.9
Foot breadth	10.0	9.5	9.6	8.8
Foot length	25.3	26.1	26.7	24.4
Hand breadth	8.5	9.2	8.8	7.8
Hand length (bone)	18.4	19.3	19.0	18.7
Head length	19.4	19.8	19.7	18.8
Head breadth	15.6	15.5	15.4	15.4
Bizygomatic br.	15.2	13.9	14.1	13.9
Bigonial br.	11.8	10.6	10.9	11.0
Tot. facial ht.	12.4	11.9	--	12.1
Nose height	5.4	5.4	--	5.4
Nose breadth	4.0	3.6	3.3	3.5
Ear height	7.3	6.7	6.3	6.7
Ear breadth	3.8	3.8	3.6	3.8
Rel. sitting ht.	52.8	52.9	52.0	51.9
Chest index	76.5	72.8	75.1	76.2
Tib. ht./stature	25.6	--	--	26.0
Brachial index	77.3	--	76.2	74.8
Rad. lg./stature	14.6	--	14.4	14.6
Foot index	39.5	36.4	36.0	36.1
Foot lg./stature	15.2	15.0	15.2	14.3
Hand index	46.2	47.7	46.3	41.7
Hand lg./stature	11.1	11.1	10.8	11.0
Cephalic index	80.4	78.3	78.2	81.9
Facial index	81.6	85.6	--	87.3
Nasal index	74.1	66.7	--	64.8
Ear index	52.0	56.7	57.1	56.7

[*]Hrdlička (1925) measurements on third-generation Whites living in the vicinity of Washington, D.C., between 1910 and 1924; 247 males and 210 females.

[+]Hertzberg et al. (1963) measurements on more than 4000 Air Force flying personnel. Data are 50th percentiles. Humerus length is calculated from acromiale height minus radiale height, and radius length from radiale height minus stylion height.

[‡]Todd and Lindala (1928) measurements on 100 cadavers of the anatomical laboratory of Western Reserve University. Subjects were primarily northern European, lower- and middle class industrial workers.

TABLE 4-4 *Measurements of North Alaskan Eskimo Females and of Whites (cm)*

Variable	Eskimos	Old Americans[*]	Smith College[+]
Weight (kg)	64.5	57.8	55.6
Sitting ht.	82.7	87.3	86.8
Stature	154.2	161.8	162.8
Chest breadth	27.7	26.6	25.1
Chest depth	21.6	20.0	18.8
Tibiale ht.	39.8	--	42.2
Spherion ht.	8.3	--	7.8
Humerus length	29.1	--	29.2
Radius length	22.3	--	22.3
Foot breadth	9.1	8.4	8.3
Foot length	23.1	23.3	23.7
Hand breadth	7.7	7.9	8.0
Hand length (bone)	17.1	17.3	18.7
Head length	18.7	18.6	18.6
Head breadth	15.0	14.8	14.6
Bizygomatic br.	14.2	13.0	13.0
Bigonial br.	11.0	9.8	10.0
Tot. facial ht.	11.3	11.1	11.2
Nose height	4.8	4.9	5.0
Nose breadth	3.6	3.2	3.2
Ear height	6.8	6.1	5.9
Ear breadth	3.5	3.5	3.3
Rel. sitting ht.	53.6	54.0	53.3
Chest index	78.0	75.2	74.9
Tib. ht./stature	25.8	--	25.9
Brachial index	76.6	--	76.4
Rad. lg./stature	14.5	--	13.7
Foot index	39.4	36.0	35.0
Foot lg./stature	15.0	14.4	14.6
Hand index	45.0	45.7	42.8
Hand lg./stature	11.1	10.7	11.5
Cephalic index	80.2	79.6	78.5
Facial index	79.6	85.4	86.2
Nasal index	75.0	65.3	64.0
Ear index	51.5	57.4	55.9

[*] Hrdlička (1925) measurements on third-generation Whites living in the vicinity of Washington, D.C., between 1910 and 1924; 247 males and 210 females.

[+] Steggerda et al. (1929) measurements on 100 Smith College students in 1928 and 1929. Subjects were of Western European ancestry.

TABLE 4-5 *Mean Skinfold Thicknesses of North Alaskan Eskimos and of Whites (cm)*

	Males					Females		
				U. Minn.‡			U. Minn.‡	
Skinfold	Eskimos	Northern Whites*	Firemen+	Age 23–29	Age 53–67	Eskimos	Age 18–30	Age 46–67
Flank	1.0	1.5	–	1.9	2.6	1.7	2.7	3.4
Subscapular	1.2	1.4	1.6	1.5	2.2	1.9	1.6	2.2
Triceps	0.9	1.2	1.2	1.4	1.5	2.0	2.2	2.6

*Newman (1956) measurements on 1283 northern inductees into the Army.

+Brozek (1956) measurements on 238 firemen from Minneapolis, Minn.

‡Skerlj et al. (1953) measurements on 59 male and 59 female volunteers at the University of Minnesota.

indices show that these Eskimos have narrower ears in porportion to their height than do whites.

Little subcutaneous fat. Mean skinfold thicknesses in Table 4-5 support Laughlin's (1963) addition to the description of Eskimo morphology. Eskimo males have smaller means than whites at all three measurement sites, while females average lower in all but one comparison.

To summarize then, the north Alaskan Eskimo as of 1968-71 can be described as follows:

Stature: submedium to medium.

Relative sitting height: very similar to that of whites, without especially long trunks nor short limbs. The distal segments of the limbs are *not* particularly short when expressed as a percentage of stature.

Hands and feet: of comparable size to those of whites when this size is expressed relative to stature. Feet are broad in comparison to their length.

Head form: low brachycephaly. Heads are large for body size.

Faces: large, especially in breadth.

Noses: broad.

Ears: large, particularly in height.

Skinfold thicknesses: relatively small.

This description differs from Hrdlička's 1930 description. The probable reason is that Hrdlička used absolute measurements, rather than relative or proportional ones. The smaller stature of the Eskimos would seem to require ratios and proportional statements rather than a simple comparison of means.

Sexual Dimorphism

Eskimo males are larger than females in all but skinfold measurements (Tables 4-1 and 4-2). The coefficients of variation in these tables are of perhaps more interest since they can be used to determine the relative variability of each sex for each measurement. Simpson et al. (1960) point out that for most biological data, the size of this coefficient lies between 4 and 10.

Most of the variables with coefficients of variation over ten can very likely be explained as due to fatness/leanness of the subjects (weight, skinfold thicknesses, and both mid-upper arm circumference and forearm circumference in females). Over and above the variation in body size in any group of subjects there is an additional aspect of variation in body fat; such probably contributed to the elevated coefficients in these variables. Chest depth is another measurement with a high coefficient of variation and it too might be explained in reference to body fat. Or, in conjunction with spherion height and symphyseal height, the explanation might be the imprecision associated with taking these measurements (Jamison and Zegura, 1974; Jamison, 1972). Errors in locating the measurement landmarks would contribute quite a bit of variation to such small measurements as the latter two. Finally, head circumference in women is affected by varying quantities of hair in addition to the "normal" variation in the measurement.

The least variable measurements are sitting height and stature for the body as a whole, and head length, head breadth, and byzygomatic breadth for the head. The usual explanation for reduced variability is either strong directional selection or stabilizing selection about some optimum phenotype. The reduced variability for body size and head size in the north Alaskan population is indirect evidence that selection may be operating, but direct evidence would require more thoroughgoing investigation.

Tables 4-1 and 4-2 show the values of the coefficients of variation to be generally similar between the sexes. However, for the body measurements (excluding skinfolds) twenty of twenty-three coefficients are larger in the females (average coefficient for males, 6.1; for females, 7.6). Such indicates that women have more individual variation in these measurements than men. For twelve head measurements (excluding head circumference) the coefficients are much more similar. In absolute size, the males have seven coefficients larger than the females, but the average difference is very slight and again in favor of females (means: 6.1 for males, 6.3 for females).

Another way of examining sexual dimorphism is to compare it with that in another population. Table 4-6 is an attempt to determine whether the sexual dimorphism seen in north Alaskan Eskimos is greater or less than the dimorphism seen in whites. Again, Hrdlička's Old American series is the basis of comparison. The values in Table 4-6 are the means for females as a percentage of the means for males.

Of the nineteen comparative values in Table 4-6, Eskimos have higher percentages in all except six. Overall, this table demonstrates a smaller degree of sexual dimorphism in north Alaskans than that seen in Old American whites, but the differences in the two series are not very large. Birdsell (1975) points out that smaller populations may have reduced sexual dimorphism and that alone might account for the difference in sexual dimorphism seen in these two populations.

The best way to visualize and describe the differences between male and female Eskimos is through the multivariate technique described earlier in this volume by Zegura. Figure 4-1 shows the distribution of discriminant scores for males and females along a linear function constructed so as to reflect the best discrimination between the sexes. The linear function was calculated by means of the Discriminant Analysis program in the Statistical Package for the Social Sciences (SPSS) prepared by Nie et al. (1975). A total of thirty variables was used in this analysis of 132 male and 140 female adult, nonhybrid Eskimos. As only two groups are being compared, one function accounts for

TABLE 4-6 *Sexual Dimorphism Among Eskimos and Whites (means for females as a percentage of means for males)*

Variable	Eskimo	White[*]	Diff.
Weight	90.6	84.7	5.9
Sitting ht.	94.3	94.5	-0.2
Stature	92.8	92.8	0.0
Chest breadth	91.7	89.4	2.3
Chest depth	93.5	92.3	1.2
Foot breadth	91.0	88.1	2.9
Foot length	91.3	89.3	2.0
Hand breadth	90.6	85.7	4.9
Hand lg. (bone)	92.9	90.0	2.9
Head length	96.4	94.1	2.3
Head breadth	96.2	95.6	0.6
Min. frontal br.	97.1	95.6	1.5
Bizygomatic br.	93.4	93.7	-0.3
Bigonial br.	93.2	92.6	0.6
Tot. facial ht.	91.1	93.0	-1.9
Nose height	88.9	92.5	-3.6
Nose breadth	90.0	90.0	0.0
Ear height	93.2	91.2	2.0
Ear breadth	92.1	91.6	0.5
Average	92.6	91.4	1.2

[*]Old Americans (Hrdlička, 1925).

100% of the total multivariate dispersion of the groups. The canonical correlation for this function was 0.901, indicating that 81% of the variance in group membership is explained by the single function. Its success in differentiating the sexes can be seen in the fact that only eight individuals (4.6%) were misallocated; six females to the male side and two males to the female side of the function. The difference between the means of the male and female discriminant scores is 4.1, giving a Mahalanobis' D^2 distance of 16.8. This distance is highly significant, as might be expected from the fact that univariately, all measurements were significantly different between the sexes at the 0.05 level and only two (calf circumference and forearm circumference) did not reach significance at the 0.01 level.

To clarify the relative contribution of each variable to this discrimination, Table 4-7 gives the coefficients of the discriminant function whose results are shown in Fig. 4-1. The variables with the highest coefficients, either positive or negative, are the most important in determining the discrimination on the function. Biiliac breadth, calf and upper arm circumferences, and, to a lesser

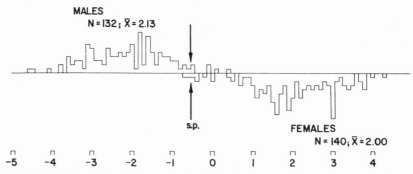

FIGURE 4-1. *Distribution of discriminate scores for nonhybrid Eskimo males and females.*

extent, hand length (crease) and total facial height have the highest positive coefficients; large measurements for these variables would be associated with "femaleness" on the sexing function in Fig. 4-1. Similarly, high negative coefficients signify "maleness," and according to Table 4-7, large values for bizygomatic breadth, foot length, wrist and hand breadths, and biacromial breadth contribute the most to this aspect of the discrimination.

In summary, then, when all of the thirty measurements are ranked by the importance of their contribution to the Eskimo sexing function, hip vs shoulder breadths, facial height vs facial breadth, and arm and calf circumferences vs bony breadths of the hands provide the major portion of the discriminant ability of the function. Eskimo women have broad hips, large faces in the vertical dimension, and large calf and upper arm circumferences when compared with Eskimo men with their broad shoulders, broad faces, and large, bony breadths.

Nonhybrid vs Hybrid Comparison

There are similarities and differences between nonhybridized Eskimos (132 males and 140 females) and those Eskimos that are known to have non-Eskimo admixture (thirty males and forty females). Most of the non-Eskimo genes in the north Alaskan population derived from crew members of whaling ships that plied the Arctic Ocean during the latter half of the nineteenth and early twentieth centuries. As early as 1850, ships from Germany, France, and England entered these waters along with vessels from both coasts of the United States and a few from the Hawaiian Islands and even Hong Kong (Van Stone, 1958; Foote, 1964). Old American or Western European genes predominate in this admixture although one village, Point Hope, has a significant amount of admixture from Americans of African descent. There is also

TABLE 4-7 *Standardized Coefficients of the Linear Function Discriminating
Eskimo Males and Females*

Variable	Coefficient	Variable	Coefficient
Sitting ht.	−0.178	Hand breadth	−0.430
Stature	0.077	Hand lg. (bone)	0.090
Biacromial br.	−0.356	Hand lg. (crease)	0.394
Arm length	−0.318	Head length	0.033
Bicondylar br.	−0.133	Head breadth	0.055
Chest breadth	−0.213	Min. frontal br.	0.073
Chest depth	−0.208	Bizygomatic br.	−0.520
Biiliac br.	0.614	Bigonial br.	−0.234
Foot breadth	0.079	Tot. facial ht.	0.375
Foot length	−0.510	Up. facial ht.	−0.213
Ankle breadth	−0.247	Nose height	−0.208
Calf. circ.	0.540	Nose breadth	−0.143
Up. arm circ.	0.438	Symphyseal ht.	−0.199
Forearm circ.	−0.305	Ear height	−0.028
Wrist breadth	−0.446	Ear breadth	−0.083

admixture from at least one Hawaiian or "Kanaka" (Milan, 1970, and personal communication).

Most of the non-Eskimo genes entered the north Alaskan population
more than fifty years ago. Therefore, the majority of the hybrids derive no
more than 1/8 to 1/4 of their genome from non-Eskimo sources. I recognize
that there is no genetic justification for forming a single group out of hybrids
whose non-Eskimo genes are so disparate, but the size of the sample precluded
further subdivision.

As far as the accuracy of the "hybrid" designation is concerned, all *known*
hybrids are included. If there are errors in this determination, they are more
likely to be hybrids placed among the nonhybrids than the converse.

Tables 4-8 and 4-9 provide descriptive statistics for the thirty anthropometric variables used to compare hybrids and nonhybrids. In general, these
two tables show that hybrids are slightly larger than nonhybridized Eskimos
in body dimensions and slightly smaller in head dimensions. Table 4-10
shows the significance of these differences by analysis of variance *F*-ratios.
Nine variables are statistically significantly different among men and six reach
this level ($P < 0.05$) among women. These results are quite a contrast to those
seen in the analysis of sexual dimorphism.

Figure 4-2 shows the distribution of discriminant scores for the single
functions separating hybrids and nonhybrids of each sex. Again, each function accounted for 100% of the total dispersion of the groups, but the canonical correlations (0.58 for males and 0.47 for females) are considerably lower

TABLE 4–8 *Body Measurements of Nonhybridized and Hybridized Eskimo Males (cm)*

Variable	Nonhybrids		Hybrids	
	Mean	S.D.	Mean	S.D.
Sitting ht.	87.7	3.2	89.6	3.4
Stature	166.1	5.4	166.7	7.0
Biacromial br.	39.0	2.0	39.2	1.6
Arm length	71.5	3.0	71.6	3.4
Bicondylar br.	7.3	0.4	7.2	0.3
Chest breadth	30.2	2.1	30.6	1.5
Chest depth	23.1	2.4	23.0	2.0
Biiliac br.	30.1	2.0	29.0	1.4
Foot breadth	10.0	0.5	10.4	2.0
Foot length	25.3	1.0	25.6	1.0
Ankle breadth	7.4	0.4	7.4	0.3
Calf circ.	34.4	2.5	35.5	1.7
Up. arm circ.	30.3	2.7	30.9	2.2
Forearm circ.	27.7	2.0	28.6	1.6
Wrist breadth	6.1	0.3	6.2	0.3
Hand breadth	8.5	0.4	8.7	0.4
Hand lg. (bone)	19.2	0.8	19.4	0.9
Hand lg. (crease)	18.4	0.7	18.6	1.0
Head length	19.4	0.7	19.4	0.6
Head breadth	15.6	0.6	15.5	0.5
Min. frontal br.	10.5	0.5	10.3	0.5
Bizygomatic br.	15.2	0.6	14.9	0.5
Bigonial br.	11.8	0.7	11.5	0.6
Tot. facial ht.	12.4	0.7	12.4	0.7
Up. facial ht.	7.4	0.6	7.4	0.5
Nose height	5.4	0.5	5.4	0.5
Nose breadth	4.0	0.3	3.8	0.3
Symphyseal ht.	4.5	0.4	4.6	0.3
Ear height	7.3	0.6	7.1	0.6
Ear breadth	3.8	0.3	3.6	0.2

than seen in the previous analysis. They indicate that only 34% and 22% of the variance in group membership, in this case hybrid and nonhybrid, is explained by the linear functions for males and females, respectively. The sectioning point of the function for men caused six nonhybrids to be allocated to the hybrid side, and sixteen hybrids to the nonhybrid side of the function. For the women, five nonhybrids were placed with the hybrids and twenty-six hybrids with the nonhybrids. These instances give misallocation frequencies of 13.5% in males and 17.2% in females.

When the Mahalanobis' D^2 distances are calculated, the distance between hybrid and nonhybrid means is 3.24 for males and 1.64 for females; neither is

TABLE 4-9 *Body Measurements of Nonhybridized and Hybridized Eskimo Females (cm)*

Variable	Nonhybrids		Hybrids	
	Mean	S.D.	Mean	S.D.
Sitting ht.	82.7	3.5	84.1	2.9
Stature	154.2	5.8	156.3	5.4
Biacromial br.	35.8	1.8	36.3	1.4
Arm length	65.9	3.0	67.0	3.1
Bicondylar br.	6.6	0.5	6.7	0.6
Chest breadth	27.7	2.2	27.7	2.0
Chest depth	21.6	3.0	21.8	3.7
Biiliac br.	29.3	2.2	29.6	2.2
Foot breadth	9.1	0.6	9.1	0.5
Foot length	23.1	1.1	23.6	1.1
Ankle breadth	6.7	0.4	6.8	0.4
Calf circ.	33.6	3.2	35.0	4.4
Up. arm circ.	29.3	4.1	30.1	4.5
Forearm circ.	25.4	2.8	26.1	2.8
Wrist breadth	5.5	0.3	5.5	0.3
Hand breadth	7.7	0.4	7.7	0.4
Hand lg. (bone)	17.8	0.9	18.0	0.8
Hand lg. (crease)	17.1	0.8	17.2	0.8
Head length	18.7	0.7	18.6	0.6
Head breadth	15.0	0.5	15.1	0.5
Min. frontal br.	10.2	0.4	10.1	0.4
Bizygomatic br.	14.2	0.5	14.2	0.5
Bigonial br.	11.0	0.6	11.1	0.5
Tot. facial ht.	11.3	0.6	11.2	0.8
Up. facial ht.	6.7	0.5	6.6	0.6
Nose height	4.8	0.4	4.7	0.5
Nose breadth	3.6	0.3	3.6	0.3
Symphyseal ht.	4.0	0.4	3.9	0.5
Ear height	6.8	0.5	6.5	0.5
Ear breadth	3.5	0.2	3.4	0.3

significant at the 0.05 level of probability. Therefore, as adults, Eskimo hybrids and nonhybrids cannot be differentiated statistically through this multivariate technique. Both the small number of hybrids and their small degree of admixture (1/8 to 1/4 of their genomes on average) must have contributed to this result.

Village Analysis

Are there differences among and between the north Alaskan villages that

TABLE 4-10 *Analysis of Variance F-Ratios Comparing Hybrids and Nonhybrids of Each Sex*

Variable	Males	Females
Sitting ht.	7.89^{+}	5.44_{*}^{*}
Stature	0.34	4.36
Biacromial br.	0.31	3.30
Arm length	0.03	3.84
Bicondylar br.	0.22	0.58
Chest breadth	1.10	0.00
Chest depth	0.01_{+}	0.24
Biiliac br.	7.94_{*}^{+}	0.63
Foot breadth	4.52^{*}	0.04_{+}
Foot length	2.72	8.35^{+}
Ankle breadth	0.08_{*}	1.16_{*}
Calf circ.	5.13	5.16
Up. arm circ.	1.35_{*}	1.08
Forearm circ.	4.90	2.11
Wrist breadth	0.12	0.07
Hand breadth	2.53	0.12
Hand lg. (bone)	0.34	1.53
Hand lg. (crease)	1.37	1.09
Head length	0.06	0.81
Head breadth	0.56	0.13
Min. frontal br.	3.51_{+}	0.00
Bizygomatic br.	10.87_{*}^{+}	0.11
Bigonial br.	5.55^{*}	0.19
Tot. facial ht.	0.04	0.77
Up. facial ht.	0.71	0.06
Nose height	0.00_{*}	2.02
Nose breadth	4.91^{*}	2.72
Symphyseal ht.	1.45	1.63_{+}
Ear height	1.56_{*}	9.20_{*}^{+}
Ear breadth	5.78^{*}	6.73^{*}

*P < .05.

$^{+}$P < .01.

might be interpreted in terms of microevolutionary processes? Thirty variables again enter into the analysis. The village sample sizes are: Wainwright, sixty-one males and forty-six females; Point Hope, twenty-five males and forty-six females; Anaktuvuk Pass, seventeen males and twenty-two females; and Barrow, fifty-nine males and sixty-six females. The Barrow sample includes a small number of Kaktovik residents who made up too small a group for independent treatment and who historically came from Barrow originally (Chance,

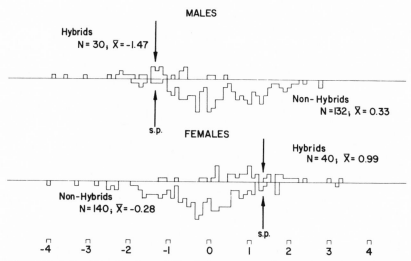

FIGURE 4-2. *Distribution of discriminate scores for nonhybrids and hybrids within each sex.*

1966). In addition, on the basis of the previous analysis, all samples except Anaktuvuk Pass contain both hybrid and nonhybrid Eskimos.

Descriptive statistics for the anthropometric measurements taken on each village sample are presented in Tables 4-11 (males) and 4-12 (females). Three previous anthropometric studies of intrapopulation variation in northern Alaska (Jenness, 1923; Seltzer, 1933; Irving, 1951) have suggested that the northern coastal villages shared more similarities with each other than any coastal village did with any inland population. The usual means of accounting for this variation was hybridization of the inland groups with Athabascan Indians or the cultural/biological differences between Nunamiut and Tareumiut. Among the genealogies collected for the subjects of the present anthropometric study, no instance of Indian admixture was reported.

The multivariate techniques used for analyzing sexual dimorphism and hybrid-nonhybrid comparisons also graphically demonstrate the anthropometric variation among the four north Alaskan villages under consideration here. For each variable, Table 4-13 shows the significance of the differences in means across all villages by analysis of variance F-ratios. These figures indicate that for males, fourteen of the thirty measurements are statistically different at the 0.05 level of significance and nine of these are also different at the 0.01 level. For females, twelve measurements reach the 0.05 level of significance and seven of these are also different at the 0.01 level. Sitting height, ankle breadth, head length, total facial height, upper facial height, and nose height have means that are significantly different at the 0.01 level in both sexes. Chest breadth and depth and nose breadth can be added to this list at the 0.05 level of significance.

TABLE 4-11 *Body Measurements of Males in the 4 Villages (cm)*

Variable	Wainwright		Point Hope		Anaktuvuk Pass		Barrow	
	Mean	S.D.	Mean	S.D.	Mean	S.D.	Mean	S.D.
Sitting ht.	88.7	3.2	87.1	3.8	86.0	3.4	88.4	2.8
Stature	167.4	5.2	163.8	5.8	164.9	6.7	166.2	5.6
Biacromial br.	39.1	2.0	38.7	2.0	39.2	1.6	39.2	1.8
Arm length	72.2	3.0	70.3	3.1	71.6	3.6	71.2	3.0
Bicondylar br.	7.2	0.4	7.2	0.4	7.2	0.5	7.4	0.3
Chest breadth	30.1	1.9	30.2	2.1	29.1	1.9	30.8	2.0
Chest depth	22.5	2.0	23.2	2.7	22.6	1.8	23.7	2.4
Biiliac br.	29.5	2.0	29.9	1.8	29.7	1.6	30.3	2.0
Foot breadth	9.9	0.5	9.9	0.6	9.8	0.4	10.3	1.4
Foot length	25.6	1.0	24.9	1.1	25.1	0.9	25.4	1.0
Ankle breadth	7.3	0.4	7.6	0.4	7.4	0.3	7.5	0.3
Calf circ.	34.3	1.9	34.5	2.9	33.2	1.7	35.4	2.5
Up. arm circ.	30.2	2.1	30.0	3.4	29.6	2.1	31.0	2.8
Forearm circ.	27.9	1.5	27.6	2.7	26.8	1.9	28.2	1.9
Wrist breadth	6.1	0.3	6.1	0.3	6.1	0.2	6.2	0.3
Hand breadth	8.6	0.4	8.5	0.4	8.5	0.4	8.6	0.3
Hand lg. (bone)	19.6	0.8	18.9	0.9	18.8	1.0	19.3	0.7
Hand lg. (crease)	18.4	0.8	18.2	0.9	18.2	0.8	18.6	0.7
Head length	19.3	0.5	19.6	0.7	19.0	0.7	19.6	0.6
Head breadth	15.6	0.6	15.5	0.6	15.6	0.3	15.6	0.6

Min. frontal br.	10.4	0.5	10.6	0.6	10.3	0.5	10.5	0.4
Bizygomatic br.	15.2	0.5	15.1	0.5	15.1	0.5	15.2	0.6
Bigonial br.	11.7	0.7	11.7	0.6	11.7	0.6	11.8	0.6
Tot. facial ht.	12.6	0.6	12.8	0.5	12.6	0.5	12.0	0.7
Up. facial ht.	7.5	0.5	7.8	0.4	7.2	0.5	7.1	0.5
Nose height	5.5	0.5	5.7	0.3	5.6	0.4	5.1	0.4
Nose breadth	3.9	0.3	3.9	0.3	4.1	0.3	3.9	0.3
Symphyseal ht.	4.4	0.4	4.8	0.3	4.5	0.3	4.4	0.4
Ear height	7.2	0.6	7.2	0.5	7.4	0.6	7.3	0.6
Ear breadth	3.8	0.4	3.7	0.3	3.7	0.3	3.7	0.3

TABLE 4-12 *Body Measurements of Females in the 4 Villages (cm)*

Variable	Wainwright		Point Hope		Anaktuvuk Pass		Barrow	
	Mean	S.D.	Mean	S.D.	Mean	S.D.	Mean	S.D.
Sitting ht.	84.2	3.2	83.6	3.3	81.8	2.7	82.2	3.5
Stature	156.0	5.9	154.1	6.1	154.9	5.5	154.0	5.4
Biacromial br.	35.6	1.8	36.1	2.0	35.9	1.2	35.9	1.7
Arm length	67.1	3.0	65.6	3.2	66.4	2.9	65.7	2.9
Bicondylar br.	6.7	0.6	6.7	0.5	6.5	0.4	6.6	0.5
Chest breadth	28.0	2.4	28.1	2.3	26.7	1.1	27.5	1.9
Chest depth	21.6	3.4	22.2	3.2	19.7	1.4	21.8	3.3
Billiac br.	29.4	2.4	29.5	2.0	29.5	1.1	29.2	2.4
Foot breadth	9.1	0.8	9.2	0.6	8.9	0.4	9.1	0.5
Foot length	23.3	1.2	23.2	1.0	23.1	0.9	23.2	1.1
Ankle breadth	6.6	0.4	6.9	0.4	6.9	0.4	6.6	0.4
Calf circ.	34.6	3.7	34.1	4.0	32.3	2.3	33.8	3.5
Up. arm circ.	30.5	4.9	29.2	4.1	28.5	3.0	29.3	4.0
Forearm circ.	25.9	2.8	25.7	2.6	24.8	1.5	25.4	3.1
Wrist breadth	5.4	0.3	5.5	0.3	5.5	0.2	5.5	0.3
Hand breadth	7.8	0.4	7.7	0.3	7.7	0.3	7.7	0.4
Hand lg. (bone)	17.9	0.9	17.9	0.8	17.8	0.9	17.9	0.9
Hand lg. (crease)	17.0	0.8	17.1	0.8	17.1	0.7	17.2	0.8
Head length	18.7	0.6	18.8	0.6	18.1	0.6	18.7	0.6
Head breadth	15.1	0.6	15.2	0.4	15.0	0.4	14.9	0.5

Min. frontal br.	10.1	0.5	10.4	0.4	10.1	0.3	10.1	0.4
Bizygomatic br.	14.2	0.6	14.3	0.6	14.2	0.4	14.2	0.5
Bigonial br.	10.9	0.6	11.2	0.5	11.0	0.5	11.0	0.6
Tot. facial ht.	11.5	0.6	11.6	0.6	11.5	0.5	10.9	0.7
Up. facial ht.	6.8	0.5	7.0	0.4	6.6	0.4	6.4	0.5
Nose height	4.9	0.3	5.2	0.4	4.9	0.3	4.5	0.4
Nose breadth	3.5	0.3	3.7	0.3	3.7	0.3	3.6	0.3
Symphyseal ht.	3.9	0.5	4.0	0.5	4.2	0.2	3.9	0.5
Ear height	6.7	0.5	6.6	0.4	6.9	0.5	6.8	0.5
Ear breadth	3.4	0.2	3.4	0.2	3.5	0.3	3.5	0.2

The multivariate portion of this analysis can be seen in Tables 4-14 and 4-15 and Figs. 4-3 and 4-4. Table 4-14 presents the group or village means on three discriminant functions calculated for maximal separation of all four villages. For males, the first function accounted for 44.6% of the total group dispersion, the second for 30.2%, and the third for 25.2%. The canonical correlation between original group membership and discriminant function scores calculated by these functions was 0.74 for the first function, 0.68 for the second, and 0.64 for the third, giving 55.4%, 45.7%, and 41.2% as the

TABLE 4-13 *Univariate F-Ratios Comparing All Males and Females from 4 North Alaskan Villages*

Variable	Males	Females
Sitting ht.	4.22^{+}_{*}	4.95^{+}
Stature	2.86^{*}	1.29
Biacromial br.	0.46	0.45
Arm length	2.39	2.51
Bicondylar br.	2.17	0.81
Chest breadth	3.40^{*}_{*}	3.08^{*}_{*}
Chest depth	2.73^{*}	3.35
Biiliac br.	1.66	0.29
Foot breadth	2.23_{*}	0.85
Foot length	3.26	0.31
Ankle breadth	5.17^{+}_{+}	6.12^{+}
Calf circ.	4.75^{+}	2.11
Up. arm circ.	1.99	1.46
Forearm circ.	2.30	0.76
Wrist breadth	2.32	1.98
Hand breadth	0.37_{+}	1.22
Hand lg. (bone)	6.38^{+}	0.05
Hand lg. (crease)	2.18_{+}	0.42_{+}
Head length	7.47^{+}	6.31^{+}_{*}
Head breadth	0.35	3.16^{*}
Min. frontal br.	2.25	4.83^{+}
Bizygomatic br.	0.49	0.44
Bigonial br.	0.19_{+}	1.40_{+}
Tot. facial ht.	17.89^{+}	13.64^{+}_{+}
Up. facial ht.	18.23^{+}	13.80^{+}
Nose height	20.53^{+}_{*}	38.25^{+}_{*}
Nose breadth	3.15^{*}_{+}	3.28.
Symphyseal ht.	5.90^{+}	2.60_{*}
Ear height	1.44	3.36^{*}
Ear breadth	0.53	0.81

* $P < .05.$

$^{+}$ $P < .01.$

TABLE 4-14 *Discriminant Functions Evaluated at Village Means*

Village	Males			Females		
	I	II	III	I	II	III
Wainwright	0.72	-0.74	0.62	0.85	1.44	-0.47
Point Hope	0.93	-0.09	-1.81	1.34	-0.86	0.77
Barrow	-1.45	0.12	-0.04	-1.46	0.10	0.39
Anaktuvuk Pass	1.09	2.40	0.59	-0.21	-1.49	-1.80

proportion of overlapping variances. For the females quite similar values are found. The first discriminant function described 46.4% of the group dispersion, the second 32.2%, and the third 21.4%. With canonical correlations of 0.77, 0.71, and 0.63 for these functions, 59.5%, 50.4%, and 40.4% of the variance in group membership is accounted for by the distribution of discriminant scores on the functions.

Table 4-14 also demonstrates that the discriminant functions accomplish their task of discrimination in roughly comparable fashion for both men and women. The first function separates Barrow from a clustering of the other three villages in both sexes. The second function does the same for Anak-

TABLE 4-15 *Mahalanobis' D^2 Distances Among Villages*

	Wainwright	Point Hope	Barrow	Anaktuvuk Pass
Wainwright		7.08	7.88	11.48
Point Hope	6.34		8.95	9.43
Barrow	5.85	8.77		8.91
Anaktuvuk Pass	10.04	12.00	12.06	

D^2 values above the diagonal are for females and below the diagonal, for males.

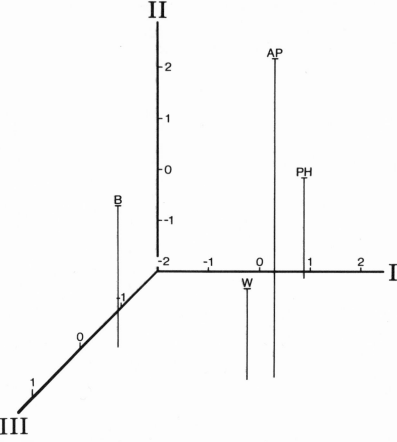

FIGURE 4-3. *Location of male samples from four north Alaskan villages in three dimensions. The endpoints of each vertical line represent village centroids based on discriminant scores on three discriminant functions. Ap, Anaktuvuk Pass; B, Barrow; PH, Point Hope; and W, Wainwright.*

tuvuk Pass among the males, while for females this function appears to cluster Anaktuvuk Pass and Point Hope at one extreme and Wainwright and Barrow at the other. Finally, in the third function, Point Hope is distinguished among males and Anaktuvuk Pass among females.

Mahalanobis' D^2 distances provide a means of expressing these distinctions using information from all three functions. The distances calculated between village centroids can be seen in Table 4-15. Also, Figs. 4-3 and 4-4 include each village centroid in the three-dimensional space formed by the three discriminant functions.

All of the distances in Table 4-15 are highly significant ($P < 0.01$). The

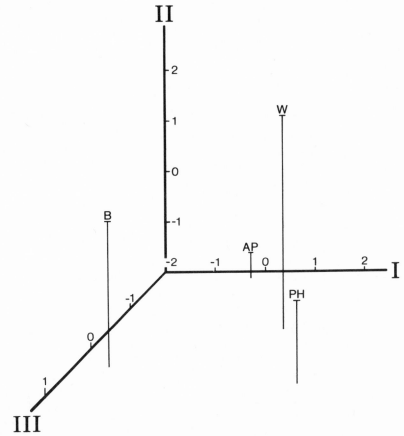

FIGURE 4-4. *Location of female samples from four north Alaskan villages in three dimensions. The endpoints of each vertical line represent village centroids based on discriminant scores on three discriminant functions. AP, Anaktuvuk Pass; B, Barrow, PH, Point Hope; and W, Wainwright.*

results for men and women are comparable in that the three coastal villages (Wainwright, Point Hope, and Barrow) tend to be the most similar and the largest values are found between Anaktuvuk Pass (inland) and the other villages. In addition there seems to be a slightly greater range of values among males than among females.

The degree of distinction that these functions reflected among these four villages may be seen by classifying individuals into village groups strictly on the basis of their discriminant scores. Overall, 82.1% of the males and 82.2% of the females were correctly allocated to their village by the discriminant function scores.

Since the first discriminant function was the only one that set off the villages in precisely the same way in both sexes, I will use it alone to examine the anthropometric variables important to the discrimination. Generally speaking there was not much comparability between the sexes in the variables chosen as the most important to the second and third functions. For men, the most important measurements in the first function are (in order of absolute magnitude of their coefficients): nose height, hand length (crease), arm length, stature, and head length. For women the "brute" discriminators in the first function are: nose height, total facial height, sitting height, wrist breadth, and hand length (crease). Vertical facial dimensions, an overall measure of body length, and upper-extremity size appear to be the best discriminators of Barrow residents from people of the other three villages.

What can be said from these results regarding the intrapopulation anthropomentric variation of north Alaskan Eskimos? First, it is tempting to point out the position of Anaktuvuk Pass in the distance results in Table 4-15 and Figs. 4-3 and 4-4 with regard to the inland coastal dichotomy. Members of coastal villages appear to be more similar to each other than they are to the inland residents of Anaktuvuk Pass. One possible explanation for this result is that it is a result of admixture since all three coastal village samples contain hybridized individuals and the inland sample does not. However, in a further analysis (not presented here) based entirely on nonhybridized individuals the same patterning was seen in all but one comparison. (In this analysis, Point Hope males were more "distant" from Barrow males than is the case in Table 4-15). Therefore, admixture with non-Eskimos does not seem to provide an explanation for these results.

Another explanation of these results may be the one suggested by Spencer (1959). If marriages were infrequent between individuals who belonged to different bands, or if inland orientation vs coastal orientation were a cultural barrier to marriage, the pattern of variation seen in the present results would be expected. Matings certainly occur across these "boundaries" but marriages may be more frequent within than between them.

On the other hand, the fact that all of the coastal villages include people from a variety of named bands (see discussion in Chapter 3) would suggest that there has been a good deal of shifting of population into these villages from a broad geographical area. It may be more important to emphasize the fact that that all of the villages can be distinguished anthropometrically at a high level of statistical significance than to resort to attempts to find patterns in the magnitude of the distances. Certainly the most important processes that have been operating are the historical circumstances of who became established in what village, regardless of his/her ancestral affiliation with one or more territorial groups. In other words, the results presented here may be best viewed as dependent on where people were drawn by the provision of social, educational, and welfare services rather than the operation of marriage and mating patterns.

In future analyses, an attempt will be made to examine the territorial affiliation of the residents of these villages to see whether new groups can be set up to reflect membership in bands that were principally oriented to either the coastal zone or the interior. Multivariate analysis of such groups might shed light on the questions raised above. In either case, however, it would appear that historical circumstances and marriage/mating patterns are more likely to provide explanations of the intrapopulation anthropometric variation of north Alaskan Eskimos than implication of the forces of natural selection, random genetic drift, or admixture with Athabaskan Indians.

GROWTH MEASUREMENTS

Measurements on children and subadults formed an integral part of the anthropometric study of north Alaskan Eskimos. Individuals between one and twenty years old were measured for stature and weight, while those between five and twenty were subjects for the complete battery of anthropometric measurements. Table 4-16 provides a breakdown of the subjects by village. Because of the size of the sample in each age category, data reported here will submerge both village of residence and hybrid vs nonhybrid status of the subjects.

All of the data reported in this section derive from measurements taken by myself. Subjects wore light, indoor clothing—usually jeans and T-shirts for boys or slacks and blouses for girls, plus undergarments. Weiner and Lourie (1969) provided the decimal method used to record age; it designates each age group by a one-year interval (for example, six-year-olds include children between the ages of 5.500 and 6.499 years).

Tables 4-17 and 4-18 list data on stature and weight, respectively, for all subjects included in the cross-sectional aspect of the growth study. In a

TABLE 4-16 *Sample Sizes for North Alaskan Eskimo Growth Study*

Sex	Wainwright	Point Hope	Anaktuvuk Pass	Barter Island	Barrow	Totals
Males	87	79	17	20	50	253
Females	83	68	15	12	57	235
Totals	170	147	32	32	107	488

previous publication (Jamison, 1976) I have compared these data to growth standards for U.S. whites taken from Watson and Lowry (1967). The comparisons indicated that north Alaskan Eskimos stature fell between the 10th and 25th percentiles and weight between the 50th and 75th percentiles of the white standard prior to adolescence. During the latter period both variables approached higher percentiles of the white growth standard. At age eighteen the Eskimo males were 6 cm shorter and 7.3 kg heavier than their white counterparts and comparable figures for Eskimo females were 4.5 cm shorter and 5.4 kg heavier. Previous studies have also remarked on the relatively high weight for stature of Eskimos (see for instance Heller et al., 1967 and Hrdlička, 1941).

Figure 4-5 shows the data on stature and weight from Tables 4-17 and 4-18. For stature, the sexes are quite similar until the age of eleven to twelve years, when girls forge ahead of boys. The distance curves for stature recross at age fourteen, and by the late teens, males are about 12 cm taller than females. For weight, the early years are comparable but less similar than was height. By age nine, females weigh more than males. At age fifteen to sixteen, the boys take the lead and at age eighteen they are about 10 kg heavier than the girls. Table 4-1 showed comparable figures, on average, for adult sexual dimorphism in stature and weight.

These cross-sectional data cannot adequately estimate parameters such as rates of growth and the age of peak growth velocity. To remedy this the article cited above (Jamison, 1976) included data from a semi-longitudinal series of measurements on Wainwright males. This was the only village in which repeated visits provided the opportunity to collect longitudinal growth data. Mean annual increments of stature for these Eskimos were slightly lower than increments for whites, taken from Watson and Lowry (1967). Peak velocity for Eskimo stature occurred between the ages of fourteen and fifteen, or approximately one year later than for whites. Compared to this standard the Eskimo males' growth spurt in stature reached a lower peak but it lasted for a longer period of time. By age seventeen to eighteen years the Eskimos' velocity was only 2 cm per year, indicating that the point of effective cessation of growth was close.

The rate curve for weight of Wainwright males was somewhat above that of the white standard at nearly all ages. Peak weight velocity occurred about one year later for Eskimos than for whites, but the magnitude of the peak was higher.

Similar data on Wainwright females (unpublished results) show that weight follows the same pattern (when compared to the white standard) as that seen among the males. For stature, however, the rate or velocity curves for Eskimos and whites were very similar. If anything, peak height velocity occurred slightly earlier in the Eskimo females, but the duration of the adolescent growth spurt was nearly the same for both populations.

With the fact in mind that Wainwright contributed the only longitudinal

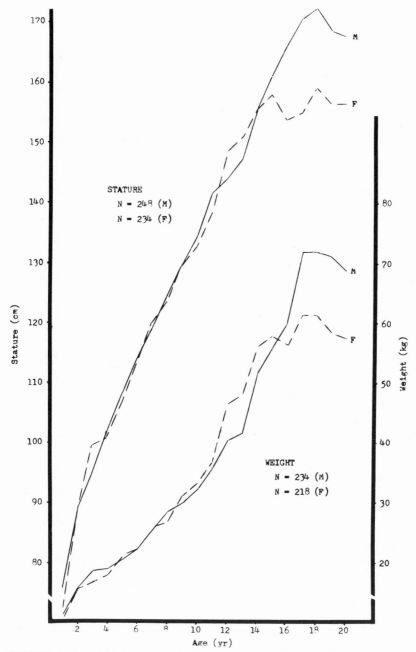

FIGURE 4-5. *Distance curves for growth in stature (cm) and weight (kg) of north Alaskan Eskimos. M, males; F, females.*

TABLE 4-17 *Stature of North Alaskan Eskimos, 1-20 Years Old (cm)*

Age (yr)	Males			Females		
	N	$\bar{X}$	S.D.	N	$\bar{X}$	S.D.
1	4	75.0	5.7	4	71.6	2.6
2	7	88.2	6.6	6	88.1	3.5
3	6	98.6	4.6	11	94.2	3.9
4	10	100.0	7.2	5	100.9	5.2
5	13	105.8	4.7	11	107.0	4.1
6	20	112.7	2.8	16	112.2	2.8
7	14	118.1	4.1	16	118.7	4.4
8	13	123.3	6.8	22	122.4	6.1
9	23	128.7	4.2	18	128.5	6.3
10	21	133.0	5.8	24	131.6	5.7
11	17	140.5	6.3	11	137.3	4.4
12	22	142.8	5.4	21	147.2	6.1
13	14	146.3	5.4	19	149.6	6.3
14	13	154.2	7.2	7	154.2	4.0
15	14	159.7	8.4	9	156.8	4.6
16	12	164.9	7.9	7	152.6	2.8
17	7	169.3	7.1	10	153.9	5.6
18	8	171.1	7.6	9	158.0	4.9
19	3	167.4	–	5	155.2	4.4
20	7	166.4	4.0	3	155.4	–

data in this study, the movement of the distance curves of stature for Eskimo males into higher percentiles of the white standard during adolescence can be partially explained by their slightly later entry into the growth spurt and slightly later peak velocities. That this is not the sole explanation can be seen especially from the comments made about the females' stature: the Eskimo and white data are quite comparable. Schaefer (1973) has implicated dietary factors, particularly increased carbohydrates, in the accelerated growth trends

TABLE 4-18 *Weight of North Alaskan Eskimos, 1-20 Years Old (kg)*

Age (yr)	Males			Females		
	N	X̄	S.D.	N	X̄	S.D.
1	7	10.5	2.0	5	10.0	1.8
2	8	15.1	1.4	6	14.9	1.1
3	6	17.7	2.2	11	16.1	1.8
4	10	18.2	3.1	5	17.2	2.3
5	12	19.6	1.9	11	20.2	2.6
6	20	21.4	1.7	16	21.4	2.3
7	12	24.7	1.7	14	24.6	2.3
8	12	27.6	4.4	19	26.0	3.5
9	19	29.1	2.7	16	30.3	5.0
10	18	31.4	4.2	23	32.3	6.8
11	17	34.8	4.5	10	35.9	4.5
12	19	39.4	6.3	17	45.3	10.5
13	14	40.6	4.5	17	47.0	8.8
14	12	50.4	7.8	7	54.9	7.4
15	13	54.7	10.2	9	56.7	7.4
16	12	58.7	9.5	7	55.1	6.2
17	7	70.5	9.2	8	60.1	8.4
18	7	70.5	4.9	9	60.2	4.8
19	2	69.8	-	5	57.2	6.9
20	7	67.4	6.0	3	56.3	-

of Canadian Eskimos. Perhaps the present data can be added as corroboration of these trends in Alaskan Eskimos.

Figure 4-6 shows growth velocity curves for stature and weight for Wainwright males and females. These semi-longitudinal data were used in the comparisons with white growth rate standards. Mean annual increments were calculated from repeated measurements taken on sixty-seven boys and seventy-five girls. The total series consists of 125 replicated measures on

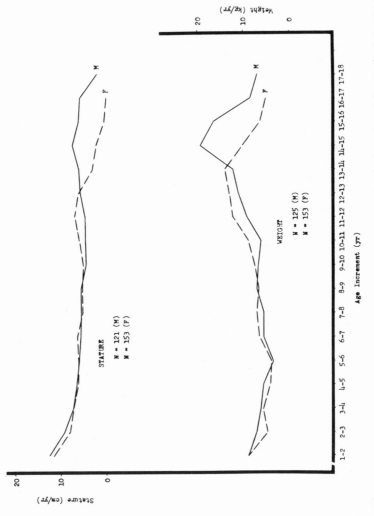

FIGURE 4-6. *Velocity curves of growth in stature (cm/yr) and weight (kg/yr) for Wainwright Eskimos. M, males; F, females.*

males and 153 on females. Stature increments indicate that the adolescent growth spurt begins at nine to ten years for females and eleven to twelve years for males. Peak height velocity occurs approximately three years earlier for females than for males.

The situation is somewhat different for weight velocities. Here the initiation of the growth spurt and the peak weight velocities are both about one year apart, with girls typically earlier in their development. Among the boys, peak height velocity and peak weight velocity occur at the same time—between fourteen and fifteen years of age. On the other hand, peak weight velocity occurs at thirteen to fourteen years and peak height velocity is earlier—between eleven and twelve years for girls. A similar pattern of peak velocity timing is seen between the sexes among whites, according to Watson and Lowry (1967).

Earlier in this chapter I used multivariate statistical methods to characterize anthropometric variation between male and female adult Eskimos. Table 4-7 listed standardized coefficients of the linear function which discriminated males from females. Examination of this table indicated that hip and shoulder breadths, facial height and breadth, arm and calf circumferences, foot length, wrist breadth, and hand breadth were the best discriminator variables. Growth distance curves for these variables delineates the developmental pattern of Eskimo sexual dimorphism.

Biiliac and Biacromial Breadths. Figure 4-7 shows cross-sectional data on hip and shoulder breadths for Eskimos between the ages of five and twenty years. The distance curves indicate that prior to eleven years these breadths are very similar in both sexes, and after age eleven females have broader lateral dimensions than males. By age fifteen to sixteen the distance curves shift position and biacromial breadth is markedly greater for males than for females (on the average) at all subsequent ages. For biiliac breadth, boys also tend to have the larger dimensions, but the sexual difference is not nearly as marked as for shoulder breadth. Broad hips relative to shoulders is a female characteristic among Eskimos as it is for most other populations.

Bizygomatic Breadth and Total Facial Height. Growth curves for facial dimensions can be seen in Fig. 4-8. The developmental pattern here seems to be one in which the dimensions are quite similar until the adolescent period. At age thirteen, bizygomatic breadths begin to differ between boys and girls, as does total facial height at age fourteen. After these ages male Eskimos have longer and broader faces than do female, and the dimorphism is slightly greater for the facial height than the facial breadth.

Upper Arm and Calf Circumference. Figure 4-9 shows the growth pattern of arm and calf circumferences in males and females. For these variables females tend to have the higher values, although the differences in the early years are slight. From eight to nine years until age sixteen girls have considerably larger limb circumferences than do boys. By sixteen to seventeen the sit-

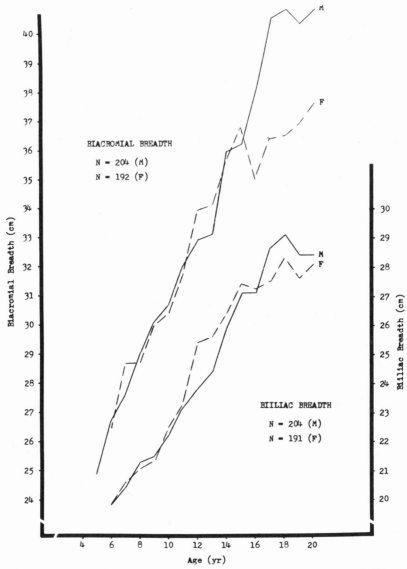

FIGURE 4-7. *Distance curves for growth in biacromial breadth (left) and biiliac breadth (right). M, males; F, females.*

uation reverses and boys surpass girls in these dimensions. A greater dimorphism can be seen for upper arm circumference than for calf circumference.

Foot Length and Breadth. The multivariate analysis of adult Eskimo sexual dimorphism indicated that foot length was a good discriminating variable while foot breadth was not. The latter measure is included here simply for comparative purposes. Figure 4-10 presents distance curves for

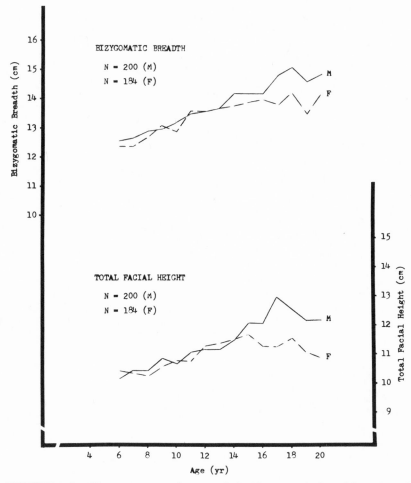

FIGURE 4-8. *Distance curves for growth in bizygomatic breadth and total facial height for north Alaskan Eskimos. M, males; F, females.*

both of these variables on boys and girls. The sexes are comparable for foot dimensions up to age thirteen, after which they begin to diverge. The difference in degree of sexual dimorphism apparent during inspection of these growth curves is probably a function of the greater absolute size of foot length over foot breadth.

Wrist Breadth. Distance curves of growth in wrist breadth are also shown in Fig. 4-10. There is a good deal of similarity in the developmental pattern of wrist breadth and foot breadth. Both sexes have similar age-group means for wrist breadth until age thirteen, when they diverge. Unlike some of the distance curves that fluctuate widely in the upper ages as a result of small sample sizes, wrist breadth is quite stable in its pattern. The standard devia-

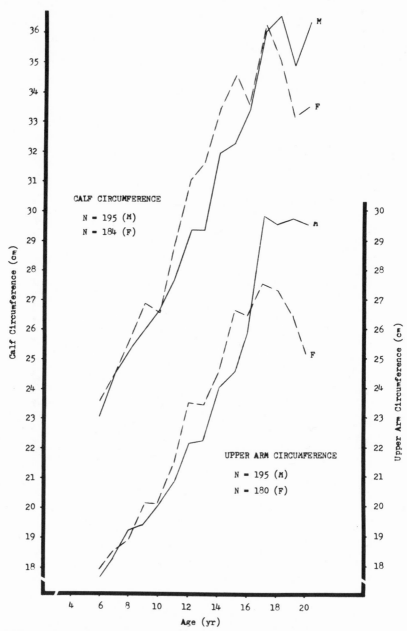

FIGURE 4-9. *Distance curves for growth in calf circumference and upper arm circumference in north Alaskan Eskimos. M, males; F, females.*

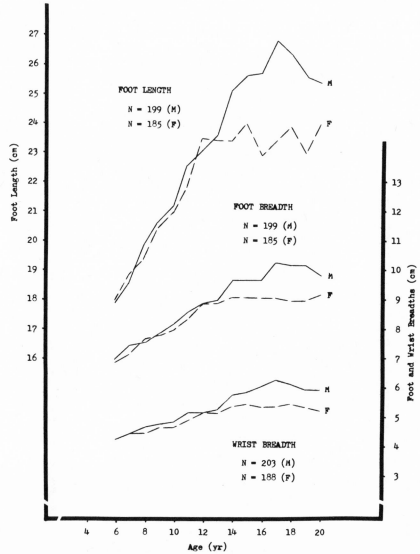

FIGURE 4-10. *Distance curves for growth in foot length (left) and foot breadth and wrist breadth (right) for north Alaskan Eskimos. M, males; F, females.*

tins of the age-group means (not reported here) suggest that the reason is a relatively low variability in the measurement in all age groups.

Hand Length and Breadth. Hand breadth (see Fig. 4-11) turned out to be a good discriminator of sex in the multivariate analysis of adults, and hand length was not. The latter is included here for comparative purposes, as was foot breadth. Hand length shows a developmental pattern in which twelve-

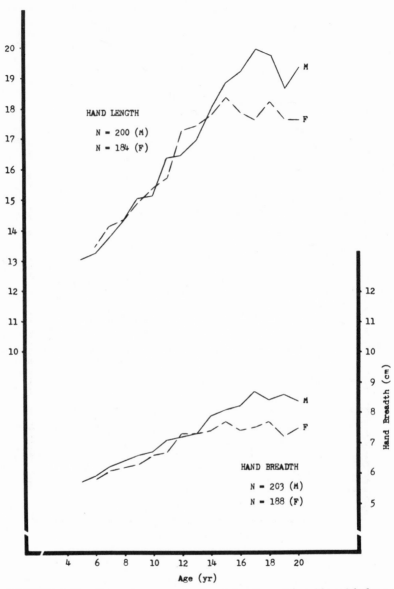

FIGURE 4-11. *Distance curves for hand length and hand breadth for north Alaskan Eskimos. M, males; F, females.*

and thirteen-year-old girls have longer hands than the same age boys. Around age fourteen the distance curves recross and males develop longer hands than females. Hand breadth gives a pattern very similar to foot breadth and wrist breadth. Males tend to have only slightly higher values until age thirteen, when the dimorphism becomes more marked.

In all of the foot and hand dimensions there is a sharp peak around age twelve in the values for females, when they approximate or even surpass the values for males. This finding is very likely indicative of the earlier adolescent growth spurt in girls, but for these variables the cross-sectional data suggest rather poorly defined spurts of short duration compared to some of the other measurements.

It must be kept in mind when viewing Figs. 4-7 through 4-11 that the majority of these variables were selected for inclusion here because of their utility in differentiating male and female adult Eskimos. In the multivariate analysis, order of variable entry and the pattern of correlations between variables affects their importance to the discriminant function ultimately produced. With this in mind, it is still of interest that there is a progression of development of sexual dimorphism throughout the growth period. Eskimo females have larger biiliac breadths and arm and calf circumferences than males for a significant portion of the growth and developmental period. The dimensions of the face and the extremities have the shortest period when girls have larger values than boys. Age-group means of boys surpass those of girls between the ages of thirteen and seventeen years. The point of final divergence occurs earliest in the extremity and facial dimensions, somewhat later for biacromial and biiliac breadths, and latest for the limb circumference.

AGE AND SECULAR TRENDS

Figure 4-12 shows trends in stature and weight across ten-year age groups for male and female Eskimos. The data are means for all individuals in each age decade, and both hybrids and nonhybrids are included. The two variables give quite different patterns. Stature means tend to decrease with each succeeding decade (thirty- to forty-year old females are the exception), and this decrease is greater among females than among males. Secular trends as well as degenerative age changes must be involved in these results. The steep decline of stature between the last two data points for each sex is probably primarily due to aging. Prior to this decline the more general decrease in stature with increasing age may be interpreted as evidence for secular trends affecting north Alaskan Eskimos. For males the trend is very slight, approximating 2.5 cm; among females it is twice as large or about 5 cm. Similar results were encountered in a previous examination of secular trends in Wainwright Eskimos (Jamison, 1970), although the trends in that data were more marked.

Weight tends to increase, in the present data, until the sixth and fifth

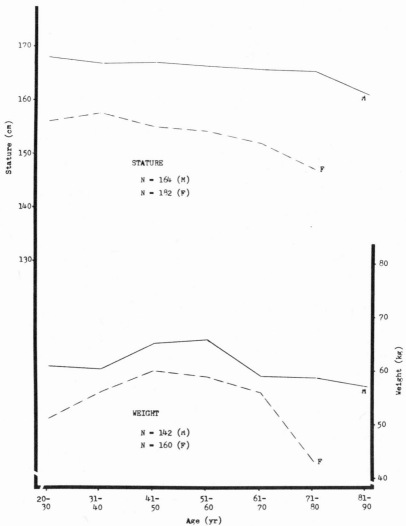

FIGURE 4-12. *Trends in stature (cm) and weight (kg) for adults. Data graphed are means for groups of individuals in 10-year age intervals. M, males; F, females.*

decades for males and females, respectively. After the seventh decade (sixty to seventy years) weight drops off slightly among men and rather sharply among women. There is no evidence from these data that a secular trend for increased body weight is occurring among north Alaskan Eskimos. From Fig. 4-10 it is apparent that the high weight for stature encountered in Eskimo growth data is maintained and even increased in the adults. Whether this finding is a manifestation of the "ecogeographic rule" of Bergmann or a result of the dietary practices of these Eskimos is not discernible.

5

Dermatoglyphic Variation

Robert J. Meier

Dermatoglyphic data on north Alaskan Eskimos were collected under the auspices of the IBP Human Adaptability Project in the villages of Wainwright (during 1969), Point Hope (during 1970), Barter Island (during 1970), Anaktuvuk Pass (during 1969 and 1970), and Barrow (during 1971). In all, nearly 800 sets of digit and palm prints were obtained from the five villages. Previous reports on this research have dealt with digital pattern frequencies (Meier, 1974a), total ridge count (Meier, 1974b), and pattern intensity (Meier, in press). In addition, in a doctoral thesis Murad (1975) utilized the palmar data from the five villages in performing univariate and multivariate analyses. This report presents the results of further research in digital ridge correlation and regression, as well as a summary of the principle findings of earlier research.

CORRELATION OF DIGITAL RIDGE COUNTS AND PATTERN INTENSITY

Until recently rather little attention had been paid to the question of relationship between dermatoglyphic patterns and the size of these patterns. One reason might be that suitable measures of pattern size were not available until Bonnevie (1924) and, later, Holt (1949) established a methodology for counting ridges from all pattern types. Cummins and Steggerda (1935, 1936) were perhaps the first to consider the matter of interpopulation variabiltiy in pattern size as determined from ridge counting. Their studies showed that Mayan Indians had loop and whorl patterns which were on the average two ridges smaller than a Dutch series. Significantly, even though whorl patterns had mean ridge counts about eight ridges higher than loops in both groups, the Mayans had twice the whorl pattern frequency of the Dutch families. This finding led Cummins and Steggerda (1936, p. 115) to suggest that ". . . types of patterns may vary interracially in their size trends."

This suggestion has been followed up in a number of fairly recent studies including Singh (1961) on Indian castes, Huizinga (1965) and Glanville and Huizinga (1966) on several African groups, Basu and Namboodiri (1971) on

An earlier version of this chapter was presented in part at the American Association of Physical Anthropologist Meetings, Amherst, Mass., April 1974.

PLAIN ARCH   PLAIN LOOP   WHORL

FIGURE 5-1. *The three basic pattern types: arch, loop, and whorl. A heavy line drawn from the pattern* core *(the centermost ridge) to the* triradius *(point of intersection of ridge systems) indicates the* ridge count *for the loop and whorl patterns.*

Haitians, Basu (1972) on Brahman Indians, Rigters-Aris (1975) on three West African tribes, and Meier (1975) on Easter Islanders. The general finding is that different populations do indeed have varying expressions of pattern size and pattern type. The study reported here explored some aspects of digital pattern size and type relationships among the five Eskimo villages listed above.

BASIC TERMINOLOGY

Definition of most digital dermatoglyphic variables rests upon the two pattern landmarks of *triradius* and *core*. By locating these two points a *ridge count* can be made, and the three basic pattern types can thereby be defined (see Fig. 5-1).

Pattern Types. The three basic pattern types are the arch, the loop, and the whorl.

The *Arch* is a patternless area having no triradius or core, or a patterned area with one core and one triradius but a ridge count of zero (referred to as a *Tented Arch*).

The *Loop* is a patterned area having one core, one triradius, and one variable ridge count. Sometimes loops are distinguished, by the direction of open ridges, as *Ulnar* and *Radial Loops*.

The *Whorl* is a patterned area having two triradii, one or two cores, and two variable ridge counts. There are several subtypes of whorls, such as *Twin Loops, Lateral Pocket Loops,* and *Concentric Whorls.*

Coded Pattern Types (TPAT). Pattern types were coded according to the number of triradii, which would assign zero to an arch, one to a loop, and two to a whorl. This coding basically represents an increasing series in pattern size and an increasing degree of pattern complexity.

Pattern Intensity Index (PII). Pattern intensity is defined as the sum of the triradii over the ten digits of an individual. PII ranges from zero (all arches) to twenty (all whorls). As an example, a PII value of fourteen might represent an individual with six loops and four whorl patterns.

Ridge Counts. Three different kinds of ridge counts were made, defined as follows:

Total Ulnar Ridge Count (TULC): The sum of ridges on the ulnar side of all patterns per individual.

Total Radial Ridge Count (TRDC): The sum of ridges on the radial side of all patterns per individual.

Total Ridge Count (TRC): The sum of the higher ridge count (either ulnar or radial) of all patterns per individual.

RESULTS

Correlation analysis was done on the five variables of TPAT, PII, TULC, TRDC, and TRC. All coefficients in the matrix were highly significant in the positive direction (probability less than 0.001). Table 5-1 shows the correlation coefficients between PII and the other four variables. The highest coefficient (r, 0.99) was found between PII and TPAT, because the number of triradii was used to define both variables. The correlation between PII and TRDC is higher than between PII vs TULC and PII vs TRC, perhaps because both PII and TRDC are quite sensitive only to whorl pattern frequency, while TULC and TRC are more influenced by the frequency of both loops and whorls. Most loop patterns are of the ulnar kind, and very few are of the radial kind. Hence, TRDC is essentially a count of the whorl patterns and only whorl patterns contribute to PII for values exceeding ten.

The relationship between pattern intensity and mean total ridge count invited a closer look for three reasons. (1) Both variables are clearly expected to follow similar paths of increasing complexity—that is, as whorl frequency increases, so will PII and TRC. (2) Both variables have been shown to have fairly high heritability estimates; Loesch (1971) obtained an H^2 value of 0.66 for PII and a value of 0.70 for TRC. (3) Comparative studies are available for these two variables, whereas the other two ridge counts used here are not reported in the literature. For a comparison in terms of correlation between PII and TRC, the values obtained in Loesch's 1971 study are included in Table 5-1. The present study is clearly in close agreement with her study.

Table 5-2 shows the correlation between PII and TRC for male and female subjects, broken down for each of the five Alaskan Eskimo villages. For Point Hope, it was necessary to maintain a separation between hybrids and non-hybrids since it was found (as will be discussed later) that racial admixture had had a significant effect upon dermatoglyphic variation. Even though there was some variability in the strength of correlation between PII and TRC

TABLE 5-1 *Correlation Between Pattern Intensity Index (PII) and Ridge Counts (TULC, TRDC, TRC) and Pattern Type (TPAT), by Sex*

Variable	Mean	S.D.	Correlation Coefficients[*]
Male Subjects (382)			
TULC	125.5	46.6	0.73
TRDC	53.0	47.4	0.93
TRC	132.9	48.6	0.77[+]
TPAT	13.7	3.4	0.99
PII	13.6	3.3	--
Female Subjects (403)			
TULC	113.6	47.1	0.78
TRDC	44.4	44.1	0.88
TRC	120.8	49.4	0.82[+]
TPAT	12.8	3.4	0.99
PII	12.8	3.4	--

[*]All coefficients are significant beyond .001.

[+]Loesch (1971) gives a value of 0.77 for male and 0.79 for female subjects.

for the five villages, all *r* values were significant beyond the 0.001 level. This intervillage comparison revealed an approximate linear relationship between PII and TRC, as can be seen in a bivariate plot in Fig. 5-2. In essence, the relationship involves pattern type (as expressed by PII) and pattern size (as measured by TRC).

Two important possibilities ensue from studying this relationship. First, it might be unnecessary to count ridges if counting only the triradii would suffice. Second, it might be possible to replace missing TRC values for persons whose patterns can be identified by type according to number of observable triradii, but whose patterns themselves are too smudged or scarred for accurate ridge counting. In order to use the relationship between PII and TRC for either of these two purposes, it is necessary to apply regression statistics to

TABLE 5-2   *Correlation Between Pattern Intensity Index (PII) and Mean Total Ridge Count (TRC)*

Population	N	PII		TRC		Correlation Coefficients*
		Mean	S.D.	Mean	S.D.	
Male Subjects						
Point Hope						
Nonhybrid	51	16.0	2.8	157.7	52.6	0.60
Hybrid	51	14.1	3.5	144.8	51.0	0.80
Anaktuvuk Pass	35	13.5	2.8	133.8	40.5	0.84
Barter Island	23	13.5	2.9	134.0	42.0	0.74
Barrow	100	13.3	3.2	133.0	45.9	0.77
Wainwright	113	12.6	2.8	115.9	45.8	0.74
Female Subjects						
Point Hope						
Nonhybrid	66	14.4	3.8	136.5	58.6	0.69
Hybrid	45	12.0	3.9	112.6	53.3	0.88
Barrow	118	13.4	3.3	129.9	47.2	0.81
Anaktuvuk Pass	37	13.1	2.7	125.8	38.0	0.86
Barter Island	16	13.0	3.0	120.4	52.4	0.83
Wainwright	122	11.7	3.0	104.6	41.9	0.81

*All correlations were significant beyond .001.

obtain prediction equations. One such application has been made by Basu and Namboodiri (1971). The major conclusion of these workers is that,

Predictions of TRC from PII on the basis of regression estimates from Haitian data gave satisfactory results for Negroid and some Caucasoid populations but less satisfactory results for Mongoloid groups suggesting that the relationships might be different in different ethnic groups. (p. 165)

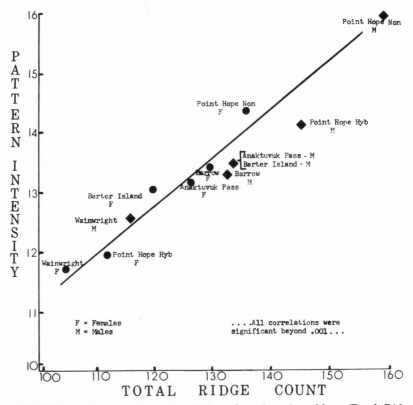

FIGURE 5-2. *Pattern Intensity Index plotted against Mean Total Ridge Count for five Eskimo groups, for male (M) and female (F) subjects. All correlations were significant beyond 0.001.*

Table 5-3 shows the results of applying the Basu and Namboodiri regression to one group originally included in their study, Tibetans, and two new groups added here, Eskimos and Easter Islanders. As can be seen, a rather poor fit exists between observed and expected TRC as estimated by PII. One explanation for this poor fit could be that the relationship between TRC and PII is not linear. Nonlinearity has been found by Glanville and Huizinga (1966) and Rigters-Aris (1975); the relationship between TRC and PII was approximately *S*-shaped in several studies of African male series. Alternatively, the relationship could be essentially linear but based upon a different slope coefficient.

To pursue this alternative, a set of prediction equations was derived from the Alaskan Eskimo data, and the results appear in Table 5-4. As expected, the Haitian observed TRC values are underestimated by about as much as the Haitian equations overestimated the Eskimo observed TRC values. Since the Haitian equations also overestimated the Tibetan observed TRC counts, the

TABLE 5-3 *Regression Estimates of Total Ridge Count from Pattern Intensity, Based upon Equations for Haitians*

Population	Total Ridge Count		
	Observed	Predicted	Difference
Male Eskimos	132.9	147.2	+ 14.3
Female Eskimos	120.8	131.9	+ 11.1
Male Tibetans	156.2	174.9	+ 18.7
Female Tibetans	138.6	152.3	+ 13.7
Male Easter Islanders	177.1	166.6	− 10.5
Female Easter Islanders	161.1	157.2	− 3.9

The Haitian equations, from Basu and Namboodiri (1971), are as follows: $\underline{Y} = -13.412 + 11.806\ \underline{X}$ for 229 males; $\underline{Y} = -12.419 + 11.246\ \underline{X}$ for 258 females; where $\underline{Y}$ is the estimated total ridge count and $\underline{X}$ the mean pattern intensity.

Eskimo equations might provide a better fit—and indeed, Table 5-4 shows only a minor difference between observed and expected TRC for Tibetans.

In general, the Eskimo equations appear appropriate for predicting Mongoloid TRC values, but are not necessarily applicable to other groups. Indeed, the predictions for Easter Islanders show that the Eskimo equations are very much worse than the Haitian equations. Perhaps this situation can be explained by characterizing the variable relationship between TRC and PII in terms of a few major categories or groupings.

The populations compared in Table 5-5 differ both in whorl pattern frequency and in size of whorl patterns such that three major kinds of relationships appear to exist: (1) some populations have low frequencies of whorls but whorl patterns of rather *large* size (seen in the Haitians, Dutch, and British series); (2) some populations have *high* frequencies of whorls that are of *small* average ridge count (seen in north Alaskan and Karluk Eskimos, and Mayan Indians); and (3) some populations have *high* whorl frequencies of *large* average pattern size (seen in Easter Islanders). The fourth combination, *low* whorl frequency with *small* ridge counts, is likely to occur in such groups as the Efe Pygmies (see Basu and Namboodiri, 1971).

In general, these results indicate that for a given increase in whorl frequency—which basically is represented by a corresponding rise in pattern intensity—there will be an increase in total ridge count, whose size will depend

TABLE 5-4 *Regression Estimates of Total Ridge Count from Pattern Intensity, Based upon Equations for Eskimos*

| Population | Total Ridge Count | | |
	Observed	Predicted	Difference
Male Haitians	132.6	119.8	− 12.8
Female Haitians	120.1	108.2	− 11.9
Male Tibetans	156.2	158.0	+ 1.8
Female Tibetans	138.6	141.7	+ 3.1
Male Easter Islanders	177.1	150.4	− 26.7
Female Easter Islanders	161.1	146.7	− 14.4

The equations are as follows: $Y = -13.093 + 10.724 \underline{X}$ for 382 males; $\underline{Y} = -27.301 + 11.539 \underline{X}$ for 403 females; where $\underline{Y}$ is the estimated total ridge count and $\underline{X}$ the mean pattern intensity.

TABLE 5-5 *Whorl Pattern Frequency and Mean Whorl Ridge Count for Seven Samples (Male Subjects)*

Population	Whorls (%)	Mean ridge count
Low Frequency, Large Whorls		
Dutch (1)	20.2	19.4
British (2)	26.7	19.6
Haitians (3)	30.1	18.2
High Frequency, Small Whorls		
North Alaskan Eskimos (4)	37.2	17.8
Karluk Eskimos (5)	42.3	17.3
Mayan Indians (6)	42.3	17.3
High Frequency, Large Whorls		
Easter Islanders (7)	53.0	21.1

Sources: (1) Cummins and Steggerda, 1935; (2) Holt, 1949, 1961; (3) Basu and Namboodiri, 1971; (4) this study; (5) Meier, 1966; (6) Cummins and Steggerda, 1936; and (7) Meier, 1975.

upon the size of the whorl patterns as measured by ridge count. In effect, this is stating that the slope of the relationship between TRC and PII can differ between populations according to differences in either whorl pattern frequency or whorl pattern size. (Loop patterns also would be expected to have an effect upon the relationship, but of a lesser magnitude than whorls.) Both TRC and PII could be of significance in investigating dermatoglyphic variation between populations, and using either whorl frequency or ridge count alone would not necessarily adequately describe interpopulation variation.

SUMMARY OF DIGITAL DERMATOGLYPHIC RESEARCH

A major feature of the digital prints was that the five villages showed considerable intervillage variability (see Table 5-6) in terms of pattern type frequencies, pattern intensity index (PII), and mean total ridge count (TRC).

Point Hope can be seen to vary from the other villages in having comparatively few loop patterns, many whorls, and hence a high PII (Table 5-7). In contrast to Point Hope, Wainwright departed in the other direction in having many loop patterns, few whorls, and a correspondingly low PII.

Univariate testing (chi-square and t-tests) on the intervillage differences was performed, after the village samples were divided by sex and hybrid status. The results generally showed Point Hope and Wainwright as highly significantly different from each other, both were significantly removed from the three-village cluster of Barrow/Barter Island/Anaktuvuk Pass.

The results were interpreted on the basis of evolutionary processes and Eskimo cultural history. First of all, because there was no direct or even circumstantial evidence, the processes of mutation, selection, and nonrandom mating were initially removed from consideration. Gene flow and random evolutionary process remained to be investigated.

For assessment of gene flow, genealogical data collected during the IBP study provided fairly good estimates for four of the villages and especially complete records for Wainwright. In brief, the family history data showed that nearly 40% of the people supplying the dermatoglyphic samples from Point Hope, Barrow, and Barter Island had some Caucasian ancestry. In Point Hope there was some American black as well as Caucasian admixture. Twenty-five percent of the Wainwright series was found to have Caucasian admixture, and no non-Eskimo ancestry was detected in the Anaktuvuk series. The degree of non-Eskimo ancestry was nearly always less than one-fourth.

Even though gene flow historically has been high in several villages, its effect upon dermatoglyphic variability was statistically significant only in the case of Point Hope. For this village, the contributing Caucasian and American black admixture apparently resulted in a marked reduction in whorl pattern frequency. To illustrate, the PII in the hybrid subsamples of both sexes was some two points lower than in the nonadmixed subsamples. This would

TABLE 5-6 *Digital Pattern Frequencies, Mean Pattern Intensities (PII), and Mean Total Ridge Counts (TRC) for 5 Alaskan Eskimo Villages, by Sex and Hybrid Status*

	No.	Digital Pattern Frequencies (%)				PII		TRC	
		Arch	Radial Loop	Ulnar Loop	Whorl	Mean	S.D.	Mean	S.D.
Male Subjects									
Point Hope									
Nonhybrid	53	2.7	2.3	33.4	61.7	16.0	3.5	157.7	52.6
Hybrid	51	2.0	2.2	53.3	42.6	14.1	3.6	144.8	51.0
Total	104	2.3	2.2	43.2	52.3	15.1	3.7	151.4	52.0
Wainwright									
Nonhybrid	91	2.7	5.6	64.2	27.6	12.6	2.9	113.5	46.8
Hybrid	26	3.1	2.7	69.5	24.7	12.4	2.5	124.3	41.9
Total	117	2.7	5.0	65.4	26.9	12.6	2.8	115.9	45.8
Barrow									
Nonhybrid	58	4.7	3.5	58.8	33.0	13.0	3.4	128.7	48.2
Hybrid	46	1.5	3.7	57.2	37.6	13.7	2.9	138.3	42.9
Total	104	3.3	3.6	58.1	35.1	13.3	3.2	133.0	46.0
Barter Island									
Nonhybrid	12	2.5	5.8	61.7	30.0	12.8	2.8	135.0	47.9
Hybrid	11	0	7.2	50.0	42.7	14.3	3.0	133.0	36.9
Total	23	1.3	6.5	56.1	36.1	13.5	2.9	134.0	42.0
Anaktuvuk Pass									
Nonhybrid	35	0.9	1.7	63.1	34.3	13.5	2.8	133.8	40.6
Totals									
Nonhybrid	249	2.9	3.9	56.1	37.2	13.6	3.4	130.3	50.0
Hybrid	134	1.9	3.2	57.5	37.4	13.7	3.2	137.6	45.7
Grand total	383	2.5	3.6	56.6	37.2	13.6	3.3	132.9	48.6

Female Subjects

	N								
Point Hope									
Nonhybrid	69	5.1	4.2	44.0	46.7	14.4	3.8	136.5	58.6
Hybrid	45	9.1	2.7	60.7	27.6	12.0	3.9	112.6	53.3
Total	114	6.7	3.6	50.6	39.1	13.4	4.0	127.1	57.6
Wainwright									
Nonhybrid	90	6.3	3.6	68.3	21.8	11.8	3.1	104.1	44.2
Hybrid	32	4.4	2.5	76.9	16.3	11.3	2.7	105.7	35.2
Total	122	5.8	3.3	70.6	20.3	11.7	3.0	104.6	41.9
Barrow									
Nonhybrid	71	3.4	3.9	56.6	36.1	13.3	3.3	130.7	50.5
Hybrid	48	3.5	2.9	54.9	38.6	13.5	3.4	128.7	42.5
Total	119	3.4	3.5	55.9	37.1	13.4	3.3	129.9	47.3
Barter Island									
Nonhybrid	4	1.7	2.5	64.2	31.7	12.3	1.3	123.8	43.1
Hybrid	12	2.5	7.5	60.0	30.0	13.3	3.4	119.3	56.9
Total	16	1.9	3.8	63.1	31.2	13.0	3.0	120.4	52.4
Anaktuvuk Pass									
Nonhybrid	36	1.7	3.9	63.6	30.8	13.1	2.8	124.6	37.8
Totals									
Nonhybrid	278	4.5	3.8	58.5	33.2	13.0	3.4	122.4	50.7
Hybrid	129	5.7	2.9	62.5	28.9	12.5	3.5	117.6	46.7
Grand total	407	4.8	3.5	59.8	31.8	12.8	3.4	120.8	49.4

89

TABLE 5-7 *Pattern Type Frequencies and Pattern Intensity Index for 5 North Alaskan Eskimo Villages*

Village	N	Pattern type (%)			Pattern Intensity
		Arches	Loops	Whorls	
Point Hope	218	4.5	50.0	45.5	14.1
Barrow	223	3.4	60.5	36.2	13.3
Barter Island	39	1.5	64.4	34.1	13.3
Anaktuvuk Pass	71	1.3	66.2	32.5	13.1
Wainwright	239	4.3	72.1	23.6	11.9

The order of the villages is based on decreasing pattern intensity; the sexes are combined.

amount to an average individual difference of two whorl patterns; on the average, an admixed Point Hope Eskimo would have four whorl patterns (and probably six loops) while the nonadmixed Eskimo from this village would have six whorls (and probably four loops). There is also an indication that nonadmixed, precontact Point Hope Eskimos were even more divergent from the remainder of the northwestern Alaskan villages than they are at the present time. For example, whorl pattern frequency for nonadmixed Point Hope Eskimos was over 60% in males (with a PII of 16) and almost 50% in females (with a PII of 14.4). These findings can be compared with those for Wainwright, at the opposite end of the range, where whorls made up only about 24% of the patterns (for a PII of 11.9) for the sexes combined.

Somewhat surprisingly, subsamples of Wainwright hybrid and nonhybrid males did not differ significantly from one another in their digital dermatoglyphics. It would have been reasonable to expect that the very low whorl frequency and low PII in this village were due to admixture from non-Eskimo sources. It should be noted again here that the genealogical records for Wainwright are extensive and particularly well documented, which would seemingly rule out any large amount of undetected gene flow that could have affected the results.

In considering the magnitude of intervillage variation, especially the marked difference between Point Hope and Wainwright (these two villages are located on the coast some 230 air miles apart; none of the other villages is located between them), any evolutionary interpretation would quite clearly implicate random processing of dermatoglyphic variables. Indeed, traditional north Alaskan Eskimo population structure involving effectively small, widely dispersed hunting bands (Milan, 1970) provided ideal conditions for the operation of random genetic drift. Furthermore, the dermatoglyphic data could be utilized as precise indicators of the manner in which random drift very probably occurred. That is, if it can be assumed that the three-village cluster of Barrow/Barter Island/Anaktuvuk Pass is presently fairly representative of an aboriginal Alaskan Eskimo dermatoglyphic "population," then Point Hope and Wainwright can be viewed as departures in opposite directions due to founder effect and/or fertility differentials (based upon chance rather than upon fitness) in generations subsequent to an initial separation and settlement. Specifically, Wainwright has apparently drifted toward a low whorl frequency while Point Hope probably initially drifted toward a high whorl frequency but more recently returned to a lower level as a result of gene flow from the outside.

SUMMARY OF PALMAR DERMATOGLYPHIC RESEARCH

An analysis of palmar dermatoglyphics showed considerable variation among the five Alaskan villages, just as did digital prints. However, the digits and palms did not completely correspond in the way in which villages were found to be associated by their degree of dermatoglyphic similarity. To illustrate, Wainwright males were rather distinct in their palmar variables, as they were in their digital variables. On the other hand, Barter Islanders turned out to be the most different from the other groups in terms of their palmar variables, whereas in digital features they closely resembled the people of Barrow and Anaktuvuk Pass. In attempting to explain the distinctiveness of Barter Island palmar dermatoglyphics it is possible, of course, to once again invoke random evolutionary processes, particularly the special case of "founder effect." Barter Island is predominantly composed of former residents of Barrow, but the small village might not be a representative sampling of the Barrow dermatoglyphic community. For this explanation to be valid it would be necessary also to assume that random processing had occurred in different directions for the palmar and digital traits, since Barter Island is not very different in digital traits. Likewise, Wainwright and Point Hope are the two villages in which drifting had apparently occurred in the digital but not the palmar traits. Unfortunately, little is known regarding the genetic-environmental interactions between digit and palm dermatoglyphic expression (see Mavalwala, 1966).

The palmar multivariate analysis detected a patterning of variation among villages which was not apparent in the digital prints (see Table 5-8). The generalized distance analysis in Table 5-8 was based on sixteen palmar variables including pattern types, main-line termination, a-b and c-d ridge

TABLE 5-8 *Mahalanbois' D^2 Values Between Pairs of Alaskan Eskimo Villages, by Sex*

Village comparison	D^2 Value Female	D^2 Value Male
Wainwright X Point Hope	0.5[*]	1.1[*]
Wainwright X Barrow	0.5[*]	0.4[*]
Wainwright X Anaktuvuk Pass	0.4	1.2[*]
Point Hope X Barrow	0.7[*]	0.3[+]
Point Hope X Anaktuvuk Pass	0.3	0.6[+]
Barrow X Anaktuvuk Pass	0.2	0.6[+]
Barter Island X Wainwright	2.4[*]	1.1[*]
Barter Island X Point Hope	2.9[*]	1.6[*]
Barter Island X Barrow	3.1[*]	1.0[*]
Barter Island X Anaktuvuk Pass	2.4[*]	0.7

Adapted from Murad (1975).

[*]Values significant at the .01 level.

[+]Values significant at the .05 level.

counts, and position of the axial triradius. *With the exception of Barter Island,* it can be seen that females from different villages tended to be alike, while males from different villages tended to differ from one another. This finding was interpreted as evidence of a historical pattern of residence and migration in Eskimos whereby a newly married couple initially resided with the wife's father (generally until the birth of their first child) and later joined the husband's father's camp or hunting band (Graburn and Strong, 1973:158-159). Under this custom there would be a tendency toward greater similarity among females from different villages, and correspondingly the patrilocal residence pattern would tend to promote greater distinctiveness between males from different villages. This finding of more homogeneous women and heterogeneous men across villages was also observed in the anthropometric data (Jamison, 1972).

The D^2 values for palmar traits given in Table 5-8 also indicate that there is currently no marked biological distinction between interior (Nunamiut) and coastal (Tareumiut) Eskimos, as once implied (Spencer, 1959, p. 129). Indeed, Anaktuvuk Pass, now representing the sole surviving interior Eskimo community, is more similar to Wainwright, Barrow, and Point Hope than any of these three are to each other. Biological differentiation in Eskimo groups appears to have been greater along the coastline than between the coastline and the interior.

PLANNED RESEARCH FOR THE ESKIMO DERMATOGLYPHIC DATA

It appears justifiable to claim a moderate degree of success in applying dermatoglyphics toward unraveling Alaskan Eskimo microevolution. To be sure, the picture which emerges does not portray very clear historical developments or relationships among the North Slope villages. This lack of clarity is probably due to the specific evolutionary nature of dermatoglyphic variables. Since these variables have not been shown to be measurably selected upon (and in any case, the total environment is rather uniform for all of the villages), gene flow and random evolutionary processes must be held accountable for explaining variation between villages. What does emerge from the dermatoglyphic study is that models for investigating interpopulation variation might well include different classes of phenotypic variables, ranging from those known to be selected for to those which, insofar as can be determined, vary randomly and are free of environmental stresses. In the research planned, this kind of approach would be followed, by combining dermatoglyphic data with anthropometrics, seriologic data, and ethnohistorical information, in the hope that a composite, clearer evolutionary picture will appear.

A second line of research would investigate possible correlations between dermatoglyphic features and various body dimensions, such as limb and extremity size. Growth processes very likely underlie some dermatoglyphic features which are developmentally associated with other parts of the body. Finding such associations would obviously raise the interesting possibility that dermatoglyphics are not totally removed from environmental pressures, at least prior to their formation during the first four months of fetal development.

Much of the dermatoglyphic research, completed and planned, is possible only because of the combined efforts of many researchers. Such application of the multidisciplinary approach does promise the means to investigate interesting problems not ordinarily accessible to the lone researcher.

6

Eskimo Craniofacial Studies

A. A. Dahlberg, R. Cederquist, J. Mayhall, and D. Owen

Craniofacial studies for the US/IBP study included five seasons of activity in Wainwright, Barrow, and Point Hope, Alaska. Matching these studies were closely allied efforts in two areas of the Canadian Arctic: northern Foxe Basin (by Colby and Cleall) and Igloolik (by Mayhall). Similarly, studies were conducted on the Ainu of Hokkaido, Japan, by Hanihara; the Eskimo of Greenland by Jakobsen; the Lapplanders of Finland by Hedegarde, Kirveskari, and associates; and Lapplanders and other northern peoples of the Soviet Union by Zoubov.

The U.S. group pursued investigations of craniofacial growth, craniofacial morphology, dental morphology, typing of salivary samples, tooth eruption sequences and timing, caries incidence, periodontal conditions, and craniofacial measurements and development.

CRANIOFACIAL GROWTH AND MORPHOLOGY

In 1968 cephalometric X-rays on the Wainwright population were taken by a team under the direction of Dotter (University of Oregon). After 1968 the X-ray team included Dahlberg, Mayhall, Walker, and Merbs; Cederquist (1975) and Dahlberg have analyzed the data. In this study, sexual dimorphism and Eskimo population comparisons were examined, along with an analysis of the adaptive significance of the Eskimo face.

The purpose of the roentgenographic cephalometric investigation of the Eskimo population at Wainwright, Alaska, was to describe the morphology of the craniofacial area as seen in *norma lateralis*. The sample consisted of 188 individuals, 92 female and 96 male. A total of 361 roentgenographic cephalograms was used for analysis. The films were divided into seventeen separate groups and seven combined groups, according to the age of the subjects at the roentgenographic examinations. Each individual was examined one to five times. For those who were examined more than once, the interval between exposures was approximately one year. Thirty-one anatomical reference points were recorded for each film, with a Science Assessories Corp. Graf/Pen Model GP-2 digitizing system. The recorded x- and y-coordinates were transformed to punch cards, and a computer program was written for the calculation of sixty-three linear and angular measurements for each film.

Most subjects were radiographed only once or twice, and thus the results are essentially based on cross-sectional data. Longitudinal records are to a large extent hidden in each of seven age groups, except from those individuals whose examination dates fell on both sides of a group boundary. The data represent differences in craniofacial morphology associated with age within the population; certainly, individual variations in magnitude and direction of growth cannot be determined from these results. However, in order to get a general picture of the developmental sequences of the Eskimo face it must be assumed that differences in mean values between two age groups are at least approximations of the changes that have taken place in the older of the two compared groups.

When a radiographic exposure is made the image on the film shows a certain degree of enlargement of the object. To correct for this phenomenon a correction factor was incorporated in the computer program that generated the measurements. The correction factor varied for each individual exposure; it equaled the distance between the midsagittal plane and the roentgenogram at each particular examination. However, it should be kept in mind that all measurements, both linear and angular, are still projections on the midsagittal plane and do not represent true values (Bjork, 1947; Sarnas, 1959; Bjork and Solow, 1962). For some roentgenograms the correction factor was not known. In these instances a mean correction factor for that specific age was used, which introduces an error in the linear measurements. However, these errors are minimal. Furthermore, they are, in all probability, evenly distributed in the sample and thus have little or no effect when the different age groups are compared.

The thirty-two variables that were tested for significance were those judged most suitable to describe gross changes of the dentofacial region. Other measurements have been included in this study in order to allow comparisons with other, similar investigations. In an attempt to reduce the effect of introduced errors and to avoid misinterpretations of data the level of significance was set high, and thus only differences of 0.01 were considered.

One parameter, midfacial flatness, here defined according to Hylander (1972), was included in the tests of significance although it was shown that a rather large error was involved in the recording of the maxillo-zygomatic line. The inclusion was determined by the existing controversy over the significance of the Eskimo zygomatic morphology, and because, as mentioned earlier, by testing for significance only at the 0.01 level the effect of the recording error will partly be eliminated. The results show that there is a significant increase with age in midfacial flatness. This is more conclusive in males, where two variables revealed significant changes, than in females.

Two main viewpoints have been advanced to explain the adaptive significance of facial flatness: (1) that the morphological features of the flat or "Mongoloid" face are related to cold adaptation—i.e., the flat face is adapted to withstand cold climate, and (2) that facial flatness is related to function—

i.e., there is a morphological adaptation in response to functional forces that are exerted on the craniofacial structures.

The most well-known theory concerning the adaptation of human facial form to conditions of extreme cold stress was put forward by Coon et al. (1950). They suggested facial forstbite as one selective force responsible for the arctic or Eskimo face. A man with thin, bony features, especially a narrow, prominent nose, would be in danger of freezing his face. From this climatic circumstance came a type of human being with a flat face, padded with fat. However, Steegmann (1967, 1970) has rejected this hypothesis, after having conducted laboratory experiments on changes in surface temperature in the facial region. He found that malar temperature increased as face width decreased. A more protrusive or larger malar is actually more exposed to cold and also does get colder. Fatty tissue padding may protect deeper structures but permits surface temperatures to fall. Actually, it may be stated that the "European" face is better protected from cold than the arctic or Eskimo face.

The second theory relates the characteristic morphological features of the Eskimo face to powerful chewing (Hrdlička, 1910). This is associated with voluminous muscles of mastication and with the positioning of these muscles (Washburn, 1963; Hylander, 1972). Thus, the Eskimo skull is especially adapted to generate and dissipate large vertical biting forces. If facial flatness indeed increases with age, as the results of the present study suggest, it is difficult to relate it to cold adaptation. The present findings would rather tend to support the interpretation that midfacial flatness is associated with function.

In the tests of sexual dimorphism many of the measurements that show significant differences in the younger age groups do not reveal similar trends in the intermediate age groups. In the older groups a few values indicate larger dimensions of the male face but these are not as apparent as in the three youngest groups. These results may reflect a leveling-out of dimensional differences between the sexes with age. However, composite facial polygons do not support such a conclusion. They rather illustrate a consistent tendency for larger measurements in men, both anteroposteriorly and vertically. This apparent inconsistency is likely to be caused by inadequate sample sizes in the groups above twenty-one years of age.

The developmental pattern of the facial region can be summarized as follows: The face emerges from beneath the cranium with increasing age. In the vertical dimension the relative changes are greatest in the posterior facial part, while anteroposteriorly there are proportionately greater increments of the inferior area of the face, causing increasing prominence of the lower face. For the younger age ranges the patterns are characterized by uniformity. However, among the older groups, the forty- to forty-nine-year group shows smaller vertical dimensions than the thirty- to thirty-nine-year group. Males in the fifty- to seventy-five year group show less facial prominence than the forty-to forty-nine-year group. Colby and Cleall (1974), in their roentgenographic cephalometric investigation of Canadian Eskimos from the northern Foxe Basin, reported similar findings and speculated whether they could be an effect of a secular trend within the population. But they concluded that small sample sizes in their older groups was the most likely cause. The same reasoning can be applied to the present study.

Further comparison of the Wainwright and the northern Foxe Basin samples reveal that cranial base flexion appears to be similar in the two populations, as does the degree of maxillary prognathism. However, the Wainwright sample shows considerably less dental protrusion, with more upright maxillary and mandibular incisors. Colby and Cleall found the mandible to be moderately retrognathic in their study. The Wainwright sample, on the other hand, shows a well-developed and forward-positioned lower jaw; a finding which is consistent with anthropometric descriptions of Eskimo mandibular morphology (Hrdlička, 1930; Oschinsky, 1964). In both the Wainwright and the northern Foxe Basin samples the gonial angle was observed to become less obtuse with increasing age, even in the adults, which is not in agreement with the statement that in adult age, provided no extensive tooth loss occurs, the size of the gonial angle is stable (Hrdlička, 1940). The size of the gonial angle in both samples was well within the range of what has earlier been reported for Eskimo skeletal material from Alaska, both before contact and from the middle of the last century (Cameron, 1923; Hrdlička, 1940; Dahlberg, 1968). It is difficult to use Colby's and Cleall's observations for further comparison because the total sample is included in their mean values of the various measurements, and both sexes are pooled in their facial polygons. Also, their polygons do not include scales.

The present study can be compared more thoroughly with the findings of two roentgenographic cephalometric investigations on Eskimo skeletal material, one by Hylander (1972) and the other by Dahlberg (1968). Hylander's material consisted of the skulls of thirty-three males and twenty-two females recovered from the northwest Hudson Bay area in the Canadian Arctic. This material, which is considered to predate European contact, is associated with the Thule culture and is dated approximately 1200–1600 A.D. Dahlberg's material comprised the skulls of fifteen males and twenty females from northwest Alaska and is dated about 1860 A.D. Concerning age, no information other than that the skulls were of "adults" was available for these samples. To allow comparison the three oldest groups of the Wainwright sample were pooled, men and women separately, and new means and standard deviations were calculated. Tests of significance of differences between means are based on Student's t-distribution. The level of significance was set at 0.01 and all tests were two-sided. Significant differences between means were tested for twenty-one variables between the Wainwright and the Hudson Bay samples. The results are presented in Table 6-1. Eight variables could be compared between the Wainwright group and the Alaskan skeletal material. The results

TABLE 6-1 Tests of Significance Between Wainwright Adults (Over 40) and Adult Eskimo Skeletal Material (Northwest Hudson Bay Area)

Measurement	Females				Males			
	Wainwright		Sig. (.01)	Hudson Bay*		Wainwright		Sig. (.01)	Hudson Bay*
	Mean	S.D.		Mean	S.D.	Mean	S.D.		Mean	S.D.
CRANIAL BASE									
Anterior cranial base length (sella-nasion)	67.4	4.1		64.4	2.9	67.0	2.4		67.2	2.2
Lateral posterior cranial base length (sella-articulare)	32.9	2.9		30.8	3.8	36.7	2.1	Yes	34.5	3.4
Ant.-post. diameter of frontal sinus (nasion-ethm.-sella pl.)	12.7	1.9	Yes	9.3	2.0	13.3	1.5	Yes	9.7	2.0
Anterior position of glabella	5.1	1.3		5.8	1.5	5.8	1.5		6.0	1.3
Median cranial base angle (nasion-sella-basion)	132.8	3.6	Yes	137.2	4.0	131.6	4.9	Yes	138.7	4.7
Saddle angle (nasion-sella-articulare)	125.4	3.5		129.8	4.6	125.7	5.5	Yes	131.2	3.8
FACIAL VERTICAL DIMENSION									
Total anterior facial height (nasion-gnathion)	116.6	6.5		111.5	6.5	125.8	5.2		123.7	4.6
Upper anterior facial height (nasion-spinal point)	52.3	3.8		50.4	3.3	55.2	4.6		53.7	2.5
Lower anterior facial height (spinal height-gnathion)	65.5	4.2		61.6	5.9	71.7	4.3		70.6	3.3
Mandibular corpus length (pogonion-gonial tangent point)	77.1	5.1		74.3	3.5	78.6	4.2		81.2	3.8

Mandibular ramus height (articulare-gonial tangent point)	45.6	4.6	44.6	2.9	51.3	4.5	48.7	4.2
Maxillary basal prognathism (sella-nasion-subspinale)	82.8	5.0	81.6	3.2	83.2	3.5	82.2	3.8
Mandibular basal prognathism (sella-nasion-pogonion)	80.6	3.3	78.5	2.7	81.7	3.1	78.6	3.6
Joint angle (sella-articulare-gonial tangent point)	147.5	3.5	145.1	5.0	142.1	4.8	142.6	5.7
Gonial angle (articulare-gonial tangent point-gnathion)	121.7	4.2	119.2	4.4	126.9	7.6	122.1	7.9
Mandibular plane angle (nasion-sella line to mandibular line)	34.6	4.0	33.5	3.7	34.8	5.8	35.8	5.1

DENTAL RELATIONSHIPS

Interincisal angle	131.5	8.5	--	--	137.3	13.1	151.8	5.0
Maxillary incisal axis (nasion-sella line)	101.3	5.2	--	--	99.9	6.4	95.3	11.4
Mandibular incisal axis (mandibular line)	92.5	4.7	93.3	0.1	88.0	7.3	88.8	8.5

MIDFACIAL FLATNESS

Maxillo-zygomatic line to nasion-sella line	51.9	5.9	48.3	5.2	51.1	6.8	52.4	6.3

Yes

*Data from Hylander (1972).

of the tests of significance between the means of these variables are shown in Table 6-2.

For females from Wainwright and the Hudson Bay area there is a significant difference in nasion to ethmoidal-sella plane (n-esp) distance, a measure of frontal sinus depth. This measurement is larger in the Wainwright sample. The cranial base is flatter in the Hudson Bay group, indicated by a significantly larger nasion-sella-basion (n-s-ba) angle. The nastion-sella-articulare (n-s-ar) angle, which is also related to cranial base flexion (and to anteroposterior position of the mandibular condyle), did not show significant differences. However, the test gave a relatively high t-value (2.61). For males the cranial base angle was also different in the two samples, evidenced by significant differences in both n-s-ba and n-s-ar. The skeletal material showed less flexion of the cranial base. The linear dimension of the posterior cranial base in males was also significantly different, being longer in the Wainwright group. Further, the skeletal material showed, for both men and women, less anteroposterior development of the frontal sinus. Significant difference was also found in the variable sella-nasion-pogonion (s-n-pg) between the two samples. The Hudson Bay material had less mandibular basal prognathism than did the Wainwright group.

Despite contrasting features, great similarities exist in the craniofacial area between the two groups, and the main difference for females can be summarized as increased cranial base flexion and larger frontal sinus in the Wainwright sample. In males, the Wainwright material showed more cranial base flexion, longer posterior cranial base, larger frontal sinus, and a more prognathic mandible than the Canadian Eskimo skulls. These differences are illustrated in Fig. 6-1. As there are no significant differences in linear dimensions of the lower jaw, it is suggested that the retrognathic position of the mandible in the skeletal material is due to the larger cranial base angle, which positions the articular fossae further posteriorly.

The comparison between the Wainwright group and the Alaskan skeletal material reveals no differences in maxillary and mandibular apical base position in relation to the cranial base. However, for males (but not females) the apical base relation (ANB-angle) is significantly smaller in the Wainwright sample. The Wainwright males have less facial convexity than do the Alaskan skulls of males, indicated by a significantly smaller nasion-subspinale-pogonion (n-ss-pg) angle. Both men and women from Wainwright have significantly more labial inclination of maxillary incisors than has the Alaskan skeletal material. This tendency for increased incisor inclination is most pronounced in the females; they also show significant differences in the interincisal angle and mandibular incisor inclination when the two groups are compared.

Thus this comparison indicated only a few major differences: The contemporary Eskimos from Wainwright show more incisor inclination. The Wainwright males also show less difference in maxillary and mandibular apical base relaion and less facial convexity than the male Alaskan skeletal material.

TABLE 6-2 *Tests of Significance Between Wainwright Adults (Over 40) and Adult Eskimo Skeletal Material (Northwest Alaska)*

Measurement	Females Wainwright Mean	S.D.	Sig. (.01)	Alaska* Mean	S.D.	Males Wainwright Mean	S.D.	Sig. (.01)	Alaska* Mean	S.D.
SAGITTAL POSITION OF MAXILLA AND MANDIBLE										
Maxillary basal prognathism (sella-nasion-subspinale)	82.8	5.0		83.4	3.3	83.2	3.5		84.3	3.3
Mandibular apical base position (sella-nasion-supramentale)	80.8	3.0		80.3	3.3	81.8	3.3		80.4	3.2
ANB-angle (supramentale-nasion-subspinale)	2.1	2.8	Yes	3.5	2.7	1.6	2.8	Yes	3.9	2.3
Gonial angle (articulare-gonial tangent point-gnathion)	121.7	4.2		125.5	6.1	126.9	7.6		125.8	6.7
DENTAL RELATIONSHIPS										
Interincisal angle	131.5	8.5	Yes	149.5	10.3	137.3	13.1		147.5	10.2
Maxillary incisal axis (nasion-sella line)	101.3	5.2	Yes	90.7	8.3	99.9	6.4	Yes	93.0	6.4
Mandibular incisal axis (mandibular line)	92.5	4.7	Yes	85.5	7.7	88.0	7.3	Yes	84.5	8.3
TOTAL FACIAL FLATNESS										
Profile angle (nasion-subspinale-pogonion)	4.7	6.2		8.8	7.3	3.4	5.7	Yes	9.6	7.1

*Data from Dahlberg (1968).

101

┌2.54 cm.┐

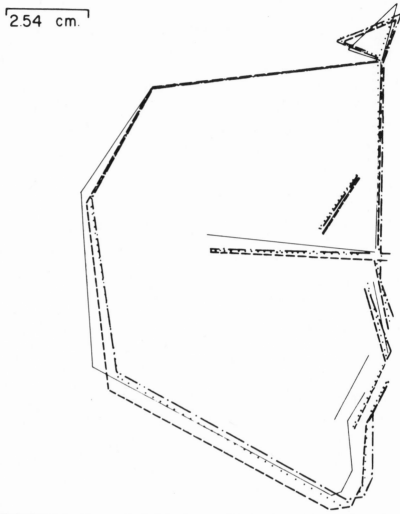

FIGURE 6-1. *Composite facial polygon with superimposition on the nasion-sella line and registered at sella. Solid line, Hudson Bay skeletal material for men (approximation based on Hylander, 1972); broken line, Wainwright men, ages 50 to 74 years, 11 months; broken line with dots, Wainwright men, ages 40 to 49 years, 11 months; dotted line, Wainwright men, ages 30 to 39 years, 11 months.*

Postmortem distortion of the cranial base of the Hudson Bay skulls might have occurred. Such distortion would have the effect of opening up the cranial base angle and thus placing the articular fossae and mandible further posteriorly. It is surprising that in these skulls, as indicated in Fig. 6-1, there is a distance of several millimeters between the maxillary and mandibular incisor tips. Hylander indicated that this distance is 6.5 mm. measured along a line parallel to the sella-nasion line, and it can be considered a measure of dental overjet. However, the possibility of such postmortem distortion is not mentioned by Hylander and thus can probably be ruled out.

The increased cranial base flexion in the contemporary Wainwright population may be due to admixture. Wei (1968), in a roentgenographic cephalometric study of adult Chinese, found a mean saddle angle of $122°$ in females and $123.9°$ in males. Bjork (1947, 1951) has shown a saddle angle of $123°$ in twenty-one- to twenty-two-year-old Swedish men. Within his data those individuals with a less obtuse cranial base also indicate a tendency toward decreased dental horizontal overbite. It is conceivable that this phenomenon is reflected in the Wainwright sample—i.e., increase in cranial base flexion resulting in more pronounced mandibular basal prognathism. Simultaneously, labial inclination of the anterior teeth has increased, as shown in the comparison between the subjects from Wainwright and the Alaskan skeletal material.

That similar results were not obtained when the Hudson Bay material was used for comparison may be explained by the fact that Hylander's values for interincisal angle, maxillary incisor to sella-nasion line, and mandibular incisor to mandibular line were based on only two, five, and seven skulls, respectively. One may speculate about the possibility that with changes in the use of the dentition, in types of foodstuffs, and in ways of preparing food (Waugh, 1937), fewer functional forces are exerted on the contemporary Eskimo anterior dentition, which thus fails to upright with age to the same degree as seen in the skulls.

In this connection the nutritional aspect of the Eskimo diet and its influence on skeletal growth and development should also be considered. The major portion of the native diet is obtained from seal, walrus, whale, caribou, and fish. This diet is extremely high in protein but low in carbohydrate (Krogh and Krogh, 1913). It is also rich in vitamins A and D and in the B-complex (Høygaard, 1940). The intake of calcium shows seasonal variations, usually being too low in the winter (Høygaard, 1940; Scott, 1956). Vitamin C also varies considerably, being sufficient in the summer but very low in the winter, when the consumption of stored food is high.

The native diet seems to be sufficient to satisfy the basic energy, vitamin, and mineral requirements, with the possible exceptions of vitamin C and calcium. In spite of the low intake of vitamin C, Høygaard (1940) reported that severe scurvy is unknown among Eskimos. However, in the springtime "sub-scurvy" could occur, indicated by, for instance, gingivitis. Høygaard also reported that rickets was very rare among Eskimos. A reason for this is probably the fact that infants suckle until they are two or three years old. But he also observed that infantile cramps were not infrequent among children, and he concluded that they might be due to calcium starvation. During difficult years, not only would the supply of vitamin C and calcium be low, but the total caloric requirement might be impossible to satisfy. This could cause retardation of both skeletal and sexual development (Lowrey, 1973).

It has been shown that malnutrition might cause, not only immediate or acute effects, but also permanent impairment of growth. McCance et al. (1961) and Widdowson and McCance (1964) have shown severe retardation of the growth of the facial skeleton as an effect of malnutrition in the pig. The mandible tended to be more affected than the maxilla. Growth was permanently retarded as a result of undernutrition early in life. No matter how adequate the nutrition after this critical period, complete recovery did not take place. If the pigs were undernourished after the neonatal period, the growth rate decreased but complete recovery was possible.

Today, probably no Eskimos subsist exclusively on native diet. Practically every Eskimo family has some source of cash income, and can thus rely more or less on imported foods, especially during the winter. Doing so insures against the worst consequences of famine, and the diet of modern-day Eskimos appears to have no nutritional disadvantages (Scott, 1956). However, the dependence on imported foods has been made responsible not only for a sharp increase in dental caries, but also for an increase in irregularities of the teeth and a decrease in jaw size (Waugh, 1937; Hooton, 1937; Klatsky, 1948). The comparison in the present study between the Wainwright sample and the skeletal material failed to show such a reduction in jaw size. The reduction may be limited to the alveolar process, with the consequence of more tooth crowding. A more important consequence of more imported food in the diet is that there will be less occlusal and interproximal wear of the teeth, which earlier was a significant adjusting mechanism for proper alignment of the teeth.

In summary, tests of significant sexual dimorphism within the combined age groups revealed:

1. great similarities in shape of the craniofacial complex in males and females;
2. differences in size of the craniofacial area, in that all linear measurements were greater in males than in females, resulting in a larger male face both vertically and in depth;
3. more dental protusion in females than in males;
4. greater anteroposterior differences in maxillary and mandibular apical base relation in younger men (although in the older groups the tendency is reversed, the differences are not significant);
5. a tendency for males to show more midfacial flatness than females; and
6. a degree of total flatness that is similar in both sexes.

The most notable changes that occur with age were found to be:

1. an increase in all linear dimensions for both males and females;
2. an increase in the posterior facial height relatively greater than the anterior facial height, causing an anterior rotation of the mandible (this phenomenon is more pronounced in men than in women);

3. an increase in mandibular basal prognathism and mandibular base position, in both sexes;
4. a reduction in apical base relation (ANB-angle) in both sexes;
5. a reduction in horizontal overbite (overjet) in both sexes;
6. a decrease in the gonial angle's obtuseness, in both sexes;
7. a decrease in the axial inclination of maxillary and mandibular incisors in males; and
8. an increase in the degree of midfacial flatness and total facial flatness, in both sexes.

The craniofacial morphology of the adults in the Wainwright sample was also compared with craniofacial data from roentgenographic cephalometric studies on two series of adult Eskimo skeletal material, one from northwest Hudson Bay area, dated as precontact (Hylander, 1972), and the other of skulls from northwest Alaska, dated 1860 A.D. (Dahberg, 1968).

The Wainwright Eskimos and the skeletal material showed great similarities in craniofacial morphology—e.g., degree of maxillary prognathism, degree of midfacial flatness, and most linear dimensions. However, some distinguishing features were also observed:

1. The contemporary Wainwright adult Eskimos have less obtuse cranial bases, and the Wainwright males have longer posterior cranial bases than do males in the skeletal material.
2. There is apositional difference in the mandible; it is more retrognathic in the skeletal material.
3. The difference in maxillary and mandibular apical base relation is less in the Wainwright Eskimos.
4. The Wainwright group shows more labial inclination of maxillary and mandibular incisors than do the Alaskan skulls.
5. The anteroposterior dimension of the frontal sinus is greater in the Wainwright group than in the Hudson Bay material.

MEASUREMENTS

For all teeth except the maxillary second premolars, the mesiodistal crown diameters (see Tables 6-3 and 6-4) of the Wainwright Eskimo males are larger than those of Wainwright females. In the maxilla, except for the first molars, no significant differences are indicated. Significant differences exist between the sexes in the first molars, both in the maxilla and the mandible.

The Alaskan Wainwright Eskimos have larger mesiodistal crown diameters in each tooth than occurs in American whites. In addition, the differences between mean mesiodistal crown diameters of Wainwright Eskimos and Aleuts were calculated for males and females separately; large differences were found. The teeth of Alaskan Wainwright Eskimos are larger than are those of

TABLE 6-3 *Mesiodistal Crown Diameters of the Permanent
Mandibular Teeth of Alaskan Wainwright
Eskimos (mm)*

Tooth	Mean	N	S.D.	S.E.
		FEMALES		
I 1.	5.61	64	0.42	0.05
I 2.	6.41	64	0.43	0.05
C	7.16	56	0.37	0.05
P 1.	7.27	35	0.55	0.09
P 2.	7.26	34	0.56	0.10
M 1.	11.20	38	0.76	0.13
M 2.	11.17	10	0.90	0.28
		MALES		
I 1.	5.62	59	0.54	0.07
I 2.	6.56	56	0.56	0.07
C	7.49	50	0.45	0.06
P 1.	7.62	45	0.45	0.07
P 2.	7.43	39	0.52	0.08
M 1.	11.85	33	0.63	0.09
M 2.	11.62	16	0.93	0.26

the Aleuts in both sexes. The Alaskan Wainwright Eskimos also have larger mesiodistal crown diameters in both sexes than do the Japanese.

INTERMAXILLARY RELATIONSHIPS

A very high percentage of the entire population seems to possess a genetic trait involving the relationships of the jaws so that in effect the lower jaw protrudes unusually (mandibular prognathism); this factor becomes a problem in the construction of dentures. In young individuals it also presents an orthodontic problem peculiar to Eskimos. For many of the children as young as

TABLE 6-4 *Mesiodistal Crown Diameters of the Permanent Maxillary Teeth of Alaskan Wainwright Eskimos (mm)*

Tooth	Mean	N	S.D.	S.E.
		FEMALES		
I 1.	8.92	59	0.63	0.08
I 2.	7.56	55	0.60	0.08
C	8.21	36	0.43	0.07
P 1.	7.72	39	0.48	0.08
P 2.	7.10	30	0.47	0.09
M 1.	10.75	49	0.73	0.01
M 2.	9.97	18	0.57	0.14
		MALES		
I 1.	9.04	56	0.63	0.08
I 2.	7.61	48	0.74	0.11
C	8.25	46	0.54	0.08
P 1.	7.63	36	0.51	0.09
P 2.	7.29	30	0.54	0.10
M 1.	11.20	36	0.74	0.12
M 2.	10.22	21	0.73	0.16

two and three years of age it was discernible that an edge-to-edge bite of Classic II malocclusion existed.

MORPHOLOGY OF THE DENTITION

Morphologically, the teeth of the Wainwright Eskimos are similar to those of other Mongoloid groups such as American Indians and Asiatics, but differ markedly from those of whites and blacks. Shovel-shaped incisors are in great evidence. The protostylid is in evidence in various categories of expression, particularly the undulating-surface type, which are almost all bilateral. In several instances, unilateral barrel-shape upper lateral incisors are to be found in the population, as well as two cases of bilateral occurrence. Carabelli's cusps are quite general but only in the very small expression type, frequently represented only by furrows. Two individuals showed enamel pearls bilaterally in the upper second premolars.

ORAL EPIDEMIOLOGY

During July of 1968 all available residents of Wainwright, Alaska, were examined for evidence of oral pathologic conditions and oral hygiene in addition to the other dental procedures reported here. A summary of dental caries rates for this group has been published earlier (Mayhall et al., 1970a), but in that report results for both sexes were combined. Another report presented the results of an examination for torus mandibularis (Mayhall et al., 1970b).

The examination for dental caries was made with a mirror and explorer aided by a battery-operated spotlight. No radiographs were available. In order to summarize the total caries experience of the population, Table 6-5 combines decayed and filled permanent and deciduous teeth, but only permanent teeth are included in the category of missing teeth. Inspection of this table reveals the efficacy of the U.S. Public Health Service's priorities of dental treatment. The US/PHS has concentrated upon school-age children for the last ten to fifteen years, and that is reflected in the relatively low rates of decayed teeth in the under-twenty age groups. It can also be seen that the number of filled teeth is large in the eleven to twenty and twenty-one to thirty groups, indicating a large amount of dental treatment in the past. However, this latter group (twenty-one to thirty) now has a high number of decayed teeth, indicating that preventive measures employed earlier have lost their effectiveness.

The number of missing teeth reaches appalling proportions at an early age. The low rates for periodontal disease (Table 6-6) would indicate that the vast majority of the missing teeth are the result of caries. There is no doubt that dental caries is the most prevalent disease in this group. The oldest male Eskimo who is caries-free is only six years of age, while the oldest female is only three. Of those over the age of thirty, twenty-three are edentulous.

In both the males and females the peak of caries involvement occurs in the twenty to thirty age group, with a leveling-off in later years in the females and a drop in the decayed, missing, and filled teeth in the males. This latter drop is indicative of dietary changes: the younger population consumes high proportions of cariogenic food, and the older people show less exposure to this type of food, subsisting primarily on "native" food.

The dietary effects on the rates of dental caries in Eskimos have been demonstrated by Russell et al. (1961), Bang and Kristoffersen (1972), Mayhall (1970) and Möller et al. (1972). The first two of these studies were conducted in Alaska and showed conclusively that a change from a diet of

TABLE 6-5 *Caries Experience in Wainwright, Alaska, Eskimos (Decayed, Missing, and Filled Teeth per Individual)*

Age	N	Decayed	Missing	Filled
MALE SUBJECTS				
0-10	37	3.27	0.11	1.59
11-20	22	1.59	1.41	7.82
21-30	8	6.38	11.00	8.25
31-40	13	2.62	14.85	1.62
41-50	10	1.10	16.70	1.00
50+	16	2.19	20.12	0.94
Av.		2.71	7.59	3.24
FEMALE SUBJECTS				
0-10	44	3.73	0.16	1.84
11-20	28	1.32	1.75	10.53
21-30	9	3.67	15.00	6.11
31-40	15	2.60	19.40	2.13
41-50	3	5.67	14.33	2.67
50+	13	0.31	25.46	0.62
Av.		2.63	7.64	4.28

locally available food to a diet of commercially processed food results in an increase in the caries rate. The same general trends have been seen in the Northwest Territories of Canada (Mayhall, 1970) and Greenland (Möller et al., 1972).

The examination for periodontal disease utilized the procedures outlined by Russell (1956) but without the aid of radiographs. The Periodontal Index is a weighted index ranging from 0, or no disease, to 8, indicating severe manifestations of periodontal involvement. In this survey, each tooth was examined. The resultant score for each patient is a mean score for these teeth. As Table 6-6 shows, periodontal disease is extremely rare in all age groups in

TABLE 6-6 *Periodontal Indices of Wainwright, Alaska,*
            Eskimos

Age	Male Subjects		Female Subjects	
	N	Indices	N	Indices
0–10	21	0.02	34	0.01
11–20	21	0.06	28	0.03
21–30	8	0.02	8	0.08
31–40	11	0.40	13	0.10
41–50	7	0.97	3	0.15
50+	10	0.54	4	0.02

Wainwright. The great majority of patients evidenced only a slight gingival inflammation around single teeth.

These results are surprising in light of the results from other studies of Alaskan Eskimos. Kristoffersen and Bang (1973) reported a much higher level of the disease in 1973, after reporting a low level in 1957. Russell et al. (1961) also noted higher levels, which may indicate that the criteria utilized in this study were different from those of the other studies. However, a comparable study of Canadian Eskimos (Mayhall, 1976) demonstrated higher levels in the less acculturated Foxe Basin people. On the basis of two examinations, four years apart, there was no significant increase in disease levels in the Canadian Eskimos, although there had been a marked shift in diet toward processed food and away from the native foods. An earlier sectional study of the same Foxe Basin groups, in which the subjects were divided into groups according to their dietary intake, failed to reveal significant differences in periodontal disease (Mayhall, 1970).

Greene and Vermillion (1960) proposed a simple system for quantifying the amount of soft debris and supragingival calculus on the teeth in order to examine oral hygiene. This system records the number of thirds of the tooth covered by these two contaminants. We recorded this for both the buccal and lingual surfaces of each tooth present and then divided by the number of surfaces examined, to arrive at the debris and calculus indices in Table 6-7. As noted earlier, a similar study was made in Canada (Mayhall, 1976) and the comparisons are interesting. In Wainwright there was three to four times more debris on the teeth, while the calculus deposition was comparable with the Canadian Eskimo values.

As might be expected, the calculus deposition increased in intensity with age but never obliterated as much as one-third of the tooth crown. This finding may partially explain the low periodontal disease rate, as calculus is one

TABLE 6-7 *Oral Hygiene of Wainwright, Alaska, Eskimos*

Age	N	Calculus Index	Debris Index
MALE SUBJECTS			
0–10	22	0.0	1.00
11–20	21	0.01	0.71
21–30	8	0.36	0.69
31–40	11	0.82	1.31
41–50	7	0.87	1.30
50+	10	0.74	0.90
FEMALE SUBJECTS			
0–10	34	0.0	0.64
11–20	28	0.0	0.75
21–30	8	0.12	0.73
31–40	13	0.55	0.86
41–50	3	0.45	0.66
50+	4	0.88	0.82

of the contributors to periodontal breakdown. The debris rates, while higher than in the Canadian group, are not extremely high. Here again, these levels may help to explain the periodontal indices.

In summary we can say that the Eskimos' primary problem with their teeth is the onslaught of dental caries. A disease that was unknown to the Eskimos only a few decades ago, now may be the most prevalent disease in Arctic populations. While it is impossible to ascribe an exact cause, there can be no doubt that the great change in diet of the Eskimo has been a major element. Studies from throughout the Arctic over the past twenty years have conclusively shown that the diet of the southern resident is ill-suited to the Eskimo dentition, perhaps because of the unique shape of the Eskimos' teeth (Mayhall, 1972) which contain a number of built-in food traps.

While the Wainwright Eskimos do not as yet show high levels of periodontal disease, it will probably be only a short time before they reach the levels seen in some other Alaskan Eskimos. This process may be beginning now, with the deterioration of the oral hygiene of these people. The Eskimo of a few years ago with his legendary good, strong teeth is now being replaced by one with large numbers of missing or diseased teeth, certainly not a trend that public health officials would like to see continue.

SALIVA ANALYSIS FOR SECRETION OF
BLOOD GROUP SUBSTANCES

Saliva samples in quantities of 10–15cc were obtained by David Owen from 221 individuals from Wainwright who were stimulated to produce saliva by chewing wax. The saliva was boiled for 15 min, and then centrifuged, the opalescent fluid was decanted and frozen. Antiserums were tested by trial runs on saliva from secretor and nonsecretor individuals of known ABO blood groups.

Twenty specimens plus four controls were tested in each series. Anti-A and anti-B serums were diluted with 0.9T saline to a 1:10 titer. For each specimen, one drop of diluted anti-A serum and one drop of saliva were placed in one tube, and one drop each of anti-B serum and saliva placed in a second tube. One drop of anti-A serum was placed in each of two of the control tubes. To one was added one drop of saline, to the other a drop of group-specific AB substance. The two remaining control tubes contained one drop of anti-B serum each; to one was added one drop of saline, and to the other one drop of group-specific AB substance.

The tubes were shaken and incubated at room temperature for 30 min. Two drops of a 2% suspension of A_2 cells were then added to the specimen and control tubes containing anti-A serum. Similarly, two drops of a 2% suspension of B cells were added to the tubes containing anti-B serum. The tubes were shaken and incubated at room temperature for 1 hr, centrifuged lightly, and read.

Tests for blood group O were run concurrently. Anti-H serum was diluted to a titer of 1:10. One drop was added to a control test tube containing one drop of saline, and one drop to each of twenty tubes containing one drop of saliva. The tubes were shaken, and incubated for 30 min at room temperature. Two drops of a 2% suspension of O cells were then added to each tube and they were incubated at room temperature for 1 hr, centrifuged lightly, and read for agglutination.

Double determinations were run on all tests showing weak agglutinations, and later, a third determination was done in the six cases which did not agree with field blood-typing data. All 221 specimens were from secretor individuals; 55.6% belong to group A, 31.7% to group O, 7.7% to group B, and 5.0% to group AB.

SUMMARY

The oral structures of the Eskimo are fundamentally Mongoloid with elements of admixture in evidence in the modern population, plus some local specialization of some traits due to small, inbred groupings. These characteristics are not of sufficient extent or prominence to have been of any significance in the survival of the natives in the Arctic. The basic Mongoloid features of the cingulum, shovel-shape character, and size are sufficient in all the known populations of Asia to have been of major good function in the northlands.

The measurements, growth and development data, and information on function, wear, morphology, and physiology of the dentitions and craniofacial structures are of great value in comparative studies and in their analysis and use in epidemiological and health programs of the circumpolar people.

7

Biochemical Variation: The Development of Biochemical Normal Ranges for Eskimo Populations

Ronald H. Laessig, Frank P. Pauls, Toni A. Paskey, and Thomas H. Schwartz

An individual's serum biochemical parameters—i.e., his glucose, urea nitrogen, or alkaline phosphatase levels—are often used as an index of health or a valuable diagnostic indicator of possible disease. Because most physicians do not have available specific biochemical norms for each person, his or her test results, particularly biochemical screening data, are referenced to population *normal values* for interpretation. The individual's results are interpreted as being "normal" (healthy) or "abnormal" (indicative of a possible disease state). Consequently, the question "What is the range of normal;" is of critical importance. Typically, such "normal ranges" are developed for general populations, often by the manufacturer of an instrument or test kit used for the determination or by the original developer of the procedure. Much of the current automated testing technology in clinical chemistry and the associated literature implies normal ranges presumably derived from "typical" or representative populations. For many types of instrumentation in the United States and Europe, ranges are derived from Caucasian adults.

In this study we evaluate apparent normal ranges for three Alaskan Eskimo village populations sampled during the International Biological Program. The normal ranges so developed are referenced for comparison to Wisconsin populations matched for age and sex, including children. The purpose is twofold: to derive specific Eskimo population normal ranges, and possibly to evaluate, via the tests, the health status of the Eskimo population.

MATERIALS AND METHODS

Blood samples were collected by one of the authors (FPP) on site in three locations (Wainwright, Point Hope, and Barrow) during the summer of 1968-

114

71. These samples were obtained by venipuncture using 15-ml evacuated blood-drawing tubes (Vacutainers, Becton-Dickinson Company, Rutherford, N.J.). The blood was allowed to clot for 30–60 min and then centrifuged, and the serum separated. The serum was then placed in plastic vials, sealed, and stored under liquid nitrogen. Serums so obtained were air-shipped to Wisconsin (State Laboratory of Hygiene, University of Wisconsin, Madison) for biochemical analysis. The shipping/storage technique is fully described and evaluated in Laessig et al. (1972). Biochemical analyses were performed on the Technicon SMA 12/60 Auto Analyzer (Technicon Instruments Corporation, Tarrytown, N.Y.). The instrument performs twelve determinations (calcium, inorganic phosphorus, urea nitrogen, uric acid, cholesterol, total protein, albumin, total bilirubin, alkaline phosphatase, lactic acid dehydrogenase, glutamic oxaloacetic transaminase, and creatinine) at the rate of sixty specimens per hour. Test methodologies are further described below.

All tests on both Eskimo and Wisconsin populations were performed on the same analyzer in the same laboratory. The analysis service is part of the State of Wisconsin, Department of Health and Social Services, Multiphasic Screening Program (Laessig et al., 1970; Schwartz et al., 1972). By producing all data in a single laboratory, and on a single instrument, the homogeneity (and hence population intercomparability) of the data is enhanced. While this approach is not an assurance of absolute accuracy (freedom from bias) the control of precision is achieved over the period of the study. This factor is critical for deciding the presence of *inter-* or *intra*population age-sex differences or trends, especially over the three-year period of the study. Routine *inter*laboratory quality control procedures indicate no significant differences between this system and other, similar analyzers; hence, accuracy may also be inferred.

Test Methodologies

All tests were performed on an SMA 12/60 instrument. In the following citations, page numbers reference the Technicon Manual (T-70-135) for each test.

Ca^{++}-Dye (Calcium); SMA, p. 5-1; cresolphthalein complexone.
IP (Inorganic Phosphorus); SMA, p. 12-1; phosphomolybdic acid.
UN (Urea Nitrogen); SMA, p. 4-1; diacetyl monoxime.
UA (Uric Acid); SMA, p. 18-1; phosphotungstic acid.
Chol (Cholesterol); SMA, p. 8-1; Liebermann-Burchard.
TP (Total Protein); SMA, p. 17-1, biuret.
Alb (Albumin); SMA, p. 2-1; HABA dye.
TB (Total Bilirubin); SMA, p. 16-1; diazosulfanilic acid.

AP (Alkaline Phosphatase); Orthophosphoric monoesterphosphodyrolase 3.13.1; SMA, p. 3–1; p-nitrophenyl phosphate.

LDH-UV (Lactic Acid Dehydrogenase); L-lactate: NAD oxidoreducatase, 1.1.1.27; SMA, p. 13–1; tetrezolium.

GOT-UV (Aspartate Aminotransferase); L-aspartate: 2-oxoglutarate amino transferase 2.6.1.1; SMA, p. 14–1; azoene dye.

Statistical Analysis

A technique first described by Harris and DeMets (1972) was utilized to derive the normal range from the raw data sets on each population. This statistical technique has also been used and modified by the authors (Laessig et al., 1973) for the adult Wsiconsin population. The technique corrects basic data for *skewness* and *kurtosis* in the gross populations of values for each test. Skewness, or tailing, is a phenomen encountered in some tests such as the one for aklaline phosphatase, where a few members of the population may evidence physiologically normal (healthy) values which are significantly higher than the usual statistical normals. Such outliers unnecessarily broaden the physiological normal range if it is calculated on the basis of mean ±2 S.D., or derived by selecting the central 95% of the data. Kurtosis is a phenomenon exhibited by tests with a very narrow (sharp) distribution of values. Bilirubin values (normal range, approximately 0.5–1.2 mg/dl), routinely exhibit excessive kurtosis. The Harris and DeMets technique "corrects" the raw population frequency distribution for more realistic normals by a series of mathematical transformations intended to reduce skewness and kurtosis to optimum levels. These optimized distributions are then used to calculate normal ranges, which are reported in this study.

Computer Programs

David E. Miran and William Zimmermann of the State Laboratory of Hygiene devised the computer programs utilized in this study. They executed these programs using the facilities of the University of Wisconsin Computing Center.

RESULTS

In Table 7–1 we have summarized the age-sex normal ranges found in the male Eskimo population, designated "E." For comparison we have included normal ranges for the corresponding age-sex group in the Wisconsin population "W." Table 7–2 supplies the same information for the female populations.

Calcium (CA)

The normal range for Eskimo children six to nine and ten to fourteen years old are slightly higher than for their Wisconsin counterparts. Wisconsin adults however (age fifteen and above), exhibit values approximately 0.6 mg/dl higher than their Eskimo counterparts. The trend is independent of sex, as are the ranges generally.

Inorganic Phosphorus (IP)

Ranges in both populations show strong age-dependence. Eskimo children show a slightly higher range than their Wisconsin counterparts. The trend is not sex-related, and is also present to a smaller degree in the adult groups. The test is strongly influenced by bone growth—hence the higher values in children.

Urea Nitrogen (UN)

Upper limits of normal are strongly age-dependent; a factor we observe in the Wisconsin population. The upper limit of normal near 30 mg/dl is consistently observed in the age sixty-five-plus group of both populations. However, there is a striking tendency to show considerable variance among the Eskimo children with respect to upper limits of UN. This test is dependent on protein intake—a factor which may be reflected here. Starvation and decreased or impared renal function can cause increased UN but these causes are ruled out (see Total Protein below).

Uric Acid (UA)

In adults of both populations, uric acid shows a strong sex differentiation in the premenopausal range (females show approximately 1 mg/dl lower) but no population differences. In children six to nine years old there is no sex or population difference, while in the ten to fourteen age group a sex difference already appears in the upper limit of normal data. Uric acid is the end point of purine metabolism. However, there is no dietary influence since ingestion of purine-containing foods does not affect blood levels in normal individuals.

Cholesterol (Chol)

In children's groups, with one exception, the Eskimos show a tendency toward slightly lower values (roughly 20-30 mg/dl which is independent of

TABLE 7-1 *Comparison of Normal Ranges for Eskimo (E) and Wisconsin (W) Males*

Age	Pop.	CA (mg/dl)	IP (mg/dl)	UN (mg/dl)	UA (mg/dl)	Chol (mg/dl)	TP (g/dl)
6– 9	E	8.7–10.4	4.2–6.2	6.8–28.0	1.8–5.7	123–288	6.1–8.1
	W	7.7–10.6	3.2–5.6	9.0–19.0	2.0–4.9	114–255	6.1–8.4
10–14	E	8.4–10.5	4.0–6.6	6.6–25.7	2.3–7.5	109–232	5.9–8.3
	W	7.9–10.3	2.8–5.4	7.5–18.2	2.1–6.1	102–260	6.3–7.8
15–24	E	6.9–10.4	2.7–6.0	7.0–26.0	2.9–9.5	130–237	6.3–8.2
	W	8.1–11.1	2.4–5.1	6.3–17.7	3.1–6.6	121–243	6.3–8.6
25–44	E	8.3–11.0	2.8–5.2	11.0–32.8	2.8–8.8	121–281	6.4–8.4
	W	9.1–11.3	2.4–4.9	8.8–23.1	3.9–8.8	144–334	6.5–8.5
45–64	E	8.4–10.1	2.6–4.9	11.3–31.7	3.5–9.9	142–318	6.3–8.1
	W	8.9–10.9	2.4–4.6	9.6–27.5	3.6–8.9	141–331	6.2–8.1
65+	E	8.3–10.2	2.3–4.5	12.7–31.1	4.5–8.7	131–334	6.6–8.9
	W	8.9–10.8	2.3–4.6	10.3–32.3	3.7–9.4	134–319	6.2–8.1

Age	Pop.	Alb (g/dl)	TB (mg/dl)	AP (μ/ml)	LDH (μ/ml)	GOT (μ/ml)	CRT (mg/dl)
6- 9	E	3.3-4.8	0-0.4	96-266	172-327	25-61	0.2-1.9
	W	3.9-5.3	0.1-0.9	126-288		22-52	
10-14	E	2.8-4.8	0-0.5	98-317	148-338	23-61	0.2-1.9
	W	3.9-5.2	0.2-0.9	119-310		15-47	
15-24	E	3.6-5.1	0-0.7	32-255	99-296	20-71	0.4-2.0
	W	4.1-5.8	0.2-1.2	39-295		12-52	0.8-1.5
25-44	E	3.1-5.1	0-0.5	30-151	103-317	20-83	0.7-1.2
	W	4.0-5.7	0.2-1.3	29-102	93-214	10-56	0.9-1.5
45-64	E	2.2-4.2	0-0.5	32-152	105-290	17-112	0.6-1.3
	W	3.7-5.4	0.1-1.3	31-114	93-224	11-55	0.9-1.6
65+	E	2.3-4.0	0-0.5	32-156	94-296	20-99	0.7-1.1
	W	3.6-5.2	0.1-1.3	32-128	96-215	10-53	0.8-1.7

TABLE 7-2 Comparison of Normal Ranges for Eskimo (E) and Wisconsin (W) Females

Age	Pop.	Ca (mg/dl)	IP (mg/dl)	UN (mg/dl)	UA (mg/dl)	Chol (mg/dl)	TP (g/dl)
6– 9	E	8.5–10.5	3.4–5.8	6.5–27.7	2.3–5.8	122–222	6.1–8.2
	W	8.0–10.7	3.8–5.6	7.6–17.5	2.1–4.5	109–231	6.0–8.1
10–14	E	8.0–10.9	3.7–5.9	7.1–33.5	2.5–6.2	137–241	6.6–8.3
	W	8.0–11.0	3.1–5.4	4.0–19.0	2.3–5.3	109–264	6.5–8.5
15–24	E	8.5–10.3	3.1–5.8	5.8–26.8	1.7–6.0	109–239	6.4–8.3
	W	7.9–10.3	2.3–5.4	4.2–15.4	2.4–5.4	109–316	6.3–8.7
25–44	E	7.4–10.7	2.7–5.3	6.6–24.6	2.4–6.4	126–325	5.9–8.5
	W	8.9–10.9	2.3–4.7	6.7–23.3	2.8–7.0	126–293	6.4–8.3
45–64	E	8.1–10.4	2.8–5.4	11.6–32.2	2.7–8.4	148–368	6.3–8.3
	W	9.0–11.0	2.6–4.9	9.1–26.3	3.0–7.8	154–357	6.3–8.1
65+	E	8.1–10.5	2.9–5.2	10.1–32.3	2.1–7.7	129–321	6.2–8.5
	W	8.9–10.9	2.6–4.7	9.8–27.6	3.0–8.5	153–356	6.2–8.1

Age	Pop.	Alb (g/dl)	TB (mg/dl)	AP (u/ml)	LDH (u/ml)	GOT (u/ml)	CRT (mg/dl)
6- 9	E	3.2-4.8	0-0.5	80-282	89-262	25-55	0.2-0.8
	W	3.8-5.3	0.1-0.8	126-325		21-48	
10-14	E	3.8-5.0	0-0.6	25-285	102-332	17-72	0.1-2.3
	W	4.0-5.7	0.2-1.2	9-309		12-46	
15-24	E	3.5-4.9	0-0.8	29-142	100-255	13-62	0.2-3.0
	W	3.1-5.3	0.2-0.9	39-113		11-31	0.7-1.3
25-44	E	2.7-4.7	0-0.5	18-129	76-286	17-78	0.2-3.6
	W	3.7-5.5	0.1-1.3	25-89	84-199	7-48	0.6-1.3
45-64	E	2.3-4.3	0-0.5	34-197	119-323	22-88	0.2-4.4
	W	3.7-5.2	0.1-1.0	32-116	99-224	10-48	0.7-1.3
65+	E	2.6-4.1	0-0.3	30-109	151-184	19-100	0.4-1.4
	W	3.5-5.1	0.1-1.0	36-124	105-229	10-48	0.7-1.5

sex. The Wisconsin males show a characteristic increase in cholesterol range with age, with a drop-off after age sixty-five, while the females do not—a factor claimed by some to reflect the tendency toward coronary incidents in middle-age males with high colesterol levels (speaking simplistically, they die off). The male Eskimo follows his counterpart closely but does not exhibit the characteristic drop off at age six-five-plus. Females in both populations show a characteristic progression with age. Regulation of cholesterol levels in the body is not well understood; however, the high correlation between elevated serum cholesterol in males and coronary risk is well documented.

Total Protein (TP)

The test shows no age, sex, or population differentiation. All proteins ingested are normally metabolized to amino acids and transported to the liver and to the reticuloendothelial system, where plasma proteins are synthesized. Total protein levels are markedly decreased in starvation—a situation not observed here.

Albumin (Alb)

This test shows little age or sex differentiation, although Eskimo norms are approximately 0.5 mg/dl lower than those of their Wisconsin counterparts. One discrepancy occurs in the Wisconsin female fifteen to twenty-four age group and is unexplained. Albumin is produced by metabolism of ingested protein (as above, TP) and functions primarily as a "carrier" for various insoluble constituents of the blood.

Total Bilirubin (TB)

The test for total bilirubin is a generalized test of liver function; the serum bilirubin level rises as an indicator of disease. The test is, however, very sensitive to light (UV), which causes a decrease in values. We feel the apparent marked decrease for Eskimos when compared with their Wisconsin counterparts reflects this phenomenon. Population normal-range inference should not be drawn from these data. The general absence of severe liver disease may be inferred.

Alkaline Phosphatase (AP)

Children of both populations show much higher values than adults, again reflecting bone growth. The Wisconsin children of both sexes tend to have higher upper limits of normal than their Eskimo counterparts. The adults of both populations have approximately equal normal ranges. The total alkaline phosphatase activity measured by these tests reflects alkaline phosphatase (iso)enzymes present in many organs including the intestinal epithelium, kidney, bone, liver, and placenta. Elevations are generally seen as an indication of a spectrum of possible diseases rather than as specific indications.

Lactic Acid Dehydrogenase (LDH)

We do not have sufficient data on Wisconsin children for comparison. The values in children are expected to be higher than for adults, as evidenced in the male Eskimos. The Eskimo children, however, also have higher values than their female counterparts. This sex differentiation is not expected and may indicate an incidence of some individuals with specific disease states in the population studied. LDH-related observations must be drawn with extreme care since red cell LDH values (which are 1,600 times as large as serum values) can easily distort findings if there has been the slightest hemolysis. We attach minimal significance to this finding—especially in view of the field collection and processing of specimens.

Aspartate Aminotransferase (GOT)

The two study populations show most striking differences in this test, Eskimos being consistently higher. The uniform nature of the difference (all sex and age groups) would point to a population dependence rather than to disease. Both populations show the same progression with age; small children have slightly higher values. Elevated GOT values are most often associated with liver disease and obstructional jaundice. The role of GOT and LDH in myocardial infarct is noted but not applicable to either screening population.

Creatinine (CRT)

Again, sufficient data on the Wisconsin children's population were not available. The adult Eskimo females tend to show values which are higher than expected by reference to their Wisconsin counterparts. The males do not show a similar trend. Generally there is no age or sex relationship expected for this test. The observed discrepancy for women is not explained. Creatinine levels are not affected by high protein (as is UN). This test is primarily an indicator of renal functions.

CONCLUSIONS

The normal range, the standard to which biochemical screening results as well as diagnostic test results are compared for interpretation, has in several instances been shown to be significantly different when Eskimo and Wisconsin populations are compared. Cholesterol, alkaline phosphatase, GOT, and creatinine show statistically significantly different ranges when compared by the t- and F- tests. These differences, described qualitatively in the present study, would be likely to lead to variations in the interpretations of screening test results. The importance of these differences to the individuals, with respect to initiating either costly follow-up tests or diagnostic workups, should not be minimized. The Eskimo specific normal ranges reported here, particularly as they influence the concept of "normalcy," should be of value to physicians.

The presence of severe abnormalities, particularly in the creatinine values for females, among the Eskimo population is a serious finding worthy of follow-up. The difference between children's cholesterol levels (Eskimo lower than Wisconsin counterpart) is noteworthy and interesting but of no immediate concern.

In general, the Eskimo incidence of grossly abnormal biochemical results is about that found in the Wisconsin population. This finding lends support to the hypothesis that there is no vast disparity between the general biochemical health of the populations as measured by the twelve screening tests. The study does not indicate grossly different incidence rates of the presence of an epidemic or hepatic or renal dysfunction. Still, the scope of the limited screen as well as the nature of the populations (particularly with respect to survival as influenced by the availability of routine or preventive medical care and treatment) must be considered.

8

Biochemical Variation: Carbonic Anhydrase

Mary Jane Moore

Human adaptability can be examined at two levels—the individual and the population. In both cases variation and heterozygosity are adaptive from an evolutionary point of view. Red-cell carbonic anhydrase is a vital respiratory exzyme and is an important protein in the investigation of human variation. It catalyzes the transport of carbon dioxide from the tissues to the lungs and the release of the carbon dioxide in the lungs. The enzyme's essential function in CO_2 metabolism indicates that quantitative assays would also be crucial in human adaptability studies.

There are many factors that can affect the level of an enzyme. Some of these factors, such as qualitative differences of the isozymes, and age and sex of the individuals in a population, are readily studied. Other parameters that require more information include health status, nutrition, climate, relationship between respiratory function and varying concentrations of the enzyme, etc. Genetic factors such as modifying genes that control enzyme levels may also play a part in quantitative variation.

This report will summarize work completed on the qualitative studies of carbonic anhydrase in Alaskan Eskimos, and will present preliminary findings on some of its quantitative aspects. A more detailed discussion of quantitative variation will be reported elsewhere.

STUDY POPULATION

During the summer of 1970, blood samples from Eskimos of Point Hope, Alaska, were collected by a segment of the IBP research team. The red cells were separated from the plasma and stored under liquid nitrogen according to the method of Rowe et al. (1968) until analysis.

The village census listed 350 current residents of Point Hope. The IBP team was successful in drawing blood from 181 individuals who came to the blood drawing station. Of these, 172 blood samples were sufficient for quantitative assay of carbonic anhydrase. The age and sex distribution of the Eskimo population is shown in Table 8-1. The ages ranged from five years to eighty-two years, and more than half of the sample (96) was less than eighteen years old. A relatively equal sex ratio was obtained.

Of the Eskimo population whose blood was drawn, 72% were hybrids. ("Hybrids" are defined here as those Eskimos with a known non-Eskimo in their genealogy.) The type and degree of admixture were determined by Dr. Fred Milan, University of Alaska, and Dr. Paul Jamison, Indiana University. There was a total of seventy-five hybrids, of whom nineteen were adults (eighteen years or older). Of these nineteen, twelve had white admixture; three were black-Eskimo; and four were white-black-Eskimo.

The health status of Point Hope Eskimos was ascertained by Dr. Thord Levine, University of Goteborg. He examined each individual and administered a short medical-history questionnaire. One-third of the children were suffering from an upper respiratory infection at the time of examination. Of the adults interviewed, 10% had had tuberculosis of the lung and had been treated for it. Two women were in the third trimester of pregnancy. According to the village public health aide, many women were using oral contraceptives, but no written records were available.

QUALITATIVE STUDY

Hemolysates were prepared from the blood samples and were subjected to starch-gel immunoelectrophoresis to determine if variant isozymes of carbonic anhydrase were present in the Eskimo population (see Moore et al., 1971, for description of method). Two major isozymes of red-cell carbonic anhydrase have been described, CA-B and CA-C (also referred to as CA I and CA II, respectively), and are products of two separate gene loci (Kindo et al., 1975; Tashian et al., 1968). This Eskimo population, however, did not show genetic variants of these two major isozymes.

Variants of the CA-B isozyme are rare and are found in low frequencies. To date, nine variants of CA-B have been found, in individuals from the following populations: Micronesian (Tashian et al., 1963), Filipino (Lie-Injo, 1967), Indonesian (Lie-Injo and Poey-Oey, 1970), American black (Shows, 1967), American white (Shaw et al., 1962; Funakoski and Deutsch, 1970), British white (Carter et al., 1972, 1973), and Japanese (Ueda, 1974).

Only one variant of the other major isozyme, CA-C has been reported, and this was found to be polymorphic in U.S. blacks (Moore et al., 1971, 1973). Additional surveys have shown that this variant (CA-H) also exists at polymorphic levels in African blacks (Carter, 1972; Hopkinson et al., 1974).

Other populations which have been surveyed for variants and in which none have been discovered are Melanesians of New Guinea (Tashian, 1969), Seminole Indians of Florida (Tashian, 1969), Xavante Indians (Neel et al., 1964), Yanomamo Indians (Arends et al., 1967), Lapps (Tashian, 1969),

TABLE 8-1 *Age and Sex Distribution of Point Hope*
Eskimos Studied

Age	Male	Female
5– 9	18	23
10–14	25	13
15–19	13	12
20–29	5	8
30–39	8	7
40–49	2	9
50–59	5	7
60–69	6	4
70–79	1	4
80–90	2	0
Total	85	87

Indonesian Chinese (Lie-Injo and Poey-Oey, 1970), West Malaysian aborigines (Welch et al., 1972), and Asiatic Indians (Hopkinson et al., 1974). As far as I know, no other Eskimo population has been examined for carbonic anhydrase variants.

QUANTITATIVE STUDY

The levels of the two major isozymes CA-B and CA-C were determined by the Mancini single radial immunodiffusion method (Mancini et al., 1965). Details of methodology as applied to carbonic anhydrase measurements can be found in Moore (1972). It is important to point out, however, that this method measures the amount of enzyme protein, not enzymatic activity. A high degree of reproducibility and reliability can be obtained by this method of antigen-antibody reaction.

Histograms were constructed with the data for adult individuals for both isozymes, to judge if the enzyme levels were distributed normally. By visual inspection and by calculation of the coefficient of skewness, the distribution of both CA-B and CA-C data was considered to be normal.

Sex

The average concentration of CA-B in adult Eskimo males was 10.7 mg/g hemoglobin (Hb), and in females, 10.3 mg/g HB. The average CA-C level was found to be 1.82 mg/g Hb, in both sexes. The adult population average was 10.5 mg/g Hb for CA-B and 1.82 mg/g Hb for CA-C. By analysis of variance it was determined that there was no significant difference in the enzyme levels between the sexes.

Age

The next factor that could contribute to variation of enzyme levels is age of the individual. Over half of the Eskimo population was under eighteen years old. When data for both children and adults (ages five through eighty-two years) were plotted against age, it was evident that both CA-B and CA-C levels increase from a low value at age five to adult levels during adolescence.

Several regression equations were formulated to more accurately describe the effect of age on enzyme levels. The first regression model used was the straight-line, $Y = a + bX$, where Y is enzyme level and X is age. The straight-line model was used on a series of different age groups for both male and female subjects. A significant linear regression between age and enzyme level was found in both sexes when all ages were included. The regression was also significant for the age group five to eighteen years in both sexes. It is note-worthy that the age regression of enzyme levels for the older groups was statistically insignificant—indicating that adult levels are reached during adolescence and remain the same during the rest of life.

Three other regression equations were used. A nonlinear exponential equation ($Y = \theta_1 + \theta_2 e^{-\theta_3 X}$) was chosen as the model that best explained the effect of age on the isozyme levels. The raw data of the regression analysis in Figure 8-1 show that there is a wide range of biological variability in enzyme levels among individuals of the same age. A wide range of levels also exists among adults of different ages. It is this extensive vari-ability that is probably contributing to the low coefficient of determination obtained by the regression analysis. (Coefficient of determination is the percentage of the variation in the dependent variable explained by the inde-pendent variable in the equation.) The best equation, the nonlinear expo-nential equation, had the highest coefficient of determination (31%). The CA-C data and the shape of the nonlinear exponential regression line are similar to that of CA-B, shown in Fig. 8-1.

With the exponential equation, at age five the model gives a CA-B level of 6.8 mg/g Hb and an adult level of 10.6 mg/g Hb. Therefore, at age five, 64% of the adult level has been reached. For CA-C, the level at age five is 1.34 mg/g Hb, which is 73% of the adult level (1.84 mg/g Hb). The dif-

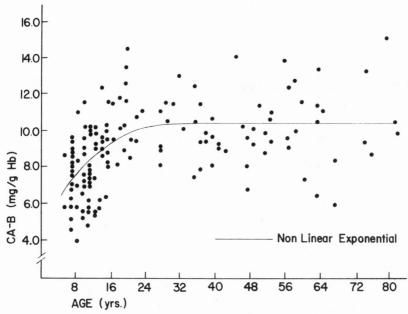

FIGURE 8-1. *Regression of CA-B levels on age in years, showing the non-linear exponential model.*

ferences in the percentages of adult levels attained for CA-B and CA-C at age five may be due to random errors, and in fact both isozymes may be increasing at the same rate with age. However, CA-C isozyme has been considered the evolutionarily older of the two isozymes and more strongly selected for because of its higher CO_2 hydrase activity (Tashian et al., 1971). Perhaps, because of its physiological "importance" over CA-B, CA-C increases faster than CA-B during childhood.

Adult levels appear to be reached during or after adolescence, or between ages eighteen and twenty-four. It is difficult to be more specific or to place too much weight on the exact age at which adult levels are attained, because there were only fourteen individuals in this age bracket (eighteen to twenty-four).

The shape of the line of the regression model chosen to illustrate the effect of age on carbonic anhydrase is similar to that of growth curves for stature. Jamison's cross-sectional data on stature of the Point Hope Eskimos (Fig. 8-2) show that at age five, approximately 65% of the adult stature is attained (62% for males, 67% for females). These percentages were obtained via a third-degree polynomial equation. It appears that carbonic anhydrase follows roughly a parallel course in development with stature. There is a steep rise in height and enzyme levels during childhood, a tapering-off in rate of increase during adolescence, and then a plateau through the adult years. Two differences between the carbonic anhydrase pattern and stature are that neither sex differences during development nor an adolescent growth spurt was detected in the enzyme concentration levels.

POPULATION COMPARISONS

During the same study of carbonic anhydrase levels of Point Hope Eskimos, two additional populations were assayed—U.S. whites and U.S. blacks. If one compares the enzyme levels of adult Eskimos (age eighteen and above) with adult whites and blacks, there are small but statistically significant differences between the populations. Results of the analysis of variance of the three populations are given in Table 8-2. Examination of the CA-B values shows that the white and black average levels are essentially the same, 11.5 mg/g Hb and 11.2 mg/g Hb, respectively. The Eskimo CA-B levels of 10.5 mg/g Hb is significantly lower. The white and Eskimo CA-C levels are essentially the same, and it is the black value of 2.08 mg/g Hb that differs significantly.

Eskimo Hybrids

Since significant population differences in CA-B and CA-C levels were found among the white, black, and Eskimo populations, it was necessary to

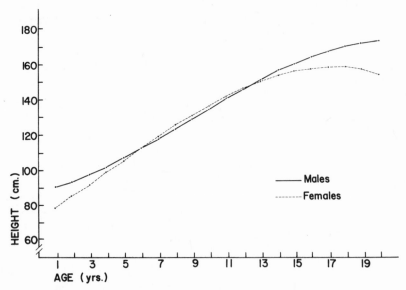

FIGURE 8-2. *Regression of height on age in years, showing both sexes.*

TABLE 8-2 *Descriptive Statistics for Population Comparisons of Isozyme Levels*

	N	$\bar{X}$ (mg/g Hb)	S.D.	Var	F-ratio
			CA–B		
White	129	11.5	1.7	2.89	$F_{(1,306)} = 1.211$
Black	179	11.2	2.4	5.98	$P = .290$
Black	179	11.2	2.4	5.98	$F_{(1,253)} = 5.704$
Eskimo	76	10.5	1.8	3.31	$P = .018$
White	129	11.5	1.7	2.89	$F_{(1,203)} = 15.998$
Eskimo	76	10.5	1.8	3.31	$P = .018$
			CA–C		
White	129	1.86	0.22	0.048	$F_{(1,306)} = 58.842$
Black	179	2.08	0.28	0.076	$P < .001$
Black	179	2.08	0.28	0.076	$F_{(1,253)} = 50.608$
Eskimo	76	1.82	0.22	0.049	$P < .001$
White	129	1.86	0.22	0.048	$F_{(1,203)} = 1.113$
Eskimo	76	1.82	0.22	0.048	$P = .293$

F-ratios were obtained by one-way analysis of variance between the populations.

examine the levels of the Eskimo individuals who were considered to be hybrid. There was a total of seventy-five hybrids, of whom nineteen were adults. The levels of the hybrid children were not compared with those of the nonhybrid Eskimo children because of the complicating effect of age on enzyme level. Of the nineteen adults, twelve had white admixture. The group of twelve had an average CA-B level of 10.6 mg/g Hb (which does not differ from the Eskimo population's mean of 10.5 mg/g Hb) and an average CA-C level of 1.92 mg/g Hb. Even though the CA-C level of 1.92 mg/g Hb is somewhat higher than the population mean (1.82 mg/g Hb), it does not differ significantly at the 5% level, using Student's *t*-test. Two other types of Eskimo-non-Eskimo associations: black-Eskimo (three adults) and white-black-Eskimo (four adults) did not have statistically significant differences in the levels of CA-B and CA-C when compared with levels of the Eskimo population.

DISCUSSION

From this study it is clear that sex of the individual does not affect the concentration of carbonic anhydrase isozymes. However, age of the individual has a marked effect upon enzyme level before puberty. There are few red-cell enzymes that have been measured systematically in different age groups as has been done in this study (Brewer, 1974). None of the enzymes that were investigated show so marked an increase with age as does carbonic anhydrase. Although the data for Eskimos do not include data for newborns, recent work has established that the level and activity of carbonic anhydrase in newborns are less than 10% of adult levels (Funakoski and Deutsch, 1971; Norgaard-Pedersen et al., 1971; Mondrup and Anker, 1975). It is tempting to suggest that the increase of carbonic anhydrase levels from birth to puberty and increase in stature are under similar hormonal control. However, there are no data to show such.

The statistically significant differences in the levels of CA-B and CA-C found between the populations are beyond the range of interassay error (0.7 and 0.11 mg/g HB of CA-B and CA-C, respectively). It is hard to attribute the population differences to a single factor. The small but significantly lower CA-B level of 10.5 mg/g Hb of the Eskimos may be linked to an elevated protein-bound iodine (PBI) level. Since CA-B concentrations are lowered in hyperthyroidism, which is accompanied by elevated PBI levels (Weatherall and McIntyre, 1967; Lie-Injo et al., 1967, 1970; Funakoski and Deutsch, 1971), plasma from the Eskimos' blood samples were used to determine PBI concentrations. The Eskimo's average PBI of 7.3 $\mu g\%$ is significantly higher than the University of Wisconsin Hospital normal value of 6.0 $\mu g\%$. Elevated PBI levels in Eskimos have been previously reported (Gottschalk and Riggs, 1952). It may be that the slightly elevated PBI level reflects a chronic increase in thyroxine which, in turn, depresses the level of the CA-B isozyme.

Since measurement of red-cell carbonic anhydrase are not performed routinely in the clinical laboratory, there are few data to link low or high levels with various physiological and pathological states. There are increased amounts of both CA-B and CA-C in emphysema, polycythemia, and pregnancy (Funakoski and Deutsch, 1971), and elevated CA-B amounts in chronic renal failure (Drukker et al., 1972). Besides hyperthyroidism, CA-B levels are also decreased in lead-exposed workers (Taniguchi et al., 1975). As far as could be ascertained, none of the individuals of the three populations suffered from any of these conditions, except for two Eskimo women who were pregnant. Schenker et al. (1972) have reported elevated CA-B concentrations in women who use oral contraceptives. This fact is probably not relevant to the significant differences in the populations, in that it can be assumed a comparable percentage of women in each of the three populations were on "the pill." Data were not available to support this assumption, however.

Quantitative studies of carbonic anhydrase in normal, healthy individuals usually involve a small number that serve as controls for a disease-state comparison. No other population surveys of Eskimo carbonic anhydrase levels have been reported.

SUMMARY AND CONCLUSIONS

Three factors—(1) presence of genetic variant isozymes, (2) sex, and (3) age—were explored as to their effects upon carbonic anhydrase quantitative variation in an Eskimo population. No genetic variants of CA-B and CA-C were found, and sex did not influence enzyme levels. Age, on the other hand, has a marked effect, with levels ranging from roughly two-thirds of the adult level at age five to maximum concentrations attained during adolescence. The relevance of the developmental pattern of the enzyme is demonstrated when it is compared to the rate of stature increase in the same Eskimo population. Even after these three factors were accounted for, there were significant differences of CA-B and CA-C values among American Eskimos, whites, and blacks. The small but significant differences may be due to environmental or genetic factors. It is not known how climate and nutrition would affect carbonic anhydrase, nor has definitive work been undertaken to study the relationship of enzyme level and respiratory function. It is possible that the differences may reflect the action of genetic factors upon a population's enzyme level response. It is becoming apparent that some enzyme systems are under partial genetic control, and it may well be that carbonic anhydrase is one of them. Future investigations hold the answer.

9

Biochemical Variation: Bone Mineral Content

Richard B. Mazess and *Warren Mather*

Measurements of bone mineral content using direct photon absorptiometry (Mazess, 1974; Cameron, 1970) have been made on Eskimos in Alaska and Canada as part of the IBP investigation of circumpolar peoples. Until recently it has not been possible to assess skeletal status by objective quantitative means, but in the last decade the photon absorptiometric method has opened up this possibility. The Eskimos, as a distinct ethnic group with a way of life and diet quite different from that of Western society, offered an interesting comparison to other North American and European populations. The results of these studies on Alaskan and Canadian Eskimos have been reported elsewhere (Mazess and Mather, 1974, 1975), and this chapter will summarize the findings.

METHODS

The direct photon absorptiometric method uses an external monoenergetic radionuclide source (^{125}I) for transmission scanning. The source and detector are passed across the limb to be investigated and the changes of the count rate when the beam traverses the bone are proportional to the mineral content at that site. The errors of precision and accuracy are about 2%. A single absorptiometric scan on a long bone is highly correlated ($r > 0.90$) with the weight of that bone, and in fact with the weight of the total skeleton (Chestnut et al., 1974; Cohn et al., 1974). Our measurements in both Canada and Alaska were made with the same portable instrument which allowed immediate digital readout of both bone mineral content and bone width. The system was calibrated in the field with the use of ashed bone sections and various standards; the calibration in the field locations remained virtually identical to that obtained in our Wisconsin laboratory.

Measurements were made on Wainwright Eskimos in 1968 and 1969 using

Supported by grants Y–NGR–50–002–051 from NASA and (11-1)–1422 from the U.S. AEC, and by the American and Canadian Human Adaptability IBP projects.

two anatomical locations on the arm: (1) the midshaft of the humerus, and (2) across the radius and ulna shafts at a site one-third of the distance between the olecranon and the styloid process of the ulna, proximal to the ulna styloid. The latter is the standard midshaft site in common use for bone mineral determination. Additional subjects were measured in Point Hope and Barrow in 1970, and additional measurements were made on the distal radius and ulna about 2 cm proximal to the tip of the ulna styloid. In 1971 measurements were made on Canadian Eskimos at Igloolik and Hall Beach. Bone scans were made at the midshaft and distal sites across the radius and ulna.

In Alaska, 413 subjects were measured of whom 217 were children (ages five to nineteen years), 89 were young adults (ages twenty to forty-nine years) and 107 were elderly (over fifty years). In Canada 335 Eskimos were measured, including 177 children, 123 young adults, and thirty-five elderly. Both sexes were about equally represented in the age groupings. Differences among the various Eskimo villages were examined and only a few scattered significant differences were found. Consequently, the village data were merged. The Eskimo data have been compared with those collected by identical methods on U.S. whites (Mazess and Cameron, 1974). In this chapter only the results on the midshaft radius are dealth with, as this site is representative of the various sites measured and it is the site for which the most comparative data are available.

Measurements on Children

Heights and weights of Eskimo children in Alaska and Canada, and of U.S. whites, are shown in Fig. 9-1. During growth Alaskan Eskimos of both

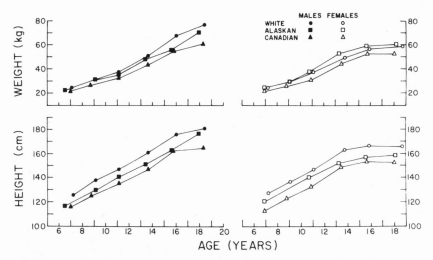

FIGURE 9-1. *Height and weight of Eskimo children and white children.*

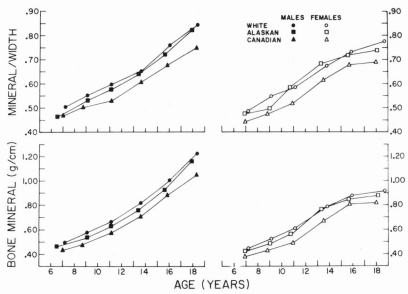

FIGURE 9-2. *Bone mineral content and the mineral-width ratio in Eskimo and white children.*

sexes were significantly shorter than U.S. white children by about 6%, while Canadian Eskimo children were about 8% shorter than the whites. Although the Canadian Eskimos were a few percentage points shorter than their Alaskan kin the differences generally were not significant. Alaskan Eskimo females were a few percentage points heavier than comparable white children, despite their smaller stature, but the differences were not significant. Preadolescent Alaskan Eskimo males were about 5% lower in body weight than whites, but again not significantly lower. The Canadian Eskimo children were about 10-15% lower in body weight than U.S. whites, and the differences at each age were generally significant.

These morphological patterns of growth were also reflected in the bone mineral content (Fig. 9-2). The Canadian Eskimo children have lower bone mineral than Alaskan Eskimos, who are in turn generally lower (5%) than U.S. whites. The differences in mineral-width ratio were even smaller.

Measurements on Adults

The Alaskan Eskimos were similar in stature to Canadian Eskimos of the same sex, and the Eskimos were in general about 7% shorter than U.S. whites (Fig. 9-3). During and after adolescence Alaskan Eskimo males are about 10% lighter in weight than U.S. whites; Canadian Eskimo males weighed about 5% less than Alaskan Eskimos and 15% less than U.S. whites. Despite the shorter

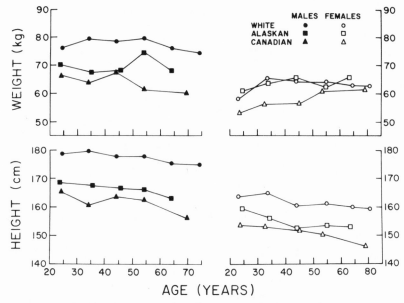

FIGURE 9-3. *Height and weight of Eskimo and white adults.*

stature of the Eskimo females their body weights were relatively close to those of U.S. white females; Alaskan Eskimo women had almost identical weights while those of Canadian Eskimo women were about 12% lower.

Canadian and Alaskan Eskimos of both sexes had very similar bone mineral content and similar age changes (Fig. 9-4). The mineral content of young Eskimo adults was most similar to that of U.S. whites (about 5-10% lower), but in the elderly the difference increased to 20%. The mineral-width ratio showed accentuation of this Eskimo-white difference. In U.S. whites and other populations it is usual to see relative stability of bone mineral until the forties in females and the fifties in males, followed by a slight loss in males and a larger loss in females. The Eskimos, in contrast, show a large bone loss with a relatively early onset.

DISCUSSION

During growth and early adulthood the Eskimos of Canada and Alaska have a relatively normal bone mineral content, but as aging proceeds there is a sharp change. Canadian Eskimos, prior to aging bone loss, have a bone mineral content about 5-10% lower than U.S. whites and this is commensurate with their smaller stature and lighter weight. In Alaskan Eskimos, body size is also smaller than in whites but bone mineral content was not reduced to the same degree. Apparently Canadian Eskimos have a normal bone mineral content

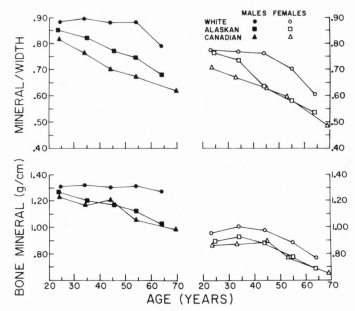

FIGURE 9-4. *Bone mineral content and the mineral-width ratio in Eskimo and white adults.*

relative to their smaller body size, and by this same reference the bone mineral content of Alaskan Eskimos may even be slightly elevated. However, in the elderly such is not the case; both Eskimo groups lose bone mineral content at an accelerated rate and the onset of bone loss is earlier than in whites.

In our previous reports we noted that the Sadlermiut Eskimo of Southampton Island showed a similar pattern of high bone loss with aging and that this bone loss seemed associated with vertebral fractures. We have also discussed the possible nutritional etiology of Eskimo bone loss and hypothesized that the high protein diet of the Eskimos, together with marginal calcium and vitamin D intakes, may be contributory. At this time, however, neither the origin nor the consequences of the large bone loss in Eskimos has been defined.

10

Nutrition Studies: The Aboriginal Eskimo Diet— A Modern Perspective

H. H. Draper

As a formula for nutritional health, modern nutritionists generally recommend a mixed diet of fruit, vegetables, cereals, meat, and dairy products. The assumption underlying this recommendation is that no single food or food group is capable of providing all the essential nutrients required for health and well-being. Yet for centuries Eskimos residing at latitudes above the Arctic Circle maintained a vigorous life-style on a diet consisting almost entirely of meat and fish.

How can this seeming paradox be explained? In one perspective the Eskimos can be perceived as belonging to the rearguard of numerous hunting societies which once populated the earth; however, most such societies received the nutritional benefits of indigenous fruits, berries, leaves, and roots. Although plant foods were available to Eskimos residing at subarctic latitudes, they were of little significance in the diet of Eskimos in the Arctic region. The remarkably restricted character of their aboriginal diet has raised the question whether Eskimos possess unique metabolic capabilities that enabled them to adapt to the all-meat regimen.

Nutritional science has demonstrated that there are no essential foods but only essential nutrients. With certain qualifications, mainly of a technical nature, the basic nutritional needs of man now can be defined in terms of discrete biochemical entities which cannot be synthesized in the body. This accomplishment makes it possible to evaluate the Eskimo diet in terms of its capacity to meet his needs for these entities. Viewed in this context, it can be concluded that the native diet, despite its lack of variety, is capable of furnishing all the nutrients essential for nutritional health, provided it is available in adequate amounts and is prepared according to traditional methods. In the historical perspective, the nutritional crises of Eskimos were mainly the result of failures in their food supply associated with the misfortunes of hunting rather than of inadequacies in the quality of their indigenous diet. That diet is evaluated in this chapter in terms of specific, essential nutrients.

VITAMIN CONTENT

The Arctic Eskimo native diet is characteristically high in protein and fat and low in carbohydrate. The "B complex" vitamins occur in animal tissues in association with enzyme proteins; hence the high protein content of the diet assures a liberal supply of these nutrients. There is no history of epidemic vitamin-deficiency diseases such as those which afflicted some cereal-based food cultures. The oils of fish and marine mammals are rich in the fat-soluble vitamins A and D. The meat diet also provides adequate amounts of vitamin K, and a recent investigation of the Eskimos' blood plasma levels of vitamin E showed that they are fully comparable to those of populations consuming a mixed diet.

The nutrition of the Eskimos with respect to ascorbic acid (a vitamin generally associated with fresh fruits and vegetables) has long held a fascination for nutritionists. In south and central Alaska, berries and green plants were harvested in the summer, and where permafrost was available berries in seal oil were preserved for use during the winter. In the northern coastal regions, however, berries were not available in sufficient amounts to constitute a substantial source of this vitamin. The rumen contents of caribou have been cited as a possible source of ascorbic acid, but studies with cattle indicate that vitamin C is rapidly destroyed by rumen microorganisms. The expeditions of early Arctic and Antarctic explorers foundered on scurvy, sometimes in spite of strict adherence to contemporary medical advice on methods of prevention. The Arctic expeditions of Vilhjalmur Stefánsson were a notable exception. The fact that Eskimos were unaffected by the disease prompted Stefánsson to condition his men to the native regimen before embarking on his explorations. Subsequently, in a celebrated experiment, he and his associate Karsten Anderson sustained themselves in good health under medical supervision for a year with a diet of meat and fat. Stefánsson's appraisal (1935-36) of the ascorbic acid nutriture of the Eskimo has successfully withstood forty years of critical evaluation, namely ". . . that if you have some fresh meat in your diet every day, and don't overcook it, there will be enough C from that source alone to prevent scurvy." This conclusion is supported by the results of subsequent experiments on the minimum requirement of ascorbic acid for the prevention of scurvy, and by analyses of Eskimo foods which have shown that some items (notably muktuk—whale blubber with skin attached) are relatively good sources of this vitamin when consumed in the fresh state.

MINERALS

Little direct information is available about the mineral content of the native diet. Since many inorganic elements (including iron, potassium, phosphorus, magnesium, and manganese) are bound to animal proteins, a high meat diet is naturally rich in these nutrients. However, meat is notably low in calcium, and dairy products (the main source of calcium in industrialized countries) were unavailable to the Eskimo until recent times. Explorers' accounts indicate that calcium was derived mainly from the soft bones of fish and the spongy portion of the bones of land and sea mammals. Recent biochemical research has elucidated a vitamin D-dependent mechanism which enables the body to adapt to a range of calcium intake by modifying the efficiency of absorption, and this mechanism undoubtedly served the need of the Eskimos to absorb efficiently the limited quantity of calcium supplied by this diet. In this respect, however, the calcium nutriture of the Eskimo was not substantially different from that of other nondairying populations.

The low calcium content of the meat regimen may be of lesser significance than its exceptionally high content of phosphorus. A high phosphorus diet, particularly when it is low in calcium, produces hypocalcemia, secondary parathyroidism, and an increased rate of bone resorption. It is of interest in this context that an unusual degree of adult bone loss has been observed among Eskimos of northern Alaska and Canada. Whether this condition is related to a high phosphorus intake (accentuated in recent years by a decline in bone calcium intake) is worthy of further investigation.

ENERGY

From an adaptational standpoint the predominant feature of the Arctic Eskimo native diet stems from its remarkably low carbohydrate content. In contrast to the modern U.S. mixed diet, which is estimated to provide 46% of calories from carbohydrate, 42% from fat, and 12% from protein, the premodern Eskimo diet contained only about 2% carbohydrate calories, the remaining energy being derived from variable proportions of fat and protein. Depending upon total caloric intake, the typical all-meat diet of adults yielded 10–20 g of glucose per day in contrast to the 250 g or more provided by the mixed diet and even larger amounts furnished by high cereal diets. The adult brain alone is estimated to consume 100 g of glucose or its equivalent per day. The central problem in adaptational bioenergetics for the Eskimo therefore was to maintain glucose homeostasis in the face of a paucity of carbohydrate in the diet.

Since glucose cannot be synthesized from fatty acids (the main constituents of dietary fat) it follows that glucose homeostasis in subjects consuming a meat diet is maintained primarily by synthesis from dietary amino acids; indeed, the biochemistry of these conversions has been well established. Given its low carbohydrate content, a high protein content therefore was an essential feature of the Eskimo native diet, since extra protein was necessary to furnish the amino acids required for glucose synthesis beyond those normally required for protein synthesis.

The low-carbohydrate, high-fat character of the native regimen is also noteworthy with respect to its influence on the composition of body fat. A high carbohydrate diet provides more glucose than can be immediately utilized by the tissues or stored as glycogen; consequently there is an active conversion of glucose to fatty acids which are stored in the adipose tissues as fat. These biosynthetic acids, which are saturated and mono-unsaturated, constitute the main components of body fat. In the Eskimo, on the other hand, lipogenesis was inhibited by a surfeit of fatty acids supplied by the diet. Dietary fatty acids, somewhat modified during metabolism and diluted by some fatty acids synthesized *de novo,* constituted the bulk of Eskimo body fat. Hence the fatty acid composition of Eskimo adipose tissue was strongly influenced by the composition of dietary fat. The long-chain polyunsaturated fatty acids typical of marine oils were prevalent in the adipose tissues of Eskimos consuming seal and whale blubber. Although runimant fats are generally characterized as being highly saturated, analysis of the fatty acids of caribou meat consumed by northern Alaskan Eskimos revealed a much higher content of polyunsaturated fatty acids (21%) than is found in the meat of modern beef animals (approximately 3%). This discrepancy is attributable to the "marbling" of beef with neutral fat, a property which has been encouraged in breeding practices as an asset to flavor and palatability. The high saturated fatty acid content generally ascribed to animal fats therefore does not apply to a diet of caribou, sea mammals, and fish. Polyunsaturated fats in native foods may have contributed to the low serum cholesterol levels of premodern Eskimos.

A subject of frequent speculation concerning the energy metabolism of Eskimos is whether they relied on ketone bodies, in addition to fatty acids and glucose, as a significant source of metabolic fuel. Under ordinary conditions fatty acids are utilized for energy production by a process involving oxidative degradation to two-carbon fragments which are combined with products of glucose metabolism and further oxidized to carbon dioxide and water (hence the biochemical adage that fats burn in a flame of carbohydrates). Ketone bodies are condensation products of these fragments which form in the liver under conditions of glucose shortage. Such conditions prevail whenever the diet is low in carbohydrate and contains insufficient protein to supply the excess amino acids required for glucose synthesis. Through processes of biochemical adaptation ketone bodies can be utilized as an alternate source of energy by most extrahepatic tissues. Recent evidence indicates that under conditions of severe glucose shortage the brain is also capable of adapting extensively to ketones for its energy requirements.

How frequently conditions conducive to ketogenesis prevailed in Eskimo dietary experience is difficult to estimate, but they seem likely to have occurred at least sporadically. In addition to dietary fatty acids, four of the twenty amino acids supplied by dietary protein are ketogenic as well as glycogenic, and another (leucine) is specifically ketogenic. It has been estimated that the capacity of the liver to metabolize amino acids as fuel is limited to about half the total energy requirement. A meat diet leads to asymptomatic ketosis and ketonuria, but this condition gradually diminishes as a result of biochemical adaptation to the use of ketone bodies for energy. Whether Eskimos have unusual adaptational capabilities in this regard is unknown.

The high protein diet also imposed on the Eskimo a need to dispose of an unusually large load of urea, a toxic compound formed during the conversion of amino acids to glucose. Animals fed high protein diets show a marked increase in water consumption and excretion, and it is of interest that early explorers commented on the high water intake of Eskimos. Evidently a feedback mechanism acts to prevent uremia under conditions of the excretion of urea.

The study of metabolic adaptation to changes in diet composition is a major theme in modern nutritional biochemistry. The current state of knowledge in this field makes it possible to characterize the basic features of biochemical adaptation to the Eskimo native diet as well as the metabolic changes necessitated by introduction of processing of foods. Discovery of the allosteric enzymes (i.e., enzymes which are activated or inhibited by substrates or products of the metabolic pathways in which they function) has provided an explanation of many rapid biochemical responses to changes in diet composition, particularly those which regulate the synthesis of glucose, fatty acids, and ketone bodies. Discoveries in the field of biochemical genetics have revealed slower adaptational phenomena which entail DNA-directed synthesis of more or less enzyme protein in response to prevailing metabolic needs. In addition to the influence of substrate supply, allosteric regulation, and genetic induction and repression of enzyme synthesis on metabolic processes, a further control is exercised by hormonal regulators.

That these intricate adaptational systems are universal is evident from the ability of all human populations to utilize the energy in diets which vary markedly in composition. The fact that the indispensable nutrients required by all populations evidently are qualitatively the same further attests to the fundamental uniformity of human nutritional needs. Nevertheless, it is still unclear whether populations habituated over centuries to a strict food culture, such as that of the Eskimo, are capable of adapting to a radical change in diet without some adverse effects. For those affected by primary sucrase deficiency, an inherited condition which appears to be unique to Arctic Eskimos, adaptation to the processed diet presents serious difficulties. Low lactase activity restricts the extent to which Eskimos can obtain from dairy products the calcium they once obtained from bones. On the other hand, the prevalence of diabetes among Eskimos remains low, even among those who have consumed a mixed diet for many years. These observations suggest that there may be numerous subtle distinctions in the biochemical adaptation of Eskimos to changes in diet composition.

IMPACT OF THE MODERN DIET

The changes in the nutritional status of Alaskan Eskimos which have taken place over the past quarter-century as a result of acculturation mirror the changes which have occurred in industrialized populations over a much longer time. The modern Eskimo has been presented for the first time with the opportunity to make significant food choices. Previously, he required no knowledge of nutritional principles in order to be well nourished. He ate a high-quality diet for one basic reason: there was nothing else to eat. Presented with an array of exotic new foods which he is unable by experience or education to evaluate adequately, he tends to choose unwisely. In general, the items he selects are below the average quality of the mixed U.S. diet and of the items they replace in his native diet.

The current nutritional problems of Eskimos arising from dietary acculturation are instructive for the rest of the U.S. population. Industrialized countries have produced a great variety of foods on the assumption that any deficit of essential nutrients in one would be compensated by surpluses present in others. Technology has contributed greatly to food preservation and safety, and has increased the number of nutritious foods available. However, it has also produced many new foods of low nutritional value. Moreover, it has made them attractive and appetizing, with the result that their consumption has increased at the expense of foods of superior quality. The prevalence of low-quality foods has created a need for consumer education to the point where, in order to be able to select a balanced diet, the public must have a better knowledge of nutrition than of any other health science.

There has been a rapid increase in recent years in the prevalence among Eskimos of those diseases which are the hallmarks of industrialized societies: obesity, cardiovascular disease, and hypertension. The hunting culture has been extensively eroded, although land and sea animals are still available and the Eskimo is better equipped than at any time heretofore to hunt them. Underemployment and the decline of hunting have contributed to a sedentary life-style. Government food programs have accelerated the erosion of the native diet culture. The nutritional status of subarctic Alaskan Eskimos today is similar to that of other segments of the U.S. population of similar social and economic status.

11

Nutrition Studies: An Appraisal of the Modern North Alaskan Eskimo Diet

R. Raines Bell and *Christine A. Heller*

To appreciate the present dietary patterns of the Alaskan Eskimo, it is necessary to understand the factors which influenced the Eskimo diet in the past. For centuries the Eskimo lived entirely from what he could obtain from his immediate surroundings. The Eskimo diet therefore varied considerably from one geographic location to another. From a dietary standpoint, the regions of Alaska inhabited by Eskimos in aboriginal times can be divided into four ecological areas, each of which provided different food staples. One such area was the northern coastal region where whale, seal, and caribou constituted the main dietary components and fish, wild fowl, and walrus were lesser ingredients. A second area was occupied by the northern inland Eskimos of the Brooks Range, who depended almost entirely on caribou to provide food and raw materials for clothing and shelter. In these two northern regions edible greens and berries contributed only minimally to the aboriginal diet.

Both inland and coastal regions can be examined in southern Alaska also. On the inland tundra of southern Alaska, Eskimos lived almost entirely on fish, whereas the coastal Eskimos of southern Alaska used considerable amounts of seal as well as fish. Both southern groups hunted small animals and wild fowl when available and they were able to gather some edible greens, roots, and berries. In all areas the Eskimo lived in a nomadic fashion, moving frequently in quest of seasonal foods.

After contact with outside civilization, the Eskimo diet changed rapidly, to the extent that today it resembles that of Western industrialized countries more than it does that of the aboriginal Eskimo. The cultural impact of modern civilization as well as the availability of outside foods have resulted in a decreased reliance on native food sources. In aboriginal times Eskimos tended to wander in small bands following the seasonal supply of food. By necessity, these groups were never larger than could be supported by the land. Within recent times, Eskimos have gathered in permanent villages surrounding government schools, post offices, churches, and stores. The populations of these villages are usually larger than can be supported by the surrounding countryside. Families no longer travel extensively in search of native food, since the children are in school from September to May. Men frequently leave the villages during the summer months for seasonal employment on construction projects and in canneries in more urban areas. This concentration of the population in small areas and its relative immobility put a stress on the local food supply.

In the course of nutritional studies conducted under the International Biological Program, information on the dietary intakes of Eskimos was obtained from residents of Wainwright and Point Hope, Alaska. Both Eskimo villages are located on Alaska's northwest coast and are accessible only by air during most of the year. The native dietary staples of Wainwright Eskimos are caribou, seal, and baleen and beluga whale; walrus, fish, and birds are lesser food items. At Point Hope the main native foods are baleen and beluga whale, seal, and fish, and minor items are caribou, polar bear, and birds. Both villages are located north of the Arctic Circle where few edible plants or berries are available.

Each village has a cooperative store which provides a wide variety of goods including a large selection of processed food items. A few families have food shipped in on their own, but most of the villagers purchase their food from the cooperative store or from one of several smaller family-operated stores. Money for the purchase of food and other material goods comes from a variety of sources. Some families receive welfare payments such as Bureau of Indian Affairs general welfare, aid to dependent children, and old age assistance as well as Social Security payments and unemployment insurance. Some men regularly seek summer employment outside the village, and there are a limited number of jobs available in the village, including health aide, school janitor, postmaster, store manager, school cook, teachers' aide, and service in the National Guard. Some cash is obtained from the sale of furs and native crafts. Food stamps are provided in both Wainwright and Point Hope to increase food-purchasing power.

During the summer of 1971 and the winter of 1972, three- to four-day dietary records were obtained from residents of Wainwright and Point Hope, Alaska. The records were collected under the supervision of one of us (CAH) with the help of assistants recruited from the village who acted as interpreter-helpers.

The intake of eleven nutrients was calculated from these dietary records, using values for processed foods taken from USDA Agriculture Handbook No. 8 (Watt and Merrill, 1950) and values for native foods from analyses carried out at the Arctic Health Research Center, Anchorage, Alaska (Heller and Scott, 1967). Calcium intakes were compared with FAO/WHO standards (1962). The intake of all other nutrients was compared with the Recommended Dietary Allowances (RDAs) set forth by the National Research Council (1974). In interpreting our results, it is important to realize that the RDAs are not estimates of requirements for nutrients, but recommended intakes designed to meet the nutritional needs of practically all healthy persons. With the exception of energy allowances, the RDAs exceed the nutrient requirements for most individuals; therefore, an intake below the RDA is not necessarily an indication of nutritional inadequacy. The contribution of native foods to total nutrient intake was calculated and the consumption of native food was compared with the data reported in *The Alaska Dietary Survey of 1956-1961* (Heller and Scott, 1967).

EVALUATIONS OF NUTRIENTS

Calories

Caloric intake data are presented by age and village in Fig. 11-1. The values indicated that 54% of the children at Wainwright and 58% of those at Point Hope consumed less than the RDA for calories. Similar values were recorded for the adults in Wainwright and Point Hope, where 65% and 59%, respectively, fell below the RDA. Comparable data were recorded during *The Alaska Dietary Survey of 1956-1961* (Heller and Scott, 1967), which indicated that 73% of the men, 60% of the women, and 72-87% of persons under twenty years of age consumed less than the RDA. Because of day-to-day variations in caloric intake, it is to be expected that a portion of the population will not meet the RDA in any one sampling period and that a similar portion of the population will consume more than the RDA during the same period. In such a case, the population as a whole has a mean intake close to the RDA and is in caloric balance. In the present survey, however, the fact that 25-35% of the population appeared to consume less than 70% of the RDA (Fig. 11-1) would suggest that a segment of this population was in caloric deficit. Clinical examinations, however, revealed no evidence of caloric deficiency, and indeed the women tended to be moderately over-

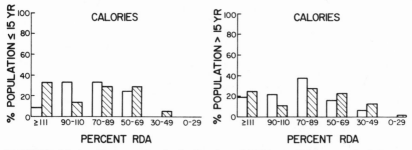

FIGURE 11-1. *Estimated caloric intake of Eskimo children and adults, as percentages of RDAs. Shaded bars, Wainwright; open bars, Point Hope.*

TABLE 11-1   *Calories from Protein, Fat, and Carbohydrate (%)*

Population	Protein	Fat	Carbohydrate
Wainwright			
Adults	25.0	43.1	31.9
Children	18.3	38.4	43.3
Point Hope			
Adults	21.6	35.5	42.8
Children	15.2	37.6	47.2

weight. Hence it must be concluded that whereas the kinds of foods reportedly consumed were probably accurate, as in many other diet surveys the amounts consumed were underestimated. Dietary records obtained by methods other than direct weighing are subject to such errors.

Table 11-1 shows the sources of calories in the Eskimo diet. In both villages the children obtained a greater percentage of their calories from

TABLE 11-2   *Nutrient Intake from Native Foods (%)*

Subjects	No.	Calories	Protein	Fat	Carbo-hydrate	Ca
Wainwright						
1971						
Males	9	42.6	79.4	47.7	0.5	27.5
Females	7	52.2	83.3	62.7	0	29.7
Children	16	23.2	55.6	30.0	0.05	6.4
1972						
Males	17	33.0	68.1	44.7	0.5	24.4
Females	15	45.5	73.2	60.3	0.9	18.6
Children	21	25.3	55.6	42.0	0.7	18.1
Average	85	34.1	66.0	45.8	0.5	19.2
Point Hope						
Males	16	23.9	62.0	25.9	0.5	10.3
Females	16	19.8	51.8	22.3	0	11.4
Children	12	8.1	22.0	12.5	0	2.5
Average	44	18.1	47.4	20.9	0.2	8.6

carbohydrates and a lesser percentage from protein than did the adults. Wain-wright adults obtained more of their calories from protein and fat and less from carbohydrates than did Point Hope adults, probably because the Wain-wright population makes greater use of native foods that are high in protein and fat and low in carbohydrates. Table 11-2 indicates that 34% of calories were obtained from native foods in Wainwright and only 18% in Point Hope. The diet survey of 1956-1961 on a selected group of Eskimo and Indian villages (including Point Hope but not Wainwright) indicated that at the time 31.7% of calories were derived from native foods. The consumption of native foods by residents of Wainwright today is as high as that in the Eskimo and Indian study villages fifteen years ago, while the consumption of native foods has decreased markedly during the past fifteen years at Point Hope.

The Alaska Dietary Survey of 1956-1961 reported that adult Eskimos and Indians consumed approximately 31% of their calories as protein, 36% as fat, and 33% as carbohydrates. Assuming the present survey and the earlier data are comparable, Point Hope and Wainwright adults now consume fewer calories as protein than in the recent past. In Wainwright protein calories have been replaced by calories from fat, while in Point Hope protein calories have been replaced by carbohydrate calories (Table 11-1). The adult Eskimo diet is still somewhat higher in protein than the average U.S. diet, which provides approximately 12% of calories from protein, 42% from fat, and 46% from carbohydrates (National Research Council, 1974).

P	Fe	Vita-min A	Vita-min C	Thiamin	Ribo-flavin	Niacin
74.1	78.0	72.5	0	56.8	78.5	75.4
76.8	83.4	53.9	0	59.4	77.7	74.4
41.1	57.6	41.1	0	31.7	46.6	52.0
49.0	78.1	76.3	0	43.5	63.4	57.9
59.8	72.8	82.9	1.4	58.4	68.4	69.6
37.8	78.6	69.7	1.1	22.6	45.9	51.3
51.6	73.8	67.0	0.5	41.5	59.6	60.4
39.5	70.3	40.9	19.1	36.7	30.3	63.2
36.9	58.5	28.5	0	27.3	47.5	53.0
9.5	38.6	11.0	0	7.8	17.7	26.2
30.4	57.4	28.2	6.9	25.4	33.1	49.4

Protein

Even though the dietary records evidently underestimated total food consumption, the estimated protein intake met or exceeded the RDA in nearly all cases (Fig. 11-2). All groups except the Point Hope children obtained more of their protein from native than from processed foods (Table 11-2). Adults at Wainwright and Point Hope obtained approximately 75% and 57%, respectively, of their protein from native foods. The estimate for Wainwright adults is comparable to the 72% derived from the 1956-1961 survey of eleven Eskimo and Indian villages in southern and central Alaska (Heller and Scott, 1967). Since that time, however, there has been a marked shift toward processed foods in these latter villages. A rapid erosion of the traditional diet culture at Wainwright and Point Hope is also evident in the smaller percentages of calories and protein derived from native foods in the diet of children than in that of adults (Table 11-2). Caribou and sea mammal meat (and to a lesser extent fish) contributed most of the native dietary protein.

Carbohydrate and Fat

Carbohydrates provide a much greater portion of the calories in the Eskimo diet today than they did in aboriginal times. Most of the carbohydrates come from breads, cereal products, rice, and refined sugar. Canned fruits are used in small quantities and vegetables are used only occasionally. Fresh fruits and vegetables are expensive and are available only in limited quantities. The contribution of native foods to carbohydrate intake is negligible (Table 11-2). It is noteworthy that the proportion of calories derived from carbohydrates by children at Point Hope is comparable to that of the general U.S. population (National Research Council, 1974).

Over half of the fat in the diet is imported, largely as hydrogenated fat and margarine. Vegetable oils are seldom used. The 1956-1961 survey of

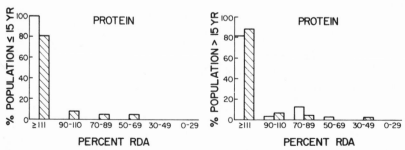

FIGURE 11-2. *Estimated protein intake of Eskimo children and adults, as percentages of RDAs. Shaded bars, Wainwright; open bars, Point Hope.*

Alaskan Eskimos and Indians indicated that 40% of dietary fat came from native foods. In the present survey 46% and 21% of the fat came from native foods in Wainwright and Point Hope, respectively. Most of the native fat is obtained from sea mammals. Muktuk (the outer skin and attached blubber of baleen or beluga whale) is a popular food when available, and caribou and dried fish are often eaten dipped in seal oil.

Calcium and Phosphorus

The Eskimo diet is low in calcium. Figure 11-3 indicates that 61% of Wainwright adults and 47% of Point Hope adults consumed less calcium than FAO/WHO standards (1962) recommend. Only 17% of the Point Hope children consumed less than the recommended intake of calcium, whereas 62% of the Wainwright children were below the FAO/WHO standard. If the US/NAS-NRC standard (1974) is employed, a greater proportion of the population appears to be in low calcium status. Much of the calcium in the diet is now derived from imported dairy products. Canned evaporated milk is used by many families but often in small amounts. The school lunch program provides at least one cup of milk per day for schoolchildren. In Wainwright 19.2% of the calcium came from native foods, while at Point Hope only 8.6% came from native foods (Table 11-2).

The aboriginal Eskimo diet was low in calcium but did contain some relatively good sources of calcium. Certain native foods such as animal blood, crushed animal bones, fish heads, developing embryos of wildfowl eggs, and putrefied fish products contain significant amounts of calcium. These foods are seldom used today.

The Eskimo diet is relatively high in phosphorus (see Fig. 11-4) because of its high meat content. A high phosphorus intake, together with a low calcium intake, can be detrimental to skeletal integrity. The overall calcium to phosphorus ratio for all subjects was 1:2.85. The ratio was somewhat

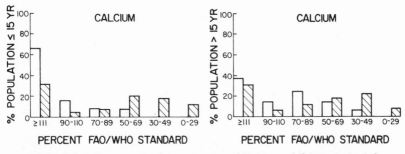

FIGURE 11-3. *Estimated calcium intake of Eskimo children and adults, as percentages of FAO/WHO standard. Shaded bars, Wainwright; open bars, Point Hope.*

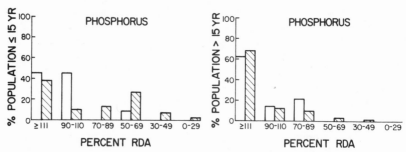

FIGURE 11-4. *Estimated phosphorus intake of Eskimo children and adults, as percentages of RDAs. Shaded bars, Wainwright; open bars, Point Hope.*

lower for Wainwright adults (1:3.68) whose diet more closely resembles that of the aboriginal Eskimo.

Iron

Iron intake by adult Eskimos appears to be generally adequate (Fig. 11-5). A greater proportion of children failed to meet the RDA for iron. This is probably a reflection of the lower consumption of native foods by children than by adults. A majority of the dietary iron comes from native food sources. Native foods provided 74% of the dietary iron at Wainwright and 57% at Point Hope (Table 11-2). Meat, especially the flesh of sea mammals, is a good source of dietary iron; hence in these northern coastal villages, where sea mammals are used abundantly, little iron deficiency would be expected among subjects consuming the native diet. In the southern tundra villages, where fish is the main native food, lower iron intakes can be expected.

Vitamin A and Vitamin C

Individual daily intakes of vitamin A varied widely (Fig. 11-6). Relatively high intakes by a few individuals show that rich vitamin A sources are consumed. Since this vitamin is readily stored in the body, adequate vitamin A nutriture can be maintained in spite of a variable intake. Figure 11-6 shows that the vitamin A intake for a large portion of the children fell considerably below the RDA. However, these values represent only the vitamin A consumed in the diet. In addition, schoolchildren received vitamin A and D supplements (4000 IU of vitamin A and 400 IU of vitamin D) daily at school. Meat and fat from native food sources provided much of the dietary vitamin A. Vegetables and fruit supplied lower amounts of vitamin A activity than they do in the U.S. mixed diet.

A large portion of the Wainwright children and a majority of adults at

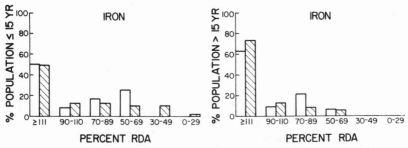

FIGURE 11-5. *Estimated iron intake of Eskimo children and adults, as percentages of RDAs. Shaded bars, Wainwright; open bars, Point Hope.*

Wainwright and Point Hope consumed less than the RDA for vitamin C (Fig. 11-7). Their intake values, however, reflect only the vitamin C present in imported foods. Reliable values for the ascorbic acid content of native foods are not available. Since there is no history of scurvy among Eskimos, native foods must be capable of providing enough vitamin C to prevent a deficiency. The Eskimo practice of eating meat either raw or lightly cooked helps to conserve the ascorbic acid present in the meat. Certain imported foods rich in ascorbic acid are now popular among Eskimos. Such food items include a variety of vitamin C-supplemented natural and simulated fruit juices. Schoolchildren also receive fruit or fruit juices as a part of the school lunch program. Despite the low intakes of ascorbic acid indicated by the diet survey, there were no clinical signs of vitamin C deficiency, and biochemical analysis of blood serum revealed no evidence of low vitamin C levels.

Thiamin, Riboflavin, and Niacin

The high meat diet of Eskimos provides liberal amounts of thiamin, riboflavin, and niacin. Although Figs. 11-8-11-10 suggest that a considerable

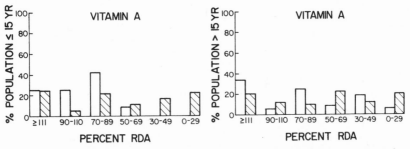

FIGURE 11-6. *Estimated vitamin A intake of Eskimo children and adults, as percentages of RDAs. Shaded bars, Wainwright; open bars, Point Hope.*

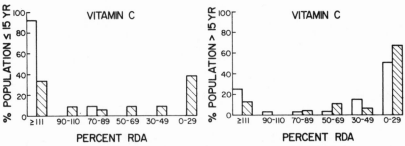

FIGURE 11-7. *Estimated vitamin C intake of Eskimo children and adults, as percentages of RDAs. Shaded bars, Wainwright; open bars, Point Hope.*

number of subjects fell below the RDA for these vitamins, it must be remembered that since the dietary records underestimated the intake of total calories they also underestimated the intake of B vitamins. If the calculated intake of these vitamins is adjusted to reflect an adequate caloric intake (as indicated by the height and weight records) an adequate consumption of thiamin, riboflavin, and niacin is also indicated. Biochemical assessment of the vitamin status of this population supported this conclusion. Further, it should again be noted that a value lower than the RDA (which contains a safety factor) does not necessarily reflect an inadequate intake. Native foods provided a large portion of the dietary intake of these B vitamins: 40-60% at Wainwright and 25-50% at Point Hope (Table 11-2).

SOUTHWESTERN TUNDRA VILLAGES

In addition to the dietary records obtained at Wainwright and Point Hope, general dietary information was collected during a nutrition survey at Kasigluk and Nunapitchuk, two villages on the inland tundra region of southwest Alaska. Fish is the native dietary staple in this region. During the summer months families often camp near the mouth of the Kuskokwim River

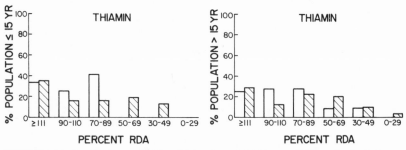

FIGURE 11-8. *Estimated thiamin intake of Eskimo children and adults, as percentages of RDAs. Shaded bars, Wainwright; open bars, Point Hope.*

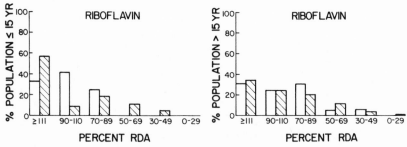

FIGURE 11-9. *Estimated riboflavin intake of Eskimo children and adults, as percentages of RDAs. Shaded bars, Wainwright; open bars, Point Hope.*

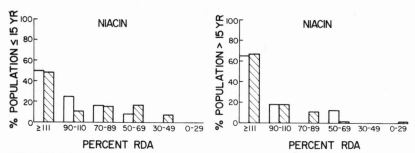

FIGURE 11-10. *Estimated niacin intake of Eskimo children and adults, as percentages of RDAs. Shaded bars, Wainwright; open bars, Point Hope.*

and fish for salmon. Large quantities of salmon are dried for use in the winter and significant quantities are sold to canneries. Both villages are located near the Johnson River, where residents are able to fish for whitefish and pike during much of the year. These fish are either eaten fresh or dried for future use.

In the past the sole dietary staple of this population was fish, which provided a lower iron and thiamin intake than the diet of northern coastal Eskimos. Most of the available fish have a relatively low iron content, and thiamin is also low in such fish as blackfish, herring, and smelt. Certain other native fish are known to contain the heat-labile enzyme thiaminase which destroys dietary thiamin; hence the traditional Eskimo practice of eating raw fish or dried uncooked fish could reduce the amount of dietary thiamin available. While Eskimos in this region eat large amounts of fish, some of it without cooking, biochemical assessment of their thiamin nutriture revealed no evidence of thiamin deficiency.

The more southerly location of these villages enabled the inhabitants to gather significant amounts of cloudberries, low-bush cranberries, crowberries, blueberries, and mouse nuts (edible roots of certain tundra plants). In the past, families would gather several hundred pounds of these foods and store them for use in the winter. While most of these foods are still used today, they are seldom gathered in significant quantities and constitute only an occasional item in the diet.

It was not possible to evaluate the relative amounts of native and imported foods consumed at Kasigluk and Nunapitchuk. It was evident, however, that these villages relied more heavily on imported foods than did the inhabitants of Wainwright and probably those of Point Hope. It is possible to travel by river from these tundra villages to Bethel, an urbanized settlement, where many more food and material items are available. Some food is also transported into the villages on barges, a less expensive method than the air freight frequently used in the northern villages.

12

Nutrition Studies: Biochemical Assessment of Nutritional Status

J. G. Bergan and *R. Raines Bell*

A biochemical evaluation of the nutritional status of Alaskan Eskimos was conducted in four villages, two in northern Alaska (Wainwright, 1971, and Point Hope, 1972) and two in southern Alaska (Kasigluk, 1973, and Nunapitchuk, 1973). Blood and urine samples were obtained from 740 Eskimos out of a potential population of about 1,100.

According to standards proposed for the U.S. National Nutrition Survey (O'Neal et al., 1970), low hemoglobin values were present in approximately one-third of children and adults at Wainwright, Point Hope, and Kasigluk and in one-half of the sample at Nunapitchuk (Table 12-1). The hematocrits showed similar tendencies. The prevalence of low and deficient values in the total adult sample was twice as frequent in males as in females (58% and 29%, respectively). Earlier studies (Mann et al., 1962; Sauberlich et al., 1972) in these villages yielded lower estimates of the frequency of anemia and revealed no significant differences between men and women. The present findings indicate that low levels of hemoglobin and hematocrit are now a frequent problem among Alaskan Eskimos as they are among other segments of the U.S. population. This condition probably is being aggravated among Eskimos by a declining consumption of iron-rich native foods.

Plasma levels of vitamin C (Table 12-2) were found to be adequate in nearly all subjects at Wainwright and Point Hope. Mean ascorbic acid values were considerably higher in children than in adults in both villages. Ascorbic acid-fortified beverages were widely consumed in these villages and were provided as part of the school lunch program.

Table 12-3 shows that plasma vitamin A levels were acceptable except among children at Wainwright and Nunapitchuk. Plasma β-carotene concentrations were below those found in the U.S. population in general and reflect a limited intake of fruits and vegetables indicating that a high proportion of the vitamin A activity in the diet was derived from the preformed vitamin present in animal foods.

As would be expected of a population consuming a high-protein diet,

157

TABLE 12-1 *Hemoglobin and Hematocrit Status (%)*

Population (ages)	Hemoglobin				Hematocrit			
	N	Accept.	Low	Def.	N	Accept.	Low	Def.
Wainwright (1971)								
2- 5	4	75	25	0	6	33	67	0
6-12	41	59	39	2	48	59	41	0
13-16	23	70	30	0	21	81	14	5
Men	35	40	49	11	35	31	48	20
Women	40	78	20	2	40	60	35	5
Point Hope (1972)								
2- 5	-	-	-	-	11	100	0	0
6-12	46	89	11	0	73	79	21	0
13-16	15	48	40	12	16	57	31	12
Men	44	36	61	2	44	34	59	7
Women	45	89	9	2	47	77	23	0
Kasigluk (1973)								
6-12	-	-	-	-	61	74	26	0
13-16	-	-	-	-	20	40	35	25
Men	10	30	50	20	10	40	60	0
Women	28	68	28	4	30	77	20	3
Nunapitchuk (1973)								
6-12	64	51	47	2	63	90	10	0
13-16	29	17	52	31	29	59	38	3
Men	12	8	67	25	12	25	75	0
Women	41	49	49	2	41	78	22	0

Standards of acceptability are based on guidelines of O'Neal et al. (1970).

TABLE 12-2 *Plasma Vitamin C Levels*

Population	Age (yr)	N	Mean ± S.D. (mg/100 ml)	Status (%) Accept.	Low	Def.
Wainwright (1971)	6–17	66	1.67 ± 0.53	100	0	0
	> 17	64	1.25 ± 0.59	98	2	0
Point Hope (1972)	6–17	28	1.52 ± 0.52	100	0	0
	> 17	50	0.74 ± 0.46	98	2	0

TABLE 12-3 *Plasma Vitamin A and β-Carotene Levels*

Population	Age (yr)	N	Mean ± S.D. (mg/100 ml)	Status (%) Accept.	Low	Def.
VITAMIN A						
Wainwright (1971)	6–17	63	40.9 ± 11.8	90	10	0
	> 17	66	47.0 ± 8.5	100	0	0
Point Hope (1972)	6–17	47	56.4 ± 14.5	100	0	0
	> 17	77	89.9 ± 26.3	100	0	0
Kasigluk (1973)	> 17	37	39.6 ± 10.0	100	0	0
Nunapitchuk (1973)	6–17	92	34.5 ± 10.4	69	22	9
	> 17	48	37.2 ± 12.3	98	2	0
β–CAROTENE						
Wainwright (1971)	6–17	63	66.3 ± 24.9	94	6	0
	> 17	66	63.4 ± 25.2	85	15	0
Point Hope (1972)	6–17	47	78.6 ± 23.6	98	2	0
	> 17	77	48.6 ± 21.8	70	22	8
Kasigluk (1973)	> 17	37	56.0 ± 20.6	100	0	0
Nunapitchuk (1973)	6–17	92	38.3 ± 11.5	41	59	0
	> 17	50	28.2 ± 11.1	14	58	28

TABLE 12-4 *Serum Protein Concentrations*

Population	Age (yr)	N	Mean ± S.D. (mg/100 ml)	Status (%) Accept.	Low	Def.
Wainwright (1971)	> 17	39	7.80 ± 0.60	100	0	0
Point Hope (1972)	6-17	52	7.80 ± 1.30	98	2	0
	> 17	82	7.65 ± 0.69	98	2	0
Nunapitchuk (1973)	6-17	78	8.55 ± 1.50	96	4	0
	> 17	40	9.60 ± 2.00	100	0	0

TABLE 12-5 *Thiamin and Riboflavin Status*

Population	Age (yr)	N	Status (%) Accept.	Low	Def.
		THIAMIN			
Wainwright (1971)	4-15	65	98	2	0
	> 15	69	100	0	0
Point Hope (1972)	4-15	70	97	3	0
	> 15	81	99	0	1
Kasigluk (1973)	4-15	79	94	5	1
	> 15	41	85	10	5
Nunapitchuk (1973)	4-15	85	100	0	0
	> 15	53	100	0	0
		RIBOFLAVIN			
Wainwright (1971)	4-15	69	95	4	1
	> 15	65	100	0	0
Point Hope (1972)	4-15	83	71	28	1
	> 15	89	97	2	1
Kasigluk (1973)	4-15	80	96	4	0
	> 15	41	100	0	0
Nunapitchuk (1973)	4-15	85	99	0	1
	> 15	54	100	0	0

serum protein values were in the acceptable range (Table 12-4). Values for urinary riboflavin and thiamin excretion (Table 12-5) also were in the acceptable category for most of the sample. However, 29% of the children at Point Hope were low or deficient in riboflavin, and 9% of the Kasigluk sample showed evidence of inadequate thiamin nutriture.

The nutritional status of this sample of Alaskan Eskimos with respect to the biochemical parameters measured was generally satisfactory except for a pervasive incidence of low hemoglobins and hematocrits. There appear to be some shifts in the biochemical indices since the time of earlier studies (Mann et al., 1962; Sauberlich et al., 1972). For instance, plasma ascorbic acid levels are higher and the prevalence of apparent anemia is greater. There is also evidence of specific nutritional inadequacies in certain population subsamples (e.g., in the vitamin A status of children at Nunapitchuk). As their diet continues to change, the nutritional condition of Eskimos is likely to shift toward that of other segments of the U.S. population of similar socioeconomic status.

13

Nutrition Studies: Clinical Observations on Nutritional Health

M. J. Colbert, G. V. Mann, and *L. M. Hursh*

Four villages were surveyed in two areas of Alaska: Wainwright and Point Hope on the northwest coast, and Kasigluk and Nunapitchuk in the southwest portion of mainland Alaska (Bethel area). These villages were selected to represent two major environmental areas inhabited by Alaskan Eskimos. They also reflect rather different stages of cultural disruption.

CHARACTERISTICS OF THE VILLAGES AND VILLAGERS

All examinees were Eskimos. Those on the northwest coast speak Inupik and those in the southwest portion speak Yupik. The former were found to have greater familiarity with the English language than the latter. While all the schoolchildren were learning English in school, it was often necessary to have an interpreter in order to communicate with the adults in the villages in southwest Alaska.

Probably the most striking characteristic of Eskimo village life at this time (as seen by outside observers) is the virtually complete lack of daily schedule. Because of the endless days in summer and the endless nights in winter, individuals tend to eat, sleep, play, and work on their own personal schedules. A visitor to almost any house is likely to find one or more members sound asleep, others busy at work, and others at meals. This lack of adherence to a schedule or clock timing may have some interesting implications for health. Certainly it allows one to speculate that life-style may have a bearing upon some chronic diseases.

The energetic and expensive insertion of school systems into the villages is impressive. The schools and teachers probably constitute the most important foreign influence in Eskimo life.

PROVISION FOR MEDICAL CARE

Each village has at least one health aide (a native who has received some months of training at a regional hospital). The aide has a stock of standard medications and basic medical equipment. Also, the aide has radiotelephone access to a physician at the nearest regional hospital who may be consulted regarding medical problems at a prearranged time each day. The aide maintains a medical history file on every resident of the village. These files were generally found to be very well maintained.

When a medical problem is encountered which is beyond the training and/or equipment of the aide (even with radiotelephone consultation), the patient must be evacuated to a regional hospital. For all practical purposes evacuation is possible only by air. Limitations are thus placed by weather conditions. The remoteness of these villages means that some public health programs are of necessity sporadic. When a public health nurse visits a village, the children get their immunizations. When a dentist visits, much dental care is concentrated in a few days for a large proportion of the village residents.

The medical-aide system, developed in Alaska through the necessity of logistic circumstances, is a strong endorsement of a notion now being tried in the lower forty-eight states. That is the substitution of paramedical people for physicians in the delivery of health care. The Eskimo experience indicates that the system can be effective.

EXAMINATIONS

Permission was obtained in advance from the village councils for examination of the residents of each village. In the Bethel area, Drs. Daniel Blumenthal and Daniel Sexton (both of the Center for Disease Control) assisted in the examinations. When the survey team arrived, the health aide used a telephone system, which includes each home, or runners to notify the residents. Total or amost total participation of schoolchildren was obtained. Among those persons older or younger than school age, participation was still quite complete, though there did seem to be paucity of men examined who were of ages to be family heads. There was also a notable deficit of teenagers and young adults, because these people had either been sent out to school or were away at seasonal work. Still, the age-census plots show the typical high mortality at early ages which leads to small populations of aged persons. In Alaska this trend is compounded by two unique additional factors. The rates of emigration out of the villages are high for young adults, and the occupational mortality of adult men is high. Hunting in the arctic environment is a high-risk enterprise.

CLINICAL CONDITIONS

No clinical entities were recognized as being specifically due to nutritional deficiencies.

Infectious Diseases

Infectious diseases continue to be a major cause of disability as they were reported to be in the 1958 study of Mann et al. (1962). Many persons had a history of tuberculosis but no new active cases were noted. Some persons were taking isoniazid because of conversion of their tuberculin tests. Streptococcal infections were rampant.

Ear Disorders

Eardrum perforations were almost as common as intact drums. In some instances the perforation was the residual of an earlier otitis media, no longer active. In many other instances chronic otitis media was present. The hereditary dry form of ear wax in these Mongoloid people may be a contributing factor to the present epidemic of otitis media.

Dental Disorders

Dental caries were numerous in virtually every schoolchild, despite the efforts of the schools to teach dental hygiene. The role of diet changes vs the proposal that dental caries is a response to a spreading epidemic of *Streptococcus mutans* cannot be resolved with these measurements. There are still large between-village variations of caries prevalence which invite explanation.

The older examinees were frequently edentulous. Women often exhibited teeth which were worn down symetrically to the gum line. Inspecting such a tooth from above could be likened exactly to seeing a horizontal cross-section of a tooth.

Lung Disorders

Arrested tuberculosis, as mentioned earlier, was common. Also common were bronchitis and emphysema in adults. Smoking was a frequent habit.

Skin Disorders

Heavy pigmentation of exposed areas, as has been reported previously in Eskimos, was again noted. Often the skin appeared to be quite dry, but invariably, when pruritus was inquired about it was denied. A recent increase in acne vulgaris, at least among Canadian Eskimos, has been reported (Schaefer, 1971b); however, it was not a common finding among the adolescents examined in this survey. Pyoderma was common in winter, probably because of the shortage of water for bathing.

Gastrointestinal Disorders

A frequent cause of diarrhea in the villages is infection related to sanitation problems. Some of the women had a history of cholecystectomy. This is interesting in light of the report of Schaefer cited above, in which he stated that cholelithiasis is being recognized more frequently in Canadian Eskimos in recent years.

Reproduction

Many of the older women gave histories of many pregnancies, with frequent loss of children, particularly in the neonatal period. Contraception is now available, and the younger women appear to be having smaller families than their mothers.

Injuries

Injuries remain a major cause of disability. Cold injury is fairly common. Falls on ice are frequent causes of lacerations and/or fractures. Several scars from old gunshot wounds were seen. Other major sources of trauma are dog bites and knife wounds.

Alcoholism

While the sale of alcohol in the villages studied is prohibited, alcohol does enter the villages to some extent. No instances of alcoholic hepatitis or other disorders directly attributable to alcohol were seen. On the other hand, there were several instances of depression in female survivors of males who were reported to have drowned or been frozen to death while intoxicated. A drunken Eskimo who appeared in one of our clinics was a source of profound embarrassment to the other Eskimos.

Diabetes Mellitus

Diabetes mellitus is said to be rare in Eskimos, and juvenile diabetes to be unknown (Mouratoff and Scott, 1973). Quick (1974) feels that the occurrence of diabetes in an Eskimo should prompt inquiry about racial background: "Most of the diabetic Alaskan natives that I have encountered have European or Russian ancestors . . . ." (p. 1383). Fisher (1974) reported seven diabetic Eskimos among the native population of Barrow (2,313 persons). He reported that the onset of the diabetes in these seven occurred between fifty-seven and seventy-five years of age. He implies that as Eskimos live longer (with the control of neonatal deaths and infectious disease), diabetes may be found more frequently. In our study, only one person, a teenage girl, was found with documented diabetes mellitus and it was controlled by diet alone.

Obesity

The data for height, weight, and skinfold thickness of adults are shown in Tables 13-1 and 13-2. Weights were recorded for subjects wearing light clothing and without shoes. For purposes of comparison, the data are presented in a form similar to that used by Mann et al. (1962) to report results from a 1958 survey on National Guard personnel and their families. The southern Eskimos examined by these investigators were from the Bethel region, which encompasses Kasigluk and Nunapitchuk; their northern subjects included residents of Point Hope and two neighboring villages but not Wainwright. The finding that northern Eskimo males were taller and heavier than their southern counterparts in 1958 was again observed in the present study in a small sample of males and larger sample of females. The "percentage of standard weight," based on U.S. Medico-Actuarial Tables, and skinfold thicknesses were substantially higher for females than for males. These measurements confirmed the subjective impression that obesity was more prevalent in women (Mann et al., 1962).

The "percentage of standard weight" by age and sex is presented in Table 13-3. The average values for Kasigluk and Nunapitchuk male subjects were slightly higher than those for male subjects as Wainwright and Point Hope over the age of ten, but overall were not significantly different from those found previously (Mann et al., 1962). However, the values for female subjects rose progressively with age and were substantially higher than those recorded for a comparable population sample approximately fifteen years earlier by Mann and coworkers. The data indicate that there has been a sharp increase in obesity among female Eskimos in recent years.

TABLE 13-1 *Mean (± S.E.) Stature and Weight of Adults*

Age (yr)	Sex	N	Stature (in.)	Weight (lb.)	Percentage of Standard Weight*
			WAINWRIGHT AND POINT HOPE		
17–19	M	4	66.8 ± 0.6	139.5 ± 8.3	96 ± 6
17–19	F	3	62.0 ± 0.6	138.0 ± 5.4	115 ± 3
20–39	M	32	66.6 ± 0.4	151.0 ± 3.1	103 ± 8
20–39	F	36	62.0 ± 0.3	139.7 ± 4.9	115 ± 2
40–54	M	14	65.6 ± 0.9	155.1 ± 5.1	109 ± 4
40–54	F	23	61.8 ± 0.8	160.3 ± 6.8	133 ± 5
All	M	50	66.3 ± 0.4	151.2 ± 2.5	104 ± 2
All	F	62	61.9 ± 0.3	147.3 ± 4.0	122 ± 3
			KASIGLUK AND NUNAPITCHUK		
17–19	M	1	62.0	120.0	92
17–19	F	6	61.0 ± 0.3	147.3 ± 8.9	127 ± 8
20–39	M	4	62.1 ± 0.7	142.5 ± 9.5	109 ± 6
20–39	F	29	59.8 ± 0.3	135.1 ± 4.6	120 ± 4
40–54	M	5	62.8 ± 0.7	133.8 ± 2.4	101 ± 3
40–54	F	21	58.0 ± 0.5	140.9 ± 7.8	129 ± 7
All	M	10	62.5 ± 0.5	135.9 ± 4.3	104 ± 3
All	F	56	59.2 ± 0.3	138.6 ± 3.9	124 ± 3

*From US Medico-Actuarial Tables (National Center for Health Statistics, 1969).

The obesity index employed in Table 13-4 also documents the greater prevalence of obesity in women than in men, and indicates, in contrast to the 1958 findings, that this condition is now as frequent among northern as among southern women. The indices for both males and females, moreover, are substantially greater than those recorded earlier, indicating that overweight has been on the increase since 1958 in both sexes.

Hypertension

Measurements of blood pressure (Table 13-5) showed the usual rise with age. The data for Wainwright and Point Hope Eskimos indicate that there has been no increment in systolic or diastolic pressure in northern Eskimos since

TABLE 13-2 *Mean (± S.E.) Skinfold Thickness of Adults*

Age (yr)	Sex	N	Mean Skinfold Thickness (mm)	
			Triceps	Subscapular
WAINWRIGHT AND POINT HOPE				
17–19	M	1	6.5	8.5
17–19	F	1	15.0	11.0
20–39	M	27	8.6 ± 1.0	8.5 ± 0.7
20–39	F	27	20.4 ± 2.0	18.9 ± 2.4
40–54	M	12	11.5 ± 2.2	12.1 ± 2.2
40–54	F	13	25.9 ± 2.8	25.4 ± 4.5
All	M	40	9.4 ± 1.0	10.0 ± 0.9
All	F	41	22.0 ± 1.6	20.8 ± 2.2
KASIGLUK AND NUNAPITCHUK				
17–19	M	1	5.0	9.5
17–19	F	5	24.6 3.9	30.8 5.9
20–39	M	4	9.5 ± 2.6	12.4 ± 1.7
20–39	F	27	23.3 ± 1.7	20.0 ± 2.1
40–54	M	3	10.3 ± 3.8	11.0 ± 3.5
40–54	F	15	28.7 ± 3.8	28.4 ± 3.5
All	M	8	9.3 ± 1.8	11.5 ± 1.4
All	F	47	25.3 ± 1.5	23.9 ± 1.9

an assessment in 1958 (Mann et al., 1962); in fact, the mean values for most age groups are somewhat lower. But this difference may be attributable to the inclusion in the present study of Wainwright subjects, who were observed to have lower blood pressures than subjects from Point Hope. Both systolic and diastolic pressures were higher at Kasigluk and Nunapitchuk than in the northern villages, a difference not seen in the data collected in the same regions in 1958.

The prevalence of hypertension (defined as ≥ 160 mm Hg systolic or 95 diastolic) is summarized by sex and geographic location in Table 13-6. The data reflect a north-south gradient in blood pressures which is particularly evident in females. While there was no difference in the incidence of high blood pressure between the sexes in the northern villages, there was a substantially greater incidence among females in the southern villages. No sex difference was found in the 1958 summary. Hypertension was inexplicably more prevalent among women in Kasigluk than in Nunapitchuk. In Eskimo

TABLE 13-3 *Percentage of Standard Weight by Age and Sex*

Age (yr)	Wainwright and Point Hope				Kasigluk and Nunapitchuk			
	Male		Female		Male		Female	
	N	$\bar{X} \pm$ S.E.	N	$\bar{X} \pm$ S.E.	N	$\bar{X} \pm$ S.E.	N	$\bar{X} \pm$ S.E.
5- 9	42	112 ± 1	43	111 ± 1	37	111 ± 1	38	115 ± 2
10-14	32	111 ± 2	40	113 ± 3	45	117 ± 2	38	118 ± 2
15-44	43	104 ± 2	54	117 ± 3	16	106 ± 3	49	121 ± 3
45+	38	109 ± 2	37	113 ± 5	16	113 ± 8	31	129 ± 6

US Medico-Actuarial tables were used as standards for adults (National Center for Health Statistics, 1969), and Baldwin-Wood standards for children under 15 years of age.

TABLE 13-4 *Obesity in Eskimo Adults by Age and Sex*

Population	Age 15-44			Age 45+		
	Examined (No.)	Obese		Examined (No.)	Obese	
		No.	%		No.	%
			Males			
Kasigluk & Nunapitchuk	16	2	12.5	16	6	37.5
Wainwright & Point Hope	43	2	4.7	38	8	21.1
Total	59	4	6.8	54	14	25.9
			Females			
Kasigluk & Nunapitchuk	49	19	38.8	31	19	61.3
Wainwright & Point Hope	54	20	37.0	37	25	67.6
Total	103	39	37.9	68	44	64.7

Obesity defined as weighing $\geq$ 120 percent of standard weight according to US Medico-Actuarial Tables (National Center for Health Staistics, 1969).

TABLE 13-5 *Mean (± S.E.) Blood Pressure of Adult Eskimos by Age and Geographical Location (mm Hg)*

Age (yr)	Wainwright and Point Hope			Kasigluk and Nunapitchuk		
	N	Systolic	Diastolic	N	Systolic	Diastolic
5– 9	81	98 ± 9	50 ± 15	1	130	70
10–14	75	106 ± 10	59 ± 14	9	116 ± 7	68 ± 8
15–19	15	109 ± 12	57 ± 9	10	119 ± 10	69 ± 9
20–44	83	112 ± 13	63 ± 12	38	123 ± 15	74 ± 14
45–64	51	127 ± 21	69 ± 17	35	143 ± 30	81 ± 14
65+	25	153 ± 33	74 ± 14	16	157 ± 25	81 ± 9

males the incidence of hypertension appears still to be significantly lower than it is among the U.S. male population generally, but among females of the central and southern regions of Alaska it appears to be at least comparable to the national average for women. The traditional profile of low blood pressure, low blood cholesterol, and lean body mass is being eroded among the Eskimo inhabitants of these villages located at an interface with Western civilization.

TABLE 13-6 *Prevalence of High Blood Pressure Among Eskimo Adults, Ages 18–74*

Source	Males		Females		Both	
	N	%	N	%	N	%
Wainwright	39	5.1	43	4.6	82	4.9
Point Hope	41	12.2	42	14.3	83	13.3
Kasigluk	10	10.0	30	36.7	40	30.0
Nunapitchuk	10	10.0	36	19.4	46	17.4
Kasigluk and Nunapitchuk	20	10.0	66	27.3	86	23.3
National Health Survey (1960–62)[*]		15.0		16.7		15.9

[*]National Center for Health Statistics (1969).

Electrocardiographic Findings

Resting 12-lead electrocardiograms (ECGs) were recorded for persons forty years of age and over. The findings showed an increasing trend of abnormality with age, but at a somewhat lower frequency and rate of increase than is found in persons in the lower forty-eight states. A statistically real difference in rates of abnormal cardiograms could not be shown between Point Hope and Wainwright, although the former village did have a slightly higher frequency of abnormalities. The kinds of abnormal cardiographic findings were typical of a population with extensive atherosclerotic heart disease. While some of the bundle-branch blocks could be caused by parasitic disease, that must be an uncommon cause.

Figure 13-1 shows a comparison of the frequency of abnormal ECGs of all forms in Eskimos and two other populations. The first is the reference U.S. population studied in Tecumseh, Michigan (Ostrander et al., 1965), and the second is the Masai, an East African pastoral group of people. It is clear that the trends are similar but appear at a later age in the two non-white populations, and even at advanced ages never reach the high rates seen in the U.S. populations. This kind of finding suggests that the factors which cause these disorders are appearing either less forcefully or at a later stage of life among the Eskimo and Masai. Figure 13-2 shows the age groups forty and over in somewhat greater detail, and emphasizes again that the Eskimo population is midway between the East African pastoral people and the U.S. population in its prevalence of ECG abnormalities. For Fig. 13-3 three risk factors

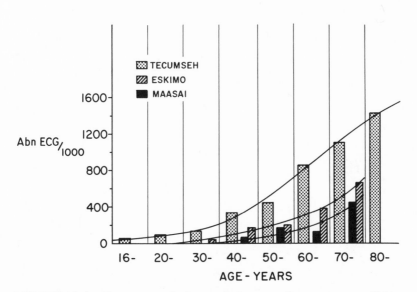

FIGURE 13-1. *Frequency of abnormal electrocardiograms among Eskimos and two reference populations.*

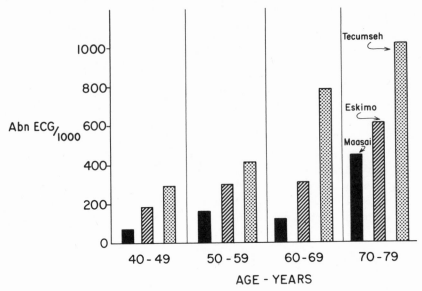

FIGURE 13-2. *Comparison of electrocardiographic abnormalities in subjects 40 years of age or older in three populations.*

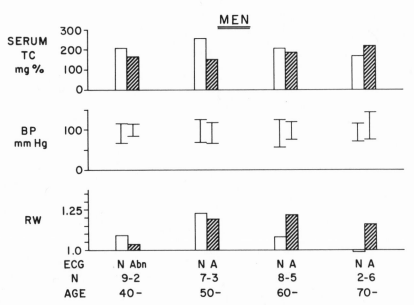

FIGURE 13-3. *Relationship between abnormal cardiograms and three risk factors for coronary heart disease in Eskimo males. TC, total cholesterol; BP, blood pressure; RW, relative weight (percentage of standard weight).*

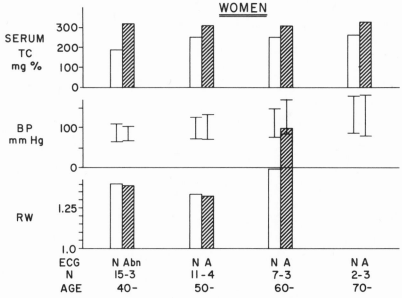

FIGURE 13-4. *Relationship between abnormal cardiograms and three risk factors for coronary heart disease in Eskimo females. TC, total cholesterol; BP, blood pressure; RW, relative weight (percentage of standard weight).*

for coronary heart disease (serum cholesterol, blood pressure, and weight relative to "standard weight") were examined in relation to abnormal cardiograms in Eskimo males over forty. The small numbers involved make this comparison somewhat hazardous, but there is no real evidence the ECG abnormality was significantly associated with any of these three risk factors. In Fig. 13-4 the similar comparison for women does show that women with abnormal ECGs tend to have consistently higher levels of cholesteremia.

Serial electrocardiography, especially if combined with controlled exercise and objective measures of physical fitness, seems a most promising way to document the continuing changes of rate of cardiovascular disease. Comparison of these relationships in populations with various degrees of acculturation might be of value in identifying the responsible factors. This approach has been used by Blackburn et al. (1967). The main requirement at present is for larger numbers of cardiograms collected in a standard way in various populations.

14

Metabolic Parameters: Aspects of Cholesterol, Lipid, and Carbohydrate Metabolism

Sheldon A. Feldman, Arthur Rubenstein, C. Bruce Taylor, Kang-Jey Ho, and *Lena Lewis*

As part of the metabolic studies described in this volume, cholesterol, lipid, and carbohydrate metabolism were investigated.

CHOLESTEROL METABOLISM

Inasmuch as the Arctic Eskimo has historically subsisted on an almost purely carnivorous diet and to a variable extent still partakes of a diet unusually rich in meat sources, his reputed lack of coronary artery disease has prompted investigations into the epidemiology of hypercholesterolemia among these people (Wilber and Levine, 1950; Corcoran and Rabinowitch, 1937; Sinclair et al., 1949; Scott et al., 1958; Pett and Lupien, 1958; Pett et al., 1961). These studies have shown a strong tendency towards normocholesterolemia (< 250 mg/100 ml) among the more unacculturated Eskimo groups but increased rates of elevated serum cholesterol among modernized Eskimos. To gain insight into the relationship between dietary intake and serum levels of cholesterol, as well as to develop a predictive measure of the Eskimos' liability to changing dietary patterns, a cholesterol balance study was carried out in Point Hope, Alaska.

Materials and Methods

Eight healthy Eskimos, thirty-nine to sixty-six years old, participated in the cholesterol balance study. While on a measured *ad libitum* diet they re-

This research was supported in part by U.S. Public Health Service grants HE 13613–02, HE 6835, HL 6853, AM 13941, PH 43–67–144, GM 1865–03, and G7093, and the Research Service of the Veterans Administration.

ceived a single injection of cholesterol-4-^{14}C (Chobanian et al., 1962). Serum samples were obtained daily in the first week, biweekly in the third through fifth weeks, and then weekly for an additional fifteen weeks. Quantification and specific activity of both free and esterified cholesterol were obtained by the methodology of Sperry-Webb (1950). Two seventy-two-hour stool specimens were obtained during the second and third weeks of the study. After extraction of neutral sterols and bile acids the specific activity of fecal neutral sterols and bile acids was determined (Abell et al., 1952; Herberg, 1965) together with the total fecal cholesterol content (Ho et al., 1972). The intake of cholesterol was calculated by measurement of the amounts of the various dietary items ingested, complemented by the determination of cholesterol content of indigenous items and reference to published values for cholesterol content of imported foods. The data were analyzed with a combination of the kinetic analysis of Gurpide et al. (1964) and the input-out analysis of Perl and Samuel (1969) as modified by Feldman et al. (1972). Furthermore, a mass sampling for serum cholesterol was performed among 85% of the Point Hope population over the age of six.

Results

Dietary Intake. The cholesterol content of the indigenous dietary elements are listed in Table 14-1. The Eskimos tested consumed, on average, 918 mg/day of cholesterol, and this rate varied between 420 and 1650 mg between subjects. This rate of ingestion is approximately that of the general U.S. population.

Serum Cholesterol Levels. The serum cholesterol concentration of the Point Hope population was 221 mg/dl ± 66 (mean ± standard deviation) with 25% nonesterified. Serum cholesterol content rose with age, but there were no significant associations with sex (Table 14-2). In this table, the linear regression between age (X) and serum cholesterol (Y) is: $Y = 201.7 + 0.7X$. The standard error of estimate (SEE) is 4.3 and the correlation coefficient (r) is 0.22, with an associated probability of less than 0.05.

Kinetic Parameters of Cholesterol Metabolism. Results of the balance study indicated that the Eskimos possessed two pools of cholesterol distributed in their bodies in a pattern like that noted among all other peoples studied with a similar experimental protocol (Fig. 14-1). One pool (A) is characterized as having a smaller mass and a more rapid turnover rate of cholesterol than does the other (B). The various kinetic parameters obtained in the balance study are listed diagramatically in Fig. 14-1. They are generally quite similar to those noted among normocholesterolemic U.S. whites.

Dietary Cholesterol and Net Cholesterol Balance. Table 14-3 summarizes regression analyses between dietary cholesterol and various parameters of cholesterol metabolism. Formula 1 in this table indicates the the amount of

TABLE 14-1 *Cholesterol Content of Indigenous Foods (g/100 g)*

Food	Cholesterol (wet tissue)
OILS AND FATS	
Prepared seal oil	0.16
Walrus fat	0.12
Bearded seal fat	0.24
Bowhead whale:	
Subdermal fat	0.15
Epimuscular fat	0.08
Prepared "whale fat"	0.09
Beluga whale:	
Subdermal fat	0.12
Epimuscular fat	0.10
Caribou fat	0.12
Seal fat	0.27
MEATS	
Walrus	0.08
Bearded seal	0.10
Bowhead whale	0.06
Beluga whale	0.08
Caribou	0.12
Seal	0.09
WHOLE FISH	
"White fish"	0.14
"Trout"	0.04
"Small salmon"	0.09
"Salmon"	0.05

TABLE 14-2 *Relationship Between Age and Mean Serum Cholesterol Concentration in 168 Point Hope Residents*

N	Age	Cholesterol (mg/dl)
62	6–12	200
28	13–17	218
18	18–24	219
12	25–35	224
32	36–60	231
16	61–82	250

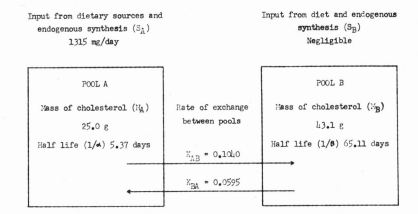

Input from dietary sources and
endogenous synthesis (S_A)
1315 mg/day

Input from diet and endogenous
synthesis (S_B)
Negligible

POOL A

Mass of cholesterol (M_A)

25.0 g

Half life (1/α) 5.37 days

Rate of exchange
between pools

K_{AB} = 0.1040

K_{BA} = 0.0595

POOL B

Mass of cholesterol (M_B)

43.1 g

Half life (1/β) 65.11 days

Rate of excretory loss from pool (K_A)
0.0544 or 1315 mg/day

Rate of excretory loss from pool (K_B)
Negligible

Mean transit time of total bodily cholesterol $\bar{T}$ = 52.6 days
Total input of cholesterol into system I_T = 1315 mg/day
Total cholesterol in body (M_T) = 68.1 g

FIGURE 14-1. *Kinetic parameters obtained in the cholesterol balance study of 8 subjects.*

amount of cholesterol absorbed was linearly proportional to the amount present in the diet, with an efficiency indicated by the slope of the equation (57%). The subjects absorbed an average of 456 mg of cholesterol per day with a maximum noted in one individual of 912 mg/day. Both the efficiency of absorption and the absolute amount absorbable were extremely high. By comparison, the maximal capacity of U.S. whites is about 300 mg/day, and among the Masai, who consume large amounts of meat and milk, the maximum absorption rate is 653 mg/day at 33% efficiency. (The Masai data, however, were obtained after supplementation with crystalline cholesterol.) The turnover rate of total body cholesterol (Formula 3) was directly proportional to the amount of cholesterol absorbed, with a slope of 1.04, which suggests that the amount of cholesterol absorbed daily contributed directly and exactly to the daily turnover of body-exchangeable cholesterol.

The Eskimos appeared to lack a facility for suppression of endogenous synthesis of cholesterol at the levels of dietary exposure measured. That is, the rate of endogenous synthesis was unrelated to the $\dot{Q}$ absorbed (Formula 2), and the total daily input (amount absorbed plus amount synthesized) remained constant at about 1,315 mg/day or 17.7 mg/kg body weight regardless of the amount of cholesterol absorbed. However, since the lowest $\dot{Q}$ absorbed was 420 mg/day it may well be that the rate of endogenous synthesis (on average 841 mg/day) would be higher if the diet were free of cholesterol. Given a constant daily input of 1,315 mg/day, on a zero-cholesterol diet the rate of endogenous synthesis of the Eskimo may be about 1,315 mg/day, indicating that at the dietary levels examined, the rate of inhibition

TABLE 14-3 *Regression Analysis Relating Absorbed Cholesterol to Kinetic Parameters of Cholesterol Metabolism*

Relationship	Regression equation (Y)	Significance
1. $\dot{Q}$ diet (X) vs $\dot{Q}$ absorbed (Y)[1]	−65.6 + 0.570X	r, 0.92 P < .001
2. $\dot{Q}$ absorbed (X) vs $\dot{Q}$ synthesized (Y)		n.s.
3. $\dot{Q}$ absorbed (X) vs turn-over rate (Y)	841.0 + 1.040X	r, 0.64 P < .01
4. $\dot{Q}$ absorbed (X) vs total cholesterol mass (Y)	51.2 + 0.045X	r, 0.56 P < .02
5. $\dot{Q}$ absorbed (X) vs serum level (Y)	211.3 + 0.048X	r, 0.56 P < .02
6. $\dot{Q}$ absorbed (X) vs Mass A (Y)	17.3 + 0.020X	r, 0.68 P < .01
7. $\dot{Q}$ absorbed (X) vs Mass B (Y)		n.s.

[1]Previously published with (X) and (Y) reversed.

of endogenous synthesis is 36% and is maximal at a $\dot{Q}$ absorption of 420 mg/day (Feldman et al., 1972).

Formula 5 in Table 14-3 indicates that serum cholesterol rose proportionately with $\dot{Q}$ absorption at a rate of 0.048. The bodily mass of rapidly exchangeable cholesterol (Formula 6) also increased, but not the slowly exchanging pool (Formula 7). This suggests that an increase in $\dot{Q}$ absorption (or $\dot{Q}$ diet) results in an increase in serum cholesterol, turnover rate, and the size of the rapidly exchangeable cholesterol pool (A).

LIPID AND CARBOHYDRATE METABOLISM

In semi-isolated Eskimo villages such as Point Hope the native diet continues to be relatively low in carbohydrate and confection, moderate in fat, and high in protein. In order to gauge the effect of low carbohydrate intake upon Eskimo metabolism, mass blood sampling and carbohydrate-linked tolerance testing were carried out both at Point Hope and among Eskimo students at a boarding high school (Mount Edgecumbe, who consumed a much higher carbohydrate diet.

Lipids and Lipoproteins at Point Hope

The mean lipid and lipoprotein values for the resident population at Point Hope are shown in Table 14-4. Triglycerides, free fatty acids, and chylomicra are listed for four postprandial time intervals. The 11- to 14- and 16- to 26-hr postprandial intervals may be considered moderate and extended fasting states.

This population shows a strikingly low concentration of serum triglyceride in the 11- to 26-hr fasted state (61.0 ± 17.0 mg/dl, with a range of 17.0–72.1 mg/dl). Neither sex nor age influenced this result. An initial rise of triglycerides at the 1- to 5-hr postprandial interval was noted, and this rise was associated with chylomicronemia which persisted to the 6- to 10-hr period. In addition to their low triglyceride concentration, the subjects had a low VLDL (very low-density lipoprotein) level, with a mean fasting value of 31.1 mg/dl. A positive linear correlation (r, $0.20, P < 0.05$) between the fasting triglycerides and very low density lipoproteins was demonstrable.

Serum fatty acid concentrations were high among the Point Hope subjects, especially in the prolonged (15- to 26-hour) fasting period when they averaged 49 mg/dl. Immediate postprandial fatty acid levels were 25 ± 3.8 mg/dl, and increased significantly to 39 ± 4.2 mg/dl (F, $8.35, P < 0.01$) by 11–14 hr after eating. A negative linear correlation between triglycerides and free fatty acids was present.

Low-density lipoprotein (LDL) concentrations of the Point Hope population averaged 319 mg/dl. There was a trend for the low-density lipoproteins to increase with age but this trend was not significant. A positive correlation was present between serum cholesterol and low-density lipoprotein concentrations (r, 0.21, $P < 0.05$). The mean high-density lipoprotein (HDL) level was 299 mg/dl (range: 184–380 mg/dl).

A negative linear association was apparent between the levels of very low-density lipoprotein and low-density lipoprotein (r, $-0.32, P < 0.001$), such that persons with the highest concentrations of VLDL also had the lowest levels of LDL. However, fasting serum triglycerides and cholesterol did not show a similar negative correlation with either LDL or VLDL.

Comparison between Point Hope and Mount Edgecumbe Samples

Thirty-two persons were tested at Mount Edgecumbe; they ranged in age from sixteen to twenty years. Their data were compared with data from forty-one persons comprising an age-matched segment from the Point Hope group. The sex ratio in these samples was 60:40 in favor of males.

Dietary Differences. The sixteen- to twenty-year-olds' diet at Point Hope indicated a total caloric intake of approximately 2,800 kcal. Their diet was estimated to contain about 250 g carbohydrate (including 75–100 g of confection), 150 g protein, and 135 g fat. Thus, in a typical adolescent diet, 40%

TABLE 14-4 *Mean (± S.D.) Serum Lipid Moieties of Point Hope Eskimos (All Ages)*

Postprandial time (hr)	Triglycerides* (mg/dl)	Free fatty acids* (mg/dl)	Chylomicra* (% of total on electro-phoretic scan)	VLDL+ Sf.....20-111 S1.21..70-400 (mg/dl)	LDL+ 0-20 20-70 (mg/dl)	HDL+ 1-10 (mg/dl)	Cholesterol+ (mg/dl)
1- 5	91 ± 7.6	25.0 ± 3.8	7.9 ± 3.8				
6-10	69 ± 5.4	29.5 ± 4.0	3.8 ± 5.1				
11-14	56 ± 17.1	39.0 ± 4.2					
15-26	65 ± 18.1	49.0 ± 7.3					
11-26							
Male subjects				28 ± 9	299 ± 18	288 ± 34	
Female subjects				36 ± 11	345 ± 21	310 ± 37	
Total				31 ± 13	319 ± 28	299 ± 34	
All times							
Male subjects							226.0 ± 31
Female subjects							217.1 ± 19
Total							222.0 ± 26

*N, 164.

+N, 55.

of calories were derived from carbohydrate, 20% from protein, and 40% from fat. The Mount Edgecumbe subjects liberally supplemented their diet with soda and candies. They ingested about 3,400 kcal daily, composed of approximately 600 g carbohydrate (about 50% from confection), 70 g protein, and 80 g fat. Of their total caloric intake, therefore, 65% was derived from carbohydrates, 10% from protein, and 25% from fat. Dietary cholesterol content, also estimated in both locales, indicated typical daily intakes of about 900 mg/day at Point Hope and less than 350 mg/day at Mount Edgecumbe.

Lipid and Lipoprotein Comparisons. Table 14-5 compares the fasting lipid and carbohydrate levels in Point Hope and Mount Edgecumbe age-matched subjects. Serum triglycerides are significantly higher ($P < 0.001$) in the Mount Edgecumbe subjects (112.5 ± 12.7 mg/dl) than in the Point Hope group (70.5 ± 9.7 mg/dl). No sex differences were present. Very low-density lipoprotein (VLDL) concentrations were somewhat higher in the Mount Edgecumbe sample, averaging 26.0 ± 10 mg/dl as compared with 19.0 ± 8.5 mg/dl at Point Hope ($P < 0.07$). Serum cholesterol was significantly lower at Mount Edgecumbe (114.3 ± 32.3 mg/dl) compared with Point Hope (219 ± 49.1 mg/dl) (with a probability less than 0.001).

Formulae generated from a detailed analysis of the relationship between dietary intake of cholesterol and serum levels would have predicted a reduction of serum cholesterol in the face of Mount Edgecumbe dietary intake,

TABLE 14-5 *Mean (± S.D.) Fasting Lipid, Glucose and Insulin Values of 32 Mount Edgecumbe and 41 Point Hope 15- to 20-Year Old Subjects*

Substance	Point Hope	Mount Edgecumbe	Significance
Cholesterol (mg/dl)	219.0 ± 49.1	144.3 ± 32.3	P < .001
Triglyceride (mg/dl)	70.5 ± 9.7	112.5 ± 12.7	P < .001
VLDL (mg/dl)	19.0 ± 8.5	26.0 ± 10.0	n.s.
LDL (mg/dl)	269.2 ± 30.4	279.4 ± 34.3	n.s.
HDL (mg/dl)	214.0 ± 42.0	214.0 ± 51.0	n.s.
Plasma glucose (mg/dl)	86.2 ± 18.1	71.8 ± 18.4	n.s.
Serum insulin (μu/ml)	18.2 ± 6.1	10.2 ± 4.8	n.s.

to about 185 mg/dl, somewhat less than the magnitude of fall demonstrated (Feldman et al., 1972). The concentrations of low- and high-density lipoproteins showed no significant differences between the two groups. The mean value of LDL at Mount Edgecumbe was 279.4 ± 34.3 mg/dl while at Point Hope it was 269.2 ± 30.4 mg/dl.

Glucose and Insulin. Fasting plasma glucose and insulin concentrations were also determined for forty-one Eskimo youths residing in Point Hope and for thirty-two Eskimos at Mount Edgecumbe, all of whom were sixteen to twenty years old. Mean plasma glucose and insulin values (Table 14-5) were not significantly different between these samples and were within the range observed for healthy subjects in the United States. Mean fasting glucose and insulin concentrations were 86.2 ± 18.1 mg/dl and 18.2 ± 6.1 μu/ml, respectively, at Point Hope, and at Mount Edgecumbe these values were 71.8 ± 18.4 mg/dl and 10.2 ± 4.8 μu/ml, respectively.

Glucose tolerance tests (Table 14-6) revealed that Point Hope subjects had significantly higher plasma glucose levels at 60 min (t, 2.47; $P < 0.05$) than those at Mount Edgecumbe. However, the percentage increment of

TABLE 14-6 *Mean (± S.D.) Results of Glucose Tolerance Tests in 7 Point Hope and 5 Mount Edgecumbe Subjects*

Test	Point Hope	Mount Edgecumbe	Significance
Plasma glucose			
0 min.	87.0 ± 7.6	69.2 ± 6.3	n.s.
60 min.	117.8 ± 5.0	91.6 ± 8.1	t, 2.47; P < .05
120 min.	100.0 ± 6.6	81.8 ± 5.8	t, 2.06; P < .07
Serum insulin (μu/ml)			
0 min.	19.0 ± 9.5	10.4 ± 1.4	n.s.
60 min.	62.3 ± 2.6	66.8 ± 2.6	n.s.
120 min.	36.2 ± 1.4	49.3 ± 3.7	n.s.
Integrated areas			
Glucose	213.4 ± 11.1	167.3 ± 13.7	t, 2.61; P < .05
Insulin	84.5 ± 12.9	95.5 ± 13.0	n.s.
Insulin/glucose	0.38± 0.05	0.56± 0.04	t, 2.54; P < .05

TABLE 14-7   *Mean (± S.D.) Results of Tolbutamide Tolerance Tests on 9 Point Hope Residents*

Time from injection (min)	Glucose		Insulin (μu/ml)
	mg/dl	% reduction from 0 time	
0	86.0 ± 3.6	---	20.2 ± 5.9
2	80.2 ± 3.9	5.3 ± 1.8%	142.4 ± 19.9
5	66.5 ± 4.1	15.9 ± 3.1%	126.1 ± 71.4
10	53.9 ± 5.6	33.3 ± 4.4%	96.0 ± 21.1
15	58.7 ± 2.3	30.8 ± 4.5%	80.3 ± 14.5

plasma glucose over the basal level was not significantly different between the two groups at either the 60- or 120-min sampling time.

To demonstrate the overall relationship between plasma glucose and serum insulin, the integrated insulin and glucose areas were calculated for each subject. The ratio of insulin to glucose areas in the Point Hope group (0.38 ± 0.05) was lower than that for the Mount Edgecumbe subjects (0.56 ± 0.04); here, *t,* 2.61; $P < 0.05$. This difference is accounted for by the smaller glucose areas in the Point Hope subjects compared with those at Mount Edgecumbe (213.4 vs 167.3); here, *t,* 2.54, and $P < 0.05$.

The results of the tolbutamide tolerance tests performed on subjects at Point Hope are listed in Table 14-7. Since the test was arbitrarily terminated at 15 min the data cannot be directly compared with data from other studies in which 20- and 30-min intervals are reported. Nevertheless, it is apparent that the initial decrement in glucose concentration is within the normal range, falling to 53.9 ± 5.6% of the baseline by 10 min. Accompanying the prompt decline in plasma glucose, there was also a rise in insulin, reaching a peak of 142 μu/ml at 2 min. All subjects peaked at either 2 or 5 min, and the range extended up to 200 μu/ml. Thus, despite the low carbohydrate intake preceding the test, insulin reserves were adequate and sensitivity of plasma glucose to circulating insulin appeared.

15

Metabolic Parameters: Lactose and Sucrose Tolerance

R. Raines Bell, H. H. Draper, and *J. G. Bergan*

Peoples whose cultures have not included dairying are often intolerant, to some extent, to lactose. Eskimo populations appear unique in manifesting sucrose intolerance as well. Tolerance to these two sugars was studied in Wainwright and Point Hope.

LACTOSE INTOLERANCE

Adults

Twenty subjects (eleven males and nine females) between the ages of twenty-five and fifty-nine were recruited from the Wainwright and Point Hope populations to participate in a study of lactose tolerance in adult Eskimos (Bell et al., 1973). To avoid the trauma which may follow administration of the usual 50-g lactose load to intolerant individuals, graduated amounts of lactose (10, 20, and 30 g) were given on consecutive days after an overnight fast. These amounts approximate the quantities of lactose present in one, two, and three cups of milk, respectively. The test sequence was discontinued when the first definite symptoms of intolerance appeared (gastrointestinal distress, flatulence, mild diarrhea).

The findings are summarized in Table 15-1. Seven of the twenty subjects (35%) completed the series without adverse effects. Eight experienced symptoms of intolerance after a 20-g lactose load and an additional four after a 30-g load. Ten grams induced symptoms in only one subject. Hence 95% of the sample were asymptomatic after consuming an amount of lactose equivalent to that present in one cup of milk.

The results suggest that 20 g of lactose was the approximate threshold tolerance load in this sample of Eskimo adults. A majority were tolerant to nutritionally significant amounts of dairy foods. Only two of the twenty subjects reported that they neither drank milk nor used it in meal preparation.

TABLE 15-1 *Results of Graduated Lactose Load Tests*
Performed on 20 Eskimo Adults

Subjects	Lactose load (g)		
	10	20	30
Number first experiencing intolerance	1	8	4
Number intolerant (cumulative)	1	9	13
Percent intolerant (cumulative)	5	45	65

The remainder used modest amounts, mostly in conjunction with other foods, and none regarded themselves as intolerant to milk.

Children

Lactose tolerance tests also were conducted on twenty-seven healthy Eskimo children ranging in age from seven to fourteen years. After an overnight fast, each subject was given a standard 50-g lactose load. Capillary blood samples were taken by finger prick immediately before, and 30 and 60 min after the dose, for determination of glucose.

The results are summarized in Table 15-2. Nineteen subjects (70%) failed to show a rise in blood glucose of 20 mg/100 ml or more, the usual biochemical index of lactose intolerance. Fifteen subjects (56%) experienced gross symptoms of intolerance. However, all but one (a ten year old) reported that they normally consumed one or more cups of milk each day, usually as part of their school lunch.

Evaluation of Lactose Tolerance Tests

The foregoing results indicate that Alaskan Eskimos share with other cultures lacking a history of dairying (Kretchmer, 1972) a limited capacity for lactose digestion. The findings on adults are compatible with those of Duncan and Scott (1972) on a mixed sample of Alaskan Eskimo and Indian adults, 80% of whom were found to be intolerant to a 50-g lactose load.

Several considerations should be taken into account in evaluating the nutritional significance of studies on lactose intolerance. The 50-g lactose

TABLE 15-2 *Results of 50-g Lactose Load Test Performed on 27 Eskimo Children*

Age (yr)	Tested	Showing 20 mg/100 ml rise in plasma glucose	Showing symptoms of intolerance
7	2	0	0
8	4	2	3
9	5	3	2
10	4	4	2
11	3	2	3
12	3	2	2
13	4	4	2
14	2	2	1
Total	27	19 (70.4%)	15 (55.6%)

load employed in the conventional test represents the amount of lactose in a liter of milk. This amount is used because any lesser load leads to a rise in blood glucose which is too small to be reliably estimated. The nutritionally relevant question, however, is what proportion of a given population is tolerant to one or two cups of milk (10 or 20 g of lactose) or its equivalent in dairy products. By this criterion, a much higher proportion of the Eskimo population may be regarded as lactose-tolerant. The 50-g-load test also has been reported to yield a 20% incidence of false-positive results. Moreover, lactose in milk evidently is tolerated better than lactose in water. It appears, therefore, that most Eskimo adults are capable of consuming nutritionally significant amounts of dairy foods provided they are taken in moderate portions at intervals of several hours so as not to overload the digestive capacity of the intestine for lactose.

SUCROSE INTOLERANCE

In the course of diet interviews relative to lactose intolerance, information supplied by several subjects suggested that they were intolerant to sucrose. Typically, they reported that they developed abdominal cramps, flatulence, and diarrhea after eating cake or drinking carbonated beverages. In six individuals sucrose intolerance was confirmed by oral load tests. Figure

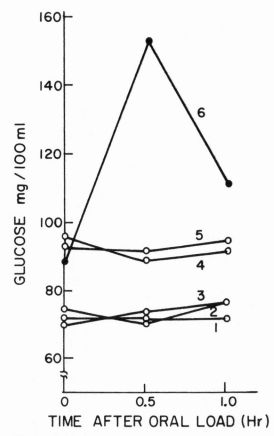

FIGURE 15-1. *Plasma glucose response in 5 sucrose-intolerant subjects (1-5) and 1 tolerant subject (6) after a 50-g oral sucrose load.*

15-1 illustrates the lack of response in blood glucose titer observed for five intolerant subjects after a 50-g sucrose load, in contrast to the normal response observed in a tolerant subject. Intolerance was also manifested in gastrointestinal disturbances beginning about 2 hr after administration of the dose and lasting a similar period. Symptoms in the sixth subject were induced by 17 g of sucrose (the amount present in one 12-oz bottle of a popular carbonated beverage to which he reported that he was intolerant). After a 50-g glucose tolerance test this subject exhibited a normal blood glucose and insulin response, showing that his intolerance to sucrose was not due to impaired monosaccharide absorption.

There was a familial pattern to the occurrence of sucrose intolerance among the individuals tested. Two were brothers and two were brother-sister siblings. The three-year-old daughter of a fifth subject, as well as the sister of another, were reportedly intolerant to sweet foods and beverages. All the sub-jects had made dietary adjustments to the problem. In the older individuals this adjustment took the form of adherence to the native diet. One younger subject had learned by experience that he could consume raisins (in which the predominant sugar is glucose) without adverse effects.

Sucrose intolerance has also been identified in independent studies on Greenland Eskimos (McNair et al., 1972). At the present time this form of sucrose intolerance is unique to Eskimo populations. Previously, only isolated cases of congenital origin have been reported. The incidence of intolerance among Eskimos is still unknown. McNair and coworkers have reported an incidence of 10.5% in a sample of Greenland Eskimos with a history of diarrhea. On the basis of documented and strongly suspected cases, the incidence in the Wainwright population is not more than 3%. Although this incidence is lower than that generally cited for lactase deficiency, the conse-quences for the individuals affected are more severe. Sucrase deficiency is not confined to adults and older children, as is lactase deficiency, and the degree of sucrose intolerance appears to be more acute. In addition, the current influx of processed foods into the Eskimo diet makes it increasingly difficult to avoid sucrose. It may be necessary to develop a class of proprietary foods for sucrose-intolerant individuals analogous to those now available for diabetics.

It is possible that sucrase deficiency among Alaskan Eskimos is indigenous to the northern region. In Nunapitchuk and Kasigluk in southwestern Alaska, dietary questioning and administration of 50 g of sucrose to ninety-six schoolchildren yielded no symptomatic evidence of intolerance. In this region berries have contributed significant amounts of sucrose to the native diet for centuries. In the arctic region, where sucrose was virtually absent from the diet, a lack of intestinal sucrase may have constituted a negligible factor in natural selection.

16

Metabolic Parameters: Plasma Vitamin E and Cholesterol Levels in Alaskan Eskimos

H. H. Draper and *Catherine C.K. Wei Wo*

Plant oils, which constitute the richest source of vitamin E in the general U.S. diet, are lacking in the native diet of the northern Alaskan Eskimo. In the subarctic region, where fish constitutes the native food staple, berries and the vegetative parts of plants make a small but significant contribution to the indigenous supply of vitamin E. Although processed foods have made substantial inroads into the native diet in recent years, the intake of vitamin E by Eskimos is still lower than that of the general U.S. population. In addition, the marine oils and fats consumed by Eskimos are high in polyunsaturated fatty acids, which are known to increase the vitamin E requirement; indeed, fish oils are used in the diet of experimental animals to produce vitamin E deficiency. The practice of drying fish in open air also leads to extensive oxidation of vitamin E along with polyenoic fatty acids. Caribou fat, like that of other ruminants, contains a low concentration of this vitamin. In view of these considerations the vitamin E status of Alaskan Eskimos was investigated.

METHODS

Blood samples were obtained from residents of the nothern coastal villages of Wainwright and Point Hope and from inhabitants of the southwestern inland villages of Kasigluk and Nunapitchuk, with the assistance of Drs. L. M. Hursh, G. V. Mann, and M. P. Colbert. The samples were collected at Wainwright in August 1971; at Point Hope in March 1972; at Kasigluk in April 1973; and at Nunapitchuk in September 1973. Kasigluk and Nunapitchuk are twin villages which have since been incorporated into the community of Akolmiut. The samples obtained at Kasigluk were all from adults whereas those obtained at Nunapitchuk were from children, and consequently the data for these villages were combined. Serum or plasma was taken from non-

fasting subjects ranging in age from six to seventy-four years and was immediately frozen and shipped to the laboratory in insulated cartons. In addition,
to evaluate more thoroughly the vitamin E status of these subjects, samples of
major native foods were collected and analyzed for vitamin E content, fatty
acid composition, and iodine value.

RESULTS

Figures 16-1-16-3 show the plasma tocopherol concentrations of 116
subjects residing in Wainwright, 111 in Point Hope, and 88 in Kasigluk and
Nunapitchuk. With a few exceptions, α-tocopherol was the only isomer
present in significant amounts. The range in values was 0.38 to 3.33 mg/100
ml plasma or serum. None of the 315 subjects had a vitamin E level below
0.35 mg/100 ml, a value suggested by Leonard and Losowsky (1967) to
represent a deficiency state.

There was a significant increase in plasma vitamin E level with age in all
three populations $(P < 0.01)$, the correlation coefficients for the Wainwright,
Point Hope, and Kasigluk-Nunapitchuk subjects being 0.50, 0.52, and 0.59,

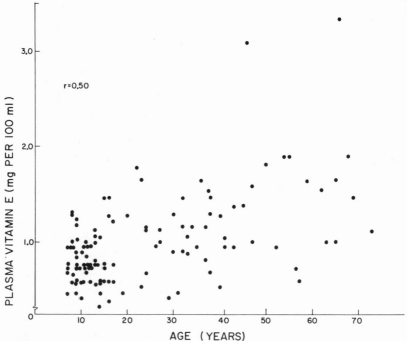

FIGURE 16-1. *Concentration of α-tocopherol in the blood plasma of 116
Wainwright Eskimos (August 1971).*

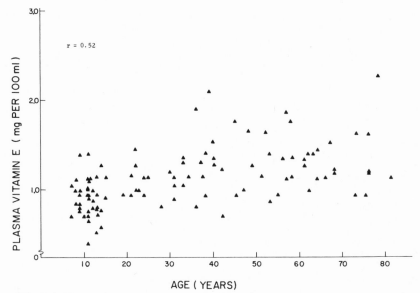

FIGURE 16-2. *Concentration of α-tocopherol in the blood plasma of 111 Point Hope Eskimos (March 1972).*

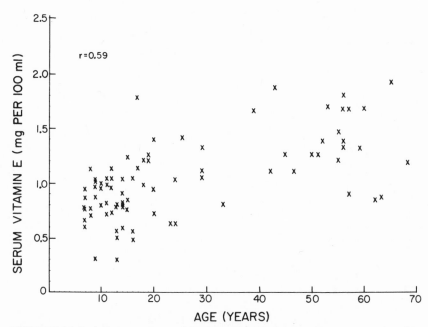

FIGURE 16-3. *Concentration of α-tocopherol in the blood serum of 88 Kasigluk and Nunapitchuk Eskimos (April and September 1973).*

TABLE 16-1 Mean and Range of α-Tocopherol Content of Some Native Alaskan Foods (Air Dry Basis)

Sample	N	Lipid (%)	α-Tocopherol (mg/100 g lipid)	PUFA (% w/w)	5- + 6-ene (% of PUFA)	Wijs (I.V.)	E:PUFA Ratio (mg/g)
Seal oil	5	100.0	8.9 5.0–14.4	30.0 20.6–34.8	87.0 82.0–91.0	170 139–187	0.30 0.17–0.52
Seal meat	3	3.2 2.7– 3.6	4.7 3.2– 5.6	20.2 20.1–20.3	74.5 69.0–80.0		0.24 0.20–0.28
Walrus blubber	3	66.0 60.4–74.7	1.80 0.80–2.40	25.0 22.6–29.1	84.0 80.0–86.0	151 144–156	0.07 0.03–0.10
Walrus meat	1		0.9	12.0	66.0		0.07
Caribou tallow	3	72.0 66.5–77.1	0.52 0.42–0.63	5.2 5.0– 5.3	0*	16 5–11	0.10 0.08–0.12
Caribou muscle	2	3.0 2.0– 3.6	0.7 0.6– 0.8	22.2 16.8–27.6	10.8 4.0–17.9		0.03 0.02–0.05
Whale blubber	3	62.0 48.6–79.3	1.5 1.2– 2.0	23.0 20.6–24.0	86.0 83.0–89.0	127 126–129	0.07 0.05–0.08
Whale meat	3	2.6 1.5– 4.6	2.5 1.8– 3.6	17.0 16.4–17.9	68.0 52.0–85.0	94 72–115	0.15 0.13–0.20
Polar bear meat	1	3.5	1.0	15.0	9.2		0.07

*Composed of 61% lineoleic acid and 39% linolenic acid.

respectively. The relationship between age and plasma vitamin E level is further illustrated in Fig. 16-4. No clear trend was discernible in the concentration of plasma α-tocopherol among the six- to seventeen-year-old subjects. However, between approximately eighteen and seventy years there appeared to be a steady increase in concentration with age. The values (mg/100 ml) for the six- to seventeen-year-old groups at Wainwright, Point Hope, and Nunapitchuk were 0.81 ± 0.26, 0.90 ± 0.20, and 0.84 ± 0.25, respectively (means ± standard deviations). The mean values for the adults at Wainwright, Point Hope, and Kasigluk were 1.21 ± 0.57, 1.23 ± 0.27, and 1.27 ± 0.33 mg/100 ml, respectively. There was a statistically significant difference ($P < 0.01$) in plasma vitamin E concentration between the six- to seventeen-year-old and the adult groups, but there was no difference attributable either to sex or to geographic location within either age group.

The α-tocopherol and polyunsaturated fatty acid (PUFA) content of the native food samples is given in Table 16-1. The concentration of α-tocopherol, expressed in mg per 100 ml lipid, ranged from 0.52 for caribou tallow to 8.90 for sea oil. The proportion of PUFA (w/w) in the edible fats and oils varied from 5.2% for caribou tallow to 30.0% for seal oil. The ratio of α-tochopherol to PUFA was 0.30 for seal oil and 0.24 for seal meat; the ratio for the other native foods was substantially lower.

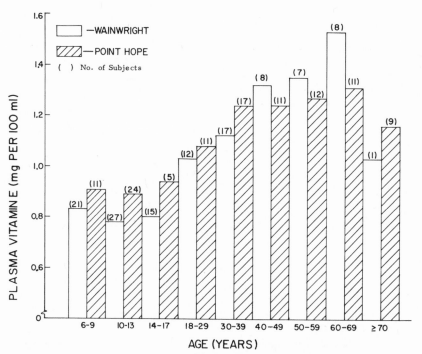

FIGURE 16-4. *Relationship of plasma α-tocopherol concentration and age in 227 subjects from Wainwright and Point Hope.*

TABLE 16-2 *Plasma Cholesterol Levels in Alaskan Eskimo Adults*

Age (yr)	N	Mean ± S.D.				N with ≥ 260 mg/100 ml		
		M	F	Both		M	F	Both
				Wainwright				
18–24	10	181±51	161±33	171±42				
25–34	15	179±24	174±32	176±28				
35–44	14	179±31	212±53	207±47				
45–54	7	160±38	258±61	202±69				
55–64	11	220±50	230±40	225±44				
65–74	9	177±36	245±91	208±71				
18–74	66	187±41	205±57	197±51		2 of 30 (6.7%)	5 of 36 (13.8%)	7 of 66 (10.6%)
				Point Hope				
18–24	9	202±33	205± 7	203±29				
25–34	15	198±50	188±31	191±37				
35–44	20	223±31	193±30	206±33				
45–54	10	177±23	219±40	202±39				
55–64	14	215±38	232±36	224±37				
65–74	14	237±41	240±39	239±38				
18–74	82	212±39	210±38	211±38		4 of 39 (10.3%)	6 of 43 (14.0%)	10 of 82 (12.2%)
			Kasigluk and Nunapitchuk					
18–24	16	188± 8	232±44	228±43				
25–34	11	222± 0	242±28	240±28				
35–44	11	243±32	265±40	261±38				
45–54	13	294±30	284±62	286±56				
55–64	19	255±22	279±45	270±39				
65–74	9	222±17	270±49	259±48				
18–74	79	247±36	260±48	256±45		7 of 13 (38.9%)	26 of 61 (42.6%)	33 of 79 (41.8%)
		US National Health Survey Data (1960–62)						
						17.6%	22.7%	

Plasma cholesterol concentrations for adults residing at the three survey sites are summarized by age in Table 16-2. The data are marked by a striking difference between the northern villages and the southwest tundra villages. Point Hope data were supplied by Dr. G. V. Mann; the remaining samples were analyzed by Bio-Science Laboratories, Van Nuys, Ca. Cholesterol levels

TABLE 16-3 *Mean (± S.D.) Plasma Cholesterol Levels in Alaskan Eskimo Children (7-16 Years)*

Site	N	Cholesterol (mg/100 ml)			Hypercholesterolemia (% ≥ 230 mg/100 ml)		
		Male	Female	Both	Male	Female	Both
Wainwright	63	145±21	151±29	149±26	0	2.4	1.6
Point Hope	56	164±22	168±27	166±24	0	0	0
Nunapitchuk	83	201±25	205±30	202±27	14.9	25.0	19.3

at Wainwright and Point Hope were substantially lower than those found in the U.S. National Health Survey of 1960-62, whereas those at Kasigluk and Nunapitchuk were substantially higher. Females had higher plasma cholesterol levels than males, although at Kasigluk-Nunapitchuk the sex difference was insignificant. Hypercholesterolemia was generally correlated with obesity, which was more prevalent in the southern villages and in women.

The data for the concentration of cholesterol in plasma of children are summarized in Table 16-3. As for the adults, there was a significant difference between the northern and the southern villages. The increments in plasma cholesterol were generally correlated with the degree of dietary acculturation, which was least at Wainwright, intermediate at Point Hope, and greatest at Nunapitchuk. A concurrent diet survey showed that the incursion of processed foods into the diet of children was substantially greater than into that of adults.

In Fig. 16-5 the plasma vitamin E concentrations of the Wainwright subjects are plotted against their cholesterol concentrations. The relationship between the levels of these plasma constituents appears to be linear (r, 0.74). The equation for the linear regression of plasma α-tocopherol level (Y in mg/100 ml) on cholesterol level (X in mg/100 ml) was $Y = 86.7 + 85.4X$. A similar relationship was evident in the data for subjects living in the other villages.

DISCUSSION

Data for U.S. adults consuming a mixed diet indicate that plasma or serum typically contains about 1.0 mg vitamin E per 100 ml. The values of 1.21 ± 0.57, 1.23 ± 0.27, and 1.27 ± 0.33 mg/100 ml for Wainwright, Point Hope, and Kasigluk adults therefore indicate that the level of vitamin E in the blood of Eskimos is at least as high as that of the general U.S. adult popu-

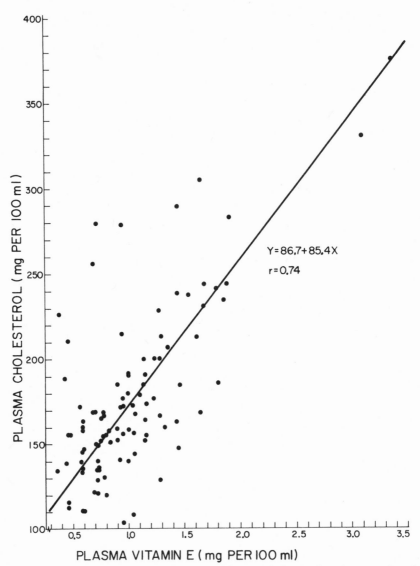

FIGURE 16-5. *Relationship between plasma cholesterol and α-tocopherol concentrations in Wainwright Eskimos (August 1971).*

lation. The means and standard deviations for the Eskimo children (six to seventeen years old) are similar to those reported by Lewis et al. (1973) for children in Los Angeles and by Baker et al. (1967) for children in New York.

A diet survey conducted in conjunction with the present study indicated that approximately 45% of the calories in the diet of Wainwright adults were derived from native foods. There were increments in the consumption of processed foods from Wainwright to Point Hope to Kasigluk and Nuna-pitchuk, and children consumed a significantly higher proportion of processed foods than did adults. This gradient was not accompanied by any discernible change in vitamin E status.

It has been estimated (National Research Council, 1974) that 64% of the α-tocopherol in the general U.S. diet is supplied by salad oils, shortening, and margarine, 11% by fruits and vegetables, and 7% by grain products (aggregate, 82%). All such foods can be said, for practical purposes, to be lacking in the native diet of the Arctic Eskimo.

Despite the magnitude of the contribution of seed oils to the α-tocopherol content of the U.S. mixed diet, much of the vitamin E in these oils is in the form of other less active isomers (particularly γ-tocopherol). In contrast, sub-stantially all of the vitamin E in the Eskimo native diet is in the form of α-tocopherol, the most active form of the vitamin. Hence, although the total vitamin E content of the Eskimo native diet is substantially less than that of the mixed diet, it appears to be comparable in α-tocopherol content. It is noteworthy that γ-tocopherol, which commonly constitutes 10–15% of the plasma vitamin E in U.S. subjects consuming a mixed diet, was undetectable in most of the Eskimo samples.

The high concentration of PUFA in caribou muscle, a mean of 5.6% arachidonic acid and 15.4% linoleic acid, is in sharp contrast to values re-ported for beef cattle fed a mixed ration, approximately 0.5% arachidonic acid and 2.5% linoleic acid (Link et al., 1970a). Caribou tallow also contains about three times the concentration of PUFA reported for beef subcutaneous adipose tissue (Link et al., 1970b). The values for caribou muscle lipids are similar to those reported for beef muscle phospholipids (Link et al., 1970a). This difference between the two ruminant species may be because caribou muscle is less "marbled" with neutral fat and hence has a greater proportion of membrane phospholipids. The caribou meat samples were noticeably lean and dark in color.

A linear relationship between plasma cholesterol and vitamin E levels has been observed in previous investigations and was evident in all three popula-tions sampled in this study. This relationship indicates that the concentration of both constituents is markedly influenced by the level of serum lipoproteins.

It is evident that the picture of low blood cholesterol levels and low blood pressures is no longer valid for many Alaskan Eskimos. Although Eskimos residing in remote villages still have a lower incidence of hypercholesterolemia and hypertension than that seen in the general U.S. population, those living in the larger towns and urban centers are now essentially indistinguishable in these respects from non-Eskimo inhabitants of the same communities. Maynard (1974) has reached a similar conclusion on the basis of a recent study on a large sample of Alaskan Eskimo men and has questioned the asser-tion that they have an unusually low prevalence of coronary heart disease.

17

Exercise Physiology

Donald W. Rennie

The extensively documented study of R. K. Nelson (1969) indicated that the north Alaskan Eskimo communities of Point Hope, Wainwright, and to a lesser degree, Barrow, were still largely dependent in 1968-70 upon the wildlife living within a limited perimeter of the town, despite a rapid decline in hunting activity during the last decade. It was the purpose of this investigation to apply standardized methods for evaluating physical work performance to as large a segment of this population as possible, to determine if any differences existed between it and other circumpolar hunting societies or more sedentary populations elsewhere. Such data might also serve as a base of comparison for any future studies of these remarkable people as the tide of modern events engulfs them.

Few studies of muscular power or endurance had been conducted on Eskimos prior to the onset of the Human Adaptability Project of the International Biological Program (IBP). Those that had been reported were in some disagreement, possibly because the daily activity level of the groups studied varied widely, with consequent differences in physical conditioning. As reported by Rodahl (1958), Rennie in 1954 administered the Harvard treadmill test (Johnson et al., 1942) to six active Eskimo hunters (ages eighteen to forty-five from the village of Anaktuvuk Pass, Alaska. He found that respective "fitness scores" for these Eskimos, well-trained army troops on duty at Fort Wainwright, and sedentary air force personnel from Ladd Air Force Base to have the ration 3.5:2.5:1. However, Erikson (1957) reported similar respiratory and heart rate responses to standard exercise in Eskimos and non-Eskimos at Barrow, Alaska. Andersen and Hart (1963) found that maximal aerobic power of a few adult male Eskimos in Paringtung on Baffin Island was, if anything, inferior to that of well-conditioned non-Eskimos.

Out of the studies associated with the IBP/Human Adaptability Program extensive new data have emerged on circumpolar Eskimos and Ainu, summarized in a detailed review by Shephard (1974). The present report therefore is confined to results obtained as a component part of the U.S. Research program. It extends observations previously reported by Rennie et al. (1970).

Whenever possible, the standardized methods are those agreed upon by

Supported in part by a grant-in-aid from the Smithsonian Institution.

coworkers at the November 1967 Working Party Conference for the IBP/HA Study of Circumpolar Populations. The tabulated data, arranged according to an individual family and census code so it can be correlated with data provided by other contributors to this volume, is available from the author on request. Summaries are presented here.

METHODS

Respiratory Function and Anaerobic Muscular Power

The subjects for this aspect of the study were sixty-two Eskimos from the village of Wainwright, ranging in age from six to sixty-four years. Fifty men and boys participated in the respiratory-function and muscle-power tests. Anaerobic power was also measured in twelve girls ranging in age from eight to fourteen. The subjects were chosen from thirty of the fifty-two family groups in Wainwright in an attempt to test a wide age span and a cross-section of the families in town. Each subject was examined by medical and dental teams. Anthropometric measurements were performed by personnel from the Department of Anthropology at the University of Wisconsin, including height, weight, and four skinfold thicknesses (subscapular, flank of ninth rib, and right and left triceps), from which the perfentage of body fat was estimated as described by Durnin and Rahaman (1967).

Pulmonary Function Tests

Vital capacity (VC), forced expiratory volume ($FEV_{1.0}$), and forced expiratory rate ($FER_{1.0}$, calculated as a percentage of VC), were measured with a 13.5-liter, two-speed (32 and 1920 mm/sec) recording Collins spirometer from which the soda lime canister was removed. The procedure described by Kory et al. (1961) was followed in detail. Vital-capacity measurements were repeated three times and the highest value was converted from ATPS to BTPS. Forced expiratory volume was also measured three times and the highest volume at 1 sec was designated $FEV_{1.0}$ BTPS. Maximum breathing capacity (MBC) was measured by collecting expired gas in a 200-liter Douglas bag over a 15-sec period, without controlling respiratory frequency or tidal volume. The expired gas was expressed manually from the Douglas bag through a dry gas meter calibrated with a 600-liter Tissot spirometer. The expired gas for all tests passed through an oversized rubber mouthpiece, a Collins triple "j" low-resistance valve, and plastic rubing 1-1/2 in. in internal diameter.

Maximal Anaerobic Power

Maximal anaerobic power was determined by the method of Margaria (1966), with the collaboration of Dr. Pietro di Prampero from Margaria's laboratory (the Institute of Human Physiology, Milan, Italy). The test consisted of measuring the vertical velocity of a subject running at top speed up the steps of the town schoolhouse; for the measurement, a specially designed electronic chronometer, sensitive to 0.01 sec, was kindly lent by the Institute of Human Physiology where it had been designed and built for this anaerobic test.

Two light beams, aligned parallel to the steps, activated photocells that started and stopped a digital timer. The vertical distance between the electric cells was 70 cm. The photocells were placed on the second and fourth steps so that the subject crossed light beams with the same stride in each case. The subject's power was expressed in kg·m/kg·sec or, more simply, as the vertical velocity, V_v, in m/sec. Total elapsed times were of the order 0.4–0.6 sec.

Maximal Aerobic Power

A total of 347 Eskimos, 195 males and 152 females, were studied by step test and motor-driven treadmill to determine their maximal O_2 consumption, $\dot{V}_{O_2 max}$. Of this total eighty-two (fifty-three male and twenty-nine female) subjects were from Wainwright, 118 (fifty-nine male and fifty-nine female) subjects from Barrow, and 110 (sixty-four male and forty-six female) subjects from Point Hope. The sample comprised roughly 30% of the villages of Wainwright and Point Hope and 10% of Barrow. The age range of all subjects was ten to seventy years old.

Step Test. A standardized submaximal "steady-state" step-test method was used in Wainwright. The subjects stepped up and down a single 30-cm or 40-cm step at a frequency of 15, 25, and 30 times a minute, using a metronome to set the cadence. A 10-min rest was interposed between each exercise. Heart rate was monitored from minutes 3.45–4 and 4.35–5 of each exercise period with a telemeter and portable electrocardiograph. (E & M telemeter Model FM-1100–#2, receiver Model FM-100-E2, and Cambridge ECG were lent by Dr. Albert Rekate, Department of Medicine, State University of New York at Buffalo.) Expired gas was collected from minutes 4–5 of each exercise period in a 200-liter Douglas bag and the volume measured as described for the MBC test. Aliquots of gas for oxygen analysis were taken from the Douglas bag as the mixed expired gas was being expressed through the gas meter. The gas sample was analyzed by passing it through a Beckman paramagnetic oxygen and analyzer calibrated in the field at zero gas flow by subjecting the analysis chamber to a range of pressures from ambient to 450 torr, producing a PO_2 range from 160 to 95 torr.

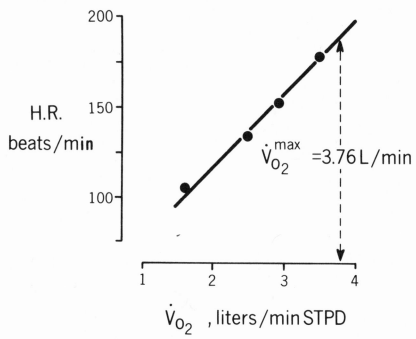

FIGURE 17-1. *Estimation of* $\dot{V}_{O_2 max}$ *from submaximal heart rate–* $\dot{V}_{O_2}$ *relationship. Subject was a 30-year-old Eskimo male for whom a maximal heart rate of 190 beats/min was assumed.*

$\dot{V}_{O_2}$ was calculated as: $\dot{V}_{O_2}$ equals $\dot{V}_E (F_{I_{O_2}} - F_{E_{O_2}})/(1 - F_{I_{O_2}}(1 - R))$, assuming R equal to 0.9.

Maximum oxygen consumption, $\dot{V}_{O_2 max}$, was determined by extrapolation of the heart rate/$\dot{V}_{O_2}$ relationship to maximal heart rate, HR_{max}, for each group. HR_{max} was taken to be as follows: over fifty years, 170 beats/min; thirty-six to fifty years, 180 beats/min; twenty-one to thirty-five years, 190 beats/min; under twenty-one years, 200 beats/min. Figure 17-1 illustrates the technique. A thirty-year-old subject exercised at four submaximal work loads and his steady-state $\dot{V}_{O_2}$ and HR were determined for each. Assuming a HR_{max} of 190 beats/min, his predicted $\dot{V}_{O_2 max}$ was 3.8 liters/min.

Treadmill Test. For all subjects studied at Point Hope and Barrow a motor-driven treadmill was used to establish the work load. Walking or jogging proved to be a more natural and comfortable form of exercise for the Eskimos and permitted a finer gradation of work load than was possible with the step test described above. In general, three broad levels of work loads were achieved: light ($\dot{V}_{O_2}$ of 10–20 ml/min·kg; slope of zero; speed of 2–3 mph), moderate ($\dot{V}_{O_2}$ of 15–35 ml/min·kg; slope of 0–5%: speed of 3–6 mph), and heavy ($\dot{V}_{O_2}$ of 20–45 ml/min·kg; slope of 1–10%; speed of 3–6 mph). On rare occasions a fourth work load was achieved if the subject was willing and appeared capable. A 10-min rest period was allowed between each exercise. Heart rate and $\dot{V}_{O_2}$ were measured as described for the step test above and $\dot{V}_{O_2\,max}$ was estimated from the calculated regression of HR on $\dot{V}_{O_2}$ extrapolated to the HR_{max} for each age group.

15-Min Run. A 15-min run along the lines suggested by Balke (1963) was conducted in Wainwright to determine the correlation between maximal aerobic power and endurance in a distance run. The town airstrip was used as the track, with oil drums spaced 1/4 mile apart. The men's division ran in age groups: forty-one to fifty, thirty-one to forty, twenty-one to thirty, and fifteen to twenty. The women ran all at once. A prize of gasoline was offered proportional to the number of laps completed, in order to motivate the competitors to run as far as possible. The predicted distance was compared to the actual distance run.

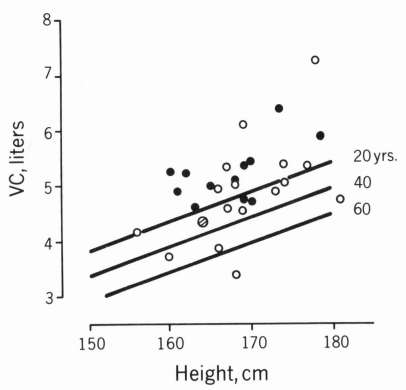

FIGURE 17-2. *Vital capacity as a function of height. Solid lines indicate the predicted relationship for U.S. males from the formula of Kory et al. (1961) for ages 20, 40, and 60 years. Values for individual male Eskimos are plotted for the age groups 15–30 years (solid circles), 31–50 years (open circles), and above 50 years (shaded circles).*

RESULTS

Respiratory Function

Total and timed vital capacity and maximal breathing capacity for the male Eskimos are depicted in Figs. 17-2 to 17-4. Since the age ranged from fifteen to fifty-six years and the height from 146 to 181 cm, the data have been plotted as a function of height and subdivided into three age groups; fifteen to thirty years, thirty-one to fifty years, and above fifty years.

To compare the Eskimo pulmonary function with normal U.S. adult male standards, we utilized the prediction formulas derived empirically by Kory et al. (1961) based upon age and overall height of 468 normal males aged eighteen to sixty-six. These formulas are as follows: For vital capacity (Fig. 17-2), VC (liters) equals $0.052\ H_{cm}$ minus 0.022 Age minus 3.60 (r, 0.64, SEE, 0.58 1). For $FEV_{1.0}$ (Fig. 17-3), $FEV_{1.0}$ (liters) equals $0.037\ H_{cm}$ minus 0.028 Age minus 1.59 (r, 0.63; SEE, 0.52 1). For maximal breathing

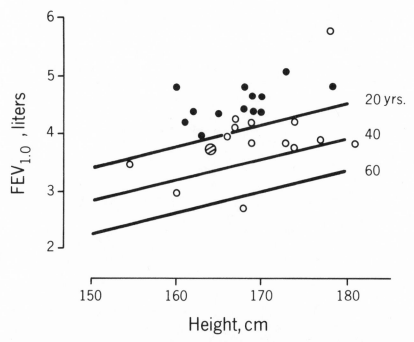

FIGURE 17-3. $FEV_{1.0}$ as a function of height. Solid lines indicate the predicted relationship for U.S. males from the formula of Kory et al. (1961) for ages 20, 40, and 60 years. Values for individual male Eskimos are plotted for the age groups 15-30 years (solid circles), 31-50 years (open circles), and above 50 years (shaded circles).

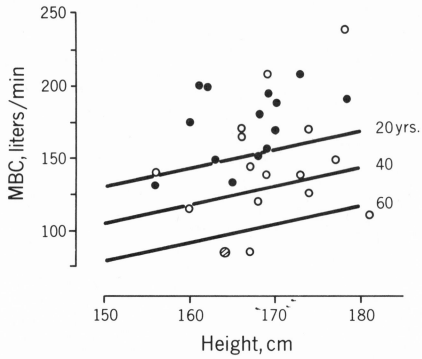

FIGURE 17-4. *Maximal breathing capacity as a function of height. Solid lines indicate the predicted relationship for U.S. males from the formula of Kory et al. (1961) for ages 20, 40, and 60 years. Values for individual male Eskimos are plotted for the age groups 15-30 years (solid circles), 31-50 years (open circles), and above 50 years (shaded circles).*

capacity (Fig. 17-4), MBC (liters per minute) equals 1.34 H_{cm} minus 1.26 Age minus 21.4 (*r*, 0.53; SEE, 29 1/min).

The solid lines in Fig. 17-2 to 17-4 show the predicted relationship between each measure of pulmonary function and height for ages twenty, forty, and sixty years. It is apparent that the measures of pulmonary function in Eskimos tend to lie above the predicted norm of U.S. males. A similar result was subsequently reported by Rode and Shephard (1973) for the Igloolik Eskimo population.

When predicted and observed values for VC and MBC are compared for each individual the observed value exceeds the predicted by an average of 10%—e.g., average observed VC equaled 4.94 1 (SD, 0.82), whereas average predicted VC equaled 4.41 1 ± 0.36, and average observed MBC equaled 181 1 ± 37 while average predicted MBC equaled 164 1 ± 14.

Certain individuals stand out within the Eskimo group, whether compared with their peers or with the Kory standards. The vital capacities of six subjects (ages sixteen to forty-four years) were over three standard deviations above the predicted VC for their age and height; and only one subject (age thirty-six) had a VC sufficiently below the predicted U.S. norm to warrant special mention. Contrary to expectations, the pulmonary-function results bear no correlation to maximal aerobic power in these individuals. We are left with the enigma of a superior pulmonary apparatus with no functional correlate.

These pulmonary-function studies were not an integral part of the work-performance measurements. They were undertaken to explore the possibility that the pulmonary component of oxygen transfer might differ from standards avilable elsewhere, in which case a more systematic study would be justified. Such appears to be the case, and one would hope that future studies of work performance among these people will include these and other tests of pulmonary function.

Maximal Anaerobic Power

Individual values for maximal anaerobic power of all male subjects are plotted in Fig. 17-5 as a function of age. In this figure maximal anaerobic power is expressed in the left ordinate in terms of the maximal vertical velocity (V_v) in m/sec (power/kg equals kg·meters/sec·kg equals meters/sec) and in the right ordinate as its corresponding energy equivalent ($\dot{W}_p{}^{max}$) in ml O_2/kg·min, calculated on the basis of a 25% efficiency (assuming 1 1 O_2 equals 5 kcal and overall mechanical efficiency of stair climbing equals 0.25 [Margaria et al., 1966]). $\dot{W}_p{}^{max}$ increases dramatically in the age range eight to twenty, attains a maximal value equivalent to 200-250 ml O_2/kg·min or about four times maximal aerobic power, and decreases after age twenty. The linear regressions for the ascending and descending parts of the function have the following formulas:

below age 17: V_v (m/sec) = 0.145 (±0.151) + 0.105 Age (years)
above age 17: V_v (m/sec) = 2.05 (±0.076) - 0.016 Age (years)

Maximal Aerobic Power

Oxygen Cost of Step Test. The relationship between $\dot{V}_{O_2}$ and rate of work for thirty-seven male Eskimos (age eleven to sixty-four years) performing the submaximal step test was linear over a range of power from 150 to 1020 kg·m/min and over a range of $\dot{V}_{O_2}$ from 0.9 to 3.5 1/min. The relationship had the formula: $\dot{V}_{O_2}$ (liters/min) equals 3.05 · 10^{-3} (Power) + 0.384 (SE, 0.251). The overall efficiency for performing this type of work averaged 15.4%, which is similar to results reported by Shephard (1974). No calcula-

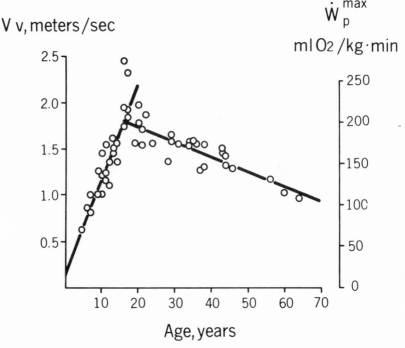

FIGURE 17-5. *Maximal anaerobic power of male Eskimos as a function of age. At left, anaerobic power as maximal vertical velocity,* V_v. *At right, anaerobic power in terms of its equivalent oxygen utilization,* $W_p max$.

tions were made of the efficiency of treadmill walking or running in the towns of Point Hope or Barrow.

Ventilatory Response to Work. The ventilatory volume per minute $(\dot{V}_E)$ corresponding to each level of step test work was a linear function of $\dot{V}_{O_2}$ up to 2.5 1/min, with the formula: $\dot{V}_E$ (1/min) equals 24.6 · $\dot{V}_{O_2}$ + 3.5. The slope, 24.6, represents liters of pulmonary ventilation per liter of O_2 uptake (ventilatory equivalent). The value is higher than that of 20.6 reported by Åstrand (1952) for Swedish men between the ages of twenty and thirty-three years but similar to the range of twenty-one to thirty-eight reported by Anderson et al. (1962) in nomadic Lapps and by Anderson et al. (1960) in Indian men.

Maximal O_2 Consumption. The relationship between $\dot{V}_{O_2 max}$ and age is summarized for all male subjects in Fig. 17-6 and for all female subjects in Fig. 17-7. For comparison, data reported by Shephard (1974) on Igloolik (Canadian) Eskimos are also shown, by sex.

Male Eskimos from each Alaskan town reached an average peak $\dot{V}_{O_2 max}$ of 50–52 ml/kg·min in their late teens, followed by a linear decline with age to an average value of 35–40 ml/kg·min at age fifty. By contrast, male Igloolik subjects had an average $\dot{V}_{O_2\,max}$ of 70 ml/kg·min in their late teens, followed by a more rapid rate of decline to 40 ml/kg·min by age fifty-five. The maximal aerobic power of the Igloolik Eskimo is significantly greater than the Alaskan groups for the age range ten to thirty-five years but not in older age groups.

Female Eskimos from each Alaskan town had an average peak $\dot{V}_{O_2\,max}$ of 35–40 ml/kg·min in their early teens and a slow decline thereafter to 35 ml/kg·min by age fifty. Again by contrast, the female Igloolik subjects had an average peak $\dot{V}_{O_2\,max}$ of 55 ml/kg·min in their early teens and a more rapid rate of decline to 35 ml/kg·min in the fifty- to sixty-year-old range. Again, the Igloolik women had maximal aerobic power clearly and significantly greater than the Alaskan women until after age forty. In fact, the maximal

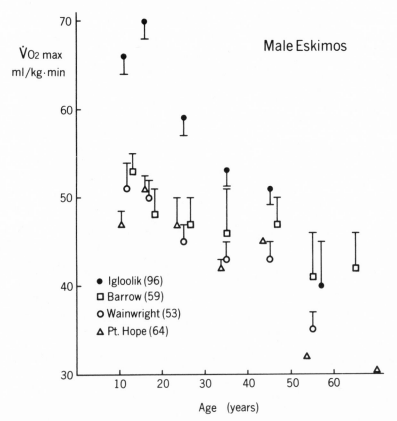

FIGURE 17-6. *Maximal aerobic power,* $\dot{V}_{O_2\,max}$, *as a function of age for male Eskimos. The mean and standard error are shown for age groups: 10–15, 16–20, 21–30, 31–40, 41–50, 51–60, and 61–70 years.*

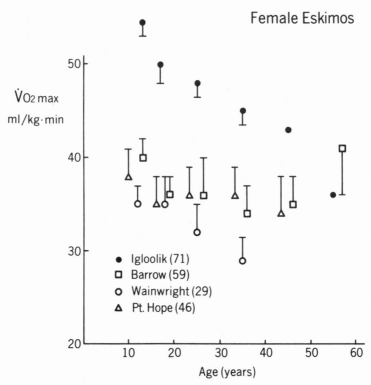

FIGURE 17-7. *Maximal aerobic power,* $\dot{V}_{O_2\,max}$, *as a function of age for female Eskimos. The mean and standard error are shown for age groups: 10-15, 16-20, 21-30, 31-40, 41-50, and 51-60 years.*

aerobic power of Igloolik women was equal to Alaskan men over the age range twenty to sixty, a rather astonishing observation.

Maximal Aerobic Power of Arm Work. Since coastal hunting practices include a high degree of arm work (Nelson, 1969) we elected to deviate from the standard protocol to include a measurement of maximal aerobic arm work in the Wainwright male Eskimos. We used three steady-state levels of submaximal "paddling-like" work. During the fifth minute the ECG and $\dot{V}_{O_2}$ were measured by the same methods employed in the step test. An exerciser was utilized that enabled the subject to draw a cord back and forth past an adjustable friction plate. The plate was mounted on the wall with the subject seated on the floor, his legs extended in front exactly as in a kayak-paddling posture. The "paddling" frequency was kept constant at 30 or 40 strokes/min, and the tension load on the plate was increased to produce subjectively "light," "medium," and "heavy" work.

Data were obtained on twenty-one male subjects (age eleven to forty-eight for whom step test data were also available. Figure 17-8 illustrates comparative $HR/\dot{V}_{O_2}$ data for the step test and arm work on a fifteen year old for whom a maximal heart rate of 200 beats/min was assumed. The linear relationship between heart rate and $\dot{V}_{O_2}$ is evident for both types of work, but the relationship is shifted to the left for arm work, leading to a smaller $\dot{V}_{O_2\,max}$ for this kind of work.

Figure 17-9 summarizes the $\dot{V}_{O_2\,max}$ obtained from leg work and arm work for each of twenty-one individuals. On the average, $\dot{V}_{O_2\,max}$ for arm work was 70% that for leg work, a result that is characteristic of populations not engaged in a high degree of arm training (Åstrand and Saltin, 1961).

15-Min Run. The relationship between distance covered in the 15-min run and the maximal oxygen consumption previously determined from the step test is plotted in Fig. 17-10. Shown are data for thirteen male Eskimos and four male members of the investigation team. The diagonal line in the figure indicates the hypothetical distance that could have been run assuming the runner utilized 100% of his maximal oxygen consumption for the entire

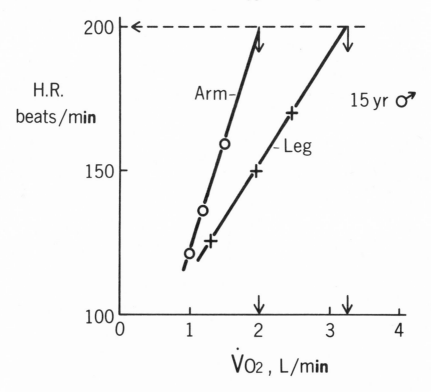

FIGURE 17-8. *Relationship between heart rate and steady-state oxygen consumption during leg work (step test) and arm work (simulated paddling) in a 15-year-old male Eskimo. The HR/$\dot{V}_{O_2}$ relationship was extrapolated to a maximal heart rate of 200 to determine the $\dot{V}_{O_2\,max}$ for each type of work. In this example $\dot{V}_{O_2\,max}$ for arm work was 2.0 1/min and for leg work, 3.2 1/min.*

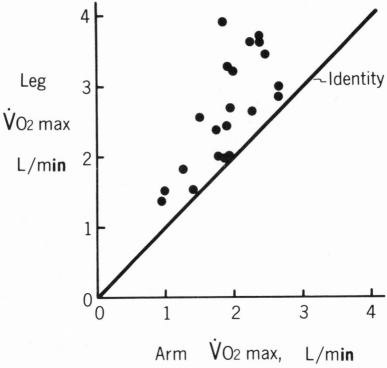

FIGURE 17-9. *Comparison of $\dot{V}_{O_2 max}$ measured in 21 male Eskimos during leg work* (ordinate) *and arm work* (abscissa). *The diagonal line indicates the locus for identical $\dot{V}_{O_2 max}$. It is evident that the $\dot{V}_{O_2 max}$ achieved by arm work is consistently less than that by leg work.*

15 min. This prediction is based on the observation that the cost of running on a level treadmill averages 200 ml O_2/kg/min/km, independent of the speed over the speed range achieved in the present study (Margaria et al., 1963).

It is apparent (Fig. 17-10) that almost half of the Eskimo runners fell far short of their predicted goal. As an extreme example, one subject with a $\dot{V}_{O_2 max}$ of forty-one ml/min·kg covered only 800 meters in the time alloted instead of the 3,000 meters one would predict. This particular individual had the highest vital capacity and maximal breathing capacity in the village but for reasons that are not clear his $\dot{V}_{O_2 max}$ was quite average and his endurance, as measured by this run, was unusually low. In contrast, all of the investigators achieved their predicted distance within 200 meters. In fairness to the Eskimo group it should be pointed out that the investigator to the far right in Fig. 17-10 was Dr. Robert Fitts, an experienced runner with a best time of 2 hrs 23 min in the marathon.

There are several reasons for failure to run as far as predicted, but by far

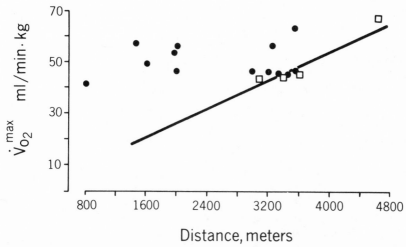

FIGURE 17-10. *Relationship between the distance run in 15 min and the previously measured* $\dot{V}_{O_2 max}$ *for Eskimo males (circles) and members of the investigation team (squares). The team member to the far right was an accomplished marathon runner.*

the most important, in our judgment, was the failure of the Eskimos to pace themselves in the early part of the run. They sprinted out of the starting gate under the stimulus of their cheering supporters and without full appreciation of the time element, and rather quickly exhausted themselves. For those Eskimos who did set a more modest pace, and for the investigators, the distance run appears to correlate well with measured $\dot{V}_{O_2 max}$.

DISCUSSION

The present study was undertaken to assess the physical fitness of as large a portion of three Alaskan Eskimo communities as possible. *Maximal aerobic power* is generally considered an important component of physical fitness because it establishes the uppermost limit of muscular power a person can theoretically support by his oxygen-transfer system. *Maximal anaerobic power* has been less frequently studied and evaluated because few techniques have been developed to measure it; however, it is well known that the muscle power generated for maximal work of short duration can greatly exceed what can be supported aerobically. Bursts of high muscular power of relatively short duration could be of great importance in successful hunting, and a high level of maximal anaerobic power would therefore be a valuable adaptation. Therefore it seemed worth while to measure this aspect of muscle function in Eskimos as well as the more commonly measured aerobic power of muscle.

Anaerobic Power

In contrast to maximal aerobic power, which is dependent upon the entire series-linked oxygen-transfer systems of the body, maximal anaerobic power depends much more upon local musculoskeletal factors such as the muscle mass/body weight ratio, the concentration and availability of phosphagens within the muscle cell, the mechanical advantage of the muscle on its tendonous attachment, the leverage which muscles can exert on the bones of the feet, legs, and lower body, and the coordination of the subject in moving rapidly on the level or uphill.

The test designed by Margaria et al. (1966), which we used in this study, measures the power generated during the first few seconds of vertical stair climbing at maximal speed. Margaria has shown that this power reaches a peak within 2 sec of the beginning of the climb and begins to decline after 5 sec. In the present study we were fortunate to have the help of Dr. di Prampero, who used the same chronometer and essentially the same technique used in previous studies in Italy and Africa. The present results are therefore quite comparable with those of the previous studies. The principal difference was the short staircase (eight steps) we had to use in Wainwright. According to Margaria's analysis this did not allow the Eskimos sufficient time to attain more than 85% of their maximal vertical velocity. However, we have not made any correction for this difference.

Figure 17-11 compares the data for Eskimos with the type of relationship between maximal anaerobic power and age that was described by Margaria et al. (1966) and di Prampero and Cerretelli (1968). Beginning with low values at age five—e.g., 0.6 kg·m/kg·sec, maximal anaerobic power achieves its peak values during the late teens and early twenties. At this age it has a value of about 1.8 to 2.5 kg·m/kg·sec in the Eskimo subjects, which is four to five times the power they can sustain aerobically, and comparable to the results reported for trained Italian track stairs. Beyond age twenty a slow decline in maximal anaerobic power sets in, which evidently (by extrapolation) would render the man of 130 years as incapable as the babe in developing this type of muscle power.

The reasons for the striking change of maximal anaerobic power with age are not known and should provide a rewarding area for basic research. It is clear from Fig. 17-11 that the Eskimos have higher values at any given age than sedentary Italian city dwellers and especially African natives (Nilo-Hamitic and Bantu) living in the vicinity of Mount Kenya. Since we have probably underestimated maximal vertical velocity, the true differences could be even greater. Possible explanations are: (1) larger leg muscles of Eskimos, (2) greater mechanical advantage of muscle attachments across joints of Eskimos, (3) a higher level of visual-motor coordination in Eskimos, and (4) the possibility of a different chemical composition of the Eskimos' muscles.

Di Prampero and Cerretelli, in discussing the results of earlier studies,

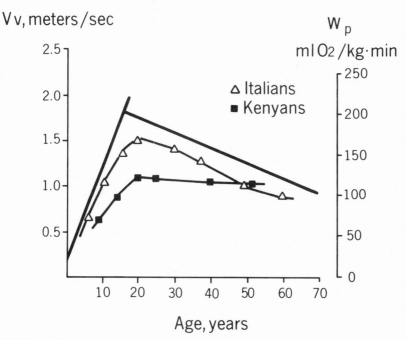

FIGURE 17-11. *Maximal anaerobic power of Eskimos (solid lines) compared with that of sedentary Italian city dwellers and African natives (di Prampero and Cerretelli, 1968).*

ruled out differences in muscle size between Africans and Italians since both had the same fat-free diameter of thigh and calves. Calf circumference of 128 Wainwright Eskimos over the age of twenty-five averaged 34.18 cm with a standard deviation of 2.05 (Jamison and Zegura, 1970); however, lacking comparable measures we do not know how this finding compares with that for the subjects studied earlier. The Africans, with unusually long and thin legs relative to body weight, were thought to be at a disadvantage mechanically in performing this step-climbing test; and it could be that the relatively short, well-muscled legs of the Eskimo place him at an advantage, at least on steps of average height. We have no way of assessing possibilities 3 and 4, but the chances seem remote that either of these could play a role.

Maximal Aerobic Power

To estimate maximal oxygen uptake a submaximal step test was chosen initially at Wainwright as most suitable, because of its simplicity, the familiarity of the Eskimos with this type of muscle work, and the relatively close agreement between this and other tests designed to measure maximal oxygen uptake directly (Shephard, 1966). In subsequent summers at Point Hope and Barrow, a motor-driven treadmill was available and was used in preference to the step test because it felt more natural to the subjects. We chose to measure $\dot{V}_{O_2}$ and heart rate directly at two or more "steady-state" work loads, as recommended by Shephard (1966), rather than rely upon indirect methods which might not be applicable to Eskimo subjects untrained in the test technique. To some degree, subjects were reluctant to perform this test any more frequently or any longer than necessary; therefore we dispensed with preliminary trials or duplicate performances. Despite their lack of practice with the test, the overall efficiency of Eskimos performing a single 30- or 40-cm step test at frequencies of 15–25/min averaged 15.4%, which is almost identical with efficiencies reported by Shephard (1966) and Rovelli and Aghemo (1963) for a similar step test.

Measurements of maximal aerobic power have been reported for male population groups with wide differences in daily life habits, nutrition, and physique. The group averages are remarkably similar, declining from approximately 50 ml O_2/min·kg at age twenty, to 40 in the fourth decade of life, and to 30 after age sixty. The outstanding exceptions are, as one would suspect, elite athletes trained in events requiring high oxygen expenditure, for example, Swedish "orienteers" who averaged 80 ml O_2/min·kg in their youth and still have a $\dot{V}_{O_2 max}$ of 47 ml/min·kg in their sixties. When our present results are compared with those of most other population groups, it is clear that no appreciable difference exists between the mean values for $\dot{V}_{O_2 max}$ of male Alaskan Eskimos and fit male population groups elsewhere, whether they be hunters or nonhunters (Andersen et al., 1960; Andersen et al., 1962; Andersen and Hart, 1963; Åstrand, 1952, 1960; Cumming, 1967; di Prampero and Cerretelli, 1968; Lammert, 1972; Margaria et al., 1965; Rennie et al., 1970; Robinson, 1938; Wyndham et al., 1963). A remarkable exception are the Eskimos of Igloolik, reported on by Shephard (1974). This latter group clearly has a superior $\dot{V}_{O_2 max}$, which ranks them among competitive athletes of other countries.

Several factors may conspire to lower the apparent $\dot{V}_{O_2 max}$ of Alaskan Eskimos below its true value. The submaximal step test and treadmill test depend upon extrapolation to a maximal heart rate that may be higher than the norms used here. However, except for well-conditioned athletes, there appear to be only minor variations in average maximal heart rates among different population groups. A disproportionately large heat load may have increased heart rates of the Eskimos and hence led to an underestimate of $\dot{V}_{O_2 max}$. We had the impression that the Eskimos sweated excessively, as compared with members of the investigating team who were also tested, and the Eskimos complained of being hot even doing moderate work. Observations made by Rodahl and Rennie (1957) indicated that heat production and sweating at rest is higher in Eskimos and that the difference is exaggerated in exercise.

Lastly, a "deconditioning" process may have occurred over the past generation as modern hunting implements are used more extensively. Nelson (1969) describes the general lack of enthusiasm for the rigors of the hunt among the younger men of the village and the increased use of modern vehicles by those who do hunt. That deconditioning may have occurred is supported by my own observations, reported by Rodahl (1958), on six Eskimo male hunters ages eighteen to forty-five who were flown into the Arctic Aeromedical Laboratory in Fairbanks from their village of Anaktuvuk Pass. Within 24 hr of arrival, they were tested on a motor-driven treadmill with a standard test described by Johnson et al. (1942). Six U.S. Army basketball team members and six sedentary U.S. Air Force clerical staff members were also tested by comparison. The usual test consists of an uphill run on a grade of 8.6% at a speed of 7 miles per hour until exhausted or for 5 min. Recovery pulses and the duration of the run are used to score the test. Because each of the Eskimo subjects could easily run for 5 min we arbitrarily increased the duration to 15 min. Only one of the army or air force personnel ran 10 min, and most of them were exhausted before 5 min, which is a common experience with this test. Each Eskimo ran the full 15 min, calmly dismounted, and proceeded to eat a large dinner without distress. Since the O_2 requirements of such a run are known to be approximately 63 ml/min·kg (Shephard, 1969), this result would place these Anaktuvuk Pass hunters well within the upper ranges for $\dot{V}_{O_2 max}$ described by Shephard (1974) for Igloolik Eskimo males. Unfortunately, the Anaktuvuk Pass individuals were not available for restudy in 1968–71, and we have no similar body of data for the coastal Eskimo twenty or more years ago; thus there is no direct longitudinal comparison available to indicate a process of deconditioning.

Many other physiological features determine success or failure to live in the Arctic. Perhaps we should not be obsessive about one type of measure of physical fitness but instead concede that brains and not brawn, at least not aerobic brawn, more likely distinguish the successful Eskimo hunter. Patience, experience, wisdom, skill in the interpretation of small signs, and skill in the fabrication and use of weapons are more apt to be features of successful arctic hunting (Nelson, 1969) than an oxygen-transport system comparable to that of a champion distance runner.

SUMMARY

The physical fitness of 176 male and 134 female Alaskan Eskimos was evaluated by submaximal tests for maximal aerobic power. A smaller number of subjects was tested for maximal anaerobic power, maximal aerobic arm work, and a 15-min endurance run. Also, a limited number of men was tested for respiratory function. With the exception of maximal anaerobic power and respiratory function, the tests were within normal limits for nonhunting and most hunting populations reported in the past.

Values for maximal anaerobic power of these Eskimos were clearly superior to those of African natives and Italian city dwellers, and more comparable with those of trained Italian athletes. Vital capacity, timed vital capacity, and maximal breathing capacity also were some 10% higher in male Alaskan Eskimos than values predicted from height-weight standards for Americans as a whole. Whatever the reason for the superior values, we are left with the intriguing enigma of one link in the O_2 transport system that appears to have a potential much greater than its present use. Given the evidence of Shephard (1969) for an unusually high $\dot{V}_{O_2 max}$ in the more active hunters of Igloolik, and previous observations (Rodahl, 1958) on more active Alaskan Eskimo hunters, it seems most likely that a process of deconditioning in maximal aerobic power has occurred as a result of a less active life-style.

18
General Health

Anthony B. Way

A population maintains itself in a particular environment by achieving a balance between its fertility and its mortality. Since mortality is importantly influenced by environment, and since the health of a population is directly reflected in its mortality, health should be an indirect indicator of a population's environmental adaptation.

The Eskimos ought to be an interesting population to study in terms of their health. Their unique high-protein, low-carbohydrate diet may have resulted in various metabolic adaptations. These adaptations, or their absences, might alter the nature of various diseases such as atherosclerosis and diabetes. Similarly, living in a relatively sterile environment, with the bulk of contagious contact occurring in the crowded living quarters of a single household, might have consequences in the area of infectious diseases. One might expect to find that the pattern of respiratory and gastrointestinal diseases is different from that of people living in more temperate climates. Any adaptation to the cold, insofar as it has changed metabolic or circulatory processes, may also have had influence on some metabolic or circulatory diseases.

On a different plane, the overall level of health of the Eskimos, relative to any other population, should tell us something about the general level of adaptation of the population to this environment as a whole. Finally, studying their general health may be useful in helping to interpret other aspects of adaptation, such as fertility and exercise capacity.

REVIEW OF LITERATURE

The bulk of the information on Eskimo health is provided by isolated studies of single diseases. Nevertheless, a fairly consistent picture of at least the highlights of Eskimo health does emerge.

Bang and Dyerberg (1972) reported that Eskimos in Greenland had low serum lipid levels compared with Danes in Denmark. However, they also

Supported in part by National Institutes of Health Fellowship 5F02GM41005–01, from the National Institute of General Medical Sciences, U.S. Public Health Service, Bethesda, Md.

noted that these serum lipids did rise to Danish levels in Eskimos living in Denmark. Consistent with these low serum lipid levels, they also reported a low level of coronary atherosclerosis. Mann et al. (1962) noted that Alaskan Eskimos did not seem to have much hypertension.

In general, Eskimos in Alaska (Mouratoff et al., 1967) and Greenland (Bang and Dyerberg, 1972; Dreyer and Hamtoft, 1966) are reported to have very little evidence of diabetes mellitus. However, Schaefer (1973) reported that some Canadian Eskimos had a very high incidence of abnormal glucose tolerance. It seems likely that these Canadian Eskimos may have been experiencing one of the consequences of access to foods high in starch and sugar. In fact, Schaefer (1973) suggested that dietary sugar may by implicated in the causation of accelerated growth patterns, myopia, caries, and atherosclerosis.

Respiratory diseases, including pneumonia, tuberculosis, bronchiectasis, and other diseases of both adults and children are widely reocognized as a major problem for the Eskimos in Alaska and Canada (Fleshman et al., 1968; Grzybowski et al., 1972; Herbert et al., 1967; Maynard and Hammes, 1964; Schaefer, 1973; Schonell, 1972). Beaudry (1968) noted that some Eskimos in Canada had markedly low pulmonary function. However, Rode and Shephard (1973) found much higher pulmonary functions in Canadian Eskimos. They suggested that these Eskimos might have experienced a marked improvement in health since Beaudry's (1968) earlier study. This suggestion was supported by Schaefer's (1973) report of a declining rate of tuberculosis.

Otitis media is also recognized as a major source of morbidity for Alaskan and Canadian Eskimo children (Brody et al., 1965; Fleshman et al., 1968; Johonnott, 1973; Maynard and Hammes, 1964; Reed et al., 1967; Schaefer, 1971a). Maynard and Hammes (1964) noted a correlation with respiratory illnesses. Schaefer (1971a, 1973) noted a similar correlation in Canada, which he related to bottle- instead of breast-feeding. Johonnott (1973), however, found that otitis media was less prevalent in urban than in rural Alaskan Eskimos.

Eskimos throughout the Arctic have a high incidence of environmental eye damage such as pterygium, pingueculae, and corneal scarring (Forsius et al., 1970; Mann, 1972; Mann et al., 1962). They also have a high prevalence of angle-closure glaucoma and shallow anterior chambers (Alsbirk, 1973; Drance, 1973; Forsius et al., 1970; Mann, 1972). Myopia is a problem that may be increasing among the Eskimos (Boniuk, 1973; Forsius et al., 1970; Schaefer, 1973).

Other diseases that may be common among the Eskimos are iron deficiency anemia (Maynard and Hammes, 1964; Rausch et al., 1967), congenital heart disease (Harvald and Hels, 1972), esophageal cancer (Fortuine, 1969), and caries (Schaefer, 1973).

As may be noted from this review, none of the reports provided an overall picture of Eskimo health, and only a few investigated the causes or relationships of these diseases.

INTERNATIONAL BIOLOGICAL PROGRAM STUDY

From 1968 to 1972, the IBP Alaskan Eskimo study collected health data from a limited segment of Eskimos on the North Slope of Alaska. While some of these data may be presented in greater detail in other chapters, this section will be limited to an overview of the general health of these Eskimos.

Feldman et al. (1972) looked at the Eskimos from Point Hope. They found that the mean serum cholesterol level was not greatly different from that of U.S. Caucasians. However, the Eskimos did lack some of the high levels often found in U.S. Caucasians. Feldman et al. (1972) also reported lower levels of serum triglycerides, but higher levels of free fatty acids than in U.S. Caucasians. These investigations noted that the reportedly low incidence of atherosclerosis in the face of a moderately high serum cholesterol levels suggested some disruption of the usual association between the two.

Bell et al. (1973) studied sugar tolerance in both Point Hope and Wainwright. They found the highest incidence of sucrose intolerance of any population studied. They also found many cases of lactose intolerance, but no abornomal glucose-tolerance curves. These normal glucose-tolerance tests imply a situation differenct from that of some Canadian Eskimos; diabetes is not yet a problem on the North Slope of Alaska.

Rennie et al. (1970) studied pulmonary function in Wainwright Eskimos. Like Rode and Shephard (1973), but in contrast to Beaudry (1968), they found higher vital capacities, timed vital capacities at 1 sec, and maximum breathing capacities, than would have been expected from U.S. Caucasians of similar age and height.

Mayhall et al. (1970), working in Wainwright, found a high rate of caries. Kristoffersen and Bang (1973) in a "repeat" study, found that severe periodontal disease had developed in the past eight years in Anuktuvuk Pass. (Dahlberg et al. in this volume report low levels of periodontal disease in Wainwright.) Both sets of investigators suggested that access to nontraditional foods, especially carbohydrates, may have been causative. Alsbirk and Forsius (1973) confirmed that, as in Greenland and Canada, the Wainwright Eskimos have shallow anterior chambers of the eye and thus may be prone to angle-closure glaucoma. Sauberlich et al. (1970, 1972) confirmed that anemia was a problem among the modern children of Wainwright. Mazess (1970) provided the novel insight that the older Wainwright Eskimos may have suffered from a remarkable degree of bone loss.

The general health of this Eskimo population has been examined in only two studies. Robinhold and Rice (1970) did complete physical examinations and recorded partial medical histories. Thet provided a list of some of the disease entitites they found. In general, their findings supported the earlier reports that pulmonary tuberculosis and otitis media were common, but that cardiovascular disease was uncommon. Interestingly, the combination of a high incidence of arcus senilis with a low incidence of cardiovascular disease supported Feldman et al's (1972) suggestion of a possible breakdown in the link between serum cholesterol and atherosclerosis in the Eskimos.

I also collected some general health data in Wainwright (Way, 1970). My study was limited to the history of chronic disease symptomatology reported by each person. The sample was limited to the older adults in the population. Out of fourteen categories of organ system, the five most common sets of complaints related to the female genitourinary; the ear, nose, and throat; the bone and joint; the gastrointestinal; and the respiratory systems. The two least common sets of complaints related to the cardiovascular and the endocrine systems. These results were at least consistent with the previously mentioned evidence from other studies that chronic otitis media and chronic pulmonary disease were quite frequent, while atherosclerosis and diabetes were uncommon. They furthermore emphasized that Mazess's (1970) suggestion of a possibly high rate of bone loss with age should be pursued.

I also summed up all of my findings to produce an index of general health (Way, 1970). While there are no comparable data on Western Caucasians, I did collect similar data on Quechua peasants in Peru (Way, 1972). Recognizing that there were likely to be major cultural and linguistic factors influencing these data, the fact that the Quechuas had proportionately more than twice the number of symptoms as the Eskimos supported the impression that the Eskimos were a relatively healthy population. Since the Quechuas under study were either living under the stress of high altitude or of recent migration to low altitude, it is reasonable to assume that the Eskimos are better adapted to their environment than are the Quechuas to theirs.

As an independent check of my index of morbidity, the data showed that, as expected, older people were significantly more sick than younger people. There also was a possible positive association between morbidity of Eskimo women and the pre- and perinatal deaths of their offspring. Recently, again as a check on the validity of this measurement of health, I compared the index of morbidity with two measurements of exercise capacity. For ten subjects, I found that maximal *aerobic* capacity as measured by Rennie et al. (written communication, 1973) was not significantly associated with health. However, for seven Eskimos, higher maximal *anaerobic* power was significantly associated with a higher level of health. As might be expected, this association, in turn, is closely tied to age. These incidental studies of a measurement of morbidity support the thesis that studies of general health can provide insights into a population's environmental adaptation.

CONCLUSIONS

The health data collected during the IBP study of Alaskan Eskimos support other evidence of a unique pattern of disease among the Eskimos. Under the environmental conditions associated with traditional Eskimo culture the cardiovascular (Bang and Dyerberg, 1972; Feldman et al., 1972; Mann et al.,

1962) and pancreatic (Bang and Dyerberg, 1972; Bell et al., 1973; Dreyer and Hamtoft, 1966; Mouratoff, 1967; Schaefer, 1973) systems seem to be partly protected from chronic disease. On the other hand, the respiratory system (Beaudry, 1968; Fleshman et al., 1968; Grzybowski et al., 1972; Herbert et al., 1967; Maynard and Hammes, 1964; Robinhold and Rice, 1970; Schaefer, 1973; Schonell, 1972; Way, 1970), including the closely related middle ear (Brody et al., 1965; Fleshman et al., 1968; Johonnott, 1973; Maynard and Hammes, 1964; Reed et al., 1967; Robinhold and Rice, 1970; Schaefer, 1971a, 1973; Way, 1970) seems to be particularly susceptible to pathological changes. However, there is some evidence that conditions are improving for the respiratory system (Rode and Shephard, 1973; Schaefer, 1973; Rennie et al., 1970). For both environmental and morphological reasons, the eye appears to be prone to disease (Alsbirk, 1973; Alsbirk and Forsius, 1973; Boniuk, 1973, Drance, 1973; Forsius et al., 1970; Mann, 1972; Mann et al., 1962; Schaefer, 1973). Other pathological conditions common to the North Slope and other Eskimos include anemia (Maynard and Hammes, 1964; Rausch et al., 1967; Sauberlich et al., 1970, 1972) and caries (Kristoffersen and Bang, 1973; Mayhall et al., 1970; Schaefer, 1973). There are also isolated reports of increased frequencies of congenital heart disease (Harvald and Hels, 1972); esophageal cancers (Fortuine, 1969), and possible senile bone demineralization (Mazess, 1970).

Unfortunately, only Feldman et al. (1972) have taken the next step of trying to define the mechanism behind one unusual disease frequency. Their evidence suggested that the Eskimos may be handling cholesterol deposition differently from Western Caucasians.

Robinhold and Rice (1970) and I (Way, 1970) have tried to describe the general pattern of disease. The findings of these studies tend to support the conclusions outlined above. However, more comparable data are needed to define how much this pattern differs from that of other populations. I provided some support for the idea that, at least compared with some Peruvian Quechua Indians, the Eskimos were in good health and were thus probably well adapted to their environment. I also provided data showing that health is a measurable characteristic that correlates well with other biological variables of inerest.

Based on this review of health studies of the Eskimos, I believe that other studies, either of greater depth or of broader perspective, would contribute measurably to the understanding of the relationship between human disease and the environment.

19

Demography and Population Parameters of the Present Inhabitants of Northwest Alaska

Frederick A. Milan

During the International Biological Program (1968–74), multidisciplinary human biological studies were conducted in several of the Eskimo villages of northwest Alaska. Coastal villages and their estimated population numbers at that time were: Point Hope (303), Wainwright (308), Point Lay (10), Point Barrow (2,300), and Barter Island (150) according to village census figures. These villages are strung out over great distances and are separated by 240, 90, 80, and 305 statute miles, respectively. In the past, except for seasonal gatherings for summer trading at places like Kotzebue, or *tulagiaq* (at the mouth of the Utokok River) or *nigilik* (at the mouth of the Colville River), "nature abhorred a crowd" in this region. The earlier population was widely dispersed both inland and along the coast. Gubser's book on the Nunamiut Eskimo of northern Alaska illustrates with exactitude the location of this population in 1900 (1965:338).

HISTORICAL BACKGROUND OF THE POPULATION

There are a number of well-known historical sources which describe the meeting of Eskimos and Europeans in this region and which document the deleterious effects on the native population of the communicable diseases introduced by Europeans. These sources also describe the breakdown of long-term genetic isolation of the population, trace the movements of the inland Eskimo people out to the coast during the early period, and detail the eventual settling down of the Eskimo people in their present locations.

The north coast of Alaska was visited by the British vessel H.M.S. *Blossom*, under the command of Captain Beechey, in 1826. On August 17 while

Blossom anchored south of Icy Cape due to heavy ice, Mr. Elson sailed the ship's boat north to Point Barrow, which he attained on the twenty-third of the month (Beechey, 1831). Captains Dease and Simpson, while in the employ of the Hudson's Bay Company, reached Point Barrow in 1837 by sailing down the Mackenzie River and walking along the shore of the Arctic Ocean (Simpson, 1843). The H.M.S. *Plover,* commanded by Captain Maguire, wintered at Point Barrow in 1852, 1853, and 1854.

The first whaling ships came to Point Barrow in 1854. Ships that made it around Point Barrow would frequently overwinter frozen in the ice at Herschell Island in order to be ready for the bowhead whaling season in the spring. The return journey to San Francisco was 4,000 miles. After 1888, whaling ships regularly visited the Arctic Coast. Ships converted to steam about 1893 and utilized the extensive coal deposits at Cape Lisburne and Wainwright Inlet. During the decade 1895–1905 it has been reported that there were fifty-one registered whalers sailing out of San Francisco.

Whaler crews were racially mixed with every West Europen racial and national entity represented. Ships' crews included Japanese, Chinese, Filipino, Hindu, Kanaka, Portugese, and African sailors (Sanderson, 1956). One can understand why the old whaling settlement at Point Hope was named "Jabber Town"! Charles Brower, in his unpublished autobiography, wrote of a journey he made aboard the whaling ship *Beda* in 1884. He visited Point Hope on July 3 and noted, "There must have been seventy ships laying there" (Brower, n.d.:119). Ejnar Mikkelsen (1910) visited Point Hope on July 29, 1906 and he wrote, ". . . went ashore the day after we anchored off the houses, and were rather surprised to see so many white men. There were about ten of them living with Eskimo women; they had rather large families—pretty and intelligent-looking children."

Although American whaling persisted until 1916, the so-called golden age, which began in 1835, was over by the end of the Civil War and thereafter whaling in the western Arctic played a minor role in the whaling industry at large (Sanderson, 1956).

In 1881 the U.S. War Department sent a ten-man detachment under Lieutenant Ray to Point Barrow. He counted some 410 people in seventy-two family groups between Wainwright Inlet at the mouth of the Kuk River and Point Barrow. This included the Eskimos living in the two settlements at Point Barrow. The coastal village at Point Hope reported 276 people in 1880 (Petroff, 1884) and 295 people in 1890 (Porter, 1893). Alva Nashoalook, who was born in 1898 at Point Franklin, told me that he remembers hearing that there were about forty-five people living at Kilimantavik, a coastal village south of Wainwright, in 1900. There were no people between there and Point Hope. According to the above information, there would have been about 750 persons living in coastal settlements from Point Barrow to Point Hope in 1900.

Charles Brower sailed past "Oolo-ru-nic" (*ulugunik* or Wainwright) in

1884 and visited the village of "Se-da-roo" (*sinaagaq*) at Point Belcher. He wrote,

> I counted twelve igloos that were occupied and quite a number of old unused ones. Kea-wak, the head man, was a fine old fellow. He told me that a few years before there had been many more people here, but that they had all died just after the large shipwreck several years before. Some time along, as near as I could make out, during the seventies. Two other villages, one south and one north of Se-da-roo had been deserted. Almost the whole population having died at the time and the remainder going to other villages. (n.d., p. 119)

When Brower arrived at Barrow on December 6, 1884, he remarked in his autobiography that "Ut-kie-a-vic" (*utkiagvik*) was at that time the largest settlement on the Alaskan coast.

Ensign Roger Wells of the U.S. *Thetis,* and his interpreter, J. W. Kelley, mapped the "tribal" boundaries of the Eskimos in Alaska as of 1889. They remarked, "the coast tribes between Point Hope and Point Barrow have been cut down in population, so as to be almost obliterated. Nooatoks, orginally called Napaktomiut, moved east and west, they have a foothold in Point Barrow, at Point Hope they have accomplished the same end" (Wells and Kelley, 1890).

Sheldon Jackson (1894), when describing the people living at Wainwright in 1890, said,

> Their original homes were along the sea coast from Wainwright Inlet to Point Lay, but disease and mortality reduced their numbers. By the process of intermarriage they have become closely allied to and assimilated in language and culture with the inland people. . . . From Point Lay south to Icy Cape north, and the riverine districts, Colville and Ikpikpun, to the eastwards, there is a nomadic tribe composed of a mixture of coast natives and inland people, styling themselves as Otookachahmutes. (p. 182)

The first government schoolhouses along the northwest coast were erected at Point Hope and Point Barrow in 1890 (Richards, 1949). The Wainwright school was established in 1904, "for the security of the one at Barrow, 100 miles further north. Every few years the ice prevents supply ships from reaching Barrow, and it was found necessary to provide a place where supplies and mail for Barrow could be landed" (Jackson, 1906). The early schoolteachers were frequently missionaries as well, although the first teacher at Barrow was a physician. The establishment of the whaling stations, schoolhouses, churches, and stores encouraged the settling down of northwest coast Eskimos after 1900 at the established places of Barrow, Wainwright, Point Hope, and nearby settlements.

The village of Wainwright was the major community studied during the IBP. An attempt was made to obtain complete information on the historical demography and population parameters of this village which would serve as baseline data for the other biological studies.

Demography

Wainwright, named after Beechey's navigator, attracted people from coastal and inland areas after the construction of the schoolhouse. Yet, as recently as 1910, the people were still seasonal migrants going inland in the fall for fishing and hunting and then returning to the coast at Christmas. Wainwright's population over time is shown in Fig. 19-1. Data were derived from censuses taken by government schoolteachers. Figure 19-1 shows both a slow population increase from 1890 (U.S. census figure) to 1940, when many families moved elsewhere in Alaska for war-related work, and a more general population increase since 1950. This latter increase was due to im-

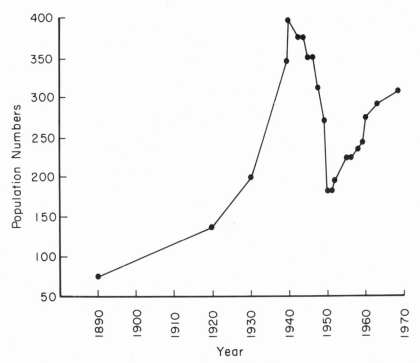

FIGURE 19-1. *Wainwright population size according to census data collected by village schoolteachers (1890 to 1970).*

provements in health care as well as the return of former migrants (Milan and Pawson, 1975).

In the census for June 30, 1919, James E. Gregg, the U.S. government teacher, enumerated a total village population of 137. Birth places for the thirty-nine male family heads were equally divided between coastal and inland locations; 44% of their wives were born in inland locations. One-half of all those born inland were listed as coming from the Utokok River (*utaqaġmiut*). The average family size was 3.61 ± 1.72 persons.

The registration list of births and deaths at the Wainwright schoolhouse covering that village, Point Lay, Icy Cape, and Atanik (a small village to the north of Wainwright), was examined for the twenty-year period 1917-37 to obtain early vital statistics. During this period, according to the registration list, 114 males and 101 females were born while 108 males and 84 females died. The net increase over twenty years was twenty-three persons. Assuming a mean population size of 206 persons for this period (137 persons in 1917 and 275 in 1937), the crude birthrate was calculated at 52.18 per

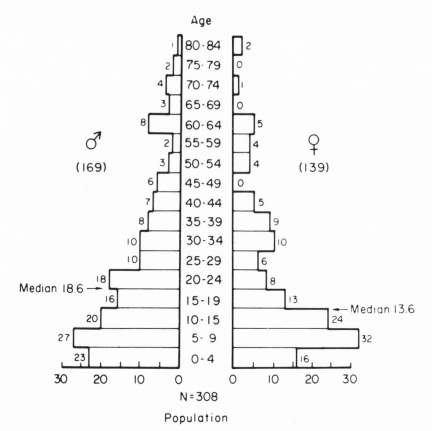

FIGURE 19-2. *Population profile for Wainwright as of July 1968.*

thousand and the crude death rate at 46.60 per thousand. Forty-eight percent of all deaths listed were children under five years of age.

Contemporary Period

In 1968 at the time of the IBP studies, the Wainwright population numbered 333 in forty-nine family groups according to the Bureau of Indian Affairs (BIA) census. Of this number, 308 persons were present in the village (Fig. 19-2). Mean family size was 6.71 ± 3.17 persons and the median age of the population was 16.1 years. A village genealogy revealed that about 25% of the population carried non-Eskimo genes.

Anamestic reproductive histories were obtained from forty-seven married women (Milan, 1970). The oldest was eighty-two and the youngest twenty-one. Seventeen women of this group were post-menopausal, fourteen were using birth control methods, and one woman was completely infertile. Forty-six women reported a total of 364 pregnancies of which 329 resulted in live births. The seventeen post-menopausal women reported an average 9.9 ± 4.08 pregnancies each. Twinning incidence was 2.73 per thousand live births and the sex ratio at birth was 108.2 males for every 100 females. (For the period 1917–37 the sex ratio was found to be 112.9 males per 100 females.) It is of interest to note that one-fifth of the mothers had approximately one-half of the now-living children, an example of differential survival of the generations over time.

The married women reported an average age at menarche of 13.68 ± 0.79 years. Average age when menopause occurred was 44.5 ± 4.30 years.

Consanguinity and Inbreeding

A small population size and the consequent limited numbers of mates will led to nonrandom mating and a reduction in genetic variability over time. Although Spencer (1959) wrote that cousin marriage was not considered desirable among the Eskimos of northern Alaska, 13% or four out of thirty-two marriages at Wainwright were found to be consanguinous. A coefficient of inbreeding (F) was calculated for the generation of children using the pathway method of Wright (1922) and the expression:

$$F_w = \Sigma(1/2)^{n-1}(1 + F_A)$$

where n equals the number of links connecting individuals in each path between one of w's parents and the other parent and F_A is the inbreeding coefficient of the common ancestor. According to Mange (1963), F_A can be neglected and taken to be 0 without significantly changing the results. The quantity *F,* according to Cotterman (1941), represents the probability that two allelic genes are identical by descent from a common ancestor. *F* can vary between 0 and 0.25. The latter figure is derived from the marriage between sibs.

Consanguinous matings at Wainwright involved two first cousin marriages, one second cousin marriage, and one marriage between second cousins once removed. The mean *F* for 141 out of the 210 children in the village whose biological ancestry was known with certainty was 0.014. This is equivalent to the biological relationship between third cousins. The inbred sibships had a mean *F* of 0.023; equivalent to that between first and second cousins.

POINT HOPE

Point Hope was the location of the Ipiutak site, the largest and oldest known settlement in the American Arctic (Larsen and Rainey, 1948). Two thousand years ago there were some 600 houses on the Point Hope spit. In 1880 the U.S. census listed 276 persons resident there (Petroff, 1884). The population declined until about 1930 (Foote and Williamson, 1966) and thereafter increased to the figure of 308 seen during the IBP study period. A population profile of this community can be seen in Fig. 19-3. An analysis of the village genealogies revealed that approximately 37% of the entire population carried non-Eskimo genes.

Reproductive Histories

Complete reproductive histories were obtained with the assistance of the village health aide from thirty-two married women. Of this sample, ten were post-menopausal, ten had had hysterectomies or tubal ligations which terminated their reproductive activities, and eleven, between the ages of twenty-three and forty-six, were still reproductively active. Of this latter group, 45% were using birth control methods.

The ten post-menopausal women reported an average of 10.60 ± 4.84 pregnancies and 9.4 ± 3.66 live-born children each. One woman reported sixteen live-born children. Sixty-six percent of all live-born children were still living during the study.

The ten women who had had their reproductive life artificially terminated reported 9.2 ± 2.57 pregnancies and 8.7 ± 2.45 live births each. Seventy-five percent of their children were still alive.

The younger women who were still reproductively active reported an average of 7.18 ± 4.56 pregnancies and 6.45 ± 4.57 live births each with 86% of their children still living. The effect of the family planning program can be seen in the "Christmas tree" appearance of the village population profile in Fig. 19-3. Only one consanguinous marriage was found at Point Hope.

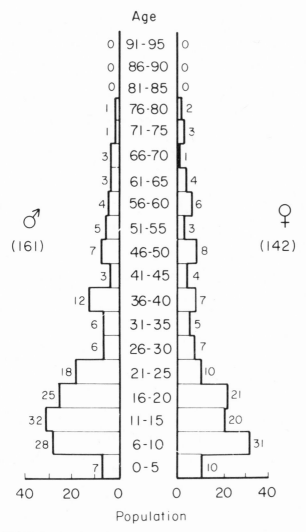

FIGURE 19-3. *Population profile for Point Hope according to the 1969 Bureau of Indian Affairs (BIA) census.*

BARROW

Recently Masnick and Katz (1976) described the historical demographic situation at Barrow using data from the censuses from 1940 to 1970. Barrow, with a population of over 2,000 in 1970 (of which about 5% are non-Eskimo), is the ninth largest city in Alaska. In 1939 when the Wainwright population numbered 341 persons, Barrow had only 362. By 1970 when Wainwright numbered 315, Barrow had increased its population six times what it was in

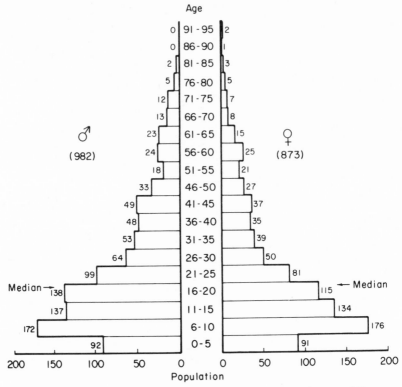

FIGURE 19-4. *Population profile for the Eskimo population of Barrow as of 1970.*

1939. This population increase was due to natural increase and the inmigration of Eskimos from other villages seeking wage work and the stimulation of the "big city."

Barrow's native population at the time of the IBP study in 1970 is shown in Fig. 19-4. Note the low median age and the "Christmas tree" appearance of the population profile. Barrow's crude birthrate over the period 1949 to 1970 is shown in Fig. 19-5. Data for this figure were obtained from the Alaska Department of Health and Social Services. The decline in the crude birthrate after 1965 is due to the introduction of family planning by state and federal health care providers.

DISCUSSION AND SUMMARY

At the time of the IBP studies, the Eskimos of northwest Alaska were living as part-time subsistence hunters in small, settled, rural communities.

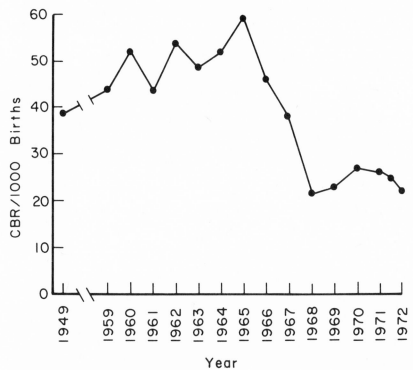

FIGURE 19-5. *Crude birthrate for the Barrow native population over the period from 1949 to 1970.*

Genealogical information revealed that between 25% and 37% of the population carried non-Eskimo genes. These genes were introduced by whalers who were on the Arctic coast at the turn of the century. Historical information and vital statistics for this population reveal that the population has recovered from the earlier effects of communicable diseases. The population had a high birthrate (at least since 1917) and the reduction of mortality rates after the 1950s allowed an unprecedented expansion until the introduction of birth control in the late 1960s. As a result of the expansion, the population has a low median age and a high dependency ratio. It is similar to many populations in underdeveloped countries.

Although consanguinity was found, it was not as high as has been reported for cultures that sanction endogamy, and the coefficiency of inbreeding was almost the same as that found among the Skolt Lapps (Vollenbruck et al., 1974). There were no evidences of any adverse effects of consanguinity although they may have been masked by the high infant mortality rate.

In their historical demography the Eskimo population of northwest Alaska is very similar to the entire native population of Alaska (Milan, 1974-

75). In Alaska, an aboriginal population originally in balance with its ecological resources, nearly became extinct due to the communicable diseases introduced by Europeans. Subsequently, it has increased rapidly due to vigorous public health programs. The population is now in a period of demographic transition with control over its own rate of increase.

20

Behavioral Studies: Cognitive Development

Carol Fleisher Feldman, Benjamin Lee, J. Dickson McLean,
David B. Pillemer, and *James R. Murray*

This report is an overview of a four-year examination of the basic cognitive skills of the Eskimo people (Feldman, 1971; Feldman and Bock, 1970). The successive phases of our investigation are discussed in their actual chronological sequence, as this organization seems most clearly to reveal the nature of the research that was undertaken.

During the summer of 1969, a number of standardized cognitive tests were group-administered to seventy-seven residents of Wainwright, Alaska, ranging in age from eleven to fifty-eight years. The tests included: (1) Sections A, B, C, and D, of the Raven Progressive Matrices, (2) a revision of the Guilford-Zimmerman Spatial Visualization IV Test, (3) a test of English, and (4) a concept induction test administered in Inupiat. Analysis of the resulting data supported the following conclusions:

1. The growth of cognitive and perceptual abilities in the Wainwright subjects appeared slower during adolescence but continued to a later age than in subjects of European origin.
2. The Wainwright subjects showed less of a sex difference in spatial visualizing ability than is typically found in subjects of European origin.
3. Evidence was found of problems of vocabulary growth which are typical of populations in which schooling is in one language and social communication is in another.
4. The Eskimos generally did well on classification tasks requiring highly abstract concepts, less well on tasks requiring functional concepts of the sort that vary between different environments. The subjects performed in a similar way in parallel English and Inupiat items on the abstract questions.
5. It was found possible to test verbal concepts in Inupiat using older, verbally fluent members of the community as a source of information about definitions and conventions of use.

Two anomalies in the results of this first testing session suggested further

233

and potentially fruitful avenues of research. First, at age fourteen the Eskimo subjects were below the established norms for the Raven's Matrices and at eighteen they were above them. Accordingly, the Block Design portion of the Wechsler Intelligence Scale for Children (WISC) was administered to 140 Eskimo children ranging in age from six to seventeen years, during a second testing session in Wainwright (summer of 1970), in order to determine whether the poor test performance characteristic of the fourteen- to seventeen-year-old subjects would also be found in younger subjects.

The results indicated performance superior to the established norms for the WISC at all ages. However, the earlier observed poor performance of Eskimo adolescents on the Raven's Matrices, indicating a possible cognitive "slump," prompted a visit to Mt. Edgecumbe School in Sitka—one of several B.I.A. boarding schools attended by the high school age Eskimos in Wainwright. Conditions observed at the school might well contribute to an adolescent cognitive slump. The life style of students in the Mount Edgecumbe School is highly regimented, in contrast with the normal living conditions of Eskimo children, who are accorded a great deal of freedom and personal responsibility. Also, there is little cognitive challenge provided, since the children are perceived as "slow" or "apathetic." Finally, there is a drastic change in diet. These conditions are discussed more fully in a report to the Mount Edgecumbe School, in which suggestions for improvement and reform are offered (Feldman, 1970).

The second of the two anomalies is the fact that the performance of Eskimo subjects on the four series of Raven's Matrices does not conform to the predicted sequential difficulty. An analysis of the results indicates that the Eskimos perform poorly on those series which test more specific—perhaps more culture-specific—skills, and introduces the problem of culture-fair testing. The tests administered during the second testing session, in the summer of 1970, represented the results of an attempt to devise culture-fair tests of cognitive function; the design of these tests was based upon a distinction between learned skills or common knowledge, on the one hand, and the ablity to transform or manipulate such skills or such knowledge, on the other.

Two different kinds of tests were developed based upon this distinction: (1) tests which establish proficiency in some skill through training and then measure the ability to transform that skill, and (2) tests which assume proficiency in a culturally indigenous skill and then measure the ability to transform such a skill. Four such tests were devised, with each test intended to provide a measure of some separate aspect of cognitive development or ability, and these were administered to seventy-eight Eskimo children ranging in age from six to eighteen.

In general, the results of the 1970 testing were in accord with our expectation that subjects' performance would be age-related. It was not possible, however, to construe the age-relatedness of these tasks as revealing a developmental sequence of abilities, because the four tests were methodologically dissimilar as well as evidently testing different cognitive levels. These problems helped us clarify our goals for 1971. In addition to making obvious the need for a single set of testing materials which could be used for assessing the complete range or sequence of cognitive development, this early exercise in test design provided valuable experience in operationalizing aspects of cognitive development for testing children in a foreign culture. This experience has contributed to both the format and to the success of a revised test, administered during the summer of 1971.

This revised test is more explicitly derived from the work of Piaget than were the 1970 tests (Feldman et al., 1974). It consists of five different sections, each section assessing some particular level of cognitive development as described by Piaget, and all five sections employ the same stimulus materials. The test was administered to sixty-seven Eskimo children from eight to nineteen years of age. The results of this administration are presented in Table 20-1.

Given that each of the five test sections is designed to assess one portion of a developmental sequence that is hierarchical in nature, the subjects should perform correctly on all test items that do not exceed their cognitive level, and fail on all subsequent items. There are six patterns of response which would be consistent with predictions based upon Piagetian theory. These patterns are: 00000, X0000, XX000, XXX00, XXXX0, and XXXXX—where 0 indicates failure and X success on one of the five sections of the test. Analysis of the results indicated that 63% of the subjects conformed to one of the six patterns allowable—a result which is highly unlikely to occur by chance, since there are thirty-two *possible* patterns of response. In addition, it is possible to produce correct responses to each section by chance, and some of the nonconforming sequences probably resulted from this. Thus, the test appears to measure an orderly sequence of cognitive abilities. Furthermore, this research is the only case known to us in which Piaget's succession of three global stages —preoperations, concrete operations, and formal operations—has been investigated in a non-Western culture (Feldman et al., 1974).

The results presented in Table 20-1 also bear upon the other aspect of Piaget's theory: the predicted relationship between cognitive stage and age. For a homogeneous population, this hypothesis would predict that the proportion of subjects performing correctly on a task should increase markedly at the approximate age of appearance of the corresponding cognitive abilities. The obtained results fit this pattern and thus provide clear support for the stage hypothesis in Piagetian theory. In addition to the primary version of this test, which employed as test materials painted wooden blocks of different shapes and colors (thus referred to as "the blocks test"), a "cultural analogue" version was devised, which presented problems structurally identical to the primary version but which employed drawings of culturally familiar arctic

TABLE 20-1 *Correct Responses for the Five Test Sections, by Age Group (%)*

Test Section	Age 8-9 (N=14)	Age 10 (N=13	Age 11-12 (N=14)	Age 13-15 (N=15)	Age 16-19 (N=11)
1	78.6	92.3	96.4	100.0	100.0
2	32.1	73.1	71.4	90.0	72.7
3	7.1	73.1	75.0	73.3	81.8
4	35.7	30.8	60.7	70.0	54.5
5	7.1	11.5	25.0	13.3	18.2

animals as stimuli. An analogue version was devised for each of sections 1, 2, and 4 of the blocks test. The results for this cultural analogue strongly corroborate the sequencing aspect of Piagetian theory. Ninety-two percent of the subjects tested conformed to one of the four "acceptable" patterns of response for three test sections. The corresponding percentage for those sections of the blocks test was eighty-four percent. Also, as in the blocks test, there are well-defined stages for sections 2 and 4, providing support for the stage aspect of Piagetian theory. More importantly, the evidence is much clearer, as would be expected from a test which is more culturally relevant.

The final outcome of this series of investigations is a clearer picture of the kinds of basic cognitive skills possessed by North Alaskan Eskimo children. Eskimo children are found to possess an intelligence which results from an adaptive process and which bodes well for their future. But there is also evidence that the Eskimos may have trouble generalizing their basic skills to the broad range of situations which are demanded by the Western culture into which they are rapidly moving. Their future adaptive success should be a matter for continued investigation so that any problems they encounter may be mitigated by the use of suitable educational materials.

21

Behavioral Studies: A Psychometric Study at Barrow Day School

R. Darrell Bock

The study reported here is one phase of the Psychology Objective of the IBP Circumpolar Peoples studies conducted on the Alaskan North Slope between 1969 and 1972. It supplements the cognitive development studies carried out by Dr. Carol Fleischer Feldman and reported elswhere (Feldman et al., 1974). Originally, it had been planned to conduct these investigations jointly in a family study including subjects of all ages, but a first attempt to proceed in this manner in Wainwright village met with limited success because of difficulty in inducing adults to take the psychological tests and an evident lack of understanding of the tests among older subjects. As a result of this experience, Dr. Feldman and I decided to limit the testing to school-age children, she pursued independently the cognitive research (based on individual testing of children of all ages in this range) while I conducted the psychometric research (based on group testing of youth).

In order to obtain the largest possible sample of youth in the twelve- to eighteen-year age range, Barrow was selected as the site for the psychometric studies. On a field trip to Barrow in the summer of 1971, I encountered difficulty in recruiting subjects in this age range as well, partly because of their absence from the village during July. However, the trip provided an opportunity to perfect the tests and to make the initial contact with Mr. James Hughes, then principal of the Barrow Day School, that led to the present study. Permission was subsequently obtained from the Bureau of Indian Affairs to conduct testing in the seventh, eighth, and ninth grades of the Barrow Day School during the 1972-73 term. Accordingly, I returned to Barrow in the second week of October 1972, assisted by Mrs. Edna McLain, and completed the psychometric testing with help from Dr. David Fauske, assistant principal at that time.

Supported in part by a grant from the Spencer Foundation.

WORKING HYPOTHESES

Various observations and investigations discussed in a review by Kleinfeld (1973b) have suggested that the special features of the environment, and the hunting and fishing subsistence that the people of the Arctic Ocean border have sustained for perhaps 3,000 years, have shaped the development of physical and intellectual skills that differ distinctively from those of the dominantly agricultural peoples of the south. Although the time span of occupancy in the region is relatively short on an evolutionary scale, the small sizes of the communities make it possible that, under stringent selection or because of founder effects, significant specialized adaptation could have been brought about by evolutionary forces. And from a cultural point of view there can be no doubt that rigorous intergenerational transmission of specialized hunting skills and technology is required for survival in this unforgiving environment. Although the young age of these subjects and the transitional character of life in Barrow make it less likely that all subjects in this study have been exposed to the detailed articles of the hunting and fishing tradition, the spirit and mentality of that tradition still permeates life in the community and shapes the attitudes of children and adults alike.

Thus, without delving into detailed consideration of the relative contribution of biological and cultural transmission of these traits, we can accept as working hypotheses the suggestions of other investigators that these subjects have relatively highly developed visual skills—skills that are exercised in the construction and use of rather sophisticated tools and equipment, and, according to Witkin, encouraged by permissive child-rearing practices. In particular, Berry (1966) presents data indicating that children in the closely related Eskimo culture of Canada show relatively better spatial ability than children of agricultural cultures elsewhere in the world. He also finds that sex differences which are so evident in spatial ability scores obtained in England and much of the United States are lacking in the Eskimo and other hunting cultures, especially those most traditional and undisturbed by modern contacts. Similarly, MacArthur (1967) and MacKinnon (1972), also working with a Canadian sample, found no sex differences on Witkins's Embedded Figures Test—a test which almost universally shows sex differences in populations of European extraction.

In an attempt to replicate these findings in the present study, a spatial test suitable for cross-cultural comparisons and known to give clear-cut sex differences in secondary schoolchildren in Illinois was selected for the test battery. In addition, and to set off more clearly the results for spatial ability, a test of auditory short-term memory span was also included. The latter test had no visual or intellectual content whatsoever, and requireed only that the subject remember a pattern of pure-tone sounds and recognize it among alternative patterns after a short delay. It was conjectured that, in view of the little emphasis on auditory skills in the Eskimo culture, subjects in this study would perform relatively poorly on this test.

A second area of investigation was that of general problem-solving ability such as required for scholastic success and verbal intellectual achievement generally. As a measure of this ability, the A, B, and C sections of Raven's Progressive Matrices were included. Although this test has no direct verbal component, it presents various types of "picture puzzles" that require the subject to recognize and use concepts that have verbal analogues. As a result, this test is represented more by the verbal factor in mental test scores than by the spatial factor (Burke and Bingham, 1969). Berry (1966) presents data showing that Canadian Eskimos score nearly as well on this test as do his Scottish samples. Although it is not clear from Berry's report the exact age level of the subjects or the manner in which the subjects were selected, his results would predict good performance of the Barrow sample relative to the Illinois sample with which it will be compared in this study.

The spatial test and Raven's Matrices cover two of the three major mental test factors found in psychometric studies of subjects of European extraction. A third important factor is measured by so-called fluency tests, such as Thurstone's Word Fluency in the Primary Mental Abilities Tests (Thurstone and Thurstone, 1947). Like the spatial and verbal factors, fluency shows evidence (in twin and family studies) of being biologically heritable. Not a great deal is known of the sources of the trait, but it is relatively independent of verbal and spatial ability and has some relationship to success on tasks demanding a flexible and creative response (see Getzels and Jackson, 1962). In the present study, the measure of fluency consists of five simple, almost geometrical, figures to which subjects respond by naming things they think these figures might represent. The score on the test is the total number of different names that the subjects can produce for all figures. From the point of view of the relatively sparse environment inhabited by the Eskimo, response to this test would be expected to be below that of subjects from the lower forty-eight states. However, from a different point of view, the permissive style of child-rearing characteristic of Eskimo communities (Feldman, 1974) may nuture a more flexible and imaginative approach to this task, especially because it is presented in a visual form, and might lead us to predict relatively good performance.

Finally, because these subjects are bilingual and speak Inupiat at home and to a large extent among themselves, and because they read, write, and receive their schooling from elementary school onward almost exclusively in English from native English-speakers, an attempt was made in this study to measure their relative proficiencies in the two languages. Generally, minority-language groups not introduced to English until elementary school tend to show a deficit in verbal ability through much of their lives. This may be generally true of the North Slope natives (Kleinfeld, 1973a). The present study, therefore, did not attempt to include a standardized test of English language knowledge or proficiency, but used instead a special test, devised by Dr. Feldman, of concept knowledge expressed in precisely parallel English and Inupiat word-classification items. The test produces a score for each subject in English concept knowledge and Inupiat concept knowledge, and the purpose of the study is to compare relative strengths on these two measures and the extent to which individual differences in these strengths are correlated.

The preceding six measures constitute the dependent variables of the present study. Data for these variables will be examined with respect to the age and sex of the Barrow subjects and, with the exception of the English-Inupiat test, will in each case by compared with data from subjects in Illinois obtained with the same tests in 1971 and 1972.

Samples

Obtaining unbiased samples for cultural comparison, never an easy task when human subjects are involved, is even more difficult in behavioral studies because of possible interactions between the method of selecting subjects and the behavioral traits being measured. To use monetary incentives to induce subjects to volunteer, for example, is to risk biasing the sample toward subjects with lower income and lower ability levels. To seek volunteers during normal working hours is similarly to overrepresent the unemployed and less able. Conversely, appeals to community spirit or public interest will attract better-informed, better-educated, and more able subjects. Although these biases are not so important in surveys in physical characteristics, such as blood groups, that have little likelihood of interacting with the sampling method, they can leave psychological or sociological studies hopelessly confounded.

The present study attempts to avoid these difficulties by concentrating on school-age samples from communities where virtually all children attend one school. This condition is obviously met in Barrow, where the Bureau of Indian Affairs Day School is the only school available. For comparative samples, two Illinois communities were found in which virtually all children attend public school. The latter communities were West Frankfort, Illinois, a town of population 8,854 in the south central region of Illinois, and Addison, a town of population 25,645 near Chicago (1970 census). Both towns consist primarily of industrial and clerical workers, tradesmen and small-business people, and such professionals as serve communities of this size.

Testing in the Illinois communities was done in the spring of the year when the weather was favorable and absences due to illness were minimal. According to the school principals, the subjects obtained in these testings represented 90% or better of all children in these age groups in the community. In the Barrow sample, the coverage is not as complete. As indicated under "Results," the largest proportion of children represented in any age and sex group is about 62%. Other children were not in the village at the time or were absent from school on the days of testing.

As a general rule, children absent from school in the lower forty-eight states tend disproportionately to represent the lower social classes where parents are less strict about their children's school attendance. In terms of school achievement, children in school on any given day are a slightly upward-biased sample. But the same may not be true in Barrow, where children not in the sample may come from more affluent and mobile families who are traveling or visiting elsewhere on the North Slope or in the south. If so, the Barrow sample may be biased downward relative to ability insofar as the correlation between ability and socioeconomic status that is seen in other parts of the United States is true of Barrow.

A second notable point is that samples obtained on a grade-in-school basis do not necessarily represent complete age groups. Because children of very low ability are often held back in school, and those of very high ability are advanced, some children are not found in the age cohort expected for each grade. Usually, the children who are a year or more younger than the modal age for the grade are those who have been advanced in school and are especially able. Indeed, these children are often not advanced as many grades as their ability would warrant and often turn up among the better students at a given grade level. Conversely, the oldest age group tends to be children who have been held back in school, often not by as many grades as their ability would warrant, and are therefore usually found among the less able in the grade to which they are assigned. As a result of these biases, the mean scores for ability tests classified by age may not show the regular pattern of increase that would be expected if all children at each age level were represented in the sample. To avoid these problems in comparisons between cultural groups in this study, scores for only those subjects who are in the modal age group for their grade are included. In the initial presentation of the Barrow data, however, means for all age groups will be reported.

The Tests

To be suitable for comparisons between cultural groups, psychological tests must have properties rather different from those of tests designed for comparing individuals within cultural groups. For widest relevance, obvious desiderata are that the tasks presented in the tests should not require the use of language, and that the instructions for the testing should make minimal demands on the subjects' comprehension and should include demonstration and practice items. Because it is often difficult or impossible to have the same persons administering the tests in the various cultural groups in question, the techniques of instruction, administration, and test scoring must be as objective as possible. It is especially important that attitudes of the test administrators toward the cultural groups, whether favorable or unfavorable, should not influence the extent of efforts to motivate the subjects or the standards of administration and scoring of the tests. The latter considerations point in the direction of objective testing rather than a more clinical approach and, where appropriate, encourage the use of group testing in school classrooms familiar to the subjects and free of distraction and extraneous influences. Group testing also makes possible, without unreasonable investment in time and effort, the type of total assessment of a school-age cohort suggested as a sampling method for intercultural studies.

In addition, certain psychometric characteristics of the test need special attention, especially when it is of interest to examine interaction of factors within cultural groups with those between cultural groups. In the present study, for example, the sex-by-cultural-group interaction in mean levels of spatial ability is of special interest. If differences between cultural groups are relatively large, as is often the case, the test score must be scaled in such a way that the differences within the groups are metrically comparable at different levels. The implication is that the test should be scored for this purpose, not by traditional right/wrong formulas, but by modern item-invariant psychometric procedures that provide estimates of ability on a well-defined interval scale (Bock, 1972). A crucial assumption of these procedures is that any given subject responds independently to separate items of the test, and that all subjects attempt all items. To conform to these assumptions, the test items should not share content or depend on information provided in previous items in the test. Moreover, if all items are to be attempted, then conventional speeded tests in which the subjects are not expected to complete all items are ruled out. Finally, the test presentation and format should be as pleasant and attractive as possible in order to engage the attention of children from those cultural groups where external pressures to perform well on the test may be lacking.

Every effort was made to incorporate the required characteristics in the tests and the method of test administration used in the study. With the exception of the English-Inupiat test, which is a direct attempt to assess linguistic proficiency, the test stimuli contain no verbal content. To maintain uniformity of presentation, all instructions are prerecorded and include a pantomime demonstration by the test administrator to accompany the auditory instructions on tape. Breaks in the tape are included at certain points in order to allow the subjects to ask questions about the instructions. Visual stimuli for the test are presented by a slide projector cued to the tape that also contains the instructions. (Instructions are on one track of a stereo-tape and the projector control cues are on the other.) Presentation of each item is individually timed, the intervals being chosen on the basis of pilot studies to determine times that yield the best distribution of item difficulties and discriminating powers in each test. For power tests, these intervals are chosen so that approximately 95% of subjects in the pilot samples are able to complete the items before the slide projector is advanced. For speeded tests, times are adjusted so that approximately 60% of subjects respond correctly to the item in the time allotted.

This method of presentation has the advantage that subjects are working at the same pace throughout the test, their attention is fully occupied by the auditory and visual display during the time the item is before them, and, because each item is presented to every subject, it is reasonable to assume that all items are attempted and that no response to an item is tantamount to inability to respond. To add to the attractiveness of the test, the items presented on slides are in color and the instructions are presented in a pleasant, unhurried manner. In all, the testing procedures satisfy the requirements for intercultural testing proposed by Vernon (1969, Chapter 15).

Raven's Progressive Matrices. This most widely used test in comparative studies of cultural groups consists essentially or a series of problem-solving tasks presented in a nonverbal form. The sample item shown in Fig. 21-1 is typical; the subject is required to find the alternative at the bottom of the item that correctly completes the missing portion of the pattern above. The

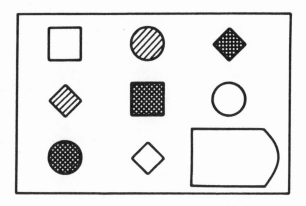

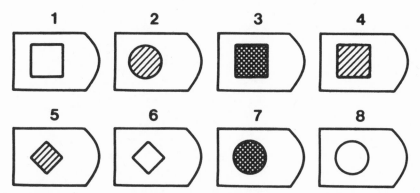

FIGURE 21-1. *An item from Form D of the Raven Progressive Matrices.*

test is organized into sets of twelve such items, each of which begins with extremely easy items and progresses in slow stages to, in some cases, quite difficult items at the end of each set. Instructions can be readily pantomimed and little formal language is required for administration of this test.

For present purposes, thirty-six matrices were presented consisting in their entirety of sets A, B, and C. Sets A and B were drawn from the colored version of the matrices; set C was in monochrome. Time limits for presentation of individual items were sufficiently generous that subjects who were able to solve an item had no difficulty in recording their response before the slide was changed. A warning that the new item was about to appear was given 5 sec before each slide change. Subjects recorded their responses in an answer booklet in which the boxes for marking the alternatives were in the same relative positions and same shape as the alternative on the slide.

The early items of Raven's Form A are simple perceptual tasks which most subjects in the age range of the present study solve correctly. In the raw score tallies for the test, we have included these items in order to make the reported scores correspond to those of other investigators (i.e., maximum number correct, 36). However, in computing scaled scores for the cultural group comparisons, only items 11 and 12 of Form A were actually scored. The item calibration for purposes of computing the scaled scores was carried out by means of the LOGOG program (Kolakowski and Bock, 1973), using the item data obtained from the subjects in the seventh, eighth, and ninth grades of the West Frankfort, Illinois, public school. The scale was adjusted to a mean of 50 and standard deviation of 10 in the calibration.

Although Raven's Matrices consist of figural stimuli, scores on the test correlate more with the general verbal-ability factor than with the spatial factor (see Bock, 1973). Factor analyses of the Raven's test suggest that, in order to complete the patterns in the matrices, subjects must draw on a store of knowledge about the figural and relational conventions employed. Thus, the test correlates highly with tests of accumulated knowledge, such as a vocabulary or general-information scale.

B-F Spatial Test. The Bock-Fitzgerald (1972) Spatial Test is a variation of the spatial test devised by Thurstone for the Primary Mental Abilities. A typical item of the test is shown in Fig. 21-2. Subjects are required to choose the two alternatives which complete the figure when placed in the opening at the top. The instructions are accompanied by a demonstration with a "formboard" model in which the alternatives can be lifted out and placed in the opening at the top, thus making it clear that the figures are to be rotated in the plane of the figure and not reflected.

Because most subjects can solve these items correctly if given enough time, these types of tests must be speeded in order to measure effectively the spatial factor. In the B-F spatial test, subjects are given 15 sec to respond to item 30 in the test and this time is gradually decreased to 8 sec near the end of the test. Responses are marked in a test booklet in which the alternatives are represented by four circles the same relative size and location

FIGURE 21-2. *An item from the B-F Space Test.*

as the circles in the items. Responses are scored as correct only if both of the correct alternatives are identified.

Auditory Span. This test, devised by Fitzgerald (1971) as a nonlanguage alternative to the familiar Digit Span Test of the Wechsler Adult Intelligence Scale, is an adaptation of Thurstone's Code Aptitude Test (Thurstone, 1944). The subjects hear a random sequence of "dots" and "dashes" followed 4 sec later by three sequences, one of which is identical to the first. The alternative sequences are separated by 3 sec of silence. The sequences increase in length as the test progresses. The subject marks the correct response in his answer book in one of three horizontally situated squares following each item number. Item numbers are heard on the tape preceding each item. Intensity level is sufficiently high for the dot-and-dash sounds to be heard easily in a classroom setting by subjects with normal hearing. The test consists of twenty-eight items and two practice items.

Associational Fluency. The associational Fluency Test is a variation of the tasks called "Pattern Meanings" or "Line Meanings" used by Wallach and Kogan in their study of creativity (1965). The shapes shown in Fig. 21-3 are projected on the screen, one at a time, and the subjects are given 1 min to write as many names as they can of things that the figures remind them of. The score on the test is the total number of names written by the subject for all five items. This test is similar to Thurstone's Word Fluency Test in which subjects are required to write as many words as they can that begin with the letter *S* or *T*. Although the constraint imposed on the response by the stimulus is quite different in the two tests, both are believed to measure some aspect of creative production that is distinct from general intellectual ability measured by conventional intelligence tests. In factor analyses, fluency measures always load on a factor distinct from verbal and spatial factors in mental test scores (Bock, 1973).

English-Inupiat Word Classification Tests. The complete English-Inupiat tests, including instructions, are shown in Appendix B. The instructions and English words were read in standard American pronunciation by William Fitzgerald. The Inupiat words were read by Edna McLain, a native Inupiat-speaker, who also assisted in the translation. In preparing the test, Dr. Feld-

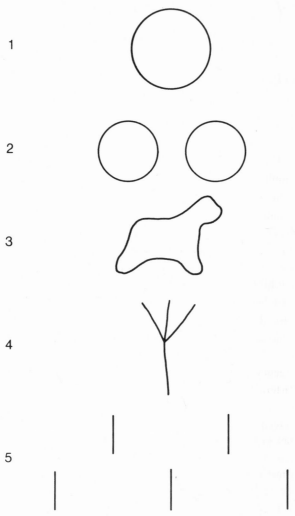

FIGURE 21-3. *The stimuli for the Associational Fluency Test.*

man made every effort to employ words of common occurrence both in English and in Inupiat having unambiguous translations in both directions.

RESULTS

The extent to which the schoolwide sampling was successful in reaching complete age cohorts can be seen in Table 21-1. The cohorts born in 1957, 1958, and 1959 are reasonably well ascertained, considering that not all persons or families on the village list were necessarily in Barrow at the time of testing. The fact that boys and girls are approximately equally represented in these cohorts leads one to believe that the sampling is unbiased with respect to sex and that a fair test of sex differences in ability should be possible. Subjects outside these cohorts, those who are advanced or held back in school, are relatively few in number and are excluded from that part of the analysis comparing the Barrow and Illinois samples.

From the distribution of subjects by year of birth in Table 21-1, it may be deduced that children in a given grade of the Barrow Day School at the junior high school level are older than is typical of other schools in the United States. This is seen more directly in Table 21-2, where the median age of children in the seventh, eighth, and ninth grades of the Barrow Day School are shown. On the basis of the December 1 birthday cutting point that is used in Illinois schools to determine when a child begins first grade, we would expect the median ages for these grades to be 12.4, 13.4, and 14.4 in Illinois schools. The children in the Barrow school are approximately one year older in these grades, with boys slightly older than girls. This tendency in grade assignment no doubt reflects the slower development seen among Eskimo children generally (Heller et al., 1967). The difference in development can be observed in the age of maximum adolescent growth observed by Jamison in Wainwright village compared with that in the published data for the Berkeley Growth Study, as estimated for the adolescent component of the two-component logistic model for human growth (Bock et al., 1973; see also Thissen et al., 1976). Estimates of age and rate of maximum adolescent growth velocity are shown in Table 21-3. There is roughly half a year's delay in the adolescent growth spurt among the Wainwright subjects. The maximum rate of growth during the spurt is, however, similar to or slightly greater than that of the Berkeley subjects.

This result may be another instance of the delayed development of rural children seen in growth studies in many parts of the world. Because it suggests that the developmental age of the Barrow sample is behind that of the Illinois sample, however, it raises a question as to the extent to which the test performance of the two groups can be compared on an age-for-age basis. Fortunately, concern on this point is alleviated somewhat by the apparent lack of any strong age effects in these data for either group. An age-by-sex

TABLE 21-1 *Number of Subjects on Village List Who Also Appear in Sample, by Year of Birth and Sex*

	1955		1956		1957		1958		1959		1960	
	M	F	M	F	M	F	M	F	M	F	M	F
Village list	34	21	26	24	33	21	32	29	21	34	27	27
Sample	2	1	9	0	17	12	17	18	13	21	1	8
Percentage	5.9	4.8	34.6	0	51.5	57.1	53.1	62.1	61.9	61.8	3.7	29.6

TABLE 21-2 *Median Age in School Grade of Barrow and*
Illinois Subjects, by Sex (years)

Sample	Grade 7 M	Grade 7 F	Grade 8 M	Grade 8 F	Grade 9 M	Grade 9 F
Barrow	13.4	13.1	14.6	14.3	15.7	15.2
Illinois	12.4	12.4	13.4	13.4	14.4	14.4

multivariate analysis of variance of the scores for Barrow subjects who completed the six tests showed no significant age or age-by-sex interaction. Similarly, when the Illinois data are included, the age-by-sex-by-cultural-group analysis of variance discussed below gives no indication of age by cultural group interaction. This finding suggests that the results of the comparisons between the groups will not be sensitive to the six-month discrepancy in developmental age and that the age-by-age comparisons can be taken at face value.

The Barrow Sample

Apart from the comparisons of the cultural groups cited below, there are a number of suggestive results in the Barrow data, the means for which appear in Table 21-4. First, the only sex effect in the table is for the variable Fluency, where girls exceeded boys in fluent production at all age levels. When fluency tests are given in written form, as was the case here, female subjects almost always exceed male subjects in number of words written. This effect is

TABLE 21-3 *Age and Rate of Maximum Adolescent Growth*
in Stature of North Slope Native Children and
of Children in the Berkeley Growth Study

Sample	Maximum adolescent growth Age (yr) M	Age (yr) F	Rate (cm/yr) M	Rate (cm/yr) F
North Slope Jamison's cross-sectional sample	13.18	11.50	5.62	6.11
Jamison's semi-longitudinal sample	13.83	11.09	6.70	5.69
Berkeley Growth Study	12.69	10.96	5.82	5.20

TABLE 21-4 *Mean ($\pm$ S.E.) of Raw Scores for Barrow Subjects, by Age and Sex*

Age	Sex	N	Raven's	B-F Space	Aud. Span	Fluency*	English	Inupiat
12	M	0	---	---	---	---	---	---
	F	7	24.0 ± 2.4	16.1 ± 2.0	15.6 ± 1.6	19.4 ± 2.2	11.1 ± 1.3	8.1 ± 1.3
13	M	11	25.7 ± 1.9	14.1 ± 1.6	12.5 ± 1.3	14.3 ± 1.7	9.0 ± 1.1	8.2 ± 1.0
	F	14	27.2 ± 1.7	12.7 ± 1.4	12.4 ± 1.1	17.2 ± 1.6	10.6 ± 0.9	8.1 ± 0.9
14	M	13	25.5 ± 1.7	13.2 ± 1.5	11.2 ± 1.2	15.5 ± 1.6	10.0 ± 1.0	8.5 ± 0.9
	F	16	26.7 ± 1.6	13.6 ± 1.3	13.0 ± 1.1	19.6 ± 1.5	10.1 ± 0.9	9.2 ± 0.8
15	M	14	26.9 ± 1.7	15.2 ± 1.4	12.9 ± 1.1	15.5 ± 1.6	9.9 ± 0.9	9.1 ± 0.9
	F	4	30.0 ± 3.1	13.5 ± 2.6	15.3 ± 2.1	22.0 ± 3.3	12.0 ± 1.8	8.7 ± 1.7
16	M	7	28.1 ± 2.4	14.7 ± 2.0	13.0 ± 1.6	15.3 ± 2.0	9.0 ± 1.3	8.4 ± 1.3
	F	0	---	---	---	---	---	---

*Six missing observations for this variable are reflected in the standard errors.

thought to be partly motivational, because female subjects tend to go along with the test administrator's directives more readily than male subjects; but it may also represent a genuine special facility of girls and women for producing words in response to stimuli. In any event, this result is in accord with findings in other cultural groups. It does not, however, extend to the other linguistic variables in this test. The girls in the Barrow sample are not significantly superior to the boys in the English or Inupiat concept test.

The only significant effect for the English-Inupiat tests is an overall superiority of subjects in English concepts relative to the parallel Inupiat concepts. The difference in number of concepts correctly identified was 1.600 ± 0.386 in favor of English ($p < 0.0001$). It is difficult to say with certainty where the source of this difference lies. One possibility is that the paired English-Inupiat items are not strictly equivalent and that one or more of the items lost clarity in translation from English to Inupiat. If so, the difference is simply an artifact of the test construction. But if the judgment of the informant is accepted, a possible implication is that the use of English as the language of instruction, and its formal study within the school curriculum, makes classification problems of this type more natural and clear-cut. Some implications of these alternative explanations will be considered under "Discussion."

The other aspect bearing on the interpretation of these data is the within-age-and-sex-group correlation matrix shown in Table 21–5. Interpretation of these correlations is aided by the principal components of the correlation matrix as shown in Table 21–6. The structure of the correlations and the pattern of signs in the principal components are, in fact, precisely as expected from previous factor research on tests of these types.

The first component is a general intellective factor that, in the present context, could be interpreted as a general ability to respond to information-processing tasks, ranging from pure recognition in the Auditory Span task to access and recovery of learned semantic and relational information in the Raven's and English-Inupiat tests. Quite as expected, the first component loads most heavily on English and Inupiat and accounts for the conventional designation of this source as the general verbal factor. The high correlation between these two tests indicates verbal ability in general and not a language-specific ability.

Next, the second component indicates a fluency factor in opposition to the spatial factor—again a typical finding in factor studies of mental tests when general ability level is held fixed, resulting in a negative partial correlation of space and fluency measures (Broverman and Klaiber, 1969).

Finally, the third component reflects the visual spatial factor in opposition to the auditory and verbal tests. In this component, tests that are presented visually are contrasted with those presented auditorily. B-F Space is weighted most heavily here, but the Raven's is also represented to some extent, showing that it is a complex test having a minor spatial component as well as a dominant verbal component.

TABLE 21-5 *Raw-Score Common Within Age and Sex Group Correlations and Standard Deviations (df, 78) (df, 78)*

Correlations	Raven's	B-F Space	Aud. Span	Fluency*	English	Inupiat
Raven's	1.0000					
B-F Space	.3020	1.0000				
Aud. Span	.3407	.2907	1.0000			
Fluency	.2589	.0210	.0191	1.0000		
English	.5531	.1942	.3652	.2849	1.0000	
Inupiat	.3408	.2056	.3584	.1328	.6208	1.0000
S.D.	6.261	5.235	4.242	5.739	3.500	3.346

*Estimates for this variable are based on 72 degrees of freedom.

TABLE 21-6 *Leading Principal Components of the Within-Group Correlation Matrix*

	Component		
Test	1	2	3
Raven's	.7504	.0944	.2222
B-F Space	.4715	-.5135	.6194
Auditory Span	.6260	-.4194	-.1084
Fluency	.3568	.7695	.3842
English	.8362	.1951	-.2375
Inupiat	.7383	.0051	-.4461
% of Variance	42.5	18.0	14.1

The results of the principal component analysis are consistent with the findings of Defries et al. (1974) and MacArthur (1973) that, in spite of differences in the mean level of performance on mental tests from one cultural group to another, the factor structure of mental tests is highly invariant. One interpretation is that, while average level of performance is highly susceptible to cultural differences in exposure to the content of the tests and in motivation for achievement, variation among individuals within groups tends to arise from dimensions of biological differentiation that are universally human. This view of within-group individual differences is supported by the results of twin studies which identify the verbal, spatial, and fluency factors as major dimensions of heritable variation (Bock, 1973). Although this interpretation is not especially relevant to the present study, which is concerned primarily with the group differences, the fact that the correlation among the tests appears much as expected lends confidence in the validity of the tests when applied to these subjects. It justifies the assignment of the same qualitative meanings to the tests for the Barrow and the Illinois populations.

Group Comparisons

Summary data for the study in the form of group means are shown in Tables 21-4 and 21-7. Means for the fluency measure are also shown separately in Table 21-8 because their statistical treatment is somewhat different than that of the other tests. Whereas the Raven's, B-F Space, and Auditory Span tests have been scored by means of a psychometric scaling model calibrated in the Illinois samples, the fluency measure gives a quantitative score (number of names written by the subject) that does not require scaling. Because the distributions of the fluency scores are typically skewed toward high values and approximately log-normally distributed, however, it is desirable that they be subjected to a log transformation before analysis of variance and estimation of means. To make the transformed scores more interpretable, they have been adjusted in the total data to a mean of 50 and a within-group standard deviation of 10, and are shown in this form in Table 21-8.

As can be seen from the age-by-cultural-group-by-sex analysis of variance in Table 21-9, clearly significant effects in these variables are confined to main-class differences. For the Raven's test, only the cultural group difference, which favors the Illinois population, is significant. It may seem surprising that an overall age effect is not observed when a test of general ability is given to subjects in this age range, but its absence can be attributed to the poor psychometric properties of the Raven's Matrices in this age range. The items of the test tend to have a bimodal distribution of item difficulty, with many items too easy for subjects of this age and others too hard. As a result, the effective ceiling of the test of the A, B, and C forms is around thirty out of thirty-six answers correct. The effect of this ceiling is apparent in the present data and a similar effect is seen in the table of norms published by Raven (1960) for the group version of the full form of the test. There is essentially no change in the percentile points in the norm table above the age of 12.5 or 13 years.

Table 21-10 shows the best estimate of the overall differences between the Barrow and Illinois samples for the Raven's scaled score to be about 7/10 of a standard deviation. This discrepancy is not especially large, and could be attributed easily to the tendency of the Barrow community in general, and the Barrow Day School in particular, to place less emphasis on scholastic competition and achievement than do Illinois schools generally. It has also been shown that Raven's Matrices is sensitive to the subject's familiarity with appropriate problem-solving strategies and that scores improve markedly when children disadvantaged in this respect are instructed in how to think about this class of problem (Ginaugh, 1971). It is not too surprising that an isolated community, representing a culture that prizes physical rather than formal intellectual skills, should contain children that perform at a somewhat lower average level on a rather abstract test such as Raven's Matrices. The test appears to have, nevertheless, a certain validity for identifying those individuals within the cultural group who have more intellectual- and achievement-oriented abilities and attitudes. The moderately high correlation between Raven's Matrices and the English test in Table 21-5 suggests that such is the case.

In the results for the B-F Space test, the point of chief interest is the lack of any evidence of a cultural group by sex interaction ($p = 0.429$), while the main class sex effect is clear enough ($p < 0.0001$). This finding is at odds with

TABLE 21-7 *Observed Means and Ns for the Age X Cultural Group X Sex Classification: Raven's, B-F Space and Auditory Span Scaled Scores (Mean, 50; S.D., 10)*

Age	Sample	Raven's Males Mean	N	Raven's Females Mean	N	B-F Space Males Mean	N	B-F Space Females Mean	N	Auditory Span Males Mean	N	Auditory Span Females Mean	N
12	Barrow	--	0	--	0	--	0	--	0	--	0	--	0
	Illinois	50.8	15	51.2	40	53.2	89	47.2	88	47.5	15	49.6	40
13	Barrow	44.3	16	47.2	21	47.2	16	44.0	23	41.4	16	40.9	21
	Illinois	49.9	51	51.9	47	54.7	195	48.0	179	52.0	51	50.6	47
14	Barrow	41.6	13	44.8	15	44.3	14	42.1	16	36.4	13	39.2	15
	Illinois	53.4	41	53.2	62	54.2	103	51.1	76	53.0	41	49.5	62
15	Barrow	44.3	18	41.6	5	50.4	18	56.3	7	41.6	18	48.9	5
	Illinois	55.2	20	41.5	16	--	0	--	0	51.8	20	45.2	16

TABLE 21-8   *Observed Means and Ns for Log-Transformed Fluency*
Scores (Standard Score Units x10+50; Mean, 3.066;
Within-Group S.D., .2962; df, 496)

		Males		Females	
Age	Sample	Mean	N	Mean	N
12	Barrow	--	0	--	0
	Illinois	55.6	44	58.7	53
13	Barrow	34.3	11	41.4	13
	Illinois	59.1	113	61.3	107
14	Barrow	39.0	13	45.7	14
	Illinois	58.9	76	63.0	48
15	Barrow	38.5	13	51.5	3
	Illinois	--	0	--	0

Based on a 50% sample of Illinois subjects in study.

those of Berry and MacArthur in that it shows no evidence that a sex effect
does not exist in the Barrow data. Inasmuch as there is no evidence of a sex
effect in the Barrow data shown in Table 21-4, this conclusion may seem
paradoxical, for it is just such failure to find sex differences in Eskimo samples that the literature reports. The explanation is, of course, that failure to
demonstrate significant sex differences in the typically small samples of such
studies does not imply that the differences do not exist nor that they would
not be detected in larger size samples. In spite of its high level of statistical
significance, the sex effect shown in Table 21-9 is only half a standard deviation for this particular test and could easily go undetected in a small-scale
study.

Neither do these data suggest that the Barrow sample has any special
facility in spatial visualization, for the cultural group effect favors the Illinois
sample, and by an amount almost exactly equal to that of Raven's Matrices.
Such could again be attributed to motivational effects in taking this speeded
spatial test requiring a level of concerted attention in a group-testing situation
seldom required of students in the Barrow school.

For the Auditory Span Test, on the other hand, it is barely possible that

TABLE 21-9 *Age (A) x Cultural Group (C) x Sex (S) Analysis of Variance: F Null Probabilities*

Source of Variation*	df	Raven's	Aud. Span	B-F Space	Fluency
A	3	.355	.856	.233	.0001
C	1	<.00001	<.00001	<.0001	<.0001
S	1	.245	.392	<.0001	<.0002
A x C	1	.219	.102	.238	.218
A x S	3	.317	.358	.059	.245
C x S	1	.152	.094	.429	.196
A x C x S	1	.354	.316	.677	.923
Error S. D.		.9703	1.0474	1.1743	10.0
df		366	366	812	496

*Additive, nonorthogonal analysis; effects eliminated from top downward. Only linear age-effects were tested in A x C and A x C x S. Results were computed with the Multivariance program, Version 5.3 (Finn, 1974).

there may be a cultural group by sex interaction ($p = 0.094$). If so, it would be due to the tendency (Table 21-7) for boys to excel in this test in the Illinois sample and girls in the Barrow sample. The extent of such a tendency, however, is extremely small relative to the very large cultural group effect of nearly 1 standard deviation, again favoring the Illinois sample (Table 21-10). That this discrepancy is larger than those for Raven's and B-F Space lends some support to belief that the Arctic Eskimo is less attuned to auditory discriminations because the climatic conditions and dress make it difficult to rely on auditory cues in outdoor activities. Although it is well known that the

TABLE 21-10 *Mean (± S.E.) of Estimated Effects (Rank 6 Models)*

	Raven's	B-F Space	Aud. Span
Cultural group (Barrow-Illinois)	−7.3 ± 1.2	−7.2 ± 1.5	−9.4 ± 1.3
Sex (male-female)	−1.2 ± 1.0	5.1 ± 0.8	0.9 ± 1.1

incidence of hearing difficulties as a sequel to otitis media is high in Barrow and the other North Slope villages, that is unlikely to explain the present result in view of the high level of sound intensity at which the test was given. The children able to function in school without special compensation for hearing loss would not have difficulty hearing the items on this test.

In an unpublished dissertation, Whang (1971) showed that a digit span test was a useful predictor of the ability of sixth-grade pupils to learn words of a foreign language (French). It is perhaps therefore of interest that the Auditory Span Test (Table 21–4) has its highest correlation with the English test. The indication may be that Auditory Span, which is seldom found to be correlated with achievement measures, is a predictor of an ability to make the kind of discriminations among sounds necessary to learn a second language. Of course, it is also possible that the presentation of these tests by tape recording (also in Whang's study) introduces a factor specific to the presentation of words and sounds on tape. Nevertheless, the widespread use of audio aids in language instruction lends a possible practical significance to these results.

Turning finally to the Fluency Test, one sees in Table 21–9 clear evidence for age, cultural group, and sex effects but no interactions. The mean values presented in Table 21–8 show that the age effect, although highly significant, represents but a small increase from year to year. Similarly the sex effect, favoring the female subjects, is quite small, amounting to about one-third of a standard deviation. Thus, there is no marked disagreement of this result with the finding of no sex effect by Wallach and Kogan for their Pattern Meaning and Line Meaning Test. Although Thurstone's Word Fluency Test, in which subjects try to write as many words as they can think of beginning with the letters S or T, shows a marked sex effect, in the more visually oriented task used here the sex differences are not as great. Some of the sex difference that is found could, of course, merely indicate that girls and women are more compliant in this somewhat onerous task of writing lists of words. But the fact that word fluency and the visually stimulated fluency of the present test do not show large sex differences suggests that the rather large individual differences one sees in these types of fluent production are not purely motivational in origin. Some subjects seem to block on these tasks and are unable to think of additional words, whereas others can move flexibly from one line of ideas to another and produce many examplars.

In the fluency measure, the Barrow subjects are a full 2 standard deviations below the mean for the Illinois sample; the estimated effects for the log-transformed fluency scores in standard score units $\times$ 10 yielded -10.3 for the Barrow-Addison comparison and -3.5 for the male-female comparison. Of the hypotheses one might have entertained about the cultural effect in fluent production, the view that the relative featurelessness of the North Slope environment leads to a paucity of content for fluent production would seem to be supported. An alternative interpretation, however, would be that this is essentially a "second language" effect, and would be true of any group that uses one language in school and another for common parlance. Since the associations draw on ideas from in-school as well as out, it may be that if the response to the test is in the school language, an entire domain of objects and ideas is excluded. Lending some support to this interpretation is the fact that the fluency test has its highest correlation with the English test and relatively little correlation with the Inupiat test (Table 21-5).

DISCUSSION

For purposes of discussion, it would be convenient to regard this study as a comparison of two highly distinct populations, separated biologically and culturally during much of the human epoch. But in actuality, the North Slope Eskimo culture has been penetrated and transformed profoundly by contacts with Western culture since the second half of the nineteenth century. As is true in all the coastal villages of the North Slope, the genealogies of the Barrow residents record an appreciable biological admixture from European sources. And to even a greater degree, the dress, diet, habitation, transportation, occupation, entertainment, and education are a varied mixture of a modern technological society and a traditional hunting and fishing culture. A more accurate view of the present study is that of a comparison, in terms of abilities that have been found to be basic to achievement in the complex occupations of modern society, between a minority American culture and the majority culture.

In these terms, the difference in performance that is observed for the four tests where comparison is possible is large only for Fluency, which is probably the measure most affected by the sparseness of the arctic environment and the intellectual limitations of life in an isolated village. By comparison, the deficiency of the Barrow subjects in performance on Raven's and B-F Space, which are the most important of the four tests for predicting scholastic and occupational success, is modest and can be attributed to the subjects' lack of experience with group tests involving novel material. It is not inconsistent with Feldman's (1974) results based on individual testing, in each of nine age groups, of sixty-eight children from Point Hope. For the Block Design Test of the *Wechsler Intelligence Scale for Children,* a test which combines elements of general problem-solving and spatial perception, she found mean scores at U.S. norm levels in all groups. Taken together with Kleinfeld's (1973a) observation that individual intelligence test performance of Eskimo children is sensitive to interpersonal affect with the test administrator, results of Feldman's study and of the present study suggest that as movement into the majority culture continues, the youth of Barrow will soon be at U.S. norm levels for visually presented nonlanguage tests of intellectual ability.

The results are perhaps less encouraging for the auditory perception and linguistic tests. In spite of the almost total absence of cultural content in the auditory span test, the Barrow subjects perform relatively more poorly on this task. A genuine lack of development of auditory attention and discrimination may be involved that could have implications for learning a second language (in this case, English). This result presents something of a dilemma because, like other minority-language cultures, the Eskimo children have to receive the bulk of their formal education in the second language. The dilemma is further compounded if, as the English-Inupiat test results seem to indicate, the development of formal concepts (in this case, class membership), and perhaps even vocabulary, tends to lag in the first language. Thus, the educational problems that are encountered by most linguistic minorities may be especially difficult among the Inupiat-speakers of the North Slope.

These problems may also be reflected in another form in the results for Fluency, which require making a verbal association to a nonverbal visual stimulus and writing the product in English. Spontaneous written production is not an entirely natural and easy task for many monolinguistic speakers, and may be even more difficult for the bilingual if translation between the languages is required. When there is little need to translate in everyday activities, as is largely the case for the Inupiat-speakers (the domain of spoken language for home and peers and the domain including written language for school remain separate), then fluency of word production in the written language suffers. Much of the verbal learning problems in the North Slope schools (Kleinfeld, 1973a) can be understood in terms of this division of resources and effort of linguistic development which inevitably confronts minority-language groups.

SUMMARY

Students in the seventh, eighth, and ninth grades of Barrow Day School were administered a set of six psychological tests during the second week of October 1972. The tests included (1) Forms A, B, and C of the Raven Progressive Matrices, (2) the Bock-Fitzgerald Space Test, (3) an Auditory Span Test, (4) a test of associational fluency, and (5, 6) parallel English and Inupiat word-classification tests.

Means for Tests 1 through 4, when compared with results from administrations of the tests under the same conditions in schools of two small Illinois communities, showed significantly lower levels of performance in the Barrow sample. The disparity was about 0.72 SD for Raven's Matrices and the Spatial Test, 0.94 SD for Auditory Span, and 2.0 SD for the Fluency Test. The Spatial Test and Fluency Tests showed a significant sex effect favoring male and female subjects, respectively. There was marginal evidence of a sex by cultural group interaction for the Auditory Span Test, but no such interaction for the other tests, including the Spatial and Fluency Tests.

The English and Inupiat word-classification tests, which were correlated 0.62 within age and sex groups, revealed a small but significant tendency for better performance in English than in Inupiat. Such trends in the results may be explained in terms of "minority-language" effects.

Finally, the factor structure of the sex tests in the Barrow sample appears very similar to that found in many other populations.

22

Multidisciplinary Research: A Case Study in Eskimo Human Biology

Stephen L. Zegura and *Paul L. Jamison*

The purposes of this chapter are twofold: (1) to specify how some of the lacunae in our knowledge of Eskimo biology have been filled by this project and (2) to provide a synergistic synthesis of the research. As mentioned by Milan in Chapter 1, Laughlin (1966) and Hildes (1966) published summaries of the knowledge available in the mid-1960s pertaining to the genetics and biological anthropology (Laughlin) and to the health and physiological adaptations (Hildes) of arctic populations. Hildes (1966) concluded with a section entitled "Areas of ignorance," in which he stated:

> Although scientific interest in the circumpolar people has existed for a long time and has been particularly active in recent years there remain large gaps in our knowledge concerning the microclimate of the people of all ages and both sexes, their level of activity, details of the diet, physical fitness, and cold tolerance, not to mention the underlying biochemical and hormonal basis of their physiological responses. (p. 505)

This volume directly addresses some of these gaps in our knowledge. Specifically, the topics of diet (Chapters 10-16), biochemistry (Chapters 7-9), and physical fitness (Chapter 17) are treated by diverse portions of the research team.

RESULTS FROM THE IBP ESKIMO STUDY

Diet

Bell and Heller (Chapter 11) point out that the consumption of native foods is as important in the diet of Wainwright residents today as it was in the diet of Eskimos surveyed fifteen years ago; however, the consumption of native foods has decreased markedly during this time at Point Hope. Although

262

their diet is still somewhat higher in protein than the average U.S. diet, the study populations now consume fewer calories as protein than in the recent past. While Wainwright protein calories have been replaced by calories from fat, the Point Hope protein calories have been replaced by carbohydrates. Erosion of the traditional diet culture at these two villages is further evidenced by the smaller percentages of calories and protein derived from native foods in the diet of children compared with the values in the diet of adults. This erosion is also demonstrated by the fact that carbohydrates from imported foods provide a much greater portion of the Eskimo diet today in these villages than they did in aboriginal times. Other dietary assessments suggest a diet that is low in calcium, high in phosphorus, adequate in iron, variable in vitamin A, low in vitamin C, and adequate in thiamin, riboflavin, and niacin.

Bergan and Bell (Chapter 12) found low hemoglobin and hematocrit values in both adults and children at Point Hope and Wainwright. They concluded that anemia is now a frequent nutritional problem among these Eskimos. Plasma levels of vitamin C were found to be adequate in nearly all subjects. Plasma vitamin A levels were generally satisfactory (except among children from Nunapitchuk). Serum protein values were in the acceptable range, as were values for urinary riboflavin and thiamin excretion (with the exceptions of low riboflavin levels in Point Hope children and inadequate thiamin levels in the Kasigluk sample). In summary, Bergan and Bell state that the nutritional status of this sample of Alaskan Eskimos was generally satisfactory in the biochemical parameters studied except for an apparently pervasive incidence of anemia. This high prevalence of anemia seems to be greater than that reported in earlier assessments.

Colbert et al. (Chapter 13) state that no clinical entities could be specifically ascribed to nutritional deficiencies in their review of clinical observations on the residents of Wainwright, Point Hope, Kasigluk, and Nunapitchuk. They felt that the roles of dietary change vs a proposed spreading epidemic of *Streptococcus mutans* in the etiology of the high prevalence of dental caries in these populations (documented in Chapter 6) could not be resolved by their study. They found no instances of alcoholic hepatitis or other disorders directly attributable to alcohol consumption. Only one case of diabetes mellitus was discovered, and this one was controlled by diet alone. Obesity has increased over the past fifteen years, more prevalent among women than men; however, the dietary components that may be implicated in these trends were not specified. In fact, the traditional profile of low blood pressure, low blood cholesterol, and lean body mass is being eroded among these Eskimos, especially in those villages located at an interface with Western culture.

S. Feldman et al. (Chapter 14) document the cholesterol content of the indigenous diet at Point Hope. The rate of ingestion proved to be approximately that of the general U.S. population. In contrast, the Point Hope subjects showed low concentrations of serum triglycerides and very low-density lipoprotein. Serum free fatty acid concentrations, however, were high. Mean plasma glucose and insulin values were not significantly different from those observed for healthy U.S. subjects.

Bell et al. (Chapter 15) performed lactose tolerance tests in Wainwright and Point Hope and found that Alaskan Eskimos share with other cultures lacking a history of dairying, a limited capacity for lactose digestion. However, it appears that most Eskimo adults are capable of consuming nutritionally significant amounts of dairy foods in moderate portions at intervals of several hours. Sucrose intolerance was also confirmed in six individuals by oral load tests. At the present time this form of familial sucrose intolerance seems to be unique to Eskimo populations. Except for this study and earlier work on the Greenland Eskimo, only isolated cases of congenital origin have been reported. Sucrase deficiency is not confined to adults and older children, as is lactase deficiency. In addition, the degree of intolerance seems to be more acute. The influx of processed foods into the Eskimo diet makes it increasingly difficult to avoid sucrose and it may become necessary to develop a class of proprietary foods for sucrose-intolerant individuals analogous to those now available for diabetics.

Draper and Wei Wo (Chapter 16) studied plasma vitamin E in residents of Wainwright, Point Hope, Kasigluk, and Nunapitchuk and found no evidence of vitamin E deficiency. They also studied serum cholesterol and found that cholesterol levels at Wainwright and Point Hope were substantially lower than those in the U.S. National Health Survey of 1960–62 whereas those at Kasigluk and Nunapitchuk were substantially higher than the U.S. values. Hypercholesterolemia was generally correlated with obesity, being more prevalent in females than in males and in the southern rather than in the northern villages. Children showed a similar pattern of increased cholesterol levels in the southern villages, which also showed the greatest degree of diet acculturation. The concentrations of both vitamin E and cholesterol were markedly influenced by the level of serum lipoproteins.

Biochemical Parameters

In addition to the biochemical parameters studied in conjunction with diet and nutrition, Laessig et al. (Chapter 7) developed a set of biochemical normal ranges for a series of twelve serum parameters based on subjects from Wainwright, Point Hope, and Barrow. These ranges were compared with those of a sample from Wisconsin; the following parameters showed statistically significant differences in ranges: cholesterol, alkaline phosphatase, aspartate aminotransferase, and creatinine. The creatinine results may be of special interest since the high values shown by Eskimo women may be an indication of renal dysfunction. The normal ranges of calcium, phosphorus, urea nitrogen, uric acid, total protein, albumin, total bilirubin, and lactic acid dehydrogenase do not differ between the Eskimo and Wisconsin populations.

Moore (Chapter 8) reports qualitative studies of the red-cell enzyme, carbonic anhydrase, performed on blood samples taken from Point Hope and Wainwright residents. Carbonic anhydrase levels showed a marked increase with age, and the developmental pattern of carbonic anhydrase level generally parallels that of stature. No genetic variants of the CA-B and CA-C isozymes were detected; however, there were significant differences in these isozyme values among Eskimos and other ethnic groups in the United States.

Mazess and Mather (Chapter 9) measured bone mineral content from Wainwright, Point Hope, and Barrow Eskimos. During growth and early adulthood these Eskimos have relatively normal bone mineral content; however, as aging proceeds there is a sharp change. In the elderly there is an accelerated rate of loss of bone mineral content and the onset of this bone loss is earlier than in U.S. whites. The possibility of a nutritional etiology for this bone loss in Eskimos should be pursued. Specifically the intakes of protein, vitamin D, phosphorus, and calcium should be thoroughly investigated within the framework of developing an understanding of the mechanisms responsible for extensive bone loss in Eskimos.

Physical Fitness

Rennie (Chapter 17) has evaluated the physical fitness of Eskimos from Wainwright, Point Hope, and Barrow. Tests for maximal aerobic arm work and a 15-min endurance run yielded results within the normal limits of nonhunting populations reported in the past. Tests for maximal anaerobic power and respiratory function, however, yielded significantly different values from those achieved by most non-Eskimo populations. Eskimo values for maximal anaerobic power were clearly superior to those of African natives and Italian city-dwellers. In fact, they were comparable with values recorded for trained Italian athletes. Vital capacity, timed vital capacity, and maximal breathing capacity were also approximately 10% higher in male Eskimos than were the values predicted from height-weight standards for Americans. As Rennie points out, we are thus left with the enigma of having one link in the O_2 transport system that appears to have a greater potential than its present use indicates. Perhaps a process of deconditioning of maximal aerobic power has occurred as a result of the less active life-style of the modern North Slope residents.

BIOLOGICAL CHANGE: EVOLUTION, GROWTH, AND AGING

Skeletal-Living Comparisons

As a quotation from Hildes (1966) provided a point of departure for the discussion of results from the IBP Eskimo study, so a statement of Laughlin's

(1966) provides a framework for a discussion of biological change. Laughlin recommends that "skeletal populations related to living populations should be studied. . . ." (p. 491). In the absence of historical records there is no way to identify positively the genetic relationship between skeletal remains found in a particular location and a living population occupying the same location. Detailed historical records with substantial time depth are lacking for North Slope populations. The vicinities of Barrow and Point Hope have been inhabited for approximately 1,000 and 2,000 years, respectively (Chapter 2). Unfortunately the phenomena of continuity, movement, and replacement are all probably involved in the population history of these areas. Without historical records it is possible only indirectly to assess the various contributions of these processes to the make-up of the present-day populations at Barrow and Point Hope. For this reason the time depth for the skeletal-living comparisons at these locations will remain rather shallow.

In Table 2-3 Zegura cites craniometric data from Point Hope and Barrow that can be compared with anthropometric data from the modern villages cited by Jamison in Tables 4-11 and 4-12. The craniometric findings date from the eighteenth and nineteenth centuries at Point Barrow (Nixeruk) and from the late nineteenth to early twentieth centuries at Point Hope. The comparatively recent temporal distribution of these skeletal series increases the probability of a genetic relationship between some of the nonliving and living members of these samples.

Table 22-1 provides comparative data on four craniometric and anthropometric variables along with two indices derived from each type of data. Obviously the soft tissue covering the anthropometric landmarks introduces a complication to the direct comparison of these measures. However, skinfold measurements can provide a partial solution to this complication. Skinfold measurements rarely fall below a minimum of 3 mm. Since this measure is of compressed tissue, and soft tissue overlying anthropometric landmarks of the head is also compressed when measuring, perhaps it can serve as an approximation of the "correction" factor that should be applied to the craniometric data in Table 22-1 to make them comparable with anthropometric measurements.

The measurement data in this table demonstrate (with one exception) an increase in size over time. This increase is particularly marked for head breadth and contributes to the increase in cephalic/cranial index. Such brachycephalization through time has been remarked upon repeatedly (see for instance Laughlin, 1958 and 1966), so it is not too surprising here.

A more interesting feature of the data in Table 22-1 is the relationship of upper facial heights for the skeletal and living individuals from Barrow. Upper facial height is a linear dimension and the correction factor of 3 mm proposed for compression measurements would probably overestimate the difference due to measurement variation expected between the skeletal and living samples. In contrast to the trend toward size increase seen in the other three measurements, upper facial height shows virtually no difference through

TABLE 22-1 *Craniometric and Anthropometric Data from 2 North Alaskan Eskimo Villages (mm)*

| Variable | Barrow Subjects | | | | Point Hope Subjects | | | |
| | Male | | Female | | Male | | Female | |
	Mean	SD	Mean	SD	Mean	SD	Mean	SD
N in Sample								
Skeletal	15		12		61		32	
Living	59		66		25		46	
Head length								
Skeletal	186.6	3.5	178.1	5.1	183.6	4.8	174.6	5.3
Living	196.0	6.0	187.0	6.0	196.0	7.0	188.0	6.0
Head breadth								
Skeletal	138.6	2.8	134.2	3.5	138.8	4.3	134.9	2.8
Living	156.0	5.0	149.0	5.0	155.0	6.0	152.0	4.0
Bizygomatic breadth								
Skeletal	140.5	3.7	130.8	3.3	143.0	4.6	133.1	3.7
Living	152.0	6.0	142.0	5.0	151.0	5.0	143.0	6.0
Upper facial height								
Skeletal	70.4	2.5	66.0	3.2	69.4	4.0	65.7	4.0
Living	71.0	5.0	64.0	5.0	78.0	4.0	70.0	4.0
Cephalic/cranial index								
Skeletal	74.3		75.4		75.6		77.3	
Living	79.6		79.7		79.1		80.8	
Upper facial index								
Skeletal	50.1		50.5		48.5		49.4	
Living	46.7		45.1		51.7		49.0	

time for male Barrow subjects and, indeed, the comparison for female subjects shows a decrease over time. It is tempting to suggest that the modern Barrow population contains a large inland component and therefore was at least partially replaced in the 200-300 years that intervened between the two samples compared here. However, the overall anthropometric results shown in Table 4-15 and Figs. 4-3 and 4-4 do not support such a conclusion. In addition, more data than one measurement would be necessary to support this conclusion, but unfortunately they are not available.

For Point Hope, data in Table 22-1 suggest that over a period of 200-300 years there was an overall increase in the dimensions of the head and face, particularly for head breadth and to a lesser extent for face breadth. The vertical facial dimension was altered less, especially among female subjects. For Barrow, the skeletal-living comparison suggests a similar increase in head length and in head and facial breadths through time but no difference or a slight decrease in the vertical facial dimension. While the trend towards brachycephalization is a common finding among recent populations, the anomalous result in the Barrow upper facial heights might be explained by sampling error or admixture or a degree of population replacement from the interior over the time period examined.

A more precise skeletal-living comparison can be made with cephalometric X-rays, as is seen in Chapter 6. Dahlberg et al. studied Wainwright residents cephalometrically and compared them with a series of crania from northwestern Alaska. The investigators found a rather high level of similarity in craniofacial morphology through time, particularly in linear measurements, the degree of maxillary prognathism, and the degree of midfacial flatness. The crania and living Eskimos were distinguished from each other by the increased labial inclination of the incisors in Wainwright residents, and the male Wainwright Eskimos had less facial convexity and less difference in the maxillary and mandibular apical base relation than the crania. Dahlberg et al. implicate admixture as a possible cause of difference seen in apical base relation, and changes in the use of the dentition were implicated as a cause of the labial inclination of the incisors. Changes in type of foodstuff and in ways of preparing food could mean less functional force on the anterior teeth in the living Eskimo, leading to a failure of the incisors to upright with age.

Thus we are left with something of a paradox by the results of morphological comparisons of living Eskimos and crania found in the same general vicinity. On the one hand, the Point Hope and Point Barrow comparisons suggest that there has been a change in linear dimensions of the head—resulting in increasing breadth through time. The Wainwright-northwest Alaskan comparison, however, revealed no differences in linear dimensions. The existence of both anthropometric and cephalometric data on living Eskimos and the number of northwestern Alaskan crania that exist in collections scattered around the United States would appear to provide a good opportunity for future research on this question.

Growth

Ontogenetic change—growth—reflects an interplay between inherited genetic potential for growth and environmental circumstances influencing the expression of this potential. Many investigators in this volume have attempted to answer such basic questions as: (1) How long do Eskimo children grow? (2) How much do they grow? (3) How fast do they grow? (4) What factors in the environment affect this growth?

Jamison (Chapter 4) presents the most comprehensive account of the growth process in these Eskimo populations. The sample for his cross-sectional anthropometric growth study includes 488 children. When Eskimo stature and weight are compared with standards for U.S. whites, north Alaskan Eskimo stature falls between the 10th and 25th percentiles and weight falls between the 50th and 75th percentiles prior to adolescence; however, during adolescence both variables approach higher percentiles of the white growth standards. At age eighteen Eskimo males are 6 cm shorter and 7.3 kg heavier than the white standards, while females are 4.5 cm shorter and 5.4 kg heavier. High weight for stature characterizes Eskimos throughout the period of growth and development. Distance curves for stature show that males and females are similar until the age of eleven to twelve years, when females forge ahead. Subsequently, the distance curves recross at age fourteen and by the late teens males are about 12 cm taller than females. Distance curves for weight show that females surpass males from age nine until age fifteen to sixteen, when males become heavier. At age eighteen males average about 10 kg heavier than females.

Information on rate (velocity) of growth in stature is presented both by Jamison (Chapter 4) and by Bock (Chapter 21), who further analyzed Jamison's data. A semilongitudinal study on Wainwright children showed that the adolescent growth spurt begins at ages nine to ten among females and at ages eleven to twelve for males. Peak height velocity (maximum rate during adolescent growth spurt) occurred at age fourteen for males and at age eleven for females. According to Bock, this value for males is one year later than that of whites from the Berkeley Growth Study. By age seventeen to eighteen the stature velocity for Eskimo males was only 2 cm per year, indicating that the point of effective growth cessation was close. This result is important because it contradicts the often-mentioned belief that Eskimo growth cessation occurs very late (in the mid-twenties).

The weight rate (velocity) curves for Wainwright children show that these Eskimos have values above the white standard at all ages. Peak weight velocity occurred one year later in Eskimos than in whites but the magnitude of the peak was higher for the Eskimos. In Wainwright peak weight velocity occurred for males at ages fourteen to fifteen; for females it occurred at ages thirteen to fourteen.

Jamison also presents distance curves based on cross-sectional data for biiliac breadth, biacromial breadth, bizygomatic breadth, total facial height, upper arm circumference, calf circumference, foot length, foot breadth, wrist breadth, hand length, and hand breadth (see Figs. 4-7 to 4-11). These figures demonstrate the progressive development of sexual dimorphism throughout the growth period. Jamison finds that Eskimo females have larger biiliac breadths, arm circumferences, and calf circumferences than males for a large portion of the growth period. Facial dimensions and extremity measurements have the shortest period when females have larger values than males. Age group means for males surpass those for females between the ages of thirteen and seventeen years. The earliest appearance of larger values for boys occurs in extremity and facial dimensions, followed by biacromial and biiliac breadths. The limb circumferences manifest this phenomenon latest of all.

Dahlberg et al. (Chapter 6) also studied growth parameters of Wainwright children. Their data are primarily cross-sectional, involving radiographs of the craniofacial complex. They characterize the developmental pattern of the Wainwright facial region as one in which the face emerges from beneath the cranium with increasing age. In the vertical dimension relative change is greater in the posterior part of the face while in the anteroposterior plane there are proportionately greater increments in the inferior facial area, causing increasing prominence of the lower face. The most notable growth-related changes in the total craniofacial complex were the following: increase in all linear dimensions; relatively greater increase in posterior facial height than in anterior facial height, causing an interior rotation of the mandible (especially in males); increase in mandibular basal prognathism; reduction in apical base relation; reduction in horizontal overbite (overjet); reduction in obtuseness of the gonial angle; increase in midfacial and total facial flatness; and decrease in axial inclination of incisors in males.

Laessig et al. (Chapter 7) attempted to derive a series of normal ranges for serum biochemical parameters for both children and adults at Wainwright, Point Hope, and Barrow. The data are essentially cross-sectional and show the following developmental patterns: children show higher ranges of inorganic phosphorus and alkaline phosphatase than adults (both parameters are influenced by bone growth); children also show higher values of lactic acid dehydrogenase and aspartate aminotransferase (GOT); adults show higher ranges than children for uric acid and cholesterol. S. Feldman et al. (Table 14-2) and Draper and Wei Wo (Tables 16-2 and 16-3) also present data on the increased blood cholesterol content encountered during growth in these Eskimo populations.

Moore (Chapter 8) analyzed the age-dependence of carbonic anhydrase in Point Hope Eskimos. She found that both CA-B and CA-C levels increase from a low value at age five to adult levels during or slightly after adolescence. At age five the CA-B level is 64% of the adult level while the CA-C level is 73% of the adult level. Adult levels are reached before age twenty-four. The shape of the regression lines illustrating the effect of age on carbonic anhydrase is similar to Jamison's (Chapter 4) growth curves for stature. At age five approximately 65% of adult stature is attained, according to the cross-sectional data for Point Hope. It appears that stature and carbonic anhydrase follow similar developmental courses except that sex differences during development are absent in the case of carbonic anhydrase, and an adolescent growth spurt was not detected in the enzyme concentrations. Moore makes the provocative suggestion that the increases in carbonic anhydrase level and stature from birth to puberty may be under similar hormonal control.

Mazess and Mather (Chapter 9) present data on the increase in bone mineral content during growth. The Alaskan Eskimos show increases until early adulthood, followed by a rapid decline with advancing age. The distance curves for bone mineral content are very similar to those for stature during the entire growth period (see Figs. 9-1 and 9-2).

Rennie (Chapter 17) studied the association of age with various physiological parameters. Maximal anaerobic power for North Slope Eskimo males increased dramatically between the ages of five and about twenty years and then decreased after about age twenty. Peak values were thus reached in the late teens and early twenties. For maximal O_2 consumption a sex difference was noted in the age of attainment of peak values: females reached their $\dot{V}_{O_2 max}$ values in their early teens, while males were delayed until their late teens. Both sexes demonstrated a linear decline with age after achieving their peak $\dot{V}_{O_2 max}$ values.

Cognitive development is the final growth-related topic discussed in this volume. The reports by C. Feldman et al. (Chapter 20) and Bock (Chapter 21) deal with intellectual maturation. C. Feldman et al. found that growth of cognitive and perceptual abilities in Wainwright subjects appears to be slowed down during adolescence. This cognitive slump may be environmentally engendered and involved individuals between the ages of fourteen and seventeen years, according to data based on the Raven Progressive Matrices Test. Overall the results of Feldman et al. support the sequencing and stage aspects of Piagetian theory for cognitive development. Bock (Chapter 21) found clear evidence for an age effect in only one test, fluency. Although the age effect was highly significant, the mean values presented in Table 21-8 show small yearly increases. Thus, the ability to make verbal associations to a nonverbal stimulus increases steadily between the ages of twelve and fifteen years in the Barrow subjects, without a spurt.

Aging

As Laughlin points out, "Harsh conditions in the Arctic area are imposed directly on the very young and the very old" (1966:485). Many of the chapters in this volume contain information directly related to the aging process in these Eskimo populations. Aging may be regarded as a breakdown in individual homeostasis. Individual adjustments to environmental constraints become less efficient. The consequences of this impairment are often a reduced contribution to community functioning and a severe drain on community resources in harsh environments.

The early onset of bone loss and the accelerated rate of this loss in Eskimos are described by Mazess and Mather (Chapter 9). The implications of these findings for the development of osteoporotic complications are clear, especially in a harsh arctic environment where accidents frequently lead to broken bones. Another cause for concern involving the North Slope populations is the large number of missing teeth reported by Dahlberg et al. in Chapter 6. Of the seventy individuals at Wainwright over the age of thirty whose dentitions were studied, twenty-three are edentulous. In fact, the average individual at Wainwright (including children) is missing 7.6 teeth. The low periodontal rates indicate that the vast majority of these missing teeth are due to the progressive deterioration of the dentition brought about by caries. The Eskimo of a few years ago with his legendary good, strong teeth is being rapidly replaced by one with large numbers of missing and decayed teeth, a very inauspicious trend.

The frequencies of abnormal electrocardiogram (ECG) findings in the Eskimo groups studied by Colbert et al. (Chapter 13) were below those found in a reference population from Tecumseh, Michigan; however, there was a definite trend of increasing abnormality with increasing age in the Eskimos. The kinds of abnormalities were typical of a population with extensive atherosclerotic heart disease. There was no real evidence that ECG abnormalities in men were related to serum cholesterol, blood pressure, or weight, three key factors often implicated in coronary heart disease. Females with abnormal ECG readings did, however, tend to have consistently higher levels of hypercholesterolemia.

In Chapter 16 Draper and Wei Wo show serum cholesterol content increasing with age. As indigenous diets change to modern diets the amount of cholesterol consumed can be expected to increase, with the concomitant effect of increasing the incidence of hypercholesterolemia, especially in the elderly. Although cholesterol levels at Wainwright and Point Hope were substantially lower than those found in the U.S. National Health Survey of 1960–62, those at Kasigluk and Nunapitchuk (the more acculturated villages) were substantially higher. Data in Chapter 13 also show that hypercholesterolemia was generally correlated with obesity, another age-related trend in Eskimo females. Thus, the interaction of changing diet, obesity, hypercholesterolemia, and ECG abnormalities should be carefully monitored in Eskimo populations (especially in women) as the phenomenon of aging unfolds. Again, the possible ramifications for the future coronary health of these people are ominous, given the presently emerging trends.

Jamison (Chapter 4) describes age changes in two anthropometric variables—stature and weight—for Eskimo adults from Anaktuvuk Pass, Barrow, Point Hope, and Wainwright. Using cross-sectional data, a reduction in stature that is probably due to aging is found among males after age eighty and for females after age seventy. Weight, on the other hand, tends to increase in these Eskimos until age forty to fifty years in women and fifty to sixty in men. After the eighth decade, weight begins to fall off slightly among men and more sharply for women. A tendency towards high weight for stature during the period of growth and development thus extends also into the majority of the adult lifespan. To the extent that high weight contributes to the complex of factors involved in coronary heart disease, this factor must be added as a further complication in the interaction of diet, cholesterol, obesity, and ECG abnormalities mentioned above.

A final statement about the effects of the aging process comes from Rennie's work (Chapter 17) on physical-fitness parameters. Male Eskimos from Barrow, Point Hope, and Wainwright reached peak values of $V_{O_2 max}$ in their late teens, followed by a linear decline with age. Female Eskimos showed a pattern of peak values in their early teens, followed by a slow decline thereafter. Maximal aerobic power is generally considered an important component of physical fitness because it establishes the uppermost limit of muscular power that theoretically can be supported by a person's oxygen transport system. The decline in $\dot{V}_{O_2 max}$ with age indicates that maximum aerobic power starts to decline soon after adolescence in these Eskimo populations. In addition, maximal anaerobic power in a sample of Wainwright residents increased dramatically in the age range five to twenty years and then decreased after age twenty. These results indicate that middle-aged Eskimos (like their counterparts in the lower forty-eight states) are, indeed, past their prime in terms of physical fitness.

BIOLOGICAL VARIABILITY WITHIN NORTHWESTERN ALASKA

The remarkable tenacity of arctic populations in accommodating to change and the general population's increase, much in hybrid populations, gives assurance of their importance for scientific studies in the future, though the strategy of studies must include several new methods. (Laughlin, 1966:470).

One of the new methods seen in the present study is the application of multivariate statistical analysis to questions of morphological variation in both skeletal and living series of Eskimos. Investigations of sexual dimorphism, analyses of hybridized vs nonhybridized Eskimos, and examinations of the pattern of morphological variation across several north Alaskan villages are three areas where this statistical method and others were applied.

Sexual Dimorphism

Examinations of sex differences in Eskimos have been detailed in this volume by Laessig et al. (clinical chemistry), Moore (carbonic anhydrase), Mazess and Mather (bone mineral content), Dahlberg et al. (dental traits and conditions), Rennie (physical fitness), C. Feldman et al. (cognitive development), Bock (psychometric parameters), Jamison (anthropometric variables), and Meier (dermatoglyphic patterns). In Chapter 7 Laessig et al. found no sex differences among individuals from Wainwright, Point Hope, and Barrow in normal ranges of calcium, inorganic phosphorus, urea nitrogen, cholesterol, total protein, albumin, total bilirubin, alkaline phosphatase, and aspartate aminotransferase. They did note differences for uric acid (particularly in premenopausal ages), lactic acid dehydrogenase (minimized as possibly due to technical difficulties), and creatinine. The difference in creatinine was unexplained but Laessig et al. felt it was worthy of follow-up.

Moore (Chapter 8) found no sex difference in carbonic anhydrase levels in Point Hope Eskimos. Likewise, Mazess and Mather in Chapter 9 found that for bone mineral content both sexes had similar levels and similar age changes in Wainwright, Point Hope, and Barrow, in contrast to U.S. whites, in whom the loss of bone mineral with age is greater among women than men.

Dahlberg et al. (Chapter 6) cite a number of sex comparisons in the craniofacial complex. They point out that shape of this complex is quite similar between the sexes while size (both vertical and depth measures) is greater among male subjects. Female subjects tended to have more dental protrusion, and male subjects to have more midfacial flatness. Dimorphism in size did not carry over extensively to the teeth. Comparisons of mesiodistal crown diameters indicated that while teeth were generally larger in males than in females, only for the first molars (maxillary and mandibular) did this difference achieve statistical significance.

Investigations of oral epidemiology in Chapter 6 also provide an opportunity to examine sex differences. The peak caries-involvement age period is the same (young adult), but subsequently the number of decayed, missing, and filled teeth drops somewhat for men and levels off among women. In contrast, Table 6–9 demonstrates that oral hygiene, as monitored by calculus and debris indices, appears to be slightly better among females than among male Eskimos.

Rennie discusses sexual dimorphism in one section of Chapter 17. Most of his physical-fitness data relates to males, but in Figs. 17–6 and 17–7 he cites values for maximal aerobic power in both sexes. Not surprisingly, the peak value of $\dot{V}_{O_2 max}$ in female subjects is 70–75% of that in male subjects. Maximal O_2 consumption reaches its peak in the early teens for females and the late teens for males. From these peaks, the values decline more sharply among men, so that by age fifty the $\dot{V}_{O_2 max}$ values are quite comparable. Interestingly, Rennie shows greater physical fitness among Igloolik, Canada, Eskimos than among the north Alaskans, but the sexual dimorphism in maximal O_2 consumption is approximately the same.

C. Feldman et al. in Chapter 20 allude to sexual dimorphism very briefly. They state that among Wainwright residents who took a series of standardized cognitive tests, less sex difference (level of significance not stated) was found in spatial visualizing ability than is typical of European subjects. In Chapter 21 Bock also discusses sexual dimorphism in relation to his battery of psychometric tests. In his Barrow sample, girls exceeded boys in fluent production at all age levels. Also, a significant sex effect favoring males was seen in the Bock-Fitzgerald Spatial Test.

For morphological parameters, Chapter 4 (Jamison) provides an extensive examination of sexual dimorphism in anthropometric measurements on Eskimos. His data show that all body-size dimensions are larger among males than females, except for skinfold measurements and head circumferences.

Variability within each sex, as measured by the coefficient of variation, is greater for females in body measurements, while head measurements show similar values in both sexes. Table 4-6 listed a series of proportions (values for women as a percentage of values for men) to compare the degree of sexual dimorphism among Eskimos with that among whites. The results indicated that north Alaskan Eskimos had less dimorphism than did whites.

The "new-method" multivariate techniques indicated that adult males and females could be statistically differentiated at a high level of probability using Mahalanobis' D^2 statistic. In this perspective, the best discriminators proved to be broad hips, relatively large faces in the vertical dimension, and large calf and upper arm circumferences, for females, and broad shoulders, broad faces, and large bony breadths, for males.

Finally, Meier (Chapter 5) includes some data on sexual dimorphism in his examination of digital dermatoglyphic variation. As Table 5-6 shows, female Eskimos have nearly twice as many arches as male Eskimos; both sexes have very similar radial loop counts; ulnar loops are again more frequent in female than in male Eskimos; and male subjects have more whorls than female subjects. These differences result in both a higher pattern intensity index and a considerably higher total ridge count among male Eskimos.

From all this information on sexual dimorphism, what can be said? If one wanted to distinguish male and female Eskimos (without looking in their jeans) the best characteristics to use would be fingerprint patterns and anthropometric measurements. Even with the latter, however, the degree of sexual dimorphism may be slightly less than that encountered in other populations (notably whites). Clinical biochemistry, bone mineral content, dental traits, physical fitness parameters, psychometric tests, and cognitive development show slight, but not marked differences. From the data presented here, the suggestion can be made that whatever the differences in role and behavior that Eskimos recognized as being patterned by sex, today they present more marked similarities than differences in their biological variation.

Hybrid vs Nonhybrid Comparisons

The effects of hybridization were reported by three investigators in this volume: Jamison (anthropometrics), Meier (dermatoglyphics), and Moore (carbonic anhydrase). Most of the non-Eskimo genes entered the study populations from crew members of whaling ships during the period between about 1850 and 1920. Old American and Western European genes predominate in this admixture, although American blacks have contributed to the gene pool at Point Hope and admixture from at least one Hawaiian has also occurred. Twenty-five percent of the Wainwright sample had Caucasian admixture, with the degree of non-Eskimo ancestry equaling 1/4, 1/8, or less for most individuals. No admixture was detected at Anaktuvuk Pass.

Jamison (Chapter 4) compared the anthropometric results of 272 nonhybridized Eskimos with those of seventy positively defined hybrids. In general he found that hybrids were slightly larger in body dimensions but slightly smaller in facial dimensions than their nonhybridized counterparts. Specifically, analysis of variance showed male hybrids to have greater sitting height, foot breadth, calf circumference, and forearm circumference values, while male nonhybrids had larger values for biiliac breadth, nose breadth and ear breadth. Female hybrids had larger values for sitting height, stature, foot length, and calf circumference, while female nonhybrids had larger ear heights and ear breadths (see Table 4-10). In a comparison of hybrids and nonhybrids in a multivariate context, the Mahalanobis' D^2 values between these groups failed to reach statistical significance for either sex, and the percentages of misallocation using discriminant functions were 13.5 for male and 17.2 for female subjects.

Meier (Chapter 5) compared digital dermatoglyphic measurements for the four villages which contained both hybrid and nonhybrid individuals. The only statistically significant difference involved Point Hope, where there was a marked reduction in the whorl pattern frequency of hybrids, resulting in a pattern intensity index that was 2 points lower for the hybrids in both sexes.

Moore (Chapter 8), studying carbonic anhydrase, failed to detect any statistically significant differences between hybrids and nonhybrids, although the CA-C level for hybrids was slightly higher than the Eskimo mean (1.92 mg/g Hb vs 1.82 mg/g Hb).

A final observation on hybridization effects comes from Dahlberg et al. (Chapter 6), who hypothesize that the increased cranial base flexion in the contemporary Wainwright population may be due to admixture, but there is no documentation of this trend.

Interdeme Comparisons

The third dimension of intrapopulation comparison possible in this research is that among and between village populations. Zegura (Chapter 2) demonstrated the range of craniometric variation of Eskimos across their geographical distribution through the use of multivariate statistical techniques. Figures 2-3 and 2-4 point out that within this total range of phenotypic variability, Point Hope and Point Barrow cluster very close together. Since the crania used in this analysis dated from the last two centuries, we would assume a degree of correspondence between these results and those from living populations (as mentioned earlier in this chapter). Thus, there is phenotypic as well as cultural justification (Chapter 3) for treating the Eskimos of northwestern Alaska as a single population. Variation within this population is the next item of interest.

Two contributors to this volume (Meier in Chapter 5 and Jamison in Chapter 4) provide data that can be used to describe and analyze morphological variation across villages in northern Alaska. These data are anthropometric measurements and two types of dermatoglyphic variables: palmar traits and digital patterns. Table 4-15 provides Mahalanobis' D^2 distances between all pairs of the following villages: Wainwright, Point Hope, Barrow, and Anaktuvuk Pass. These distances are based on thirty anthropometric measurements on adult hybrid and nonhybrid individuals. Similarly, Table 5-8 lists Mahalanobis' D^2 distances for the same pairwise comparisons of villages, based on sixteen palmar dermatoglyphic variables among hybrid and nonhybrid residents of all ages.

There are no comparable data available for digital dermatoglyphic variables, but Meier does present data in Table 5-6 on two composite measures—pattern intensity index and total ridge count—for each village sample. (Due to the high correlation between these two measures, either one could have been used individually.) Again, hybrid and nonhybrid data are presented and all ages are represented in the four villages mentioned above. Sneath and Sokal (1973) describe a summary statistic called the "taxonomic distance" which can be applied to the two digital dermatoglyphic variables to develop data for comparison with the anthropometric and palmar dermatoglyphic distances.

The following formula for taxonomic distance is adapted from Sneath and Sokal (1973):

$$d^2 = \frac{\Sigma[(X_1 - X_2)^2 + (Y_1 - Y_2)^2]}{N = 2} \qquad (22.1)$$

where X and Y are variables, and 1 and 2 are villages. Table 22-2 gives digital dermatoglyphic distances between all pairs of the four villages based on this formula. For each of comparison, this table also presents the Mahalanobis' distances for these pairwise comparisons, using anthropometric and palmar dermatoglyphic variables. It must be kept in mind when viewing all three sets of data that the anthropometric distances are based on a different sample (all adults) from that used for the dermatoglyphic distances (subjects of all ages).

The last body of data in Table 22-2 is the air-mile distance between the four villages. Air miles are used here strictly as an approximation of the distance traveled by an Eskimo moving between these villages. The use of foot-travel, dog-sled, or boat, and the route chosen would certainly affect these distances, but their only purpose here is to provide a simple basis for comparing geographical distance and morphological differentiation. A glance at the Mahalanobis and taxonomic distances compared with air miles suggests that the pattern of morphological variation is not explained simply by geographic distance. There appears to be little correspondence between the air-mile distances and any of the morphological distances.

There also appears to be a surprising lack of correspondence between the three sets of data. In all of them the *range* of distances is greater within the

TABLE 22-2 *Intervillage Comparisons*

Distance	Wainwright	Point Hope	Barrow	Anaktuvuk Pass
Anthropometry[*]				
Wainwright		7.08	7.88	11.48
Point Hope	6.34		8.95	9.43
Barrow	5.85	8.77		8.91
Anaktuvuk Pass	10.04	12.00	12.06	
Palmar dermatoglyphics[+]				
Wainwright		0.50	0.50	(0.40)
Point Hope	1.10		0.70	(0.30)
Barrow	0.40	0.30		(0.20)
Anaktuvuk Pass	1.20	0.60	0.60	
Digital dermatoglyphics[‡]				
Wainwright		25.50	32.20	20.10
Point Hope	63.30		0.40	0.30
Barrow	14.60	17.10		1.40
Anaktuvuk Pass	16.10	15.60	0.30	
Air miles[δ]				
Wainwright				
Point Hope	234			
Barrow	88	318		
Anaktuvuk Pass	263	384	247	

Distances for male subjects are below the main diagonals, and for female subjects above them.

[*]Mahalanobis' D^2 values from Chapter 4.

[+]Mahalanobis' D^2 values from Chapter 5 (values in parentheses, not significant at the .05 level).

[‡]Taxonomic distance (adapted from Sneath and Sokal, 1973) values calculated from pattern intensity and total ridge count data in Chapter 5. No significance test is given for this metric.

[δ]Air miles calculated from map of Alaska (Grosvenor, 1975).

male groups than within the female groups. However, the actual pairwise anthropometric distances tend to be larger between villages among female subjects, the palmar dermatoglyphic distances between villages tend to be larger among male subjects, and there is no apparent trend emphasizing either sex in the digital dermatoglyphic distances between villages.

Anthropometry provides the only data set in which the distances are generally comparable between the sexes. Here, as mentioned in Chapter 4, the coastal villages bear closer similarities to each other than any do to Anaktuvuk Pass, the inland village (one exception to this statement is the distance for female subjects, between Barrow and Point Hope, a slightly larger distance than to Anaktuvuk Pass). This result is in direct contrast to those for palmar dermatoglyphics for female subjects. Here the distances between Anaktuvuk Pass and the coastal villages are the smallest ones found. For male subjects, results for palmar dermatoglyphics do not show any discernible inland-coastal pattern nor do the digital dermatoglyphic results in either sex. Interestingly, for female subjects digital dermatoglyphic distances do display a pattern, whereby Wainwright is the most anomalous in its data and the other three villages cluster very close together.

It is important to recall the qualification that these distances are not based on the same samples of individuals. One explanation for the results, then, is that the inland-coastal dichotomy, while valid for the older adult residents, has been swamped by mating patterns and movements when individuals of the next two generations are included. Alternatively, interpreting these variables may require elucidating different biological mechanisms for each. Most researchers would agree that the environmental component in the expression of anthropometric traits is larger than the environmental component in dermatoglyphic traits. Following this line of reasoning, one might suggest that environmental variables such as diet have led to results seen in the anthropometric variation, as opposed to the random genetic forces to which Meier attributes his digital dermatoglyphic results. The pattern of blood-group genetic markers would add immeasurably to this discussion; unfortunately they are unavailable due to loss of specimens and lack of analysis. The result is that we are left with differences in the pattern of variation among anthropometric and palmar and digital dermatoglyphic distances across four villages in northern Alaska. These differences may be accounted for by a combination of historical patterns of movement and mating patterns among and between regions, as well as by the suggestion that both adaptation to different regions (anthropometry) and random processes (dermatoglyphics) were in operation.

SYNERGISTIC RELATIONSHIPS: DIET INTERACTIONS

We have chosen the topic of diet to illustrate the potential synergistic action of multidisciplinary results because of the diverse biological effects which can be related to the Eskimo dietary. As Draper cogently points out in Chapter 10, there are no essential foods but only essential nutrients, and the native north Alaskan Eskimo diet is capable of furnishing all the nutrients essential for nutritional health provided the diet is available in adequate amount and that the foods are prepared according to traditional methods. However, as the chapters on nutrition in this volume have repeatedly emphasized, the traditional Eskimo diet no longer obtains: Acculturation is proceeding at an ever-increasing rate. These dietary changes have affected many biological parameters and some essential nutrients are now in short supply while others are present in excess. Aboriginal and modern dietary components may have interacted with metabolism, the dental and craniofacial complexes, growth, behavioral parameters, and general health.

Diet and Metabolism

The restricted character of the aboriginal Eskimo diet has caused nutritional biochemists like Draper to question whether Eskimos possess unique metabolic capabilities which enable them to adapt to an all-meat regimen. Meat is notably low in calcium and in aboriginal times other sources of dietary calcium like dairy products were scarce. Calcium was derived mainly from the soft bones of fish and from the spongy portion of land and sea mammal bones. According to Draper (Chapter 10) a vitamin-D-dependent mechanism which enables the body to adapt to a range of calcium intake by modifying the efficiency of absorption undoubtedly served the need of the Eskimo to absorb efficiently the limited capacity of calcium supplied by the diet.

The unusual composition of the traditional north Alaskan Eskimo diet also poses interesting questions concerning the sources of metabolic energy. In Draper's view the central problem in adaptational bioenergetics for the Eskimo was the maintenance of glucose homeostasis in the face of an extremely low-carbohydrate diet. This homeostasis was maintained primarily by glucose synthesis from dietary amino acids since glucose cannot be synthesized from fatty acids. Thus, a high protein content was a necessary feature of the aboriginal Eskimo diet. Extra protein was needed to furnish the amino acids required for glucose synthesis in addition to those normally required for protein synthesis.

The low-carbohydrate, high-fat content of the native regimen is also important with respect to its influence on body fat composition. Unlike the case in most populations, dietary rather than biosynthetic fatty acids constituted the bulk of these Eskimos' body fat. Lipogenesis from glucose sources was inhibited because of lack of excess glucose in the diet and because of an excess of fatty acids in the diet. Hence, the composition of dietary fat influenced the fatty acid composition of their adipose tissue. Long-chain polyunsaturated fatty acids typical of marine oils were prevalent. Indeed, the high saturated fatty acid content generally ascribed to animal fats does not seem to apply to a diet of caribou, sea mammals, and fish. The relatively large proportion of polyunsaturated fats in native foods may have, in turn, contributed to the low serum cholesterol levels of premodern Eskimos.

The high-protein diet also imposed a need to dispose of a large urea load. Animals faced with this metabolic problem can adapt by increasing water consumption and excretion. Early explorers noted the high water intake of Eskimos. Perhaps a feedback mechanism is operating here to prevent uremia under conditions of high protein intake by stimulating water consumption and thereby enhancing urea excretion.

The aboriginal diet is fast disappearing. The metabolic consequences of such a change are as yet unclear. Some adverse effects of this change have already been documented. For instance, adaptation to a processed diet presents serious difficulties for those affected by primary sucrase deficiency (Chapter 15). Also, low lactase activity restricts the extent to which North Slope Eskimos can obtain calcium from the dairy products which have replaced animal bones as calcium sources in their diet. It is imperative that comprehensive biochemical studies of the modern Eskimo diet, like those contained in many of the chapters on nutrition in this volume, be conducted to document the continuing biochemical adaptations of Eskimos to changes in dietary composition.

Diet and Dental and Craniofacial Complexes

The Eskimos's zygomatic morphology is characterized by extreme facial flatness. The adaptive significance of facial flatness has often been related to function. Specifically, the morphological features of the Eskimo face can be related to powerful chewing, to the position and size of the muscles of mastication, and to the need to generate and dissipate large vertical biting forces. These functional considerations can, in turn, be related to requirements imposed by the composition of the diet. Evidence to support the possible role of diet as an important influence in Eskimo facial morphology comes from the work of Dahlberg et al. in Chapter 6. They conclude that since midfacial flatness seems to increase with age, the adaptive significance of this trait can be more readily associated with function than with cold adaptation, the other major explanation for the origin of the Eskimo facial form.

Diet also directly influences the dentition. Changes in the use of the teeth, in type of food, and in food preparation have combined to reduce the functional forces exerted on the contemporary Eskimo anterior dentition. Perhaps this change explains the finding of Dahlberg et al. that the modern north Alaskan Eskimo's anterior dentition fails to upright with age to the same degree as seen in adult skulls. This phenomenon is exemplified by the increased labial inclination of the maxillary and mandibular incisors of Wainwright residents compared with that of Alaskan skeletal material.

The increase in imported food also has consequences for proper alignment of the teeth. The processed foods will lead to less occlusal and interproximal wear of the teeth, which earlier was a significant adjusting mechanism for proper alignment. In addition, the new dietary may be implicated in a possible reduction of the alveolar process, which in turn can result in a higher incidence of tooth crowding. Again, improper alignment of the teeth is suggested.

The most significant effect of the modern dietary has been a sharp increase in dental caries. Decayed teeth are numerous in North Slope residents, and the number of missing teeth reaches very large proportions at an early age. Low periodontal disease rates indicate that the vast majority of these missing teeth are the result of caries. In terms of oral epidemiology, caries is the most prevalent disease in thse Eskimos. Peak caries involvement occurs in the twenty-one to thirty age group, with a drop in the caries rate for men in older age groups (see Table 6-7). Dahlberg et al. take this drop as indicative of dietary changes, with the younger groups consuming more cariogenic food than older people. Table 11-1, which documents the increased intake of carbohydrates by children in Wainwright and Point Hope, tends to substantiate the assertion by Dahlberg et al.

Relatively low rates of tooth debris and calculus deposition may explain the low periodontal disease rates. However, Dahlberg et al. caution that it will probably be only a short time before periodontal disease levels on the North Slope reach levels seen in more acculturated Alaskan Eskimos to the south. The modern dietary of the southern resident has been shown to be ill-suited to the Eskimo dentition. The unique shape of Eskimo teeth contributes to the gloomy prognosis, because of their built-in food traps. Dental caries were unknown in Eskimos only a few decades ago. Now it is the most prevalent oral disease in arctic populations. While exact causation is impossible to ascribe, Dahlberg et al. feel that the great dietary change in the last few decades has been a major factor in this process.

Diet and Growth

Growth and maturation are influenced by dietary composition, in terms of both amount of growth achieved and timing of the growth process. Jamison (Chapter 4) implicates the increased carbohydrate content of the acculturated diet as a possible explanation for the accelerated growth trends shown by Wainwright adolescents. For instance, the velocity curve for weight of Wainwright males was somewhat above that of the white standard for all ages. Although peak weight velocity occurred one year later at Wainwright than for whites, the magnitude of the peak was higher for the Eskimos. Also, peak velocity for height in Wainwright females occurred relatively early for a rural population.

Obesity has become a significant problem for adult Eskimo women. Although the stereotype of the "fat" Eskimo is incorrect (compared with most human groups the Eskimos are quite average in their skinfold thicknesses, and males are actually relatively lean), there is a definite trend toward increased obesity with increased age, especially for females. Jamison's weight velocity curves (Fig. 4-6) imply that starting at about thirteen years of age Eskimo girls increase their rate of fat deposition. Colbert et al. (Chapter 13) present data that show that 37.9% of the women they studied between ages fifteen and forty-four were obese. For the women over forty-five years of age the figure climbed to 64.7%. Detailed dietary studies on food consumption differences between male and female Eskimos are badly needed to ascertain the etiology of the sex difference in obesity and the possible dietary correlates of obesity in Eskimo women.

Interactions between diet and growth probably involve many more factors than just increased carbohydrate intake. Many other nutritional parameters mentioned in this volume interact with growth and development but the interactions have not been systematically studied. For instance, imported foods decrease occlusal and interproximal tooth wear (necessary for proper tooth alignment during growth); new foods have increased the caries rate of both children and young adults and may have affected dental development; low calcium intakes for children may affect bone growth; lowered protein intake because of adoption of nontraditional foods may affect growth patterns long adapted to high intakes of protein; low iron intakes by children may be implicated in the high incidence of nutritionally caused anemia found in modern Eskimo villages, which in turn may affect the amount of growth achieved; low plasma vitamin A and E levels in some Eskimo children may have implications for the growth process; the high incidences of lactose and sucrose intolerance may deprive children of nutrients because of excessive diarrhea, thereby affecting achievement of their growth potential.

Diet and Behavioral Parameters

C. Feldman et al. (Chapter 20) found a cognitive "slump" in adolescent test performance at Wainwright. At age fourteen the Eskimo subjects were below established norms for the Raven Progressive Matrices Test, while at age eighteen they were above the norms. Poor test performance characterized the fourteen- to seventeen-year-old subjects. This result as well as later tests performed by C. Feldman prompted a visit to Mount Edgecumbe School in Sitka. Conditions at this and similar boarding schools may well contribute to the cognitive slump implied by the test results. Feldman et al. implicate the highly regimented life-style of the school, the lack of cognitive challenge at the school, the perception of the children as "slow" or "apathetic" by the schoolteachers, and the drastic change in diet as possible contributing factors to the adolescent cognitive slump seen in Eskimo children.

Indirect involvement of the native dietary in the development of intellectual skills is also pointed out by Bock in Chapter 21. The spirit and mentality of the hunting and fishing subsistence tradition that the Eskimos of the Arctic Ocean coast have sustained over the last 2,000–3,000 years have helped to shape the attitudes of both children and adults—even in transitional villages like Barrow. Thus, highly developed visual skills related to their environmental setting are hypothesized to characterize Eskimo populations. It was also conjectured that tests of auditory skills would result in rather poor performance because of the relative lack of emphasis on auditory skills in the traditional Eskimo hunting and fishing adaptation.

The results of the Bock-Fitzgerald Spatial Test suggest that the Barrow sample shows no special facility in spatial visualization. In fact, the Illinois sample outperformed the Barrow sample not only on this test, but also on the Raven Progressive Matrices Test, which also has a spatial component. Bock points to possible motivational effects in an attempt to explain these unexpected results. The Auditory Span Test results, however, tend to support the conjecture that the Arctic Eskimo is less attuned to auditory discriminations because climate and hooded clothing make it difficult to rely on auditory cues in outdoor activities. A genuine lack of development of auditory attention and discrimination while engaged in traditional Eskimo food procurement activities could have implications for modern Eskimos when they attempt to learn a second language like English.

Diet and General Health

General health is a composite indicator of adaptation, and morbidity represents a failure or lack of adaptation to environmental pressures. The Eskimo dietary has diverse ramifications for the general health and morbidity of the Eskimo. As mentioned, the most significant effect of the modern Eskimo dietary in terms of oral health has been a sharp increase in dental caries. There have been other substantial dietary influences on health and morbidity.

Mazess and Mather (Chapter 9) hypothesized that the high-protein diet of Eskimos coupled with marginal calcium and vitamin D intakes may be contributory to the accelerated rate and early onset of bone loss observed in Eskimo populations. Draper (Chapter 10), however, points to the high phosphorus content of a meat regimen as an important factor in the etiology of bone loss. A high-phosphorus, low-calcium diet is known to lead to an increased rate of bone resorption. Documentation of the calcium and phosphorus intake data can be seen in Table 11-2 and Figs. 11-3 and 11-4. The exact causation of this rapid and extensive bone loss in Eskimos is a topic worthy of further research, as is the possible dietary involvement in the high rates of age-progressive lumbar defects of Eskimos (Chapter 2), along with the possible osteoporotic effects of the Eskimo dietary.

Bergan and Bell in Chapter 12 found a higher incidence of apparent anemia than earlier studies on the same populations. Their findings indicate that anemia is now a frequent nutritional problem among Alaskan Eskimos. The condition is probably aggravated by a declining consumption of iron-rich native foods. At the same time these authors noted that plasma vitamin C levels are on the increase, especially in children who have benefited from the ascorbic acid-fortified beverages provided as part of school lunch programs. As traditional food-preparation techniques change and as native food sources high in vitamin C content like fresh muktuk are gradually replaced, these alternative vitamin C sources are a necessary protection against scurvy.

Problems associated with low lactase activity and primary sucrase deficiency were discussed by Bell et al. (Chapter 15). Although most adult Eskimos are capable of consuming nutritionally significant amounts of dairy foods in moderate, well-spaced portions, sucrose intolerance represents a potential problem for both children and adults. The degree of sucrose intolerance appears to be more acute than that of lactose intolerance. The current influx of processed foods makes it increasingly difficult to avoid sucrose. The effects of this dietary addition are most severe in the arctic region where sucrose was virtually absent from the native diet and where lack of intestinal sucrase was not harmful in aboriginal times. Now, however, it may be necessary to develop a class of proprietary foods for sucrose-intolerant individuals.

The traditional profile of low blood cholesterol, low blood pressure, and lean body mass no longer obtains for all the Eskimo groups investigated in this project. Draper and Wei Wo (Chapter 16) suggest that those Eskimos living in more acculturated surroundings are essentially indistinguishable in hypercholesterolemia and hypertension rates from non-Eskimo inhabitants of the same communities. Colbert et al. (Chapter 13) also indicate that there has been a sharp increase in obesity among women in recent years, and Draper and Wei Wo (Chapter 16) state that hypercholesterolemia was generally correlated with obesity. The interaction of changing diet, obesity, hypertension, hypercholesterolemia, cardiovascular disease, atherosclerosis, and ECG abnormalities represents a potentially fruitful avenue for future research among Eskimos. Indeed, plasma cholesterol levels at Kasigluk and Nunapitchuk (Table 16-2), relatively acculturated villages with nontraditional diets, were actually higher than those found in the U.S. National Health Survey of 1960-62.

S. Feldman et al. (Chapter 14) have attempted to analyze the relationship between dietary intake and serum cholesterol levels by performing a cholesterol balance study in Point Hope. They also wanted to develop a predictive measure of the Eskimo's liability to changing dietary patterns. Table 14-1 lists the cholesterol content of various indigenous foods. S. Feldman et al. note that the rate of cholesterol ingestion is similar to that of the general U.S. population. The results of their cholesterol balance study (Table 14-4) indicate that the amount of cholesterol absorbed was linearly proportional to the amount present in the diet. Both the efficiency of absorption and the absolute amount absorbable were found to be extremely high. Also, the Eskimos appeared to lack a facility for suppression of endogenous cholesterol synthesis at the levels of dietary exposure measured. The conclusions give an unhealthy prognosis for the Eskimo. Specifically, they expect that in the face of a continually increased cholesterol content in the diet, the Eskimo will develop sustained hypercholesterolemia, the effects of which may contribute to an increased morbidity in Eskimo populations.

OVERVIEW

In the first chapter of this volume, Milan notes that an important feature of the planning for the IBP was an emphasis on the multidisciplinary approach to research. Baker (1965a), in an article included within the *IBP Guide to the Human Adaptability Proposals,* is more explicit. He notes, ". . . no single discipline has sufficient techniques or conceptual frameworks with which to study all the aspects of human adaptation" (p. 7). That comment is aptly demonstrated in this volume. Papers included here span research that was carried out within the confines of the following disciplines:

biochemistry	orthodontics
demography	osteology
dentistry	psychology
ethnohistory	physical anthropology
genetics	physics
human biology	physiology
medicine	serology
nutrition	

Another advantage of the multidisciplinary approach to research that is often cited is increased efficiency—more work accomplished at a lower investment of time and money per researcher. This increased efficiency assumes teams of investigators working in multidisciplinary research, versus single investigators doing the same work over extended periods of time or at different times. When numerous tests are conducted on the same group of subjects, there appears to be an advantage from the subjects' point of view as well. By concentrating the tests over a short span of time, the population should be less disrupted than it would be if the tests were carried out on repeated visits over longer time spans. Certain types of research did require repeated visits, especially to Wainwright. However, generally speaking, the entire village population was not sampled more than once in each year. The same amount of research conducted by individual disciplinary teams or individuals visiting Wainwright at separate times would surely have eroded the cooperative spirit that we met with in this village. This is not to say that there were no problems associated with a large research team descending upon a village of 300-plus inhabitants, but only that friction, misunderstandings, and resentment appeared to us to be minimal.

Baker (1965) does, however, include a rather sobering thought in his discussion of the multidisciplinary approach to research. He writes:

. . . . the majority of multidisciplinary studies have failed in their full purpose. . . . most often the results obtained on different aspects of the problem are never integrated. The reason for these failures of integration are diverse but appear often to stem from the lack of a firm structure and the subsequent fact that the members of one discipline do not trust the ability of other discipline members to interpret their data. Other problems include publication privileges and the failure of some investigators to prepare their results.

All of these problems are present to some extent in this multidisciplinary study. Perhaps the most serious weakness resulted from problems encountered by the serological team, leading to the virtual exclusion of serological data from this synthesis. Thus, many genetic explanations for our results could not be substantiated or even pursued.

Finally, the point should be made that an integration of results, mentioned by Baker as an overriding goal of the multidisciplinary approach to research, was at least partially achieved here. This argument, that a synergism should occur in such research where the ultimate product will be greater than the sum of its parts, is exemplified in the section of this chapter on diet interactions. Diet was seen to have important ramifications for the study of metabolism, the dentition and craniofacial complex, growth, behavior, and general health and morbidity.

Thus, we are presenting here an approximation of what the multidisciplinary approach holds as its potential. The ultimate judgment of our success or failure will be made by our scientific colleagues. The IBP was a resounding success in the area of international exchange and cooperation among researchers and in the training of young investigators. In addition, projects such as this one increased the avenues of communication between members of the "academic" community and relatively isolated populations in many parts of the world. The friendships made, the memories of good times, and the personal satisfactions achieved cannot be measured, or displayed on a graph. For these we again express our appreciation and gratitude to the villagers of northern Alaska. Our hope is that our scientific and nonscientific activities will be remembered and even perhaps prove useful to them in the coming years of continued transition.

Appendix A

Funding Sources for the IBP Project

The Eskimo study whose results are reported in this volume became a recognized US/IBP Human Adaptability project at the meeting of the U.S. National Committee in October of 1967. A proposal was then submitted to the National Institute of General Medical Sciences (NIGMS) of the National Institute of Health. A site visitation team from NIGMS came to the University of Wisconsin in March of 1968. Subsequently, this proposal was approved but not funded because of higher priorities elsewhere. F. A. Milan then located sufficient funds at the U.S. Air Force Office of Scientific Research (AFOSR) to commence the first year at Wainwright. Other scientists obtained additional funds for the first year. Early in 1969 the NIGMS proposal was funded.

Total grant support for the Eskimo study can be seen in Table A-1. It should be pointed out that two NIH training grants to W. S. Laughlin at the University of Wisconsin as well as other grant funds supported some of the graduate students and scientists until the NIGMS funding came through.

TABLE A-1 *Grant Support for Eskimo Program, by Year and University ($)*

Agency	1968 Wisconsin	1969 Wisconsin	1970 Wisconsin	1971 Alaska	1972 Alaska	1973 Alaska	Total
AFOSR	25,000 (L&M)	4,300 (L&M)					
NIDR	8,847 (L)						
Smithsonian	2,685 (R)*						
Wenner–Gren	4,000 (L)						
ONR (in kind)	10,000 (M)						
Subtotal							54,832
NIGMS		117,174 (L&M)	102,489 (M)	105,594 (M)	Extended, no addit. funds	Extended, no addit. funds	325,257
NSF		42,000 (D)+					42,000
Total							422,089

Principal Investigators: W. S. Laughlin (L), F. A. Milan (M), D. W. Rennie (R), H. H. Draper (D).

*SUNY at Buffalo.

+University of Illinois, Urbana.

Appendix B

Tapescript of English-Inupiat Concept Knowledge Test

Carol Fleischer Feldman

Please turn to Section 1 of your answer sheet. This is a test of your knowledge of words. In this test some of the words will be read in English and some in Eskimo. In each Problem I will read four words. Three of the words will belong together and one will be different. For example, I might read, (1) yellow, (2) green, (3) red, (4) small. (Pause). Which word is different? (Pause). The word is number 4—small—because yellow, green, and red all tell what color something is but small tells what size it is. (Pause).

Now let's do a practice problem. In the space for problem 1 mark the number of the word that is different from the other three.

(1) Wainwright, (2) Anchorage, (3) Point Hope, (4) Barrow. (Pause). Which word is different? (Pause). The word is number 2—Anchorage. Anchorage is different because it is the name of a big city. Wainwright, Point Hope, and Barrow go together because they are the names of Eskimo villages.

Now please do the rest of the problems as I read each problem to you. To help you find the answer I will read each problem twice. Problem number 2 is next.

(1) arm, (2) leg, (3) body, (4) head	(Repeat)

Problem number 3 is next.

(1) store, (2) food, (3) ammunition, (4) clothing	(Repeat)

Problem number 4 is next.

(1) hook, (2) fishing, (3) net, (4) line	(Repeat)

Problem number 5 is next.

(1) happy, (2) sad, (3) frightened, (4) cold	(Repeat)

Problem number 6 is next.

(1) house, (2) stove, (3) bed, (4) table	(Repeat)

Problem number 7 is next.

(1) eyes, (2) mouth, (3) face, (4) nose	(Repeat)

Problem number 8 is next.

(1) blanket, (2) bed, (3) pillow, (4) sleeping	(Repeat)

Now please go to section 2. The next problems are like the ones you have just finished except that they will be read in Eskimo. In these problems you should also mark the number of the word that is different from the other three.

Problem 9 is next.

   (1) ukkoak, (2) iglu, (3) natek, (4) igalorok   (Repeat)
     [door]   [house] [floor]   [window]

Problem 10 is next.

   (1) nauligon, (2) supon, (3) anguneak, (4) nanereak   (Repeat)
    [harpoon]   [rifle]   [hunting]   [trap]

Problem 11 is next.

   (1) kaaktok, (2) aleanyok, (3) allapitok, (4) omichuctook (Repeat)
    [hungry]   [lonely]   [confused]   [angry]

Problem 12 is next.

   (1) emik, (2) nikepeak, (3) utkussik, (4) tareok   (Repeat)
    [water] [meat]   [pot]   [salt]

Problem 13 is next.

   (1) isumalluktok,   (2) pialuktuk,   (3) ipektuchuk, (4) emiruktuk
    [worried]   [excited]   [upset]   [thirsty]
                                                  (Repeat)

Problem 14 is next.

   (1) tuvok, (2) kuya pirok, (3) toniktuak, (4) tuareke   (Repeat)
    [tusks]   [backbone]   [soapstone]   [carving]

Problem 15 is next.

   (1) tuvok, (2) ivik, (3) aivek aminga, (4) aivek tallera (Repeat)
    [tusks]   [walrus] [walrus skin]   [walrus flippers]

Problem 16 is next.

   (1) iglu (2) kunnechuk, (3) kukevik, (4) sinikvissi   (Repeat)
    [house] [porch]   [kitchen]   [bedroom]

Please go to section 3. These words will be in English again.

Problem 17 is next.

   (1) rifle, (2) hunting, (3) trap, (4) harpoon   (Repeat)

Problem 18 is next.

   (1) lonely, (2) confused, (3) hungry, (4) angry   (Repeat)

Problem 19 is next.

   (1) window, (2) door, (3) floor, (4) house   (Repeat)

Problem 20 is next.

   (1) pot, (2) water, (3) salt, (4) meat   (Repeat)

Problem 21 is next.

   (1) thirsty, (2) excited, (3) worried, (4) upset   (Repeat)

Problem 22 is next.

   (1) soapstone, (2) whalebone, (3) carving, (4) tusks   (Repeat)

Problem 23 is next.

   (1) kitchen, (2) porch, (3) bedroom, (4) house   (Repeat)

Problem 24 is next.

    (1) skin, (2) walrus, (3) tusks, (4) flipper   (Repeat)

Please go to section 4. The words will be in Eskimo again.

Problem 25 is next.

    (1) agklunok, (2) niksik, (3) kuvrok, (4) ekalukseoktuk   (Repeat)
      [line]   [hook]   [net]   [fishing]

Problem 26 is next.

    (1) nieevik, (2) ignavik, (3) iglu, (4) sinigvik   (Repeat)
      [table]   [stove]   [house]   [bed]

Problem 27 is next.

    (1) neoo, (2) naakok, (3) timi, (4) talik   (Repeat)
      [leg]   [head]   [body]   [arm]

Problem 28 is next.

    (1) elapa, (2) isumaluk, (3) kuversuk, (4) eksiruk   (Repeat)
      [cold]   [sad]   [happy]   [frightened]

Problem 29 is next.

    (1) karrat, (2) sinik, (3) akisee, (4) ulikrok   (Repeat)
      [mattress] [sleep]   [pillow]   [blanket]

Problem 30 is next.

    (1) kagarok   (2) nikgit, (3) anurak   (4) tauksigneakvik   (Repeat)
      [ammunition] [food]   [clothing]   [store]

Problem 31 is next.

    (1) kinyak, (2) kanuk, (3) ire, (4) kinnuk   (Repeat)
      [face]   [mouth]   [eye]   [nose]

This is the end of this test.

References

Abell, L. L., B. B. Levy, B. B. Brodie, and F. E. Kendall. 1952. A simplified method for the estimation of total cholesterol in serum and demonstration of its specificity. *J. Biol. Chem.* 195:357–366.

Alsbirk, P. H. 1973. Angle-closure glaucoma surveys in Greenland Eskimos: A preliminary report. *Can. J. Ophth.* 3:260–264.

—— and H. Forsius. 1973. Anterior chamber depth in Eskimos from Greenland, Canada (Igloolik) and Alaska (Wainwright): A preliminary report. *Can. J. Ophth.* 8:265–269.

Andersen, K. L., A. Bolstad, Y. Løyning, and L. Irving. 1960. Physical fitness of arctic Indians. *J. Appl. Physiol.* 15:645–648.

——, R. E. Elsner, B. Saltin, and L. Hermansen. 1962. Physical fitness in terms of maximal oxygen uptake of nomadic Lapps. Tech. Rept. AALTDR-61-53, AAML, Fort Wainwright, Alaska.

—— and J. S. Hart. 1963. Aerobic working capacity of Eskimos. *J. Appl. Physiol.* 18:764–768.

Arends, T., G. Brewer, N. Chagnon, M. L. Gallango, H. Gershowitz, M. Layrisse, J. V. Neel, D. Shreffer, R. Tashian, and L. Weitkamp. 1967. Intratribal genetic differentiation among the Yanomama Indians of Southern Venezuela. *Proc. Nat. Acad. Sci.* 57:1252–95.

Asmussen, E. and U. Hemmingsen. 1958. Determination of maximal working capacity at different ages in work with the legs or with the arms. *Scand. J. Clin. Lab. Invest.* 10:1.

Åstrand, P. O. 1952. Experimental studies of physical working capacity in relation to sex and age. *Ejnar Munksgaard,* Copenhagen.

——. 1960. Aerobic work capacity in men and women with special reference to age. *Acta Physiol. Scand.* 49:1–92.

—— and I. Rhyming. 1954. A nomogram for physical fitness from pulse rate during submaximal work. *J. Appl. Physiol.* 7:218–221.

—— and B. Saltin. 1961. Maximal oxygen uptake and heart rate in various types of muscular activity. *J. Appl. Physiol.* 16:977–981.

Baker, H, O. Frank, S. Feingold, G. Christakis, and H. Ziffer. 1967. Vitamins, total cholesterol and triglycerides in 642 New York City school children. *Am. J. Clin. Nutr.* 20:850.

Baker, P. T. 1965a. Multidisciplinary studies of human adaptability, pp. 63–72. In J. S. Weiner (ed.), *Guide to the Human Adaptability Proposals.* IBP Handbook No. 1. ICSU Special Committee for the International Biological Programme.

——. 1965b. Multidisciplinary studies of human adaptability: theoretical justification and method. *Yearbook of Physical Anthropology* 13:2-12.

Baker, P. T. and J. S. Weiner (eds.). 1966. *The Biology of Human Adaptability*. Clarendon Press, Oxford.

Balke, B. 1960. Cardiopulmonary and metabolic effects of physical training. In *Health and Fitness in the Modern World*. Athletic Institute, Chicago.

——. 1963. A Simple Field Test for the Assessment of Physical Fitness. Civil Aeromedical Research Institute TD-63-6. Oklahoma City, Oklahoma.

Bandi, H. G. 1969. *Eskimo Prehistory*. Methuen and Co., Ltd., London.

Bang, G. and T. Kristoffersen. 1972. Dental caries and diet in an Eskimo population. *Scand. J. Dent. Res.* 80:440-444.

Bang, H. O. and J. Dyerberg. 1972. Plasma lipids and lipoproteins in Greenlandic West Coast Eskimos. *Acta Med. Scand.* 192:85-94.

Basu, A. 1972. Quantitative Dermatoglyphics in Mysore Brahman. News Bulletin, International Dermatoglyphics Association, June, p. 4.

—— and K. K. Namboodiri. 1971. The relationship between total ridge count and pattern intensity index of digital dermatoglyphics. *Am. J. Phys. Anthrop.* 34:165-173.

Beaudry, P. H. 1968. Pulmonary function of the Canadian Eastern Arctic Eskimo. *Arch. Envir. Health* 17:524-528.

Beechey, F. W. 1831. *Narrative of a Voyage to the Pacific and Beering's Strait*. Colburn and Bentley, London.

Bell, R. R., H. H. Draper, and J. G. Bergan. 1973. Sucrose, lactose, and glucose tolerance in northern Alaskan Eskimos. *Am. J. Clin. Nutr.* 26: 1185-90.

Bergsland, K. 1958. Is lexico-statistic dating valid?, pp. 654-657. *Proceedings of the 32nd International Congress of Americanists*, Copenhagen.

—— and H. Vogt. 1962. On the validity of glottochronology. *Cur. Anthrop.* 3:115-129.

Berry, J. W. 1966. Temne and Eskimo perceptual skills. *Inter. J. Psych.* 1:207-229.

——. 1971. Ecological and cultural factors in spatial perceptual development. *Can. J. Behav. Sci.* 3:324-336.

Birdsell. J. B. 1975. *Human Evolution*. Rand McNally, Chicago.

Bjork, A. 1947. The face in profile. *Svensk Tandlakare-Tidskrift* 40, Suppl. 5B.

——. 1951. Some biological aspects of prognathism and occlusion of the teeth. *Angle Orthodontist* 21:3-27.

—— and B. Solow. 1962. Measurement on radiographs. *J. Dent. Res.* 41: 672-683.

Blackburn, H., C. L. Vasquey, and A. Keys. 1967. The aging electrocardiogram. *Am. J. Cardiol.* 20:618.

Bock, R. D. 1972. Estimating item parameters and latent ability when responses are scored in two or more nominal categories. *Psychometrika* 37:29-51.

———. 1973. Word and image: Sources of the verbal and spatial factors in mental test scores. *Psychometrika* 38:437-457.

——— and W. Fitzgerald. 1972. Unpublished test of spatial ability. University of Chicago Department of Education.

——— and D. Kolakowski. 1973. Further evidence of sex-linked major-gene influence on human spatial visualizing ability. *Am. J. Hum. Gen.* 25:1-14.

———, H. Wainer, A. Petersen, J. Murray, and A. Roche. 1973. A parameterization for individual human growth curves. *Hum. Biol.* 45:63-80.

Boniuk, V. 1973. Refractive problems of native peoples: The Sioux Lookout project. *Can. J. Ophth.* 8:229-233.

Bonnevie, K. 1924. Studies on papillary patterns of human fingers. *J. Genet.* 15:1-111.

Brewer, G. J. 1974. Red cell metabolism and function, pp. 473-508. In D. Mac N. Surgenor (ed.), *The Red Blood Cell,* vol. 1. Academic Press, New York.

Brody, J. A., T. Overfield, and R. McAlister. 1965. Draining ears and deafness among Alaskan Eskimos. *Arch. Otolaryngology* 81:20-33.

Broverman, D. M. and E. L. Klaiber. 1969. Negative relationships between abilities. *Psychometrika* 34:5-20.

Brower, C. D. 1942. *Fifty Years Below Zero.* Dodd, Mead and Co., New York.

———. n.d. The Northernmost American: An Autobiography. Manuscript. Naval Arctic Research Laboratory, Point Barrow, Alaska.

Brozek, J. 1956. Physical and nutritional status of men. *Hum. Biol.* 28:124-140.

Burch, E. S. 1970. The Eskimo trading partnership in North Alaska. *Anthrop. Papers Univ. Alaska* 15(1):49-80.

——— and T. C. Correll. 1972. Alliance and conflict: Interregional relations in North Alaska, pp. 17-39. In L. Guemple (ed.), *Alliance in Eskimo Society.* Univ. of Washington Press, Seattle.

Burke, H. R. and W. C. Bingham. 1969. Raven's Progressive Matrices: More on constant validity. *J. Psych.* 72:247-251.

Cameron, J. 1923. Osteology of the Western and Central Eskimo. The Copper Eskimos. *Report of the Canadian Arctic Expedition 1913-1918* 12:Part C, Ottawa.

Cameron, J. R. (ed.). 1970. *Proceedings of the Bone Measurement Conference.* US AEC Conference 700515. CFSTI, Springfield, Va.

Campbell, J. M. 1962. Cultural succession at Anaktuvuk Pass, Arctic Alaska, pp. 39-54. In J. M. Campbell (ed.), *Prehistoric Cultural Relations Between the Arctic and Temperate Zones of North America.* Arctic Institute of North America Technical Paper, No. 11.

———. 1968. Territoriality among ancient hunters: Interpretations from ethnography and nature, pp. 1-21. In *Anthropological Archaeology in the Americas.* Anthropological Society of Washington, Washington, D.C.

Carter, N. D. 1972. Carbonic anhydrase II polymorphism in Africa. *Hum. Hered.* 22:539–541.

——, R. J. Tanis, R. E. Tashian, and R. E. Ferrell. 1973. Characterization of a new variant of human red cell carbonic anhydrase I, CA If London (Glu-102->Lys). *Biochem. Genet.* 10:399–408.

——, R. E. Tashian, R. G. Huntsman, and L. Sacker. 1972. Characterization of two new variants of red cell carbonic anhydrase in the British population: CA Ie Portsmouth and CA Ie Hull. *Am. J. Hum. Genet.* 24:330–338.

Cedarquist, K. R. 1975. Craniofacial Description of Wainwright Alaskan Eskimos. MA Thesis, Department of Anthropology, University of Chicago.

Chance, N. A. 1966. *The Eskimo of North Alaska.* Holt, Rinehart and Winston, New York.

Chestnut, C. H. III, E. Manske, D. Baylink and W. B. Nelp. 1974. Preliminary report-correlation of total body calcium (bone mass), as determined by neutron activation analysis with regional bone mass as determined by photon absorption. In R. B. Mazess (ed.), *International Conference on Bone Mineral Measurement.* DHEW Publication 75–683. U.S. Department of Health, Education and Welfare, Washington, D.C.

Chobanian, A. V., W. Hollander, M. Sullivan, and M. Columbo. 1962. Body cholesterol metabolism in man. 1. The equilibration of serum and tissue cholesterol. *J. Clin. Invest.* 41:1732.

Chretien, C. D. 1962. The mathematical models of glottochronology. *Language* 38:11–37.

Cohn, S. H., K. J. Ellis, I. Zanzi, J. M. Letteri and J. Aloia. 1974. Correlation of radial bone mineral content with total-body calcium in various metabolic disorders. In R. B. Mazess (ed.), *International Conference on Bone Mineral Measurement.* DHEW Publication 75–683. U.S. Department of Health, Education and Welfare, Washington, D.C.

Colby, W. B. and J. F. Cleall. 1974. Cephalometric analysis of the craniofacial region of the northern Foxe Basin Eskimo. *Am. J. Phys. Anthrop.* 40:159–170.

Collins, H. B. 1951. The origin and antiquity of the Eskimo, pp. 423–467. In *Annual Report of the Smithsonian Institution for 1951,* Washington, D.C.

Cook, J. 1818. *A Voyage to the Pacific Ocean.* Robert Desilver, Philadelphia.

Coon, C. S., S. M. Garn, and J. B. Birdsell. 1950. *Races: A Study of the Problem of Race Formation in Man.* Charles C. Thomas, Springfield, Ill.

Corcoran, A. C. and I. M. Rabinowitch. 1937. A study of the blood lipids and blood protein in Canadian Eastern Arctic Eskimos. *Biochem. J.* 31:343–348.

Cotterman, C., 1941. Relatives and human genetic analysis. *Sci. Monthly* 53:227–234.

Cumming, G. R. 1967. Current levels of fitness. *Can. Med. J.* 96:868–877.

Cummins, H. and M. Steggerda. 1935. Finger prints in a Dutch family series. *Am. J. Phys. Anthrop.* 20:19–41.

—— and M. Steggerda. 1936. Finger prints in Maya Indians. *Middle Am. Res. Series* 7:103-126.

Dahlberg, A. A. 1968. Unpublished data.

Damas, D. 1969. Characteristics of Central Eskimo band structure. In D. Damas (ed.), *Contributions to Anthropology: Band Societies.* National Museums of Canada Bulletin No. 228. Anthropological Series No. 84.

Davis. C. T. M. 1968. Limitations to the prediction of maximal oxygen intake from cardiac frequency measurements. *J. Appl. Physiol.* 24:700-706.

Debetz, G. F. 1959. The skeletal remains of the Ipiutak cemetery, pp. 57-64. *Proceedings of the 33rd International Congress of Americanists,* Copenhagen.

Defries, J. C., S. G. Vandenberg, G. E. McClearn, A. R. Kuse, J. R. Wilson, G. C. Aston, and R. C. Johnson. 1974. Near identity of cognitive structure in two ethnic groups. *Science* 183:338-339.

di Prampero, P. E. and P. Cerretelli. 1968. Maximal muscular power (aerobic and anaerobic) in African natives. *Ergonomics* 12:51-59.

Dixon, W. J. 1970. *BMD Biomedical Computer Programs.* Health Sciences Computing Facility, Univ. of California Press, Berkeley.

Drance, S. M. 1973. Angle closure glaucoma among Canadian Eskimos. *Can. J. Ophth.* 8:252-254.

Dreyer, K. and H. Hamtoft. 1966. Medicostatistical information for the years 1963 and 1964 from Denmark, Greenland, and the Faroe Islands, *Danish Med. Bull.* 13:68-80.

Drukker, A., J. W. Czaczkes, Y. Ben-Yoseph, and E. Shapira. 1972. Carbonic anhydrase B concentrations of erythrocytes in chronic renal failure. *Israel J. Med. Sci.* 8:508-510.

Dumond, D. E. 1965. On Eskaleutian linguistics, archaeology, and prehistory. *Am. Anthrop.* 67:1231-57.

Duncan, I. W. and E. M. Scott, 1972. Lactose tolerance in Alaskan Indians and Eskimos. *Am. J. Clin. Nutr.* 25:867.

Durnin, J. and M. M. Rahaman. 1967. The assessment of the amount of fat in the human body from measurements of skinfold thickness. *Brit. J. Nutr.* 21:681-689.

Erikson, H. 1957. The respiratory response to acute exercise of Eskimos and whites. *Acta Physiol. Scand.* 41:1-11.

Feldman, C. 1970. Report for Mount Edgecumbe School, Alaska. Mimeographed. Univ. of Chicago.

——. 1971. Cognitive development in Eskimos. Paper presented at the Biennial Meeting of the Society for Research in Child Development, Minneapolis, April.

—— and R. D. Bock. 1970. Cognitive studies among residents of Wainwright village, Alaska. *Arctic Anthrop.* 7(1):101-109.

——, B. Lee, J. D. McLean, D. Pillemer, and J. Murray, 1974. *The Development of Adaptive Intelligence.* Jossey-Bass, San Francisco.

Feldman, S. A., K. Ho, L. A. Lewis, B. Mikkelson, and C. B. Taylor, 1972.

Lipid and cholesterol metabolism in Alaskan Arctic Eskimos. *Arch. Path.* 94:42–58.

Finn, J. D. 1974. *MULTIVARIANCE: Univariate and Multivariate Analysis of Variance, Covariance, and Regression.* National Education Resources, Chicago.

Fisher, Q. A. 1974. Letter to the editor. *J. Am. Med. Assoc.* 227:1383.

Fitzgerald, W. 1971. Unpublished test of auditory short-term memory span. Univ. of Chicago Dept. of Education.

Fleshman, J. K., J. F. Wilson, and J. J. Cohen. 1968. Bronchiectasis in Alaska native children. *Arch. Envir. Health* 17:517–523.

Fodor, I. 1961. The validity of glottochronology on the basis of the Slavonic languages. *Studia Slavica* 7:17–58.

——. 1965. *The Rate of Linguistic Change: Limits of the Application of Mathematical Methods in Linguistics.* Janua Linguarum, Series Minor, No. 63. Mouton, the Hague.

Foote, D. C. 1964. American whalemen in Northwestern Arctic Alaska. *Arctic Anthrop.* 2(2):16–20.

—— and H. A. Williamson, 1966. A human geographical study, pp. 1041–1107. In N. Wilimovsky (ed.), *Environment of the Cape Thompson Region, Alaska.* U.S. Atomic Energy Commission, Oak Ridge.

Ford, J. A. 1959. Eskimo prehistory in the vicinity of Point Barrow, Alaska. *Anthrop. Papers Am. Mus. Nat. Hist.* Vol. 47.

Forsius, H., A. W. Eriksson, and H. Luukka. 1970. Ophthalmological characteristics of Eskimos in Augpilogtok. *Arctic Anthrop.* 7(1):9–16.

Fortuine, R. 1969. Characteristics of cancer in the Eskimos of southwestern Alaska. *Cancer* 23:468–474.

Friedlaender, J. S. 1969. Biological Divergences Over Population Boundaries in South-Central Bougainville. Ph.D. Dissertation, Harvard University.

Funakoski, S. and H. F. Deutsch. 1970. Human carbonic anhydrases. IV. Properties of a mutant B type isozyme. *J. Biol. Chem.* 245:4913–19.

—— and H. F. Deutsch. 1971. Human carbonic anhydrases. V. Levels in erythrocytes in various states. *J. Lab. Clin. Med.* 77:39–45.

Fürst, C. M. and Fr. C. C. Hansen. 1915. *Crania Grøenlandica.* Copenhagen.

Getzels, J. W. and P. W. Jackson, 1962. *Creativity and Intelligence.* John Wiley, New York.

Ginaugh, B. J. 1971. An experimental study of basic learning ability and intelligence in low socio-economic status children. *Child Develop.* 42:27–36.

Glanville, E. V. and J. Huizinga. 1966. Digital dermatoglyphics of the Dogon, Peul and Kurumba of Mali and Upper Volta. *Proc. Kon. Ned. Akad. Wet.,* Series C. Vol. 69, pp. 665–674.

Gottschalk, C. W. and D. S. Riggs, 1952. Protein-bound iodine in the serum of soldiers and of Eskimos in the Arctic. *J. Clin. Endocrinol. Metab.* 12:235–243.

Graburn, Nelson H. H. and B. Stephen Strong. 1973. *Circumpolar Peoples:*

An Anthropological Perspective. Goodyear Publ. Co., Inc., Pacific Palisades, Calif.

Greene, D. 1967. Genetics, dentition and taxonomy. *Univ. Wyoming Public.* 33(2):93-168.

Greene, J. C. and J. R. Vermillion. 1960. The oral hygiene index: A method for classifying oral hygiene status. *J. Am. Dent. Assoc.* 61:172-179.

Grimby, G. and B. Saltin. 1966. Physiological analysis of physically well-trained middle-aged and old athletes. *Acta Med. Scand.* 179:513-526.

Grosvenor, G. M. (ed.). 1975. Close-up: U.S.A.–Alaska. *Nat. Geog.,* Vol. 147, No. 6. Map insert in June issue.

Grzybowski, S., J. D. Galbraith, K. Stylbo, et al. 1972. Tuberculosis in Canadian Eskimos. *Arch. Envir. Health* 25:329-332.

Gubser, N. J. 1965. *The Nunamiut Eskimos: Hunters of Caribou.* Yale Univ. Press, New Haven and London.

Gurpide, E., J. Mann, and E. Sandberg. 1964. Determination of kinetic parameters in a two-pool system by administration of one or more tracers. *Biochemistry* 3:1250-55.

Hall, E. S. 1968. Excavations at Tukuto Lake: The late prehistoric/early historic Eskimos of interior Northwest Alaska. Unpublished manuscript.

——. 1970. The late prehistoric/early historic Eskimo of interior North Alaska. An ethnoarchaeological approach? *Anthrop. Papers Univ. Alaska* 15(1):1-11.

Hammerich, L. L. 1958. The western Eskimo dialects, pp. 632-639. *Proceedings of the 32nd International Congress of Americanists,* Copenhagen.

Harris, E. K. and D. L. Demets. 1972. Estimation of normal ranges and curriculation proportions by transforming observed distributions to Gaussian form. *Clin. Chem.* 18(2):603.

Harvald, B. and J. Hels. 1972. Incidence of cardiac malformations in Greenlandic Eskimos. *Humangenetik* 15:257-260.

Heinrich, A. 1955. A summary of kinship forms and terminologies found among the Inupiaq speaking people of Alaska. Unpublished manuscript, Univ. of Alaska, College.

——. 1960. Structural features of the Northwestern Alaskan Eskimo kinship. *Southwest. J. Anthrop.* 16:110-126.

Heller, C. A. and E. M. Scott. 1967. *The Alaska Dietary Survey 1956-1961.* Public Health Service Publica. No. 999-AH-2. Government Printing Office, Washington, D.C.

——, E. M. Scott, and L. M. Hammes, 1967. Height, weight, and growth of Alaskan Eskimos. *Am. J. Dis. Childhood* 113:338-344.

Hennigh, L. 1970. Functions and limitations of Alaskan Eskimo wife trading. *Arctic* 23(1):24-34.

Herberg, R. J. 1965. Channels ratio method of quench correction in liquid scintillation counting, pp. 1-7. *Packard Technical Bulletin 15.* Packard Instrument Co., Inc., Downers Grove, Ill.

Herbert, F. A., W. A. Mahon, O. Wilkinson, et al. 1967. Pneumonia in Indian and Eskimo infants and children. I. A clinical study. *Can. Med. Assoc. J.* 96:256-267.

Hertzberg, H. T. E., E. Churchill, C. W. Dupertuis, R. M. White, and A. Damon. 1963. *Anthropometric Survey of Turkey, Greece and Italy.* Pergamon Press, Macmillan Co., New York.

Hildes, J. A. 1966. The circumpolar people—health and physiological adaptations. In P. T. Baker and J. S. Weiner (eds.), *The Biology of Human Adaptability.* Clarendon Press, Oxford.

Hirsch, D. I. 1954. Glottochronology and Eskimo and Eskimo-Aleut prehistory. *Am. Anthrop.* 56:825-838.

Ho, K. J., S. K. Peng, and C. B. Taylor. 1972. Identification and quantitation of dietary and fecal neutral sterols by mass spectrometry. *Atherosclerosis* 15:249-264.

Holt, S. B. 1949. A quantitative survey of the finger prints of a small sample of the British population. *Ann. Eugen.* 14:329-338.

——. 1961. Dermatoglyphic patterns. In A. Harrison (ed.), *Genetical Variation in Human Populations.* Pergamon Press, London and New York.

Hooton, E. A. 1937. *Apes, Man, Morons.* Macmillan, New York.

——. 1946. *Up from the Ape.* Macmillan and Co., New York.

Hopkinson, D. A., J. S. Coppock, M. F. Muhlemann, and Y. H. Edwards. 1974. The detection and differentiation of the products of the human carbonic anhydrase loci CA I and CA II, using fluorogenic substrates. *Ann. Hum. Genet.* 38:155-162.

Høygaard, A. 1940. Studies on the nutrition and physio-pathology of Eskimos. Norske Videnskaps-Akademi Skrift. Mat.-Naturv. Kl. No. 9, pp. 1-176.

Hrdlička, A. 1910. Contribution to the anthropology of Central and Smith Sound Eskimos. *Anthrop. Papers Am. Mus. Nat. Hist.* 5, Part II.

——. 1925. *The Old Americans.* Williams and Wilkins, Baltimore.

——. 1930. *Anthropological Survey in Alaska.* 46th Annual Report of the Bureau of American Ethnology, 1928-1929, pp. 19-374. Washington, D.C.

——. 1940 Lower jaw. *Am. J. Phys. Anthrop.* 27:281-308.

——. 1941. Height and weight in Eskimo children. *Am. J. Phys. Anthrop.* 28:331-341.

——. 1942. Catalog of human crania in the United States National Museum collections: Eskimos in general. *Proc. U.S. Nat. Mus.* 91:169-429.

——. 1944. Catalog of human crania in the United States National Museum collections: Non-Eskimo people of the Northwest Coast, Alaska, and Siberia. *Proc. U.S. Nat. Mus.* 94:1-172.

Huizinga, J. 1965. Finger patterns and ridge counts of the Dogons. *Proc. Kon. Ned. Akad. Wet.,* Series C., No. 5, pp. 398-411.

Hylander, W. L. 1972. The Adaptive Significance of Eskimo Craniofacial Morphology. Ph.D. Dissertation, University of Chicago.

Hymes, D. H. 1960. Lexicostatistics so far. *Cur. Anthrop.* 1:3-44.

IAHB. 1967. International Association of Human Biologists. *Yearbook of Physical Anthropology* 15:2-5.

Ingstad, H. 1954. *Nunamiut: Among Alaska's Inland Eskimo.* Allen and Unwin, London.

Irving, W. N. 1951. Notes on some physical data on a group of inland Eskimo. Unpublished manuscript.

——. 1953. Evidence of early tundra cultures in northern Alaska. *Anthrop. Papers Univ. Alaska* 1:55-85.

Jackson, S. 1894. *Report on the Introduction of Domestic Reindeer into Alaska.* Government Printing Office, Washington, D.C.

——. 1906. *Report on the Introduction of Domestic Reindeer into Alaska.* Government Printing Office, Washington, D.C.

Jamison, P. L. 1968. The location of Eskimo settlements on the Arctic coast of Alaska from historic documents. Unpublished manuscript.

——. 1970. Growth of Wainwright Eskimos: Stature and weight. *Arctic Anthrop.* 7(1):86-94.

——. 1972. The Eskimos of Northwestern Alaska: Their Univariate and Multivariate Anthropometric Variation. Ph.D. Dissertation, University of Wisconsin, Madison.

——. 1976. Growth of Eskimo children in northwestern Alaska, pp. 223-229. In R. J. Shephard and S. Itoh (eds.), *Circumpolar Health.* Univ. of Toronto Press, Toronto.

Jamison, P. L. and S. L. Zegura. 1970. An anthropometric study of the Eskimos of Wainwright, Alaska. *Arctic Anthrop.* 7(1):125-143.

—— and S. L. Zegura. 1974. A univariate and multivariate examination of measurement error in anthropometry. *Am. J. Phys. Anthrop.* 40(2): 197-204.

Jenness, D. 1923. *The Copper Eskimos.* Report of the Canadian Arctic Expedition 1913-1918, Vol. 12, Part B.

Johnson, R. E., L. Brouha, and R. C. Darling. 1942. A test of physical fitness for strenuous exertion. *Rev. Canad. de Biol.* 1:491-503.

Johonnott, S. C. 1973. Differences in chronic otitis media between rural and urban Eskimo children. *Clin. Pediat.* 12:415-419.

Jørgensen, J. B. 1953. The Eskimo skeleton. Meddelelser om Grønland, Vol. 146, No. 2. Copenhagen.

Klatsky, A. B. 1948. Studies in the dietaries of contemporary primitive peoples. *J. Am. Dent. Assoc.* 36:385-389.

Kleinfeld, J. S. 1973a. Effects of nonverbally communicated personal warmth on intelligence test performance of Indian and Eskimo adolescents. *J. Soc. Psych.* 91:149-150.

——. 1973b. Intellectual strengths in culturally different groups: An Eskimo illustration. *Rev. Educ. Res.* 43:341-359.

Kolakowski, D. and R. D. Bock. 1973. *LOGOG: Maximum Likelihood Item*

Analysis and Test Scoring: Logistic Model for Multiple Item Responses. National Education Resources, Chicago.

Kondo, T., N. Taniguchi, M. Muras, and E. Takakuwa. 1975. Estimations of active and inactive carbonic anhydrase isozyme B in human red cells. *Clin. Chem. Acta* 60:347–353.

Kory, R. C., R. Callahan, H. G. Boren, and J. C. Syner. 1961. The Veterans Administration-Army cooperative study of pulmonary function. I. Clinical spirometry in normal men. *Am. J. Med.* 30:243–258.

Kotzebue, O. 1821. *A Voyage of Discovery into the South Seas and Beering's Straits.* Longman, Hurst, Rees, Orme and Brown, London.

Krauss, M. E. 1973. Eskimo-Aleut, pp. 796–902. In T. A. Sebeok (ed.), *Linguistics in North America.* Current Trends in Linguistics, Vol. 10. Mouton, The Hague.

Kretchmer, N. 1972. Lactose and lactase. *Scient. Am.* 227:70.

Kristoffersen, T. and G. Bang. 1973. Periodontal disease and oral hygiene in an Alaskan Eskimo population. *J. Dent. Res.* 52:791–795.

Krogh, A. and M. Krogh, 1913. A study of the diet and metabolism of Eskimos. *Meddelelser om Grønland* 51:1–52.

Laessig, R. H., F. P. Pauls, and T. H. Schwartz. 1972. Long-term preservations of serum specimens collected in the field for epidemiological studies of biochemical parameters. *Health Lab Sci.* 9(1):16.

——, T. H. Schwartz, A. Indriksons, D. Miran, and W. J. Zimmerman. 1973. Application of normalizing functions to biochemical screening data to provide realistic incidence rates and normal ranges. *Clin. Chem.* 19(6):678 (abstract 203).

——, T. H. Schwartz, and J. Preizler. 1970. State of Wisconsin Multiphasic Screening Program. *Advances in Automated Analysis* (Technicon International Congress) 1:261–269.

Lammert, O. 1972. Maximal aerobic power and energy expenditure of Eskimo hunters in Greenland. *J. Appl. Physiol.* 33:184–188.

Larsen, H. and F. Rainey. 1948. Ipiutak and the Arctic whale hunting culture. *Anthrop. Papers Am. Mus. Nat. Hist.* Vol. 42.

Laughlin, W. S. 1958. Neo-Aleut and Paleo-Aleut prehistory, pp. 516–530. *Proceedings of the 32nd International Congress of Americanists,* Copenhagen.

——. 1963. Eskimos and Aleuts: Their origins and evolution. *Science* 142(3593):633–645.

——. 1966. Genetical and anthropological characteristics of Arctic populations. In P. T. Baker and J. S. Weiner (eds.), *The Biology of Human Adaptability.* Clarendon Press, Oxford.

——. 1970. The purpose of studying Eskimos and their population systems. *Arctic* 22(1):3–13.

——. 1975. Aleuts: Ecosystem, holocene history, and Siberian origin. *Science* 189:507–515.

Leonard, P. J. and M. S. Losowsky, 1967. Relationship between plasma vitamin E level and peroxide hemolysis test in human subjects. *Am. J. Clin.
Nutr.* 20:795.

Lester, C. W. and H. L. Shapiro. 1968. Vertebral arch defects in the lumbar
vertebrae of prehistoric American Eskimos. *Am. J. Phys. Anthrop.* 28:
43-48.

Levin, M. G. 1963. *Ethnic Origins of the Peoples of Northeastern Asia.* Arctic
Institute of North America: Translations from Russian Sources No. 3,
H. N. Michael (ed.). Univ. of Toronto Press, Toronto.

Lewis, J. S., A. K. Dian, M. T. Baer, P. B. Acosta, and G. A. Emerson. 1973.
Effect of long-term ingestion of polyunsaturated fat, age, plasma cholesterol, diabetes mellitus and supplemented tocopherol upon plasma
tocopherol. *Am. J. Clin. Nutr.* 26:136.

Lie-Injo, L. E. 1967. Red cell carbonic anhydrase Ic in Filipinos. *Am. J. Hum.
Genet.* 19:130-132.

——, L. Hollander, and H. H. Fudenberg, 1967. Carbonic anhydrase and fetal
hemoglobin in thyrotoxicosis. *Blood* 30:442-448.

——, C. G. Lopez, and P. L. DeV. Hart. 1970. Erythrocyte carbonic anhydrase
activity in health and disease. *Clin. Chem. Acta* 29:541-550.

—— and H. G. Poey-Oey. 1970. Phosphogluco-mutase, carbonic anhydrase
and catalase in Indonesians. *Hum. Hered.* 20:215-219.

Link, B. A., R. W. Bray, R. G. Cassens, and R. G. Kauffman. 1970a. Fatty
acid composition of bovine skeletal muscle during growth. *J. Animal Sci.*
30:726.

——, R. W. Bray, R. G. Cassens, and R. G. Kauffman. 1970b. Fatty acid
composition of bovine subcutaneous adipose tissue lipids during growth.
J. Animal Sci. 30:722.

Loesch, D. 1971. Genetics of dermatoglyphics on palms. *Ann. Hum. Genet.*
34:277-293.

Lowrey, G. H. 1973. *Growth and Development of Children,* sixth ed. Year
Book Medical Publishers, Chicago.

MacArthur, R. S. 1967. Sex differences in field dependence for the Eskimo:
Replication of Berry's findings. *Inter. J. Psych.* 2:139-140.

——. 1968. Some differential abilities of northern Canadian native youth.
Inter. J. Psych. 3:43-51.

——. 1973. Some ability patterns: Central Eskimos and Nsenga Africans.
Inter. J. Psych. 8:239-247.

McCammon, R. B. and G. Wenninger. 1970. *The Dendrograph.* Computer
Contribution No. 48. State Geological Survey, University of Kansas,
Lawrence.

McCance, R. A., E. H. R. Ford, and W. A. B. Brown. 1961. Severe undernutrition in growing and adult animals. Part 7. Development of the skulls,
jaws and teeth in pigs. *Brit. J. Nutr.* 15:213-224.

McKeon, J. J. 1966. Canonical analysis: Some relations between canonical correlation, factor analysis, discriminant function analysis and scaling theory. *Psychom. Mong.* No. 13.

MacKinnon, A. A. 1972. Eskimo and Caucasian: A Discordant note on cognitive-perceptual abilities. *Proceedings, 80th Annual Convention, Am. Psych. Assoc.*

McNair, A., E. Gudmand-Hoyer, S. Jarnum, and L. Orrild. 1972. Sucrose malabsorption in Greenland. *Brit. Med. J.* 2:19.

Mahalanobis, P. C. 1925. Analysis of race mixture in Bengal. *J. Asiatic Soc. Bengal* 23:301-333.

——. 1930. On tests and measures of group divergence. *J. Asiatic Soc. Bengal* 26:541-588.

——. 1936. On the generalized distance in statistics. *Proc. Nat. Inst. Sci. India* 12:49-55.

——, D. N. Majumdar, and C. R. Rao. 1949. Anthropometric survey of the United Provinces, 1941: A statistical study. *Sankhya* 9:89-324.

Mancini, G., A. O. Carbonara, and J. F. Heremans. 1965. Immunochemical quantitation of antigen by single radial immunodiffusion. *Immunochemistry* 2:235-254.

Mange, A. P. 1963. The Population Structure of a Human Isolate. Ph.D. Dissertation, University of Wisconsin, Madison.

Mann, G. V., E. M. Scott, L. M. Hursh, C. A. Heller, J. B. Youmans, C. F. Consolazio, E. B. Bridgforth, A. L. Russell, and M. Silverman. 1962. The health and nutritional status of Alaskan Eskimos. *Am. J. Clin. Nutr.* 11:31-76.

Mann, I. 1972. Eye disease in the Eskimo and in the Australian Aboriginal: A brief comparison. *Acta Ophtalmologica* 50:543-548.

Margaria, R. 1966. Assessment of physical activity in oxidative and anaerobic maximal exercise. *Int. z. angew. Physiol. einschl. Arbeitsphysiol.* 22: 115-124.

——, P. Aghemo, and E. Rovelli. 1965. Indirect determination of maximal oxygen consumption in man. *J. Appl. Physiol.* 20:1070-73.

——, P. Aghemo, and E. Rovelli. 1966. Measurements of muscular power (anaerobic) in man. *J. Appl. Physiol.* 21:1662-64.

——, P. Cerretelli, P. Aghemo, and G. Sassi. 1963. Energy cost of running. *J. Appl. Physiol.* 18:367-370.

Masnick, G. S. and S. H. Katz. 1976. Adaptive childbearing in a North Slope Eskimo community. *Hum. Biol.* 48:37-58.

Mavalwala, J. 1966. Inheritance studies in dermatoglyphics. *Ann. N.Y. Acad. Sci.* 134:812-814.

Mayhall, J. T. 1970. The effect of culture change upon the Eskimo dentition. *Arctic Anthrop.* 7:117-121.

——. 1972. Dental morphology of Indians and Eskimos: Its relationship to the prevention and treatment of caries. *J. Can. Dent. Assoc.* 38:152-154.

——. 1976. Inuit culture change and oral health: A four year study, pp. 414-420. In R. J. Shephard and S. Itoh (eds.), *Circumpolar Health.* Univ. of Toronto Press, Toronto.

——, A. A. Dahlberg, and D. G. Owen. 1970a. Dental caries in the Eskimos of Wainwright, Alaska. *J. Dent. Res.* 49:886.

——, A. A. Dahlberg, and D. G. Owen. 1970b. Torus mandibularis in an Alaskan Eskimo population. *Am. J. Phys. Anthrop.* 33:57-60.

Maynard, J. E. 1974. Coronary heart disease risk factors in relation to urbanization in Alaskan Eskimo men. Abstracts of papers presented at the Third International Symposium on Circumpolar Health, Yellowknife, N.W.T., Canada, July 8-11, p. 23.

—— and L. M. Hammes. 1964. Arctic Health Research Center Infant Morbidity and Mortality Study, Bethel Area, Alaska, October 1960-December 1962. U.S. Department of Health, Education and Welfare, Public Health Service Arctic Health Research Center, Administrative Report, 48 pages, May.

Mazess, R. B. 1970. Bone mineral content in Wainwright Eskimos: Preliminary report. *Arctic Anthrop.* 7(1):114-116.

—— (ed.). 1974. *International Conference on Bone Mineral Measurement.* DHEW Publication 75-863. U.S. Department of Health, Education and Welfare, Washington, D.C.

——. 1975. Adaptation and adaptive strategies. In E. Watts, F. E. Johnston, and G. W. Lasker (eds.). *Biosocial Interrelations in Population Adaptation.* Aldine, Chicago.

—— and J. R. Cameron. 1974. Bone mineral content in normal U.S. Whites. In R. B. Mazess (ed.), *International Conference on Bone Mineral Measurement.* DHEW Publication 75-863. U.S. Department of Health, Education and Welfare, Washington, D.C.

—— and W. E. Mather. 1974. Bone mineral content of North Alaskan Eskimos. *Am. J. Clin. Nutr.* 27:916-925.

—— and W. E. Mather. 1975. Bone mineral content in Canadian Eskimos. *Hum. Biol.* 47:45-63.

Meier, R. J. 1966. Fingerprint patterns from Karluk Village, Kodiak Island. *Arctic Anthrop.* 3:206-210.

——. 1974a. Evolutionary processes in Eskimo dermatoglyphics. *Arctic Anthrop.* 11, Supplement: 20-28.

——. 1974b. Correlation between ridge count, pattern intensity and pattern type in Eskimo dermatoglyphics. *Am. J. Phys. Anthrop.* 41:493 (abstract).

——. 1975. Dermatoglyphics of Easter Islanders analyzed by pattern type, admixture effect, and ridge count variation. *Am. J. Phys. Anthrop.* 42: 269-275.

——. In press. Dermatoglyphic variation in five Eskimo groups from Northwestern Alaska. In J. Mavalwala (ed.), *Dermatoglyphics: Its Role in Anthropology and Medicine.* Mouton, the Hague.

Merbs, C. F. 1969. Patterns of Activity-Induced Pathology in a Canadian Eskimo Isolate. Ph.D. Dissertation, University of Wisconsin, Madison.

—— and W. H. Wilson. 1962. Anomalies and pathologies of the Sadlermiut Eskimo vertebral column. *Nat. Mus. Can. Bull.* 180:154-180.

Mikkelsen, E. 1910. *Conquering of the Arctic Ice.*

Milan, F. A. 1964a. The acculturation of the contemporary Eskimo of Wainwright, Alaska. *Anthrop. Papers Univ. Alaska* 11(2):1-95.

——. 1964b. Maintenance of thermal balance in arctic Eskimos and antarctic sojourners, pp. 561-562. In R. Carrick et al. (eds.), *Biologie Antarctique.* Herman, Paris.

—— (ed.). 1967. Report of the Working Party Conference Held at Naval Arctic Research Laboratory, Point Barrow, Alaska. Mimeo, Univ. of Wisconsin, Madison. 112 pages.

——. 1968. International Study of Eskimos. *Arctic* 21(3):123-126.

——. 1970. The demography of an Alaskan Eskimo village. *Arctic Anthrop.* 7(1):26-43.

——. 1974-75. Historical demography of Alaska's native population. *Folk* 16-17:45.

——. (In press). *Biology of Circumpolar People.* Cambridge Univ. Press, Oxford.

—— and E. Evonuk. 1967 Oxygen consumption and body temperatures of Eskimos during sleep. *J. Appl. Physiol.* 22:565.

—— and S. Pawson. 1975. The demography of the native population of an Alaskan city. *Arctic* 28:275.

Mitchell, J. H., B. J. Sproule, and C. B. Chapman. 1958. The physiological meaning of the maximal oxygen intake test. *J. Clin. Invest.* 37:538-547.

Möller, I. J., S. Poulsen, and V. Orholm Nelsen. 1972. The prevalence of dental caries in Godhavn and Scoresbysund districts, Greenland. *Scand. J. Dent. Res.* 80:169-180.

Mondrup, M. and N. Anker. 1975. Carbonic anhydrase isoenzymes in the erythrocytes of newborn premature and full-term infants. *Clin. Chem. Acta* 61:127-133.

Moore, M. J. 1972. Population Studies of Erythrocyte Carbonic Anhydrase in Caucasians, American Negroes and Eskimos. Ph.D. Dissertation, University of Wisconsin, Madison.

——, H. F. Deutsch, and F. R. Ellis. 1973. Human carbonic anhydrases. IX. Inheritance of variant erythrocyte forms. *Am. J. Hum. Genet.* 25:29-35.

——, S. Funakoski, and H. F. Deutsch. 1971. Human carbonic anhydrases. VII. A new C type isozyme in erythrocyte of American Negroes. *Biochem. Genet.* 5:497-504.

Morant, G. M. 1937. A contribution to Eskimo craniology based on previously published measurements. *Biometrika* 29:1-20.

Morrison, D. F. 1967. *Multivariate Statistical Methods.* McGraw-Hill, New York.

Mouratoff, G. F., N. V. Carroll, and E. M. Scott. 1967. Diabetes mellitus in Eskimos. *J. Am. Med. Assoc.* 199:961-966.

—— and E. M. Scott. 1973. Diabetes mellitus in Eskimos after a decade. *J. Am. Med. Assoc.* 226:1345.

Murad, T. A. 1975. The North Alaskan Eskimo: Intra-Population Variation for Palmar Dermatoglyphics. Ph.D. Dissertation, Indiana University, Bloomington.

National Center for Health Statistics. 1969. *National Health Survey (1960–62)*. Series 11, No. 34. U.S. Department of Health, Education and Welfare, Washington, D.C.

National Research Council, Food and Nutrition Board. 1974. *Recommended Dietary Allowances,* 8th ed. National Academy of Sciences-National Research Council, Washington, D.C.

Neel, J. V., F. M. Salzano, P. C. Junqveira, F. Keiter, and D. Mayberry-Lewis. 1964. Studies on the Xavante Indians of the Brazilian Mato Grosso. *Am. J. Hum. Genet.* 16:52–140.

Nelson R. K. 1969. *Hunters of the Northern Ice.* Univ. of Chicago Press.

Newman, R. W. 1956. Skinfold measurements in young American males. *Hum. Biol.* 28:154–164.

Nie, N. H., C. H. Hull, J. G. Jenkins, K. Steinbrenner, and D. H. Bent. 1975. *SPSS Statistical Package for the Social Sciences.* McGraw-Hill, New York.

Norgaard-Pedersen, B., J. G. Klebe, and N. Crunnet. 1971. Carbonic anhydrase activity in cord blood from infants of diabetic and non-diabetic mothers. *Biol. Neonate* 19:389–396.

O'Neal, R. M., O. C. Johnson, and A. E. Schaefer. 1970. Guidelines for classification and interpretation of group blood and urine data collected as part of the National Nutrition Survey. *Pediat. Res.* 4:103–106.

Osborne, R. H. and H. Goldstein. 1972. Errors of measurement in anthropological studies. Unpublished manuscript.

Oschinsky, L. 1964. *The Most Ancient Eskimos.* The Canadian Research Center for Anthropology, University of Ottawa, Ottawa.

Ostrander, L. D., R. L. Brandt, M. O. Kjelsberg, and F. H. Epstein. 1965. Electrocardiographic findings among the adult population of a total natural community, Tecumseh, Michigan. *Circulation* 31:888.

Oswalt, W. H. 1967. *Alaskan Eskimos.* Chandler, San Francisco.

Perl, W. and D. Samuel. 1969. Input-output analysis for total input rate and total traced mass of body cholesterol in man. *Circ. Res.* 15:191–199.

Petroff, I. 1884. Report on the population, industries and resources of Alaska, pp. 1–88. In *Tenth Census of the United States,* Vol. 8. Government Printing Office, Washington, D.C.

Pett, L. B. and P. J. Lupien. 1958. Cholesterol levels of Canadian Eskimos. *Fed. Proc.* 17:488.

——, P. Verdier, and J. E. Monagle. 1961. A review of biological data on the Canadian Eskimo. *Fed. Proc.* 20:96.

Porter, R. P. 1893. Report on population and resources in Alaska, pp. 1–282. In *Eleventh Census of the United States,* Vol. 10. Government Printing Office, Washington, D.C.

Posposil, L. and W. S. Laughlin, 1963. Kinship terminology and kindred among the Nunamiut Eskimo. *Ethnology* 2:180–189.

Powers, A. D. 1967. A review of physical anthropological data in Arctic North America and its relevance to studies of population history. Unpublished manuscript (owned by S. Zegura).

Quick, W. W. 1974. Letter to the editor. *J. Am. Med. Assoc.* 227:1383.

Rainey, F. G. 1947. The whale hunters of Tigara. *Anthrop. Papers Am. Mus. Nat. Hist.* 41:231-283.

———. 1971. *The Ipiutak Culture: Excavations at Point Hope, Alaska.* Addison-Wesley Modular Publications No. 8.

Rao, C. R. 1952. *Advanced Statistical Methods in Biometrical Research.* John Wiley, New York.

Rausch, R. L., E. M. Scott, and V. R. Rausch. 1967. Helminths in Eskimos in western Alaska, with particular reference to Diphyllobothrium infection and anemia. *Trans. Roy. Soc. Trop. Med. Hyg.* 61:351-357.

Raven, J. C. 1956. *Raven Standard Progressive Matrices.* Psychological Corporation, New York.

———. 1960. *Guide to Using the Standard Progressive Matrices.* H. K. Lewis, London.

Ray, P. H. 1885. Report of the international polar expedition to Point Barrow, Alaska. *House of Representatives Executive Document,* 48th Congress, 2nd Session, Vol. 23, No. 44.

Reed, D., S. Struve, and J. E. Maynard. 1967 Otitis media and hearing deficiency among Eskimo children: A cohort study. *Am. J. Pub. Health* 57:1657-62.

Rennie, D. W., P. di Prampero, R. W. Fitts, and L. Sinclair. 1970. Physical fitness and respiratory function of Eskimos of Wainwright, Alaska. *Arctic Anthrop.* 7(1):73-82.

Richards, E. A. 1949. *Arctic Mood.* Caxton Printers, Caldwell, Idaho.

Rightmire, G. P. 1969. On the computation of Mahalanobis' generalized distance. *Am. J. Phys. Anthrop.* 30:157-160.

Rigters-Aris, C. A. 1975. Dermatoglyphics of three West African Tribes (Fali-Cameroon, Kusasi-Ghana, Bacule-Ivory Coast). *Proc. Kon. Ned. Akad. Wet.,* Series C, Vol. 78, No. 1, pp. 47-57.

Robinhold, D, and D. Rice. 1970. Cardiovascular health of Wainwright Eskimos. *Arctic Anthrop.* 7(1):83-85.

Robinson, S. 1938. Experimental studies of physical fitness in relation to age. *Arbeitsphysiologie* 10:251-323.

Rodahl, K. R. 1958. Physical fitness. *J. Am. Geriat. Soc.* 6:205-209.

——— and D. W. Rennie, 1957. Comparative sweat rates of Eskimos and Caucasians under controlled conditions. Arctic Aeromedical Lab. Proj. No. 8-7951 #7, AAML, Ladd AFB, Alaska.

Rode, A. and R. J. Shephard. 1973. Pulmonary function of Canadian Eskimos. *Scand. J. Respir. Dis.* 54:191-205.

Rovelli, E. and P. Aghemo. 1963. Physiological characteristics of the step exercise. *Int. z. angew. Physiol. einschl. Arbeitsphysiol.* 20:190-194.

Rowe, A. W., E. Eyster, and A. Kellner. 1968. Liquid nitrogen preservation of red blood cells for transfusion. *Cryobiology* 5:119-128.

Rubel, A. J. 1961. Partnership and wife-exchange among the Eskimo and the Aleut of Northern America. *Anthrop. Papers Univ. Alaska* 10(1):59-72.

Russell, A. L. 1956. A system of classification and scoring for prevalence surveys of periodontal disease. *J. Dent. Res.* 35:350-359.

——, C. F. Consolazio, and G. L. White. 1961. Dental caries and nutrition in Eskimo Scouts of the Alaska National Guard. *J. Dent. Res.* 40:594-603.

Sanderson, I. T. 1956. *Follow the Whale.* Boston.

Sarnas, K.-V. 1959. Inter- and intra-family variations in the facial profile. *Odontologisk Revy* 10, Suppl. 4.

Sauberlich, H. E., W. Goad, Y. F. Herman, F. Milan, and P. Jamison. 1970. Preliminary report on the nutrition survey conducted among the Eskimos of Wainwright, Alaska, January 21-27, 1969. *Arctic Anthrop.* 7(1): 122-124.

——, W. Goad, Y. F. Herman, F. Milan, and P. Jamison. 1972. Biochemical assessment of the nutritional status of the Eskimos of Wainwright, Alaska. *Am. J. Clin. Nutr.* 25:437-445.

Schaefer, O. 1971a. Otitis media and bottle-feeding: An epidemiological study of infant feeding habits and incidence of recurrent and chronic middle ear disease in Canadian Eskimos. *Can. J. Pub. Health* 62:478-489.

——. 1971b. When the Eskimo comes to town. *Nutrition Today* 6:8.

——. 1973. The changing health picture in the Canadian North. *Can J. Ophth.* 8:196-204.

Schenker, J. G., Y. Ben-Yoseph, and E. Shapira. 1972. Erythrocyte carbonic anhydrase B levels during pregnancy and use of oral contraceptives. *Obstet. Gynecol.* 39:237-240.

Schonell, M. 1972. Frobisher Eskimos and tuberculosis. *Med. J. Australia* 1:1090-91.

Schwartz, T. H., R. H. Laessig, and J. Preizler. 1972. Cost analysis of Wisconsin's Program of Multiphasic Health Screening. *Health Services Reports* (U.S. Public Health Service Reports) 87:523.

Scott, E. M. 1956. Nutrition of Alaskan Eskimos. *Nutr. Rev.* 14:1-3.

——, I. V. Griffith, D. D. Hoskins, et al. 1958. Serum cholesterol levels and blood pressure of Alaskan Eskimo men. *Lancet* 2:667-668.

Seltzer, C. C. 1933. The anthropometry of the Western and Copper Eskimos, based on data of Vilhjalmur Stefansson. *Hum. Biol.* 5(3):313-370.

Shaw, C. R., F. N. Syner, and R. E. Tashian. 1962. New genetically determined molecular form of erythrocyte esterase. *Science* 138:31-32.

Shephard, R. J. 1966. The relative merits of the step test, bicycle ergometer and treadmill in the assessment of cardio-respiratory fitness. *Int. z. angew. Physiol. einschl. Arbeitsphysiol.* 23:219-230.

——. 1969. Nomogram to calculate the O_2-cost of running at slow speeds. *J. Sports Med.* 9:10-16.

—— 1974. Work physiology and activity patterns of circumpolar Eskimos and Ainu. A synthesis of International Biological Program Data. *Hum. Biol.* 46:263-294.

Shows, T. B. 1967. The amino acid substitution and some chemical properties of a variant human erythrocyte carbonic anhydrase: carbonic anhydrase Id Michigan. *Biochem. Genet.* 1:171-195.

Simpson, G. G., A. Roe, and R. C. Lewontin. 1960. *Quantitative Zoology.* Harcourt, Brace and Co., New York.

Simpson, T. 1843. *Narrative of Discoveries on the Northwest Coast of America.* London.

Sinclair, R. G., G. M. Brown and L. B. Cronk. 1949. Serum lipids of Eskimos. Effect of a high fat diet (pemmican) and of fasting (Abstract). *Fed. Proc. Fed. Am. Soc. Exp. Biol.* 8:251.

Singh, R. D. 1961. Digital pattern frequency and size variation in some castes of Uttar Pradesh. *East. Anthrop.* 14:169-188.

Skerlj, B., J. Brozek, and E. E. Hunt, Jr. 1953. Subcutaneous fat and age changes in body build and body form in women. *Am. J. Phys. Anthrop.* 11: 577-600.

Sneath, P. H. A. and R. R. Sokal. 1973. *Numerical Taxonomy.* W. H. Freeman, San Francisco.

Solecki, R. S. 1950. New data on the inland Eskimo of Northern Alaska. *J. Wash. Acad. Sci.* 40:137-157.

Spencer, R. F. 1958. Eskimo polyandry and social organization, pp. 539-544. *32nd International Congress of Americanists,* Copenhagen.

——. 1959. *The North Alaskan Eskimo.* Bureau of American Ethnology Bulletin No. 171. Smithsonian Institution, Washington, D.C.

——. 1968. Spouse exchange among the North Alaskan Eskimo, pp. 131-146. In P. Bohannon and J. Middleton (eds.), *Marriage, Family and Residence.* Natural History Press, New York.

Sperry, W. M. and M. Webb. 1950. A revision of the Schonheimer-Sperry method for cholesterol determination. *J. Biol. Chem.* 187:97-106.

Spielman, R. S., E. C. Migliazza, and J. V. Neel. 1974. Regional linguistic and genetic differences among Yanomama Indians. *Science* 184:637-644.

Steegmann, A. T. 1967. Frostbite of the human face as a selective force. *Hum. Biol.* 39:131-144.

——. 1970. Cold adaptation and the human face. *Am. J. Phys. Anthrop.* 32: 243-250.

Stefansson, V. 1935-36. Adventures in Diet. Reprinted from Harper's Magazine of November and December 1935 and January 1936 by the Institute of American Meat Packers, Chicago, Illinois.

Steggerda, M., J. Crane, and M. D. Steele. 1929. One hundred measurements and observations on one hundred Smith College students. *Am. J. Phys. Anthrop.* 13:189-254.

Stewart, T. D. 1931. Incidence of separate neural arch in the lumbar vertebrae of Eskimos. *Am. J. Phys. Anthrop.* 16:51-62.

——. 1939. Anthropometric observations on the Eskimos and Indians of Labrador. *Field Museum of Natural History, Anthropology Series,* No. 31. Chicago.

——. 1953. The age incidence of neural arch defects in Alaskan natives considered from the standpoint of etiology. *J. Bone and Joint Surg.* 35(A): 937-950.

——. 1956. Examination of the possiblity that certain skeletal characteristics predispose to defects in the lumbar neural arch. *Clin. Orthoped.* 8:44-46.

——. 1959. Skeletal remains from the vicinity of Point Barrow, Alaska, pp. 245-255. In *Eskimo Prehistory in the Vicinity of Point Barrow, Alaska,* by J. A. Ford. *Anthrop. Papers Am. Mus. Nat. Hist.* 47(1).

Stoney, G. M. 1899. Explorations in Alaska. *Proc. U.S. Naval Inst.* 25:533-584 and 799-849.

Swadesh, M. 1950. Salish internal relationships. *Inter. J. Am. Ling.* 16:157-167.

——. 1951. Kleinschmidt centennial 111: Unaaliq and Proto Eskimo. *Inter. J. Am. Ling.* 17:66-70.

——. 1952a. Lexico-statistic dating of prehistoric ethnic contacts. *Proc. Am. Phil. Soc.* 96:452-463.

——. 1952b. Unaaliq and Proto Eskimo. *Inter. J. Am. Ling.* 18:25-34, 69-76, 166-171, 241-256.

——. 1954. Time depths of American linguistic groupings. *Am. Anthrop.* 56: 361-364.

——. 1958. Some new glottochronological dates for American linguistic groups, pp. 671-674. *Proceedings of the 32nd International Congress of Americanists,* Copenhagen.

Taniguchi, N., T. Sato, T. Kondo, H. Tamachi, K. Saito, and E. Takakuwa. 1975. Carbonic anhydrase isozymes, hemoglobin-F and glutathione levels in lead-exposed workers. *Clin. Chem. Acta* 59:29-34.

Tashian, R. E. 1969. The esterases and carbonic anhydrases of human erythrocytes, pp. 307-336. In J. J. Yunis (ed.), *Biochemical Methods in Red Cell Genetics.* Academic Press, New York.

——, M. Goodman, V. E. Headings, J. DeSimone, and R. H. Ward. 1971. Genetic variation and evolution in the red cell carbonic anhydrase isozymes of macaque monkeys. *Biochem. Genet.* 5:183-200.

——, C. C. Plato, and T. B. Shaws. 1963. Inherited variant of erythrocyte carbonic anhydrase in Micronesians from Guam and Saipan. *Science* 140: 53-54.

——, D. C. Shreffler, and T. B. Shaws. 1968. Genetic and phylogenetic variation in the different molecular forms of mammalian erythrocyte carbonic anhydrases. *Ann. N.Y. Acad. Sci.* 151:64-77.

Thissen, D., R. D. Bock, H. Wainer, and A. F. Roche. 1976. Individual growth in stature: A comparison of four U.S. growth studies. *Ann. Hum. Biol.* 3:529-542.

Thurstone, L. L. 1944. *A Code Aptitude Test.* Univ. of Chicago Psychometric Lab. Rept. No. 3, Chicago.

—— and T. G. Thurstone. 1947. *Tests of Primary Mental Abilities.* Science Research Associates, Chicago.

Todd, T. W. and A. Lindala. 1928. Dimensions of the body: White and American Negroes of both sexes. *Am. J. Phys. Anthrop.* 12:35-119.

Ueda, N. 1974. New Japanese variant of human erythrocyte carbonic anhydrase. *Jap. J. Hum. Genet.* 19:161-167.

Van Stone, J. W. 1958. Commercial whaling in the Arctic Ocean. *Pac. Northwest Quart.* 49(1):1-10.

——. 1962. *Point Hope: An Eskimo Village in Transition.* Univ. of Washington Press, Seattle.

Vernon, P. E. 1969. *Intelligence and Cultural Environment.* Methuen, London.

Vollenbruck, S., T. Lewin, and W. Lehman. 1974. On the inbreeding of Skolts. *Arctic Med. Res. Rept.* No. 9/74, Oulu, Finland.

Wallach, M. A. and M. Kogan. 1965. *Modes of Thinking in Young Children.* Holt, Rinehart and Winston, New York.

Washburn, S. L. 1963. The study of race. *Am. Anthrop.* 65:521-531.

Watson, E. H. and G. H. Lowry. 1967. *Growth and Development of Children.* Year Book Medical Publishers, Chicago.

Watt, B. K. and A. L. Merrill. 1950. *Composition of Foods–Raw, Processed, Prepared.* USDA Agriculture Handbook No. 8. Government Printing Office, Washington, D.C.

Waugh, L. M. 1937. Influence of diet on jaws and face of the American Eskimos. *J. Am. Dent. Assoc.* 24:1640-47.

Way, A. B. 1970. A method of measuring general health and its relationship to effective fertility in Wainwright Eskimos. *Arctic Anthrop.* 7(1):107-113.

——. 1972. Health, Exercise Capacity and Effective Fertility Aspects of Migration to Sea Level by High Altitude Peruvian Quechua Indians. Ph.D. Dissertation, University of Wisconsin, Madison.

Weatherall, D. J. and P. A. McIntyre. 1967. Developmental and acquired variations in erythrocyte carbonic anhydrase isozyme. *Brit. J. Haematol.* 13:106-114.

Wei, S. H. Y. 1968. A roentgenographic cephalometric study of prognathism in Chinese males and females. *Angle Orthodontist* 38:305-320.

Weiner, J. S. 1975. Human adaptability, pp. 1-14. In E. B. Worthington (ed.), *The Evolution of the IBP.* Cambridge Univ. Press, Oxford.

—— and J. A. Lourie. 1969. *Human Biology: A Guide to Field Methods.* IBP Handbook No. 9. F. A. Davis Co., Philadelphia.

Welch, Q. B., L. E. Lie-Injo, and J. M. Bolton. 1972. Phosphoglucomutase and carbonic anhydrase in West Malaysian aborigines. *Hum. Hered.* 22: 28-37.

Whang, J. W. 1971. The Interaction of Short-Term Memory and Instructional Variables on Verbal Ability. Ph.D. Dissertation, Department of Education, University of Chicago.

Widdowson, E. and R. McCance. 1964. Effects of nutrition and disease on growth. *Brit. Dent. J.* 117:326-330.

Wilber, C. G. and V. E. Levine. 1950. Fat metabolism in Alaskan Eskimos. *Exp. Med. Surg.* 8:422-425.

World Health Organization. 1962. *Calcium Requirements.* WHO Tech. Rept. Series. No. 230, Geneva.

——. 1964. *Research in Population Genetics of Primitive Groups.* WHO Tech. Rept. Series. No. 279, Geneva.

Wright, S. 1922. Coefficients of inbreeding and relationship. *Am. Natur.* 56: 330-338.

Wyndham, C. H., N. B. Strydom, J. F. Morrison, J. Peter, C. G. Williams, G. A. Bredell, and A. Joffe. 1963. Differences between ethnic groups in physical working capacity. *J. Appl. Physiol.* 18:361-366.

Zegura, S. L. 1971. A Multivariate Analysis of the Inter and Intra-Population Variation Exhibited by Eskimo Crania. Ph.D. Dissertation, University of Wisconsin, Madison.

——. 1975. Taxonomic congruence in Eskimoid populations. *Am. J. Phys. Anthrop.* 43:271-284.

——. In press. Anthropometry of skeletal populations: Arctic and Subarctic. In W. C. Sturtevant (ed.), *Handbook of North American Indians.* Washington.

INDEX

Abilities
  cognitive, 233, 271
  perceptual, 271
  problem-solving, 239
  spatial, 238
  verbal, 239, 251
Acculturation, 144, 279, 285
  dietary, 144
Activity level, 198
Adaptability, human, 125
Adaptation, 1, 7, 217, 238, 279,
    281, 284
  biochemical, 142–143
  ecological, 8
  environmental, 217
  maritime, 10–11
  metabolic, 143, 217
Adaptational bioenergetics, 141
Adaptive process, 236
Admixture, 50–51, 53, 64–65, 81,
    87, 90, 103, 112, 126, 227–
    228, 231, 259, 268, 275.
    See also Gene flow; Hybridi-
    zation
Adolescent growth spurt, 71
Adoption, 39
Aerobic power, 199–200, 205–211,
    213–215, 220
  arm work, 208–209
Age changes. See also Growth
  anaerobic power, 205
  biochemical parameters, 117–124
  bone mineral content, 137–138,
    265, 270
  carbonic anhydrase, 128–130,
    132–133, 270
  cholesterol levels, 193–195
  craniofacial complex, 104–105
  electrocardiograms, 171, 272
  health index, 220
  O_2 consumption, 206–207
  physical fitness, 272

Aging, 77, 265, 271–273
  bone loss, 137, 271
Alcoholism, 165–166
Anaerobic power, 200, 205, 211–
    213, 220, 271
Archaeology, 10–11, 32–33
Arctic Coastal Plain, 31–32. See
    also North Slope
Auditory Span Test, 245, 251, 253,
    256–258, 260–261

Baker, P. T., 1, 286–287
Bands, 37–39, 64–65, 91, 145
Birth control, 231. See also Con-
    traception
Birthrate, 226, 231
Bock-Fitzgerald Spatial Test, 244–
    245, 251, 253–254, 256,
    259–260, 284
Body fat, 41, 47–48, 142, 199, 280
Body mass, 170, 263
Body size, 14–15, 43–47, 65–77,
    136–137, 272, 274
Bone loss, 137, 141, 220, 265, 271,
    284
Brachycephalization, 266, 268
Brower, C., 223–224

Caloric deficiency, 147. See also
    Malnutrition
Cognitive development, 235, 237,
    271
Cognitive function, 234
Cognitive slump, 234, 271, 283
Collins, H. B., 13
Consanguinity, 227–228, 231
Contraception, 132, 165. See also
    Birth control
Cultural comparisons, 240
Cultural disruption, 162
Culture-fair tests, 234

315

Death rate, 227
Deconditioning, 214, 216
Deformation, cranial, 30
Demographic transition, 232
Demography, 225-232
Developmental age, 247-248
Diet, 140-144, 262-264, 279-286.
    See also Food; Nutrition
  biochemical assessment, 154-155,
      157-161
  calories, 147-149
  content
    carbohydrate, 150-151
    energy, 141-143
    fat, 150-151
    mineral, 140-141, 151-152
    protein, 150
    vitamin, 140, 152-154
  surveys, 148, 153, 195-196
Dietary change, 108, 111, 145, 279
Dietary intake, 146, 174-175, 181,
    285
Dietary patterns, 145, 174
Dietary records, 146, 148, 154
Diet interactions, 279-287
Disease. *See also* Health
  communicable, 231-232
  gastrointestinal, 217
  immunity, 35
  infectious, 164
  patterns, 221
  respiratory, 217-218

Electrocardiograms, 171, 272
Emigration, 163. *See also* Migra-
    tion; Movement of People
Endogamy, 38, 231
Endogenous synthesis, cholesterol,
    177-178
English-Inupiat Word Classification
    Test, 246-247, 251, 261,
    290-292
Epidemiology, oral, 108-112, 274,
    282
Explorers, arctic, 34-35, 140-141,
    143, 280

Facial polygons, 97

Fertility, 217
Fifteen-minute run, 202, 209-211
Fluency Test, 239, 245-246, 249,
    251, 258-259, 260-261
Food. *See also* Diet; Nutrition
  dairy, 184, 186, 264, 285
  plant, 139
  seasonal, 145
  shortages, 35
  staples, 154-155, 189
Founder effect, 91, 238. *See also*
    Genetic drift

Gene flow, 38-39, 87, 93. *See also*
    Admixture; Hybridization
Genetic drift, 65, 91. *See also*
    Founder effect
Genetic isolation, 222
Growth, 135, 137, 265, 268-271,
    282-283. *See also* Age
    changes
  anthropometry, 65-77
  bone mineral content, 136
  craniofacial, 94-97, 269-270
  curves, 67-75, 129, 135-138
  process, 268
  rate, 66-71, 247, 269
  skeletal, 103

Health, 114, 126, 284-286. *See
    also* Disease
  data, 220
  ear, 164, 218
  eye, 218
  gastrointestinal disorders, 165
  hypertension, 167-170, 218, 285
  index, 220
  injuries, 165
  lung disorders, 164
  nutritional, 139
  oral, 284
  skin disorders, 165
Heat load, 214
Heritability, 81
Hildes, W. J. A., 2, 262
History
  background, 222-227
  records, 266

villages, 32–33
Hrdlička, A., 11–12, 14–16, 20, 29, 40–41, 43, 47
Hybridization, 55. *See also* Admixture; Gene flow
Hybrid vs nonhybrid comparisons, 273, 275–276
anthropometry, 50–54, 276
carbonic anhydrase, 130–131, 276
dermatoglyphics, 87–90, 276
Hypertension, 167–170, 218, 285

Inbreeding, 227
International Biological Program (IBP), 1, 31–32, 79, 87, 94, 114–125, 134, 146, 198, 219–220, 222, 225, 230, 237, 265, 286–287
planning, 2–3
Point Barrow Working Party Conference, 2, 199
U.S. National Committee, 2

Language, 162
classification, 9–10, 21–30
cognate percentages, 21–22
geographical divisions, 8, 10, 13
Laughlin, W. S., 2, 11, 41, 47, 262, 265–266, 288
Linguistic proficiency, 242
Linguistics. *See* Language

Malnutrition, 103. *See also* Caloric deficiency
Mating patterns, 65, 279
Medical care, 163
Medical examinations, 163
Medical histories, 219
Memory span, 238
Metabolism, 139, 142, 280
carbohydrate, 178, 182–183
cholesterol, 174–178
lipid, 178–182
Migration, 11, 33, 39, 92, 225. *See also* Emigration; Movement of people
Morbidity, 284

Morphology, 107–108
anthropometry, 40–47
craniofacial, 13–14, 94–105
description, 40–41, 47
fat, 41, 47–48, 142, 199, 280
midfacial flatness, 95
adaptive significance, 95–96, 281
Mongoloid features, 95, 112–113
postcranial, 12, 14–15
zygomatic, 95, 281
Mortality, 217
occupational, 163
rate, 231
Movement of people, 37, 222, 279. *See also* Emigration; Migration
Mutation, 87

Naval Arctic Research Laboratory (NARL), 2–3
Normal ranges, biochemical parameters, 264–265
North Slope, 31, 237, 258–259, 271. *See also* Arctic Coastal Plain
Nutrition. *See also* Diet; Food
crises, 139
deficiencies, 164, 263
problems, 263, 284
status, 144, 157, 161–162, 263
survey, 154. *See also* Diet surveys

Obesity, 166–167, 263–264, 272, 282–283
Occlusion, 106–107
Oral hygiene, 108, 110–112, 164
Oral pathology, 108–110, 111–112, 219, 271–272

Partnerships, 39
Perception, auditory, 259
Physical conditioning, 198
Physical fitness, 173, 211, 215, 262, 265, 274
Physiological parameters, 271
physical conditioning, 198

pulmonary function, 199, 218–219
respiratory function, 199, 203–205, 215
work performance, 198, 205
Physiological tests
fifteen-minute run, 202, 209–211
step, 200–201, 205–208, 213
treadmill, 201–202
Piaget, Jean, 235–236
theory, 271
Plant oils, 189
Population comparisons
aerobic power, 214–215
anaerobic power, 212–213
anthropometry, 54–65
Auditory Span Test, 256–258
biochemical parameters, 114, 117–124
Bock-Fitzgerald Spatial Test, 254–256
body size, 166
bone mineral content, 135–138, 265
carbonic anhydrase, 130–133
cholesterol, 190–197
craniofacial dimensions, 97–103, 105, 268
dermatoglyphics, 82, 85, 87–93
diet, 154–156, 179–181
electrocardiograms, 171, 272
Fluency Test, 258–259
glucose tolerance, 182–183
health, 162
hypertension, 167–170
interdeme, 276–279
nutritional status, 157
obesity, 166–167
oral pathology, 110
Raven's Progressive Matrices, 254
respiratory function, 203–205
skeletal vs living, 266–268
skin disorders, 165
sucrase deficiency, 188
tooth measurements, 105–106
vitamin levels, 193–195
Populations
circumpolar, 1

cultural groupings, 36–39
bands, 37–39, 64–65, 91, 145
tribes, 37, 224
geographical divisions, 8
regional groupings, 36–39
territorial groupings, 37, 64
variation, 13–14, 21–30
Population size, 8–9, 222–232
aboriginal, 34–36
census data, 34–35, 225–226, 228–229
Psychometric research, 237
sampling bias, 240–241
tests, 241–247
Auditory Span, 245, 251, 253, 256–258, 260–261
Bock-Fitzgerald Spatial, 244–245, 251, 253–254, 256, 259–260, 284
English-Inupiat Word Classification, 246–247, 251, 261, 290–292
Fluency, 239, 245–246, 249, 251, 258–259, 260–261
Raven's Progressive Matrices, 234, 239, 243–244, 251, 253–254, 259–260, 283–284
Wechsler Intelligence Scale for Children (WISC), 234, 259
Public Health Service (PHS), 4, 108
Pulmonary function, 199, 218–219

Random evolutionary processes, 87, 93, 279
Raven's Progressive Matrices, 234, 239, 243–244, 251, 253–254, 259–260, 283–284
Reproductive histories, 227–228
Research teams, 3–7, 32, 286
Respiratory function, 199, 203–205, 215

Saliva, 112
Secretor vs nonsecretor status, 112
Secular trends, 77–78, 97
Selection, 48, 65, 87, 238
Sex differences. See also Sexual dimorphism

ability, 247
  cognitive, 233
  spatial, 238
Auditory Span Test, 257
biochemical parameters, 117-124
Bock-Fitzgerald Spatial Test,
    255-256, 260
carbonic anhydrase, 128, 132-
    133, 274
cholesterol levels, 195
cognitive tests, 274
Fluency Test, 249, 258, 260
obesity, 166-167
O_2 consumption, 206-208, 271
oral epidemiology, 274
physical fitness, 274
Sexual dimorphism, 13-14, 273-
    275.
    See also Sex differences
anthropometry, 47-50, 269
body size, 274
craniofacial dimensions, 94, 96,
    104, 274
dermatoglyphics, 275
growth, 71-77
Skeletal remains, 11-21, 97-103,
    266
Skills
  auditory, 284
  cognitive, 233, 236
  intellectual, 238
  physical, 238
  visual, 238, 283
Spatial visualization, 256

Spencer, R. F., 36-39, 64
Spouse exchange, 39
Starvation, 35
Statistics
  biological distance, 21
  canonical variates, 24
  cluster analysis, 21, 26, 28-30
  coefficient of racial likeness, 12
  discriminant functions, 24, 48-
    50, 60-65
  F-test, 26, 124
  Hotelling T^2, 26
  Mahalanobis' D^2, 24-30, 49, 53,
    62, 92, 275, 277
  normal ranges, 114, 116, 124
  principal components analysis,
    251, 253
  T-test, 15, 87, 97, 124, 131
Stefánsson, V., 140
Step test, 200-201, 205-208, 213
Subsistence patterns, 36

Taxonomic distance, 277
Trading centers, 35, 222
Trading fairs, 35, 38
Treadmill test, 201-202
Tribes, 37, 224
  boundaries, 224

Verbal concepts, 233

Wechsler Intelligence Scale for
    Children (WISC), 234, 259
Work performance, 198, 205